Seymour Martin Lipset, whose best-se
was a National Book Award finalist, and
book, *Political Man,* has sold over 400,000 copies and has been
translated into over twenty languages, is past president of both
the American Political Science Association and the American
Sociological Association. He has been elected to the American
Philosophical Society, the National Academy of Sciences, and
the American Academy of Arts and Sciences. A past professor at
Harvard and Stanford, he is the Hazel Professor of Public Policy
at George Mason University and a Senior Fellow of the Hoover
Institution. He is also a Senior Scholar of the Progressive Policy
Institute and of the Woodrow Wilson Center for International
Scholars. He lives in Arlington, Virginia.

BY SEYMOUR MARTIN LIPSET

(*IN CHRONOLOGICAL ORDER*)

Agrarian Socialism

Union Democracy (with Martin Trow and James S. Coleman)

Social Mobility in Industrial Society (with Reinhard Bendix)

Prejudice and Society (with Earl Raab)

Political Man: The Social Bases of Politics

*The First New Nation: The United States in Historical
and Comparative Perspective*

Estudiantes universitarios y politica en el tercer mundo

Revolution and Counterrevolution

*The Politics of Unreason: Right-Wing Extremism
in America 1790–1970* (with Earl Raab)

Group Life in America

Rebellion in the University

Professors, Unions, and American Higher Education
(with Everett C. Ladd)

Academics, Politics, and the 1972 Election (with Everett C. Ladd)

The Divided Academy: Professors and Politics
(with Everett C. Ladd)

Education and Politics at Harvard (with David Riesman)

Dialogues on American Politics (with Irving Louis Horowitz)

*The Confidence Gap: Business, Labor and Government
in the Public Mind*

Consensus and Conflict: Essays in Political Sociology

*Continental Divide: Values and Institutions of the
United States and Canada*

Distinctive Cultures: Canada and the United States

The Power of Jewish Education

Jews in the New American Scene (with Earl Raab)

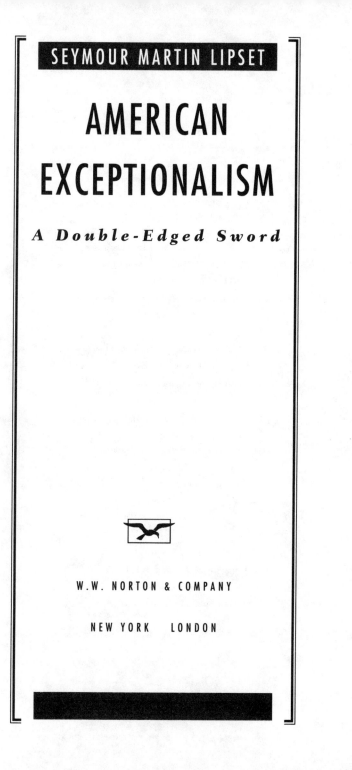

SEYMOUR MARTIN LIPSET

AMERICAN
EXCEPTIONALISM

A Double-Edged Sword

W.W. NORTON & COMPANY

NEW YORK   LONDON

Printed in the United States of America

First published as a Norton paperback 1997

The text of this book is composed in 11/13 Fairfield Light
with the display set in Fairfield bold and heavy italic
and Futura Regular Condensed
Composition and manufacturing by the Haddon Craftsman, Inc.
Book design by Margaret M. Wagner

Library of Congress Cataloging-in-Publication Data
Lipset, Seymour Martin.
American exceptionalism : a double-edged sword / Seymour Martin
Lipset.
p. cm.
Includes index.
1. National characteristics, American. 2. United States—
Civilization. I. Title.
E169.1.L5447 1995
973—dc20 95-6147
ISBN 0-393-03725-8
ISBN 0-393-31614-9 pbk

W. W. Norton & Company, Inc.
500 Fifth Avenue, New York, N.Y. 10110
W. W. Norton & Company Ltd.
10 Coptic Street, London WC1A 1PU

1 2 3 4 5 6 7 8 9 0

To Sydnee
for everything

Contents

List of Tables   11

Foreword   13

Introduction   17

AMERICAN EXCEPTIONALISM—REAFFIRMED

1   Ideology, Politics, and Deviance   31

2   Economy, Religion, and Welfare   53

3   Socialism and Unionism in the United States and Canada   77

EXCEPTIONS ON THE MARGIN

4   Two Americas, Two Value Systems: Blacks and Whites   113

5   A Unique People in an Exceptional Country   151

6   American Intellectuals—Mostly on the Left, Some
Politically Incorrect   176

PACIFIC DIVIDE

7   American Exceptionalism—Japanese Uniqueness   211

CONCLUSION

8   A Double-Edged Sword   267

Appendix: Individualism and Group Obligation   293

Notes   297

Index   337

List of Tables

1-1 *Litigiousness and Tort Costs in Six Countries* 50
2-1 *Productivity in the United States, Japan, and Germany* 56
2-2 *Attitudes Toward Absolute vs. Circumstantial Morality* 64
2-3 *Attitudes Toward Various Forms of Government Activity* 75
2-4 *Government's Responsibility in Different Areas* 76
7-1 *Differences Between America and Japan* 224
7-2 *Estimates of the Number of Jobs Held by Males Over a Lifetime in Japan and the United States* 231
7-3 *Distribution Between Women and Men of Average Time Spent per Week in Housework and Child Care: Japan, 1965–90, and the United States, 1965–86* 243
7-4 *Attitudes Toward Individualism and Equality in Japan and the United States* 255
7-5 *Attitudes Toward Freedom and Equality in Japan and the United States* 256
8-1 *Membership in Voluntary Organizations* 278
8-2 *Doing Unpaid Work for Voluntary Organizations* 279

Foreword

This book attempts to explain contemporary America, including the nature and strength of American political parties, by reference to its organizing principles and founding political institutions. These are, as Alexis de Tocqueville noted in the 1830s, exceptional, qualitatively different from those of other Western nations. Hence the United States has developed as an outlier. Yet I would add that I view the organizing principles and institutions of the United States as double-edged, that many negative traits that currently characterize the society, such as income inequality, high crime rates, low levels of electoral participation, a powerful tendency to moralize which at times verges on intolerance toward political and ethnic minorities, are inherently linked to the norms and behavior of an open democratic society that appear so admirable.

The United States was fortunate in its founders and their successors at critical junctures. George Washington proclaimed (though he did not practice it in the case of the blacks) that all ethnoreligious groups, including the Jews, were equally American, that the concept of tolerance was invidious. Thomas Jefferson noted that less government is better, and in commenting on the perpetuation of slavery voiced his concern for the future of his country in light of a just God. James Madison, who helped establish the new polity, emphasized the need to find means for government to control itself; like most of the Founders, he was suspicious of state power.

On July 4, 1826, the fiftieth anniversary of the signing of the Declaration of Independence and the date of the deaths of its authors and advocates, second and third Presidents John Adams and Thomas Jefferson, Americans felt that the hand of providence was on the young republic. How otherwise to explain these occurrences, when neither of these elderly statesmen knew what was transpiring with the other? More providential was the presence of Abraham Lincoln and Franklin Roosevelt in the White House in 1861 and 1933. The former elaborated the Declaration's meaning of equality as applying to all, and saved the Union. The latter enabled the republic to survive the most severe economic crisis in world history, put the country on the road to a new extension of the meaning of equality, and most important of all, set in motion and led the struggle to "quarantine the aggressor," to preserve and extend democracy.

The saga of American history puts into sharp relief the controversies about the role of individual greatness in history. But however one comes to this debate, there can be little question that the hand of providence has been on a nation which finds a Washington, a Lincoln, or a Roosevelt when it needs him.[1] When I write the above sentence, I believe that I draw scholarly conclusions, although I will confess that I write also as a proud American. But, I should hasten to add, not as one who thinks his country is better than other democratic societies, but as one who believes that the greatness of free polities lies in their institutionalization of conflict, of the continued struggles for freer and more humanely decent societies.

This book has been a long time in the making. In a real sense, my concern with American exceptionalism goes back to the beginning of my writing and academic career. My first book, *Agrarian Socialism* (1950), which was also my doctoral dissertation at Columbia University, took off from the issue of "why no socialism in the United States?"[2] I have subsequently dealt with the topic directly in a number of articles, the most thorough of which is a lengthy review of the explanatory variables which have been suggested to answer that query.[3] The unique American social class system was treated in another early book I wrote with Reinhard Bendix, *Social Mobility in Industrial Society*, which appeared in 1959. It emphasized the impact of ideological egalitarianism on the United States.[4] I elaborated on the topic of exceptionalism in *The First New Nation: The United States in Historical and Comparative Perspective*, which was first published in 1963.[5] More recently, *Continental Divide: The Values and Institutions of the United States and Canada* (1990) systematically analyzed the different cultures of the United States and Canada, two countries which reflect the varying outcomes of the American Revolution in different sections of what had been British North America.[6] The exceptional traits of the United States have also informed a book by Earl Raab and myself, *Jews and the New American Scene* (1995).[7]

This work originated as a plan to publish my recent articles in a book. As I read through them, I realized that a number reflected a common theoretical thread and set of questions. They elaborated my analysis of the way the organizing principles of the United States bore on the country's institutions and behavior. And much as I did thirty-five years ago in the papers which in reworked form became *Political Man: The Social Bases of Politics,* (1960, 1981), I tried to rewrite the recent ones into a cohesive book.[8] Whether I succeeded is for the reader to decide.

Various people aided me in this endeavor. They include in particular my research assistants at George Mason University, Scott Billingsley, Jeff Hayes, Marcella Ridlen Ray, and Steve Wuhs. My intellectual debts to former teachers, friends, and colleagues who have taught me about America are many. Among the most important are Robert K. Merton, the late Reinhard Bendix, Daniel Bell, S. D. Clark, Larry Diamond, Nathan Glazer, Alex Inkeles, Gary Marks, Daniel Patrick Moynihan, Earl Raab, David Riesman, and Philip Selznick. Sydnee Lipset's devotion has made it all possible. A number of scholars supplied me with relevant data. These include: Karlyn Bowman, Chikiu Hayashi, Ron Inglehart, Everett Ladd, and Tatsuko Suzuki.

Different institutions have facilitated my work over the years. These include four of which I am a member, the Hoover Institution of Stanford University, the Institute of Public Policy of George Mason University, the Progressive Policy Institute, and the Woodrow Wilson Center for International Scholars. Funds which have paid for research assistance and facilities, data collection, and travel have come over the years from the Academic Office of the Canadian Embassy in Washington, and from the Bradley, Donner, Earhart, Ford, MacArthur, and Olin foundations. I am grateful to the guiding officers of each of them.

SEYMOUR MARTIN LIPSET
Fairfax, Virginia
May 1995

Introduction

The American difference, the ways in which the United States varies from the rest of the world, is a constant topic of discussion and in recent years, of concern. Is the country in decline economically and morally? Is Japan about to replace it as the leading economic power? Why does the United States have the highest crime rate, the most persons per capita in prison? Does the growth in the proportion of illegitimate births of single-mother families reflect basic changes in our moral order? Why is our electoral turnout rate so low?

Americans once proudly emphasized their uniqueness, their differences from the rest of the world, the vitality of their democracy, the growth potential of their economy. Some now worry that our best years as a nation are behind us. Americans distrust their leaders and institutions. The public opinion indicators of confidence in institutions are the lowest since polling on the subject began in the early sixties. These concerns suggest the need to look again at the country in comparative perspective, at the ways it differs from other economically developed nations. As I have frequently argued, it is impossible to understand a country without seeing how it varies from others. Those who know only one country know no country.

The idea of American exceptionalism has interested many outside the United States. One of the most important bodies of writing dealing with this country is referred to as the "foreign traveler" literature. These are articles and books written by visitors, largely European, dealing with the way in which America works as compared with their home country or area. Perhaps the best known and still most influential is Alexis de Tocqueville's *Democracy in America*.[1] The French aristocrat came here in the 1830s to find out why the efforts at establishing democracy in his native country, starting with the French Revolution, had failed while the American Revolution had produced a stable democratic republic. The comparison, of course, was broader than just with France; no other European country with the partial exception of Great

Britain was then a democracy. In his great book, Tocqueville is the first to refer to the United States as exceptional—that is, qualitatively different from all other countries.[2] He is, therefore, the initiator of the writings on American exceptionalism.

The concept could only have arisen by comparing this country with other societies. Tocqueville looked at the United States through the eyes of someone who knew other cultures well, particularly that of his native country, but also to some considerable degree Great Britain. *Democracy in America* deals only with the United States and has almost no references to France or any other country, but Tocqueville emphasized in his notes that he never wrote a word about America without thinking about France. A book based on his research notes, George Pierson's *Tocqueville and Beaumont in America,* makes clear the ways in which Tocqueville systematically compared the United States and France.[3] At one point, he became sensitive to the fact that America was a very decentralized country, while France was reputed to be the opposite. Tocqueville commented that he had never given much thought to what centralization in France meant since as a Frenchman, he did what came naturally. He then wrote to his father, a prefect of one of the regional administrative districts, and asked him to describe the concentration of political power in France. His father apparently sat down and wrote a lengthy memorandum dealing with the subject.

When Tocqueville or other "foreign traveler" writers or social scientists have used the term "exceptional" to describe the United States, they have not meant, as some critics of the concept assume, that America is better than other countries or has a superior culture. Rather, they have simply been suggesting that it is qualitatively different, that it is an outlier. Exceptionalism is a double-edged concept. As I shall elaborate, we are the worst as well as the best, depending on which quality is being addressed.

The United States is exceptional in starting from a revolutionary event, in being "the first new nation," the first colony, other than Iceland, to become independent. It has defined its *raison d'être* ideologically. As historian Richard Hofstadter has noted, "It has been our fate as a nation not to have ideologies, but to be one."[4] In saying this, Hofstadter reiterated Ralph Waldo Emerson and Abraham Lincoln's emphases on the country's "political religion," alluding in effect to the former's statement that becoming American was a religious, that is, ideological act. The ex-Soviet Union apart, other countries define themselves by a common history as birthright communities, not by ideology.

The American Creed can be described in five terms: liberty, egalitarianism, individualism, populism, and laissez-faire. Egalitarianism, in its American meaning, as Tocqueville emphasized, involves equality of opportunity and respect, not of result or condition. These values reflect the absence of feudal structures, monarchies and aristocracies. As a new society, the country lacked the emphasis on social hierarchy and status differences characteristic of postfeudal and monarchical cultures. Postfeudal societies have resulted in systems in which awareness of class divisions and respect for the state have remained important, or at least much more important than in the United States. European countries, Canada, and Japan have placed greater emphasis on obedience to political authority and on deference to superiors.

Tocqueville noted, and contemporary survey data document quantitatively, that the United States has been the most religious country in Christendom. It has exhibited greater acceptance of biblical beliefs and higher levels of church attendance than elsewhere, with the possible exception of a few Catholic countries, such as Poland and Ireland, where nationalism and religion have been interwoven. The American religious pattern, as Tocqueville emphasized in seeking to account for American individualism, is voluntary, in other words, not state-supported. All denominations must raise their own funds, engaging in a constant struggle to retain or expand the number of their adherents if they are to survive and grow. This task is not incumbent upon state-financed denominations.

The United States, as elaborated in chapter Two, is the only country where most churchgoers adhere to *sects,* mainly the Methodists and Baptists, but also hundreds of others.[5] Elsewhere in Christendom the Anglican, Catholic, Lutheran, and Orthodox *churches* dominate. The churches are hierarchical in structure and membership is secured by birthright. Parishioners are expected to follow the lead of their priests and bishops. Sects, by contrast, are predominantly congregational; each local unit adheres voluntarily, while the youth are asked to make a religious commitment only upon reaching the age of decision. Churches outside of the United States historically have been linked to the state; their clergy are paid by public authorities, their hierarchy is formally appointed or confirmed by the government, and their schools are subsidized by taxes.

American Protestant sectarianism has both reinforced and been strengthened by social and political individualism. The sectarian is expected to follow a moral code, as determined by his/her own sense of rectitude, reflecting a personal relationship with God, and in many cases an interpretation of biblical truth, one not mediated by bishops or determined by the state. The American sects assume the perfectibility of human nature and have produced a moralistic people. Countries dominated by churches which view human institutions as corrupt are much less moralistic. The churches stress inherent sinfulness, human weakness, and do not hold individuals or nations up to the same standards as do the sectarians who are more bitter about code violations.

The strength of sectarian values and their implications for the political process may be seen in reactions to the supreme test of citizenship and adherence to the national will, war.[6] State churches have not only legitimated government, for example, the divine role of kings; they have invariably approved of the wars their nations have engaged in, and have called on people to serve and obey. And the citizens have done so, unless and until it becomes clear their country is being defeated. Americans, however, have been different. A major anti-war movement sprang up in every conflict in which the United States has been involved, with the notable exception of World War II, which for the country began with an attack. Americans have put primacy not to "my country right or wrong," but rather to "obedience to my conscience." Hence, those who opposed going to war before it was declared continued to be against it after Congress voted for war.

Protestant-inspired moralism not only has affected opposition to wars, it has determined the American style in foreign relations generally, including the ways we go to war. Support for a war is as moralistic as resistance to it. To endorse a war and call on people to kill others and die for the country, Americans must define their role in a conflict as being on God's side against Satan—for morality, against evil.[7] The United States primarily goes to war against evil, not, in its self-perception, to defend material interests. And comparative public opinion data reveal that Americans are more patriotic ("proud to be an American") and more willing to fight if their country goes to war than citizens of the thirty or so other countries polled by Gallup.

The emphasis in the American value system, in the American Creed, has been on the individual. Citizens have been expected to demand and protect their rights on a personal basis. The exceptional focus on law here as compared to Europe, derived from the Constitution and the Bill of Rights, has stressed rights against the state and other powers. America began and continues as the most anti-statist, legalistic, and rights-oriented nation.

The American Constitution intensifies the commitment to individualism and concern for the protection of rights through legal actions.

The American Bill of Rights, designed to protect the citizenry against the abuse of power by government, has produced excessive litigiousness. It has fostered the propensity of Americans to go to court not only against the government, but against each other. The rights of minorities, blacks and others, women, even of animals and plants, have grown extensively since World War II through legal action.

The American disdain of authority, for conforming to the rules laid down by the state, has been related by some observers to other unique American traits, such as the highest crime rate, as well as the lowest level of voting participation, in the developed world. Basically, the American revolutionary libertarian tradition does not encourage obedience to the state and the law. This point may be illustrated by examining the results when the American and Canadian governments tried to change the system of measurements and weights to metric from the ancient and less logical system of miles and inches, pounds and ounces. A quarter century ago, both countries told their citizens that in fifteen years, they must use only metric measurements, but that both systems could be used until a given date. The Canadians, whose Tory-monarchical history and structures have made for much greater respect for and reliance on the state, and who have lower per capita crime, deviance, and litigiousness rates than Americans, conformed to the decision of their leaders and now follow the metric system, as anyone who has driven in Canada is aware. Americans ignored the new policy, and their highway signs still refer to miles, weights are in pounds and ounces, and temperature readings are in Fahrenheit.

An emphasis on group characteristics, the perception of status in collectivity terms, necessarily encourages group solutions (see chapters Three and Four). In Europe, the emphasis on explicit social classes in postfeudal societies promoted class-consciousness on the part of the lower strata and to some extent *noblesse oblige* by the privileged. The politics of these countries, some led by Tories such as Disraeli and Bismarck, and later by the lower-class-based, social democratic left, favored policies designed to help the less affluent by means of state solutions such as welfare, public housing, public employment, and medical care. Americans, on the other hand, have placed greater stress on opening the door to individual mobility and personal achievement through heavy investment in mass education.

The cross-national differences are striking. This country has led the world by far in the proportion of people completing different levels of mass education from early in the nineteenth century, first for elementary and high schools, later for colleges and graduate institutions.

While America has long predominated in the ratio of those of college and university age attending or completing tertiary education, the numbers and proportions involved have been massive since World War II. A report on the proportion of 20- to 24-year-olds in higher education, as of 1994, indicates that it is almost double, 59 percent, in the United States to that in most affluent European countries and Japan: the Netherlands (33%), Belgium (32%), Spain (32%), France (30%), Germany (30%), Japan (30%), and Austria (29%).[8] And America spends a greater proportion of its gross domestic product (GDP) on education, 7.0 percent, than does the European Union, 5.3 percent, or Japan, 5.0 percent.[9]

Conversely, European countries have devoted a much larger share of their GNP, of their public funds, to bettering the living conditions of their working classes and the less privileged generally. The European social democrats have had frequent opportunities to hold office since the 1930s. To transform the situation of the working class, they have emphasized group improvement policies, such as public housing, family allowances and state medicine. Until recently, however, they preserved a class-segregated educational system with elite high schools and failed to focus on the expansion of university education.

American values were modified sharply by forces stemming from the Great Depression and World War II. These led to a much greater reliance on the state and acceptance of welfare and planning policies, the growth of trade unions and of class divisions in voting. While these changes continue to differentiate the contemporary United States from the pre-Depression era, the prosperous conditions which characterized most of the postwar period led the population to revert in some part to the values of the founders, especially distrust of a strong state. Support for diverse welfare entitlement policies has declined; trade union membership has dropped considerably, from a third to a sixth of the employed labor force; and class-linked electoral patterns have fallen off. Americans remain much more individualistic, meritocratic-oriented, and anti-statist than peoples elsewhere. Hence, the values which form the context for public policy are quite different from those in other developed countries, as the results of the 1994 congressional elections demonstrated.

These differences can be elaborated by considering the variations between the American Constitution and those of "most other liberal democracies . . . [which contain] language establishing affirmative welfare rights or obligations."[10] Some writers explain the difference by the fact that except for the American, almost all other constitutions were drawn up since World War II and, therefore, reflect a commitment to the welfare state, to upgrading the bottom level. But as Mary Ann Glendon has emphasized,

> The differences long predate the postwar era. They are legal manifestations of divergent, and deeply rooted, cultural attitudes toward the state and its functions. Historically, even eighteenth- and nineteenth-century continental European constitutions and codes acknowledged state obligations to provide food, work, and financial aid to persons in need. And continental Europeans today, whether of the right or the left, are much more likely than Americans to assume that governments have affirmative duties. . . . By contrast, it is almost obligatory for American politicians of both the right and the left to profess mistrust of government.[11]

In much of the writing on the subject, American exceptionalism is defined by the absence of a significant socialist movement in the United States. This again is a comparative generalization, emphasizing that socialist parties and movements have been weaker in the United States than anywhere else in the industrialized world, and also that the membership of trade unions has been proportionately smaller than in other countries. Analysts have linked those facts to the nature of the class system as well as to attitudes toward the state. Where workers are led by the social structure to think in fixed class terms, as they are in postfeudal societies, they have been more likely to support socialist or labor parties or join unions. But class has been a theoretical construct in America. The weakness of socialism is undoubtedly also related to the lower legitimacy Americans grant to state intervention and state authority. I discuss these matters in chapter Three, which deals with trade unions and socialism.

METHODOLOGY

Some who criticize an emphasis on American exceptionalism as a way of understanding current and future events have questioned the insistence that historical factors linked to the settlement of the colonies and the ideology of the founders continue to influence American behavior and values. Max Weber dealt with this topic in an interesting and insightful way, which I have relied on in earlier work. He suggested that history operates to determine the future of a nation the way a game in which the dice become loaded does. According to Weber, by conceiving of a nation's history starting as a game in which the dice are not loaded at the beginning, but then becomes biased in the direction of each past outcome, one has an analogue of the way in which culture is formed. Each time the dice come up with a given number, the probability of rolling that number again increases.[12]

Frank Underhill, a Canadian historian, suggested processes similar to Weber's in comparing the United States and Canada. He noted that, in the United States in the late eighteenth and nineteenth centuries, the left-disposed forces favoring populism, egalitarianism, and the like tended to win the major conflicts, starting with the Revolution, moving to the war hawks of 1812, the Jacksonian period, and the Civil War. The more conservative groups, the Federalists, the pro-British peace forces in 1812, the Whigs and defenders of slavery, lost out. Underhill believes that each outcome gave the egalitarian side an advantage in the next major domestic conflict. Conversely, he argues that in his native country, Canada, the conservative forces were dominant in each important struggle from the American Revolution on, through the War of 1812, the Mackenzie-Papineau Rebellion of the middle 1830s, and the founding of the Dominion of Canada in 1867 under the aegis of conservatives.[13] Those who respected authority won in Canada, while those who were more populist triumphed in the United States. Since Canadian conservatives have been Tories, believers in what a British Tory Harold Macmillan called "paternalistic socialism," statism is more acceptable north of the border than south of it. Ironically, as a result of losing the Revolution, Canadian public policy has been closer to that of social democratic countries, while the more libertarian ideology of revolutionary America has made the country the most resistant to welfare state policies and the social democratic and communitarian ethoses.

Other dissenters from the exceptionalism thesis contend that the concept is too imprecise, too unmeasurable, to be useful in explaining continuity or change in behavior on the national or group level. It may be argued that survey or polling data, available since the 1930s, provide quantitative indicators of attitudes and values which can be compared longitudinally or cross-nationally. It is important to distinguish between attitudes and values. Attitudes are much more malleable; they vary with events and contexts. They may change to reflect current social developments, recessions, corruption scandals, or violent periods, and therefore may counter assumptions about deep-rooted variations among nations. At given times, Americans may show up as more supportive than others of certain government welfare policies, less hostile to trade unions, less patriotic, or more willing to spend money to deal with a given problem.

Values are well-entrenched, culturally determined sentiments produced by institutions or major historical events, for example, a new settler society, a Bill of Rights, Protestant sectarianism, wars, and the like. They result in deep beliefs, such as deference or antagonism to authority, individualism or group-centeredness, and egalitarianism or elitism, which form the organizing principles of societies. Value-based explanations may relate to institutional differences to other countries, for example, constitutional constraints on state power, divided or united authority structures, religious systems. They also bear on behavioral outcomes, such as litigiousness or propensity to use government to deal with social problems—welfare, health, unemployment. Opinion surveys may also provide indicators of values. For example, degrees of egalitarianism may be reflected in the responses to questions in the World Values Survey conducted in 1980 and 1990 concerning equal or differentiated pay to persons of varying qualifications doing the same job. Americans are the most likely to approve of merit-based difference in reward, much more so than Japanese, Europeans, or Israelis. And indicators of basic beliefs derived from data in surveys may be used to test or elaborate hypotheses about sources of cross-national variations in behavior, such as social policy or crime rates.

Comprehensive surveys of the attitudes of 15,000 managers from many countries around the world taken from 1986 to 1993 find that American executives emphasize individualism much more than their counterparts elsewhere, and together with the Japanese are outliers with respect to different indicators of values. (See Appendix, pp. 293–96.) Charles Hampden-Turner and Alfons Trompenaars conclude that

> American managers are by far the strongest individualists in our national samples. This means that they regard the individual as the basic unit and building block of the enterprise and the origin of all its success. They are also more inner-directed, i.e., they locate the source of the organization's purpose and direction in the inner convictions of its employees. No culture is as dedicated to making each individual's dream come true. Americans believe you should "make up your own mind" and "do your own thing" rather than allow yourself to be influenced too much by other people and the external flow of events. Taken together, these are the prime attributes of entrepreneurship: the self-determined individual tenaciously pursuing a personal dream.[14]

Some critics of the concept of American exceptionalism ascribe to its exponents the belief that America had a consensual history, that its past is less marked by conflict than other countries. Nothing could be further from the truth. I have analyzed the interrelationship between consensus and conflict in social science and historical analysis in my book *Consensus and Conflict* and will not repeat the discussion here.[15] I would only note that as Sacvan Bercovitch, Richard Hofstadter, Samuel Huntington, and Gunnar Myrdal, among many, have stressed the United States is distinguished by an emphasis on adversarial relations among groups, and by intense, morally based conflicts about public policy, precisely because its people quarrel sharply about how to apply the basic principles of Americanism they purport to agree about. Conflicts which are defined in moral terms are more intense, as in America, than those which are seen primarily as reflecting interests, as in Europe.

America continues to be qualitatively different. To reiterate, exceptionalism is a two-edged phenomenon; it does not mean better. This country is an outlier. It is the most religious, optimistic, patriotic, rights-oriented, and individualistic. With respect to crime, it still has the highest rates; with respect to incarceration, it has the most people locked up in jail; with respect to litigiousness, it has the most lawyers per capita of any country in the world, with high tort and malpractice rates. It also has close to the lowest percentage of the eligible electorate voting, but the highest rate of participation in voluntary organizations. The country remains the wealthiest in real income terms, the most productive as reflected in worker output, the highest in proportions of people who graduate from or enroll in higher education (postgrade 12) and in postgraduate work (post-grade 16). It is the leader in upward mobility into professional and other high-status and elite occupations, close to the top in terms of commitment to work rather than leisure, but the least egalitarian among developed nations with respect to income distribution, at the bottom as a provider of welfare benefits, the lowest in savings, and the least taxed. And as I elaborate in the chapters that follow, the positive and the negative are frequently opposite sides of the same coin.

Here I would only like to note that those who emphasize social morbidity, who focus on moral decline, for example, or on the high crime or divorce rates, ignore the evidence that much of what they deplore is closely linked to American values which presumably they approve of, those which make for achievement and independence. As Robert Merton points out, the stress on success, on getting ahead, presses the unsuccessful or those without the means to win out legitimately—the poor and the oppressed minorities—to violate the rules of the game.[16] Individualism as a value leads not only to self-reliance and a reluctance to be dependent on others, but also to independence in family relationships, including a greater propensity to leave a mate if the marital relationship becomes troubled. America is the most moralistic country in the developed world. That moralism flows in large part from the country's unique Protestant sectarian and ideological commitments. Given this background, it is not surprising that Americans are also very critical of their society's institutions and leaders. Europeans, who take their national identity from common historical traditions, not ideologies, and are reared in a church tradition, have been unable to understand the American response to Watergate or the sexual peccadilloes of politicians.

In the seventh chapter of the book, I seek to enlarge the comparative perspective by looking at the United States and Japan. The Japanese stress the extent to which they are a unique people. They are even described occasionally as "uniquely unique." The concept of Japanese uniqueness goes back a long way. Like the Americans, the Japanese are outliers; they are usually at the opposite ends of the value and behavioral continua, as the Appendix at pp. 293–296 demonstrates. They are the most group-oriented society; the United States is the most individualistic. Japan has extremely low crime and litigiousness rates; America is at the opposite extreme among developed countries. The United States, as the data of the 1990 World Values Survey demonstrate, has the highest rates of membership and activity in voluntary associations; Japan has the lowest.[17]

The United States and other developed countries have obviously changed considerably over the past two centuries as they have industrialized, urbanized, and become democratized. But I would argue that the relative differences among them have remained. Thus, while statism has grown considerably in the United States, particularly since the Depression of the 1930s and the New Deal, and the country clearly can no longer be described as laissez-faire, it is still less welfare-oriented, less statist, and more laissez-faire than almost all the European nations, and more moralistic. Alone in the developed world, the country has not moved toward comprehensive health care under the sponsorship of the government. In general, we have hung back behind other nations with respect to state industrial policies. In November 1994, the electorate gave control of Congress to the most ardently anti-statist major political party in the world, thereby rejecting the moderate (by international standards) welfare-oriented policies of Bill Clinton and the Democrats. The Republican campaign's "Contract with America" promised to drastically cut back on taxation and the scope of government in a country which has been at the bottom among industrialized nations in terms of the proportion of national income raised in taxes, extent of public ownership, and expenditures for entitlements and welfare. The major divisive, religion-linked social controversies in America, abortion and gay rights, are non-issues in all the industrialized European countries, including the Catholic ones (non-industrialized Ireland and Poland excepted). No one burns down abortion clinics in Europe, Australasia, or Japan. But given the emphasis on moralism, American politicians define interest issues as well as value conflicts in ethical terms. Commenting on the Republican tactics in the 1994 elections, Suzanne Garment notes that the author of the GOP Contract, House Speaker Newt Gingrich, "thought the 'secular religion' he saw on the left could be successfully opposed only by equally moralistic rhetoric."[18] To understand why Americans act as they do, as distinct from the Europeans and the Japanese, it is necessary to see the ways in which the country has been exceptional all through its history.

This book addresses various aspects of American exceptionalism, such as status, statism, economic and welfare policy, trade unionism, politics, race relations, religion, crime, political participation, and economic behavior. Aside from the concluding chapter, it is divided into three sections. In the first, chapters One to Three, I examine the classic emphases of the discussion of exceptionalism, the United States as a sociological, political, and economic outlier, as well as the issue of "why no socialism in the United States?", a topic which, as noted, is taken by some as the principal meaning of American exceptionalism. In the second section, chapters Four, Five, and Six, I analyze the "exceptions on the margin," three more statist groups which illustrate the extremes: the African Americans of oppression, the Jews of success, and intellectuals of alienation from a market-driven, or for a minority of them, a populist society. In the third section, chapter Seven presents a detailed comparison of the two sociological outliers among developed countries, confronting American exceptionalism with Japanese uniqueness. And in the concluding chapter, I discuss the positive and negative outcomes of the two-edged American Creed, both fostering initiative and voluntarism, and threatening community and triggering moral decline.

AMERICAN EXCEPTIONALISM— REAFFIRMED

CHAPTER 1

Ideology, Politics, and Deviance[1]

Born out of revolution, the United States is a country organized around an ideology which includes a set of dogmas about the nature of a good society. Americanism, as different people have pointed out, is an "ism" or ideology in the same way that communism or fascism or liberalism are isms. As G. K. Chesterton put it: "America is the only nation in the world that is founded on a creed. That creed is set forth with dogmatic and even theological lucidity in the Declaration of Independence. . . ."[2] As noted in the Introduction, the nation's ideology can be described in five words: liberty, egalitarianism, individualism, populism, and laissez-faire. The revolutionary ideology which became the American Creed is liberalism in its eighteenth- and nineteenth-century meanings, as distinct from conservative Toryism, statist communitarianism, mercantilism, and *noblesse oblige* dominant in monarchical, state-church-formed cultures.[3]

Other countries' senses of themselves are derived from a common history. Winston Churchill once gave vivid evidence to the difference between a national identity rooted in history and one defined by ideology in objecting to a proposal in 1940 to outlaw the anti-war Communist Party. In a speech in the House of Commons, Churchill said that as far as he knew, the Communist Party was composed of Englishmen and he did not fear an Englishman. In Europe, nationality is related to community, and thus one cannot become un-English or un-Swedish. Being an American, however, is an ideological commitment. It is not a matter of birth. Those who reject American values are un-American.

The American Revolution sharply weakened the *noblesse oblige*, hierarchically rooted, organic community values which had been linked to Tory sentiments, and enormously strengthened the individualistic, egalitarian, and anti-statist ones which had been present in the settler and religious background of the colonies. These values were evident in the twentieth-century fact that, as H. G. Wells pointed out close to

ninety years ago, the United States not only has lacked a viable socialist party, but also has never developed a British or European-type Conservative or Tory party. Rather, America has been dominated by pure
bourgeois, middle-class individualistic values. As Wells put it: "Essentially America is a middle-class [which has] become a community and
so its essential problems are the problems of a modern individualistic
society, stark and clear." He enunciated a theory of America as a liberal
society, in the classic anti-statist meaning of the term:

> It is not difficult to show for example, that the two great political parties
> in America represent only one English party, the middle-class Liberal party.
> . . . There are no Tories . . . and no Labor Party. . . . [T]he new world [was
> left] to the Whigs and Nonconformists and to those less constructive, less
> logical, more popular and liberating thinkers who became Radicals in Eng-
> land, and Jeffersonians and then Democrats in America. All Americans are,
> from the English point of view, Liberals of one sort or another. . . .
>
> The liberalism of the eighteenth century was essentially the rebellion
> . . . against the monarchical and aristocratic state—against hereditary privi-
> lege, against restrictions on bargains. Its spirit was essentially anarchistic—
> the antithesis of Socialism. It was anti-State.[4]

COMPARATIVE PERSPECTIVES

In dealing with national characteristics it is important to recognize that
comparative evaluations are never absolutes, that they always are made
in terms of more or less. The statement that the United States is an
egalitarian society obviously does not imply that all Americans are
equal in any way that can be defined. This proposition usually means
(regardless of which aspect is under consideration—social relations,
status, mobility, etc.) that the United States is more egalitarian than
Europe.

Comparative judgments affect all generalizations about societies.
This is such an obvious, commonsensical truism that it seems almost
foolish to enunciate it. I only do so because statements about America
or other countries are frequently challenged on the ground that they
are not absolutely true. Generalizations may invert when the unit of
comparison changes. For example, Canada looks different when compared to the United States than when contrasted with Britain.[5] Figuratively, on a scale of 0 to 100, with the United States close to 0 on a
given trait and Britain at 100, Canada would fall around 30. Thus,

when Canada is evaluated by reference to the United States, it appears as more elitist, law-abiding, and statist, but when considering the variations between Canada and Britain, Canada looks more anti-statist, violent, and egalitarian.

The notion of "American exceptionalism" became widely applied in the context of efforts to account for the weakness of working-class radicalism in the United States.[6] The major question subsumed in the concept became why the United States is the only industrialized country which does not have a significant socialist movement or Labor party. That riddle has bedeviled socialist theorists since the late nineteenth century. Friedrich Engels tried to answer it in the last decade of his life.[7] The German socialist and sociologist Werner Sombart dealt with it in a major book published in his native language in 1906, *Why Is There No Socialism in the United States?*[8] As we have seen, H. G. Wells, then a Fabian, also addressed the issue that year in *The Future in America.*[9] Both Lenin and Trotsky were deeply concerned because the logic of Marxism, the proposition expressed by Marx in *Das Kapital* that "the more developed country shows the less developed the image of their future," implied to Marxists prior to the Russian Revolution that the United States would be the first socialist country.[10]

Since some object to an attempt to explain a negative, a vacancy, the query may of course be reversed to ask why has America been the most classically liberal polity in the world from its founding to the present? Although the United States remains the wealthiest large industrialized nation, it devotes less of its income to welfare and the state is less involved in the economy than is true for other developed countries. It not only does not have a viable, class-conscious, radical political movement, but its trade unions, which have long been weaker than those of almost all other industrialized countries, have been steadily declining since the mid-1950s. These issues are covered more extensively in chapter Three.

An emphasis on American uniqueness raises the obvious question of the nature of the differences.[11] There is a large literature dating back to at least the eighteenth century which attempts to specify the special character of the United States politically and socially.[12] One of the most interesting, often overlooked, is Edmund Burke's speech to the House of Commons proposing reconciliation with the colonies, in which he sought to explain to his fellow members what the revolutionary Americans were like.[13] He noted that they were different culturally, that they were not simply transplanted Englishmen. He particularly stressed the unique character of American religion. J. Hector St. John

Crèvecoeur, in his book *Letters from an American Farmer,* written in the late eighteenth century, explicitly raised the question, "What is an American?" He emphasized that Americans behaved differently in their social relations, were much more egalitarian than other nationalities, that their "dictionary" was "short in words of dignity, and names of honor," that is, in terms through which the lower strata expressed their subservience to the higher.[14] Tocqueville, who observed egalitarianism in a similar fashion, also stressed individualism, as distinct from the emphasis on "group ties" which marked Europe.[15]

These commentaries have been followed by a myriad—thousands upon thousands—of books and articles by foreign travelers. The over-whelming majority are by educated Europeans. Such writings are fruit-ful because they are comparative; those who wrote them emphasized cross-national variations in behavior and institutions.[16] Tocqueville's *Democracy,* of course, is the best known. As we have seen, he noted that he never wrote anything about the United States without thinking of France. As he put it, in speaking of his need to contrast the same institutions and behavior in both countries, "without comparisons to make, the mind doesn't know how to proceed."[17] Harriet Martineau, an English contemporary, also wrote a first-rate comparative book on America.[18] Friedrich Engels and Max Weber were among the contribu-tors to the literature. There is a fairly systematic and similar logic in many of these discussions.[19]

Beyond the analysis of variations between the United States and Europe, various other comparisons have been fruitful. In previous writings, I have suggested that one of the best ways to specify and dis-tinguish American traits is by contrast with Canada.[20] There is a con-siderable comparative North American literature, written almost entirely by Canadians. They have a great advantage over Americans since, while very few of the latter study their northern neighbor, it is impossible to be a literate Canadian without knowing almost as much, if not more, as most Americans about the United States. Almost every Canadian work on a given subject (the city, religion, the family, trade unions, etc.) contains a great deal about the United States. Many Canadians seek to explain their own country by dealing with differ-ences or similarities south of the border. Specifying and analyzing vari-ations among the predominantly English-speaking countries—Aus-tralia, Canada, Great Britain, New Zealand, and the United States—is also useful precisely because the differences among them generally are smaller than between each and non-Anglophonic societies.[21] I have tried to analyze these variations in *The First New Nation.*[22] The logic of studying societies which have major aspects in common was also followed by Louis Hartz in treating the overseas settler societies—United States, Canada, Latin America, Australia, and South Africa—as units for comparison.[23] Fruitful comparisons have been made between Latin America and Anglophonic North America, which shed light on each.

Some Latin Americans have argued that there are major common elements in the Americas which show up in comparisons with Europe. Fernando Cardoso, a distinguished sociologist and now president of Brazil, once told me that he and his friends (who were activists in the underground left in the early 1960s) consciously decided not to found a socialist party as the military dictatorship was breaking down. They formed a populist party because, as they read the evidence, class-conscious socialism does not appeal in the Americas.[24] With the exceptions of Chile and Canada (to a limited extent), major New World left parties from Argentina to the United States have been populist. Cardoso suggested that consciousness of social class is less salient throughout most of the Americas than in postfeudal Europe. However, I do not want to take on the issue of how exceptional the Americas are; dealing with the United States is more than enough.

LIBERALISM, CONSERVATISM, AND AMERICANISM

The United States is viewed by many as the great conservative society, but it may also be seen as the most classically liberal polity in the developed world. To understand the exceptional nature of American politics, it is necessary to recognize, with H. G. Wells, that conservatism, as defined outside of the United States, is particularly weak in this country. Conservatism in Europe and Canada, derived from the historic alliance of church and government, is associated with the emergence of the welfare state. The two names most identified with it are Bismarck and Disraeli. Both were leaders of the conservatives (Tories) in their countries. They represented the rural and aristocratic elements, sectors which disdained capitalism, disliked the bourgeoisie, and rejected materialistic values. Their politics reflected the values of *noblesse oblige,* the obligation of the leaders of society and the economy to protect the less fortunate.

The semantic confusion about liberalism in America arises because both early and latter-day Americans never adopted the term to describe the unique American polity. The reason is simple. The American system of government existed long before the word "liberal" emerged in Napoleonic Spain and was subsequently accepted as referring to a particular party in mid-nineteenth-century England, as distinct from the Tory or Conservative Party. What Europeans have called "liberalism," Americans refer to as "conservatism": a deeply anti-statist doctrine emphasizing the virtues of laissez-faire. Ronald Reagan and Milton Friedman, the two current names most frequently linked with this ideology, define conservatism in America. And as Friedrich Hayek, its most important European exponent noted, it includes the rejection of aristocracy, social class hierarchy, and an established state church. As recently as the April and June 1987 issues of the British magazine *Encounter,* two leading trans-Atlantic conservative intellectuals, Max Beloff (Lord Beloff) and Irving Kristol, debated the use of titles. Kristol argued that Britain "is soured by a set of very thin, but tenacious, aristocratic pretensions . . . [which] foreclose opportunities and repress a spirit of equality that has yet to find its full expression. . . ." This situation fuels many of the frustrations that make "British life . . . so cheerless, so abounding in *ressentiment."* Like Tocqueville, he holds up "social equality" as making "other inequalities tolerable in modern democracy." Beloff, a Tory, contended that what threatens conservatism in Britain "is not its remaining links with the aristocratic tradition, but its alleged indifference to some of the abuses of capitalism. It is not the Dukes who lose us votes, but the 'malefactors of great wealth. . . .' " He wondered "why Mr. Kristol believes himself to be a 'conservative,' " since he is "as incapable as most Americans of being a conservative in any profound sense." Lord Beloff concluded that "Conservatism must have a 'Tory' element or it is only the old 'Manchester School,' " i.e., liberal.[25]

Canada's most distinguished conservative intellectual, George Grant, emphasized in his *Lament for a Nation* that "Americans who call themselves 'Conservatives' have the right to that title only in a particular sense. In fact, they are old-fashioned liberals. . . . Their concentration on freedom from governmental interference has more to do with nineteenth century liberalism than with traditional conservatism, which asserts the right of the community to restrain freedom in the name of the common good." Grant bemoaned the fact that American conservatism, with its stress on the virtues of competition and links to business ideology, focuses on the rights of individuals and ignores communal rights and obligations. He noted that there has been no place in the American political philosophy "for the organic conservatism that predates the age of progress. Indeed, the United States is the only society on earth that has no traditions from before the age of progress."[26] The recent efforts, led by Amitai Etzioni, to create a "communitarian" movement are an attempt to transport Toryism to America. British and German Tories have recognized the link and have shown considerable interest in Etzioni's ideas.[27]

Still, it must be recognized that American politics have changed. The 1930s produced a qualitative difference. As Richard Hofstadter wrote, this period brought a "social democratic tinge" to the United States for the first time in its history.[28] The Great Depression produced a strong emphasis on planning, on the welfare state, on the role of the government as a major regulatory actor. An earlier upswing in statist sentiment occurred immediately prior to World War I, as evidenced by the significant support for the largely Republican Progressive movement led by Robert LaFollette and Theodore Roosevelt and the increasing strength (up to a high of 6% of the national vote in 1912) for the Socialist Party. They failed to change the political system. Grant McConnell explains the failure of the Progressive movement as stemming from "the pervasive and latent ambiguity in the movement" about confronting American anti-statist values. "Power as it exists was antagonistic to democracy, but how was it to be curbed without the erection of superior power?"[29]

Prior to the 1930s, the American trade union movement was also in its majority anti-statist. The American Federation of Labor (AFL) was syndicalist, believed in more union, not more state power, and was anti-socialist. Its predominant leader for forty years, Samuel Gompers, once said when asked about his politics, that he guessed he was three quarters of an anarchist.[30] And he was right. Europeans and others who perceived the Gompers-led AFL as a conservative organization because it opposed the socialists were wrong. The AFL was an extremely militant organization, which engaged in violence and had a high strike rate. It was not conservative, but rather a militant anti-statist group. The United States also had a revolutionary trade union movement, the Industrial Workers of the World (IWW). The IWW, like the AFL, was not socialist. It was explicitly anarchist, or rather, anarcho-syndicalist. The revived American radical movement of the 1960s, the so-called New Left, was also not socialist. While not doctrinally anarchist, it was much closer to anarchism and the IWW in its ideology and organizational structure than to the Socialists or Communists.

The New Deal, which owed much to the Progressive movement, was not socialist either. Franklin Roosevelt clearly wanted to maintain a capitalist economy. In running for president in 1932, he criticized Herbert Hoover and the Republicans for deficit financing and expanding the economic role of the government, which they had done in order to deal with the Depression. But his New Deal, also rising out of the need to confront the massive economic downsizing, drastically increased the statist strain in American politics, while furthering public support for trade unions.[31] The new labor movement which arose concomitantly, the Committee for (later Congress of) Industrial Organization (CIO), unlike the American Federation of Labor (AFL), was virtually social democratic in its orientation. In fact, socialists and communists played important roles in the movement. The CIO was much more politically active than the older Federation and helped to press the Democrats to the left. The Depression led to a kind of moderate "Europeanization" of American politics, as well as of its labor organizations. Class factors became more important in differentiating party support.[32] The conservatives, increasingly concentrated among the Republicans, remained anti-statist and laissez-faire, but many of them grew willing to accommodate an activist role for the state.

This pattern, however, gradually inverted after World War II as a result of long-term prosperity. The United States, like other parts of the developed world, experienced what some have called an economic miracle. The period from 1945 to the 1980s was characterized by considerable growth (mainly before the mid-1970s), an absence of major economic downswings, higher rates of social mobility both on a mass level and into the elites, and a tremendous expansion of higher educational systems—from a few million to 11 or 12 million going to colleges and universities—which fostered that mobility. America did particularly well economically, leading Europe and Japan by a considerable margin in terms of new job creation. A consequence of these developments was a refurbishing of the classical liberal ideology, that is, American conservatism. The class tensions produced by the Depression lessened, reflected in the decline of the labor movement and lower correlations between class position and voting choices. And the members of the small (by comparative standards) American labor movement are today significantly less favorable to government action than European unionists. Fewer than half of American union members are in favor of the government providing a decent standard of living for the unemployed, as compared with 69 percent of West German, 72 percent of British, and 73 percent of Italian unionists.[33] Even before Ronald Reagan entered the White House in 1981, the United States had a lower rate of taxation, a less developed welfare state, and many fewer government-owned industries than other industrialized nations.

THE POLITICAL VARIABLES

Fighting against a centralized monarchical state, the founding fathers distrusted a strong unified government. As the major modern theorist of classical liberal politics, Leo Strauss, noted: "The United States of America may be said to be the only country in the world which was founded in explicit opposition to Machiavellian principles," to the power of the Prince.[34] The chronic antagonism to the state derived from the American Revolution has been institutionalized in the unique division of powers that distinguishes the United States from parliamentary regimes, where parliament, or more realistically the cabinet, has relatively unchecked power, much like that held by an absolute monarch.

The American Constitution, the oldest in the world, established a divided form of government, the presidency, two houses of Congress, and a federal high court, and reflected a deliberate decision by the country's founders to create a weak and internally conflicted political system.[35] The first constitution, the Articles of Confederation, called for a Congress to pass laws, but *not* for an executive. The second and present one, ratified in 1789, divided the government into many units, each one selected differently for varying terms of office. The president was to be chosen every four years by an electoral college, basically made up of individually elected local elites, although this process was soon altered by the emergence of slates committed to party nominees who competed for the popular vote. Two senators were to be chosen by the state legislators for six-year terms, with one third of the seats open every two years, while the popularly elected House of Representatives was to be filled every two years, with the number allotted to each state roughly proportional to its share of the national population. The president could reject legislation passed by Congress, but this veto could be overridden by two thirds of each house. Changes to the Constitution required a two-thirds vote in both houses of Congress and ratification by three quarters of the states. The Constitution provided for Supreme Court justices appointed by the president for life, but their nomination, like those of other federal justices, cabinet members, and high-ranking officeholders, is subject to Senate ratification.

Almost all other democratic nations, those in Latin America aside, have much more unified governments, with a prime minister and cabinet who are supported by the majority of the elected members of parliament. Given that the executive has to be backed by the parliamentarians who placed him or her in office, prime ministers are more powerful, particularly in the domestic field, than presidents.

The American system laid down in the late eighteenth century is basically intact, although it has been amended to provide for the direct popular election of senators. The procedures for nominating presidential and other candidates have also become more populist. Potential nominees must run in party primaries (elections) held some time before the general election. These primaries first emerged in some western states around the turn of the century and became mandated for almost all posts after the 1960s. Nominees were previously chosen by party conventions, often controlled by "machines" or cabals of professional politicians. These developments were paralleled by the expansion on the state and local government levels of reliance on referenda, many of which are initiated by petitions. Such reforms reflect a commitment to populism, to the belief that the public, rather than professional politicians, should control as much of the policy formation process as possible.

In a brilliant article on "The State as a Conceptual Variable," J. P. Nettl laid out the enormous differences between the European conception of the state and the American. As he emphasized, the latter is characterized by "relative statelessness." No other elected national government apart from the Swiss is as limited in its powers. In the United States, "only law is sovereign." The weakness of the state, the emphasis on individual rights and a constitutionally mandated division of powers gives lawyers a uniquely powerful role in America and makes its people exceptionally litigious. The Bill of Rights, until recently almost unique, is indicative of a political system that has led to a steady enlargement of basic freedoms in the areas of speech, assembly, and private behavior, and to a variety of legal defense organizations to sustain such efforts, the most prominent of which has been the American Civil Liberties Union. American litigiousness is evident in the greater frequency of appeals against convictions, as well as more malpractice and environmental and occupational safety suits than elsewhere. Unlike the situation in Europe and Britain, "[I]n the United States, the law and its practitioners have perhaps been the most important single factor making for political and social change and have time and again proved to be the normal instrument for bringing it about."[36]

The institutional (constitutional) structure also inhibits the possibilities for a multi-party system by creating the base for an electoral system which comes close to requiring a heterogeneous two-party system. Other countries encourage more parties either greatly, through proportional representation of members of parliament, or somewhat, through constituency elections in which voters need only be concerned whether a party is viable in their district, not whether it can finish first or second nationally. The American system focuses on electing one individual president, who then appoints a cabinet responsible to him/her, not to Parliament. Given that only one person and party can win the presidency, voters usually recognize that effectively they must choose between the two strongest candidates running for office. Support for weaker third or fourth nominees or parties is viewed as a wasted choice. Hence, voters who are not enthusiastic about the two major candidates still wind up supporting one of them as "the lesser evil." This situation, as E. E. Schattschneider convincingly demonstrated, usually makes for a two-candidate race, for two broad electoral coalitions.[37] Those who have attempted to build third parties in America have never understood these limits, which imply the need for previously unrepresented forces to make their way to power through participation in one of the major party coalitions.[38] Third-party advocates have taken heart from the success of the Republicans, founded in 1854, but the Republicans were never a third party. They basically arose out of the break-up of the Whig Party, the major pre-Civil War opponent of the Democrats, on the slavery issue, and included most former northern Whigs.

There have, of course, been a number of strong third-party presidential candidates since World War I. Robert LaFollette, who ran in 1924, was supported by 17 percent of the electorate, while George Wallace secured over 12 percent of the vote in 1968, and John Anderson obtained 7 percent in 1980. H. Ross Perot joined this list with 19 percent in 1992. All of these candidates, except Perot, however, lost much of their support during the campaigns as voters reacted to the "wasted vote" argument. Since national opinion polling started in the mid-thirties, third-party candidates have wound up with a much lower percentage than their standing in the surveys in spring and early summer polls. In any case, no matter how many votes they received, they were not able to institutionalize themselves and become a permanent party. After each display of extra-party appeal, the two major parties successfully co-opted the protest with subsequent policies and nominees. Perot may prove himself the exception to the rule.

What makes heterogenous coalition parties possible has been the absence of party discipline, of the need for candidates and officials to follow a party line and support party leaders. This intraparty diversity is facilitated by the separation of powers, the fact that unlike a prime minister, who must resign from office and usually call a new election if he or she loses a vote for a bill in parliament, a president stays in office no matter how many of his proposals are defeated in Congress. Parliamentary parties, like the British Conservatives or the Scandinavian Social Democrats, must maintain discipline if the system is to work. Members of parliaments are expected, almost required, to vote with their party. They may have to go along with policies favored by their party leaders even when these are very unpopular in the districts they represent. American congresspersons, however, are on their own and generally must try to win their districts without much help from the weakly organized national party. The American separation of powers allows and even encourages members of Congress to vote with their constituents against their president or dominant party view. Allan Gotlieb, Canadian ambassador to the United States during the 1980s, has noted that American legislators, including congressional leaders, have voted against and helped to kill bills to carry out major international agreements in response to pressure from small groups of local constituents, such as those in the scallop-fishing industry or logging concerns.[39] As former House Speaker Thomas P. (Tip) O'Neill once put it, in Congress, "all politics is local." Various liberal or progressive reforms, enacted before World War I and after World War II, have deliberately weakened congressional party organization, thereby strengthening these tendencies.[40]

In five of the six administrations prior to Bill Clinton's election in 1992, the American electorate divided control of the government between the two parties. This pattern indicates that congressional contests are, to an extent, used to express discontent with some of the policies of those who control the national administration, even though voters do not necessarily wish to remove the president. In off-year contests (those in which a president is not elected), the president's party almost invariably loses congressional seats. The non-presidential party also wins by-elections and in recent presidential election years has secured many more votes for its congressional than presidential candidates. The results of the 1994 mid-term contests reiterated this pattern.

By dividing the government in this way, the voters seemingly reinforce the founders' desire to have the different branches of government check and balance each other. Under such conditions, the presidency remains a weaker office than the prime ministership, whose party has a parliamentary majority. American presidents control foreign policy and can order troops overseas, but often have difficulty getting their budgets and proposed legislation passed by Congress. Furthermore, the American public has often indicated in opinion polls that it continues to favor a divided government and a weak state. When samples of the population have been asked by pollsters whether they prefer the president and both houses of Congress to be controlled by one party or divided between two, majorities usually have chosen the latter response.[41] They also invariably indicate a preference for small governmental units to large ones.

The ultimate source of authority in the American system can be found in the preamble of the Constitution, which starts with "We, the People of the United States." America became more electorally democratic earlier than other countries. Its less privileged strata received the ballot without the kind of class struggle that was required in Britain, Prussia, Sweden, and most countries in Europe. The greater strength of populism in the United States is reflected in the extent to which the public has insisted on the right to elect officials or to change them with the fortunes of elections. Almost all the major figures in law enforcement on the state and local government level, including judges and the heads of the prosecutors' offices and police forces, are chosen by the voters or appointed by elected officials. In parliamentary countries, legal and police authorities tend to have life tenure and are not directly involved in politics. Judges are appointed for life. They are not fired when a new party comes to power, and since they are usually prohibited from political activity, they are not under pressure to handle cases in a way that might facilitate their reelection or attainment of higher electoral office.

In the United States, not only are more legal offices open to election but elections are held more frequently than in any other modern society. As of 1992, according to the U.S. Census Bureau, there were 511,039 popularly elected officials in the United States, or about one for every 363 members of the voting-age population. Most of them, 491,669, held local positions, with 18,828 state officeholders, about half of whom were administrative officials and judges.[42] This should mean that, including primaries and counting all offices, well over one million contests occur in every four-year cycle, since many are elected to one- or two-year terms. American states and local governments submit many proposed laws, bond issues, and constitutional amendments to popular votes; other democratic polities rarely or never do. As indicated earlier, in many states, the citizenry may propose legislation through initiative petition, a right frequently used; it hardly exists else-where. Austin Ranney, the foremost expert on the subject, has noted the effect of all this on him as a California voter:

> On November 8, I, like every Berkeley voter, was called upon to vote on twenty-nine state propositions (we had already voted on twelve proposi-tions in June), five Alameda County propositions, and eight city proposi-tions. But that was not all: I was also asked to make choices for president, U.S. senator, U.S. representative, state senator, state representative, and a number of county and city offices. In the manner of political scientists of my generation, I made a simple count and found that I had a grand total of sixty-one decisions to make![43]

The same differentiating factors are seemingly reflected in varying administrative practices at the governmental level. The dividing line between political appointees and permanent civil servants is drawn higher in most other democratic countries than in the United States. Newly elected presidents, even when they are of the same party as the person they succeeded, as with George Bush, are responsible for thou-sands of new appointments. Comparing the consequences of the divided authority in a presidential system with the more commonly used unified parliamentary government points up the way in which values and institutions interact to produce distinct political cultures. The divided government also results in numerous and powerful spe-cial interest and lobbying organizations, as well as in a greater number of social movements. The fact that congressional candidates are largely on their own, that their parties have little to do with nominat-ing or electing them, and that they must raise campaign resources per-sonally, leaves them dependent on and vulnerable to influence from those who can produce money and campaigners for them. Their leg-islative behavior reflects these needs and the characteristics of their districts, more than their party's or president's dictates. This results in American politics appearing more materialistic, more oriented toward special interests, and more personal, than elsewhere. In a discussion of the American polity, Edward C. Banfield and James Q. Wilson point out that "our government [in the United States] is permeated with politics. This is because our constitutional structure and our tra-ditions afford individuals manifold opportunities not only to bring their special interests to the attention of public officials but also—and this is the important thing—to compel officials to bargain and to make compromises. . . . [T]here is virtually no sphere of 'administration' apart from politics."[44] Such a comment underlines the effects of the populist sentiments and structures that pervade the American polity. The strong egalitarian emphasis in the United States which presses for expression in the *vox populi* makes Americans more derisive and critical of their politicians and government bureaucrats.

The civil service, which is dependent on Congress, particularly its committees, for funding and legislative support, behaves differently from the bureaucracy in parliamentary unified systems. In the latter, civil servants must conform to the will of superiors, including ultimately the political head of their department. Parliamentarians cannot affect their activity. In the United States, however, congressional committees, particularly their chairs and ranking members, have as much or more to say about the perquisites of a department or subunit than political superiors, and legislators are likely to remain around much longer than the latter. Hence, American civil servants will cooperate with congresspeople and their staffs in ways that rarely happen elsewhere. (The 1994 election results may put these generalizations in doubt, at least for two years.)

It may be argued that part of the responsibility for the lower turnout in American elections (only 55% voted in the 1992 presidential contest, while far fewer take part in primaries and lower-level elections, including those for Congress) should be attributed to populism.[45] The prolonged, multi-year campaigns, the frequency with which Americans are called to the polls (only Switzerland, which has comparably low participation, is as high), and the mud-slinging, character-assassination tactics inherent in contests which necessarily focus on individuals rather than the weak parties, all appear to discourage participation. The decline of the power of the organized parties, of the "machines" mentioned above, to nominate candidates and to mobilize people to vote has meant that fewer people take part.[46] Populism clearly does not explain all of the phenomenon. Since individual votes rarely, if ever, determine the outcome of an election, taking time to cast a ballot is not rational behavior, particularly in the United States where it takes more time to first register and then vote than in most other countries. Also, unlike America, these countries tend to hold their elections on a Sunday. Many voters elsewhere take the time to cast a ballot for the same reason they obey a sign not to walk on the grass, to wait at a red light even if no car is approaching, or not to break the law in other ways when there is little or no chance that they will be caught. Voting is encouraged as an expression of good citizenship.[47] Americans, however, being less conformist and, as we will see later in this chapter, less law-abiding than citizens of most other developed societies, vote less.

Additionally, many observers properly point to the greater difficulty Americans face in voting because of eligibility requirements, particularly the need to register to be on the voters' list.[48] But sharp reductions in such requirements since the 1960s, including in some states the elimination of the registration requirements or permitting citizens to register on election day, have been accompanied by rates of decline in voting paralleling the falloffs in less restrictive states, although the more permissive ones have higher rates of participation than states with more stringent requirements. Ironically, as the American electorate gains more formal power, the participation gap between the United States and other democracies grows.

As the United States moves into its third century under the same constitution, a world record by far, it seemingly has the same divided form of government and, compared to other Euro-Canadian polities, value emphases. It is still more classically liberal (libertarian), distrustful of government, and populist. It gives its citizens more power to influence their governors than other democracies, which rely more heavily on unified governments fulfilling economic and welfare functions. Viewed cross-nationally, Americans are the most antistatist liberal (Whig) population among the democratic nations. They continue to stand with Thomas Jefferson in believing that less government is better. But, of course, in keeping with the complexity of our times, they now favor a lot more government than he did.

CRIME, LAW, AND DEVIANCE

It may be argued that the fact that the United States "is notorious for its high crime rates" may also be linked to some of the special traits of the country as a uniquely liberal, bourgeois, and socially egalitarian society.[49] A detailed survey of comparative crime rates by Louise Shelley in developed countries for the period 1945–85 indicates that "rates for all categories of crime are approximately three times higher [in America] than in other developed nations, and the differences have been growing."[50] The country's lead is much greater for violent crimes. As of 1993, the male homicide rate was 12.4 per 100,000, contrasted to 1.6 for the European Union, and but 0.9 for Japan.[51] The same is true for imprisonment. By the end of 1993, close to 1 million persons were in state and federal penitentiaries. The United States "had an incarceration rate more than 4 times that of Canada, and more than 5 times that of England and Wales." Only Russia was higher.[52] The question is, why?

There is obviously no single answer. Shelley, who has studied the problem comparatively, mentions a number of possible factors: tensions from "postwar urbanization and population mobility, particularly as reflected among minorities and lower class persons, the drug problem, family structure and social values."[53] While all these factors seem relevant, the last set, values, has been noted by various sociologists as particularly important.[54] Robert Merton has emphasized the pressures generated by the interplay between America's basic values and the facts of social stratification in an industrial society.[55] The stress on equality and achievement in American society has meant that Americans are much more likely to be concerned with the achievement of approved *ends* (particularly pecuniary success) than with the use of appropriate *means* (the behavior considered appropriate to a given position or status). In a country that stresses success above all, people are led to feel that the most important thing is to win the game, regardless of the methods employed in doing so. American culture applies the norms of a completely competitive society to everyone. Winners take all. As Merton has put it:

> What makes American culture relatively distinctive . . . is that it is "a society which places a high premium on economic affluence and social ascent for all its members." . . . [T]his patterned expectation is regarded as appropriate for everyone, irrespective of his initial lot or station in life. . . .
>
> This leads naturally to the subsidiary theme that success or failure are results wholly of personal qualities, that he who fails has only himself to blame, for the corollary to the concept of the self-made man is the self-unmade man. To the extent that this cultural definition is assimilated by those who have not made their mark, failure represents a double defeat: the manifest defeat of remaining far behind in the race for success and the implicit defeat of not having the capacities and moral stamina needed for success. . . . It is in this cultural setting that, in a significant portion of cases, the threat of defeat motivates men to the use of those tactics, beyond the law or the mores, which promise "success."
>
> The moral mandate to achieve success thus exerts pressure to succeed, by fair means if possible and by foul means if necessary.[56]

In contrast, in nations descendant from more traditional, ascriptive, or aristocratic societies there is more emphasis on the belief that one should behave in a proper, law-abiding manner. In the morality of aristocracy, those who won generations ago, to play the game well is more important than victory. All privileged strata seek to develop norms which justify their right to high status and which limit, if not eliminate, the possibility that they may be supplanted by "new men," by the upwardly mobile who succeed by "innovating"—that is, by ignoring the conventions. To emphasize correct behavior, manners, and so forth is to reward the characteristics which those born to privilege are most likely to have. Because of its settler society and revolutionary origins, America entered the era of a capitalist, industrial, and politically democratic society without the traditions of an aristocratic or deferential order. As a result, the norms of aristocracy, though present to a limited extent among the social elite, have not been able to make much headway. Since the emphasis is on success in the United States, those individuals or groups who feel themselves handicapped and who seek to resolve their consequent doubts about their personal worth are under strong pressure to "innovate," to use whatever means they can find to gain recognition or money.

This pressure to be creative may be reflected in efforts which established groups would not make—for example, the development of new and risky industries by those of recent immigrant background and/or low status who are prevented by lack of education, skill, economic resources, and by social discrimination from advancing up economic ladders. The pressure to succeed may also lead individuals and groups to serve social needs through employment *outside* the law, in occupations usually described as "rackets." Organized vice—prostitution, bootlegging, drug selling, and gambling—has been open to ambitious individuals from deprived social backgrounds when other fields were closed. The rackets have attracted members of minority ethnic and racial groups who are strongly motivated by the American emphasis on achievement, but who are limited in their access to legitimate means of succeeding. The comparatively high crime rate in America, both in the form of lower-class rackets, robbery and theft, and white-collar and business defalcation, may, therefore, be perceived as a consequence of the stress laid on success. Daniel Bell has logically suggested that large-scale crime may be seen as a natural by-product of American culture:

> The desires satisfied in extra-legal fashion were more than a hunger for the "forbidden fruits" of conventional morality. They also are involved in the complex and ever shifting structure of group, class, and ethnic stratifica-

tion, which is the warp and woof of America's "open" society, such "normal" goals as independence through a business of one's own, and such "moral" aspirations as the desire for social advancement and social prestige. For crime, in the language of the sociologists, has a "functional" role in the society, and the urban rackets—the illicit activity organized for continuing profit, rather than individual illegal acts . . . [are] one of the queer ladders of social mobility in American life.[57]

Another source of the high American crime rate may be found in the emphasis on the "due process" guarantees for individual rights, derivative from a Bill of Rights, which has produced legal inhibitions on the power of the police and prosecutors, including the absence of serious gun-control measures.[58] This may be contrasted to the "crime-control" model, more evident in the Commonwealth, Japan, and Europe, which focuses on the maintenance of law and order and is less protective of the rights of the accused and of individuals generally.[59] But as Stephen Cole notes, "the emphasis on individual rights that makes it difficult to prosecute and punish criminals also gives Americans a degree of civil liberty not found in most other countries."[60] Great Britain, which does not have a constitutionally mandated Bill of Rights, has responded to an increase in crime through legislation enacted in 1994 which drastically reduces the legal rights of the accused in ways that would be impossible in the United States. The new law "provides strong disincentives for people questioned by the police to invoke the right to remain silent. . . . The law also contains new powers for police to stop and search vehicles and pedestrians. . . . The law increases government censorship of videos. . . . In addition to the new law, the Health Department has ordered the compilation of registers of mentally ill persons who, in the view of authorities, could perpetrate violence. . . . These individuals would be subject to extra scrutiny. . . ."[61]

The American emphasis on due process is accompanied by greater litigiousness, as well as more formal and extensive efforts to enforce the law.[62] As noted, the United States has many more lawyers per capita (312 per 100,000 inhabitants, according to the latest available statistics) than other developed countries, including all the other predominantly English-speaking common-law ones, and tort costs are much higher (see Table 1-1).

The United States is also "exceptional" with regard to high rates of divorce and single-parent families. As David Popenoe notes, its "marital breakup rate is by far the highest among the advanced societies. . . . The chances of a first marriage ending in divorce in America today are

TABLE 1-1. LITIGIOUSNESS AND TORT COSTS IN SIX COUNTRIES

	Lawyers*	Lawyers per 100,000 Population*	Tort Costs as % of GNP 1987
United States	780,000	312.0	2.4
Western Germany	115,900	190.1	0.5
England and Wales	68,067	134.0	0.5
Italy	46,401	81.2	0.5
France	27,700	49.1	0.6
Holland	5,124	35.2	—

*For latest available years.
SOURCE: Adapted from "The Rule of Lawyers," The Economist, Survey, July 18, 1992, pp. 3–4, and "Order in the Tort," The Economist, Survey, July 18, 1992, pp. 10–13.

about one in two. While . . . [the] percentage of single-parent families also ranks highest."[63] In a sophisticated effort to make sense out of divorce rates cross-nationally, which are difficult to standardize, William Goode also concludes that the divorce rate in the United States "is probably higher than that of any other nation. . . ."[64] He cites an unpublished study to the effect that "Perhaps two-thirds of all recent marriages are likely to end up in separation or divorce within thirty years."[65] As in other countries, "the United States has witnessed a rise in illegitimacy ratios and that in turn has also affected divorce rates . . . [since the] rate of divorce among . . . [mothers involved] is higher. . . ."[66] Popenoe points out that the statistics are not to be explained by the presence of a disproportionately black "underclass," though blacks have higher divorce and teenage birth rates than whites. The rate of teenage pregnancy among whites alone is "still . . . twice that of the closest European competitor," while "divorce in America today has become almost as common among the higher classes as among the lower."[67]

In seeking to explain American uniqueness in this area, he draws on the work of Robert Bellah and his colleagues, who note the importance of "self-fulfillment" and "expressive individualism" as major parts of the value system.[68] The lead of the United States in divorce rates, which goes back to the nineteenth century, presumably reflects in part the strength of individualism.

Interpreting the higher American teenage pregnancy rate, which occurs in tandem with a propensity, especially among whites, to marry to legitimize birth, is more difficult. The author of an extremely thorough comparative analysis of *Teenage Pregnancy in Industrialized Countries* seeks to account for these seemingly contradictory results as stemming from Americans being more intensely religious, individualistic, anti-elitist, and less law- and rule-conforming than the populations of other countries.[69] The expressive individualism of young Americans leads them to have intercourse at an early age. Their greater religiosity, however, undermines their developing as rational an orientation to the use of birth control as exists among the less religiously committed Europeans and Canadians. The latter groups are also more disposed to listen to the advice of authority.[70] And when pregnancy occurs, the large majority of teenage white Americans marry; Europeans (particularly in the North) and Canadians are less likely to.

PATRIOTISM AND OPTIMISM

Regardless of evidence of corruption in high places and higher violent crime rates, Americans continue to be proud of their nation, to exhibit a greater sense of patriotism and of belief that their system is superior to all others. Opinion polls taken in the late 1980s and early 1990s in most European countries, Japan, and North America, find that Americans are invariably more positive—usually much more so—on items measuring such beliefs than the citizens of the other industrialized democracies. They continue to believe in America and its superiority as a social system. As of the mid-1990s, 75 percent of American adults continue to say they are proud to be Americans. The corresponding percentages for other countries are: Britain, 54 percent; West Germany, 20 percent; and France, 35 percent.[71] The degree of patriotism is higher still for American youth. An astounding 98 percent of young Americans have reported being proud of their nationality. The numbers for youth in the United Kingdom are 58 percent, in Germany 65 percent, and in France 80 percent.[72] When asked to react to the statement, "I want to do something to serve my country," 81 percent of young Americans said yes, compared to 18 percent answering no. The numbers for British youth were 46 percent yes and 42 percent no; for West Germans, they were 29 percent yes to 40 no; while among French youth, the replies were 55 percent yes and 34 no.[73] In line with these findings, Americans, prior to the recession of the early nineties, also show up as among the most optimistic people in Gallup Polls taken annually in thirty countries between 1976 and 1992 in response to the question: "So far as you are concerned, do you think [next year] will be better or worse than [last year]?"[74] And while the proportion voicing optimism declined during the recession of the early nineties, it was still higher than in other nations.

The next chapter continues this discussion, focusing on the economy, religion, and welfare policies.

CHAPTER 2

Economy, Religion, and Welfare

The societal aspects of America's exceptionalism refer mainly to the unique class structure and religious system of the country. The first, the emphasis on egalitarian social relations, the absence of a demand that those lower in the social order give overt deference to their betters, and the stress on meritocracy, on equal opportunity for all to rise economically and socially, stemmed, as we have seen, from the twin facts that America was formed as a new settler society and emphasized equality in formulating its national identity. Tocqueville, who noted these elements in the 1830s, was, of course, aware of enormous variations in income, power, and status, and of a strong emphasis on the attainment of wealth.[1] But he emphasized that America, unlike Europe, did not require its lower strata to acknowledge their inferiority, to bow to their superiors.[2] In a discussion of social equality, Everett Carll Ladd stresses that early America consciously eschewed the symbols of aristocracy and social rank. The Constitution itself forbids the granting of hereditary titles by the government, and in "an enormous departure from 18th [century] style," the Congress of 1789 decided that George Washington and his successors would simply be called "Mr. President."[3]

The emphasis on meritocracy was present early in the ideology of the school system. As noted, the United States has led the world in the proportion of young people attending different levels of education (elementary, high school, and college) from early in the history of the republic. Martin Trow has emphasized that the "great, unique feature of American higher education is surely its diversity. It is this diversity—both resulting from and making possible the system's phenomenal growth—that has enabled our colleges and universities to appeal to so many, to serve so many different functions."[4] To this should be added their competitiveness for faculty, students, and resources in ways that do not exist elsewhere.[5]

Concern for an open and competitive society was reflected in the emergence of the concept of the common school in the early nineteenth century. It must be noted, however, that the efficacy of the American public school, which seeks to educate all young people in the same system, is low compared to those countries that seek to educate only a portion of the whole in academically oriented institutions. Cross-national achievement tests in mathematics and native language skills show American schoolchildren lagging behind their peers in Europe and East Asia. The reasons for this form of "exceptionalism" are complex, linked among other things to the greater social heterogeneity of the American population and the extraordinarily high rates of childhood poverty and single-parent families among minorities. Samuel Huntington relates the notable contrast between achievement at the level of higher education and inadequacy at the lower levels to the absence of competition in what is "overwhelmingly a public monopoly and . . . inferior as a result" and to the contrasting "intense competition" among institutions in the former.[6]

The United States, almost from its start, has had an expanding economic system. The nineteenth-century American economy, as compared to the European ones, was characterized by more market freedom, more individual landownership, and a higher wage income structure—all sustained by the national classical liberal ideology. From the Revolution on, it was the laissez-faire country par excellence. Unlike the situation in many European countries, in which economic materialism was viewed by the traditional aristocracy and the church as conducive to vulgar behavior and immorality, in the United States hard work and economic ambition were perceived as the proper activity of a moral person.

Writing in the 1850s, a visiting Swiss theologian, Philip Schaff, commented that the "acquisition of riches is to them [the Americans] only a help toward higher spiritual and moral ends."[7] Friedrich Engels and Max Weber, among many, emphasized that the United States was the only purely bourgeois country, the only one which was not postfeudal.[8] As Weber noted, "no medieval antecedents or complicating institutional heritage [served] to mitigate the impact of the Protestant ethic on American economic development."[9] Similar observations were made in the 1920s by the gifted Italian communist theoretician Antonio Gramsci.[10] America was able to avoid the remnants of mercantilism, statist regulations, church establishment, aristocracy, and the emphasis on social class that the postfeudal countries inherited. All of these writers emphasized America's unique origins and resultant value system as a major source of its economic and political development. Its secular, laissez-faire, liberal orientation was integrally related to various aspects derived from its special religious tradition; the dominance of the Protestant sects that Weber emphasized facilitated the rise of capitalism.[11]

Although many other countries in Europe and East Asia have developed economically, America is still the world leader in per capita real income and the creation of new jobs. In the early 1990s, in terms of purchasing-power parities, the GDP per head for the United States was U.S.$22,204, while Germany was second among the Group of Seven major industrialized countries at U.S.$19,500. Canada and Japan were close behind with per capita GDPs of U.S.$19,178 and U.S.$19,107, respectively.[12] Reviewing the international evidence, Sylvia Nasar notes that "the United States remains the richest and the most productive economy in the world," although the other industrialized countries have been growing more rapidly. And according to economists Allen Heston and Robert Summers, "What lets Americans live better . . . than their Japanese [and German] rivals is productivity. Contrary to the widespread view that the Japanese economy is vastly more efficient, every comparison shows that output per employee is 40 percent greater in the United States." Even if the comparisons are limited to the manufacturing sectors (since America is most efficient in service industries and agriculture), they note that the country remains clearly in the lead. "Japanese productivity is about 80 percent that of America's, while Germany's hovers at about 75 percent."[13] Economist Edward N. Wolff has also compiled productivity data for the three countries and comes to similar conclusions, as Table 2-1 demonstrates.

Stories of America's post-1970 economic decline have clearly been exaggerated. They are based on the slowdown in the rapid postwar growth, which began with the 1973 oil shock, in tandem with major structural changes. The shift to a postindustrial economy, as Daniel Bell calls it, or postcapitalist, to use Peter Drucker's term, emphasizes the role of knowledge and high technology.[14] Capital and machine or muscle power have become less important. A major outcome of the transformation has been a decline in factory production and in plant jobs for the less skilled and less educated. Proportionately, there are more of such people because of "1) reduced rate of growth in the supply of college graduates relative to less-educated workers . . . and 2) the influx of less-educated immigrants."[15] Those who fall into these categories are in less demand and less well paid. But conversely there is an increased need for the well-educated and the highly skilled. Hence jobs for which such highly trained people qualify are more numerous

TABLE 2-1. PRODUCTIVITY IN THE UNITED STATES, JAPAN, AND GERMANY

	$56.3 United States	$38.8 Japan	$39.9 Germany
Mining and oil and gas drilling	$242.5✓	$54.7	$26.5
Utilities	204.3✓	182.3	132.8
Transportation and communication	76.7✓	40.1	44.4
Manufacturing (see breakdown below)	66.9✓	52.2	36.2
Finance, insurance and real estate	45.2	57.8	59.2✓
Agriculture, forestry and fisheries	42.7✓	9.1	17.5
Wholesale-retail sales, hotels, and restaurants	41.2✓	24.0	26.4
Construction	38.7✓	34.1	27.8
Areas in Manufacturing:			
Petroleum and coal refining	$396.2✓	$321.0	$360.2
Machinery, except electrical	113.5✓	100.9	34.2
Chemicals, plastics and other synthetics	98.4	122.0✓	52.4
Cars, planes and other transportation equipment	76.7	90.5✓	36.2
Paper, printing and publishing	71.2✓	64.2	36.4
Steel, aluminum, copper and other metals	64.6	82.7✓	33.8
Scientific instruments	60.3✓	38.7	31.8
Electric machinery and electronic equipment	59.8	67.4✓	34.4
Food, beverages, tobacco	59.2✓	20.7	30.0
Stone, clay and glass products	57.9✓	44.6	39.0
Textiles	31.1✓	17.7	22.6

✓ = most efficient

Source: Edward N. Wolff, Professor of Economics, New York University. Productivity of each country measured in thousands of dollars worth of goods each worker produced. Based on gross domestic product and labor numbers from 1988, the most recent year available; calculations are shown in 1991 dollars. Table printed in Sylvia Nasar, "Cars and VCR's Aren't Necessarily the First Domino," The New York Times, May 3, 1992, p. E6.

and well rewarded. These trends have produced greater income inequalities among different levels of the employed.

In all transition periods, from agricultural to urban employment or from artisan to factory jobs, many workers have been dislocated economically, status-wise, and psychologically.[16] The recent seemingly successful effort to make the American economy leaner has also meant meaner, since many older workers and executives who have been made redundant have figuratively and actually been thrown on the scrap heap. Awareness of this phenomenon has been extrapolated to the discussion of downward trends in the occupational structure. In fact, the changes have produced more improvements in occupational status than declines. And the United States, which has been more flexible than other developed countries, including Germany and Japan, is coming through the transition in healthier shape.

The story is clear. From 1973 to 1987, 30 million jobs were created in the United States, while the Western European countries experienced a small decline. Japan and Australia also gained jobs over the period, but not nearly as fast.[17] Although the size of the American advantage fell during most of the 1970s, in part because of the incursion into the labor force of many millions of new and inexperienced young and women workers, in the 1980s, "U.S. economic performance improved markedly compared to that of other countries. . . . During the . . . five years [1983–87] the U.S. and Japanese economies grew at almost the same rate, with the United States leading in three of these years. In all five years U.S. growth exceeded that of the European Community. The biggest economy has been getting bigger, absolutely and relatively."[18] The decade saw "the creation of hundreds of thousands of new businesses and 14 million new jobs, far and away the best performance among the advanced countries."[19] After the recession of the early 1990s, job growth continued. Between the beginning of 1992 and late 1994, 5.5 million jobs were added. In the first seven months of 1994, new hires totaled almost 2 million, with approximately 100,000 of those coming from manufacturing industries, again proportionately more than elsewhere.[20] Although some contend that the great majority of these new positions are low-paying, this argument is challenged by Bureau of Labor Statistics analysis.[21] Bureau economists report that most of them are in higher-paid occupations. Sylvia Nasar reports that in 1994, "72 percent of the 2.5 million new jobs have been for managers, for professionals. . . . And despite its reputation for low wages, the service sector is adding most of the higher wage jobs."[22] And some economists even read the statistics as demonstrating that "workers as a group are fully sharing in the economic gains."[23] Basically, according to them, the increased productivity of the nineties is not only going to investors, stockholders, or other owners, or to foreigners, but to American workers as well.[24] Reporting on various economic studies, Robert Samuelson emphasizes that productivity gains have helped produce higher living standards, involving

[M]ore health care: In 1970 there were 14,000 heart bypass operations; by 1991 there were 407,000. More schooling: Sixty-three percent of high school graduates now go to college, up from half in 1980. Cleaner cars: In 1970 few cars had anti-pollution emissions controls; now all do. More gadgets and conveniences (VCRs, cable TV, home computers, car phones): between 1970 and 1992, the number of homes with cable TV rose from 5 million to 57 million. Bigger homes: The median size of new homes went from 1,385 square feet in 1970s to 1,905 square feet in 1990.[25]

The 1994 *Statistical Abstract of the United States,* produced by the Census Bureau, also reports that Americans are living longer and healthier lives in more enduring marriages. Infant mortality has dropped to from 20 per 1,000 live births in 1970 to 8.9 in 1991. The average life expectancy has increased from 70.8 years for newborns in 1970 to 75.5 in 1991.[26]

Although there are different roads to growth, the American emphasis on competitive individualism seems to have paid off. Corporate America, faced with strong foreign competition, has responded by becoming leaner and meaner, more efficient, much as in the past. These changes, it must be noted, still leave the United States with a very large trade deficit.

Other eventually successful industrial nations in Europe and East Asia, which came out of feudal, monarchical-statist traditions, took very different paths to economic development. State and economy have been much more interactive in countries which never rejected mercantilism, cartels, and guilds. As U.S. Labor Secretary Robert Reich pointed out while still an academic: "[G]overnment bureaucracies charged with mobilizing resources and directing trade were firmly established within Germany, France and Italy by the 1870s, and in Japan by the 1890s. When markets became unruly, bureaucrats organized manufacturers into groups that coordinated their investments, shared financial capital, jointly purchased raw materials, and jointly marketed their goods and fixed prices."[27] The closer links between business and government in Europe and East Asia as compared to America have been described as more functional for economic growth in today's globalized postindustrial economy than they were in the primarily agrarian and manufacturing economies before World War II.

Some emphasize that the period of exceptional success is over, arguing that as of the eighties and nineties, "American productivity is not growing as fast as it used to, and productivity in the United States is not growing as fast as it is elsewhere, most notably in Japan."[28] The reasons which have been advanced for these changes are manifold: the proportionately many more white-collar and executive staff in America than in Japan and Germany; the declining efficiency of the United States' educational system, particularly at the elementary and high school level (a development which reflects in part the changing demographic composition of the students); a greater stress on individually oriented scientific innovation (other than application among engineers); and an emphasis on consumption rather than savings.

While there can be no doubt that the relative, and in some cases the absolute, advantage of American business has declined since the oil shocks of the 1970s, the evidence, as noted, indicates that the American economy has been engaged in the late eighties and early nineties in the structural overhaul demanded by pessimistic critics, resulting in the rebirth of America's competitive standing. With the exception of some consumer electronics sectors, "American industry now is equal to or better than most of its trading competitors. Our manufacturing companies dominate, not just in mundane fields such as chemicals, wood, paper, and metals, but also in areas such as aerospace, communications, computers and semiconductors."[29] The American trade deficit has been declining, from $152 billion in 1987 to $75.7 billion in 1993, as the country's share of manufactured exports in the world market has been increasing.[30] Almost unnoticed by the media, "hundreds of American companies took drastic measures in the eighties, from slashing payrolls to dropping products on which the profit margin is low and automating simple, formerly labor-intensive tasks." A number of major American firms have been outspending the Japanese "on research and development as well as on plant and equipment and . . . [are bringing] new products to market faster than . . . [their] Asian counterparts." As a result of becoming leaner, which necessarily has meant sharply reducing the workforce in the manufacturing sector, "we regained the title of largest exporter."[31] Not surprisingly, in the fall of 1994, the World Economic Forum, located in Switzerland, which is the major analyst of comparative economic data, concluded that the United States has surpassed its rivals and clearly has "the world's most competitive economy."[32]

With U.S. unit labor costs considerably below those of its trading competitors, including Japan and especially Germany, America is well positioned to penetrate new international markets and to fend off competition in the coming years. As of mid-year 1994, *The Economist* reports, "American businesses now view Japanese competitors with growing confidence," while Japanese firms have turned "to America for lessons. They are looking at corporate downsizing, merit pay schemes, discount retailing and other ideas that might be worth importing."[33]

SECULAR AND RELIGIOUS SECTARIANISM

The strong ideological and achievement orientations in the American experience have been strengthened by its special religious character, one which was discussed in Burke's speech referred to earlier.[34] He called the sectarian Americans the Protestants of Protestantism, the Dissenters of Dissent, which predisposed them to moralism and individualism.[35] Max Weber identified sectarian beliefs as the most conducive to the kind of rational, competitive, individualistic behavior which encouraged entrepreneurial success.[36] He noted that John Wesley, who founded the Methodists, the sect which became the largest single denomination in the United States, far exceeding its success in its birthplace, Britain, explicitly exhorted "all Christians to gain all they can, and to save all they can; that is, in effect, to grow rich."[37] The epitome of bourgeois values was to be found not in the Catholic and Protestant churches, but in the Protestant sects.

In his classic work on the subject, *The Protestant Ethic and the Spirit of Capitalism* (1920), Weber noted that the Puritans brought the values conducive to capitalism with them and, therefore, that "the spirit of capitalism . . . was present before the capitalistic order."[38] His principal examples of a secularized capitalist spirit were drawn from the writings of an American, Benjamin Franklin.[39] Weber quoted extensively from Franklin's works as prototypical of the values that are most functional for the emergence of an industrialized system. Although the impact of these values on economic behavior has clearly changed over the centuries, it is noteworthy that recent comparative studies of work behavior indicate that Americans are more inclined to be workaholics than other industrialized populations. In the mid-nineties, the workweek has been going up in America, while it continues to fall in Europe and Japan. According to *The Economist,* the "average full-time American worker now toils for even more hours a year than his Japanese counterpart."[40] Linda Bell and Richard Freeman report that the typical American works much longer than the average German, takes shorter vacations and, offered the option, Americans choose to work even longer hours than Europeans, especially Germans.[41]

The American religious ethic is not only functional for a bourgeois economy but also, as Tocqueville noted, for a liberal polity. He pointed out that "[p]uritanism was not merely a religious doctrine, but corresponded in many points with the most absolute democratic and republican theories."[42] Since most of the Protestant sects are congregational, not hierarchical, they have fostered egalitarian, individualistic, and populist values which are anti-elitist. Hence, the political ethos and the religious ethos have reinforced each other.[43]

As noted above, widespread public education in America made possible extensive social mobility into elite occupations as well as the impressive economic development that Weber sought to explain. The origins of this "education ethic" can be traced back, in part, to the strong religious beliefs of the Puritans, who regarded knowledge as a key weapon against the temptation of sin:

> It being one chiefe project of that old deluder, Sathan, to keepe men from the knowledge of the scriptures, as in former times, keeping them in an unknowne tongue, so in these latter times, by perswading them from the use of tongues, so that at least, the true sence and meaning of the originall might bee clouded with false glosses of saint seeming deceivers; and that learning may not bee buried in the grave of our forefathers, in church and commonwealth, the Lord assisting our indeavors. . . .[44]

The emphasis on voluntary associations in America which so impressed Tocqueville, Weber, Gramsci, and other foreign observers as one of the distinctive American traits is linked to the uniquely American system of "voluntary religion." The United States is the first country in which religious groups became voluntary associations. American ministers and laymen consciously recognized that they had to foster a variety of such groups both to maintain support for the church and to fulfill community needs. Tocqueville concluded that voluntarism is a large part of the answer to the puzzling strength of organized religion, a phenomenon that impressed most nineteenth-century observers and continues to show up at the end of the twentieth century in cross-national opinion polls taken by Gallup and others. These polls indicate Americans are the most churchgoing in Protestantism and the most fundamentalist in Christendom.[45] One comparative survey shows 94 percent of Americans expressing faith in God, as compared with 70 percent of Britons and 67 percent of West Germans.[46] In addition, 86 percent of Americans surveyed believe in heaven; 43 percent say they attend church services weekly. The corresponding numbers for British respondents are 54 percent accepting the existence of heaven and only 14 percent indicating they attend church weekly. For West Germans, the numbers are also distinctly lower than for Americans, at 43 percent and 21 percent, respectively.[47] A remarkable 69 percent of Americans state they believe the Devil exists, as compared to one third of the British, one fifth of the French, 18 percent of the West Germans, 12 percent of the Swedes, and 43 percent of the Canadians.[48] Compared to Western Europe as a whole, Americans place a higher importance on the role of religion in their lives. Close to four fifths of Americans surveyed report that religion is very or quite important in their lives, while only 45 percent of Europeans (Germans, French, Britons, Italians, Austrians, and Dutch) on average give similar answers.[49] And it should be noted that the historical evidence indicates that religious affiliation and belief in America are much higher in the twentieth century than in the nineteenth, and have not decreased in the post–World War II era.[50]

Such quantitative data indicate the continued validity of Tocqueville's statement: "There is no country in the world where the Christian religion retains a greater influence over the souls of men than in America."[51] In so doing, the United States contradicts a statistically based generalization "that economic development goes hand in hand with a decline in religious sentiment," or the agreement among sociologists and Marxists that religion declines as a society modernizes.[52] As Kenneth Wald, reiterating an earlier analysis by Walter Dean Burnham, notes:

> The United States, however, is a conspicuous exception to the generalization. This country, with by far the highest score on the index of economic development, was also the most "religious" of countries as shown by the answers its citizens gave to the interviewers. The magnitude of American "exceptionalism" can best be gauged by comparing the proportion of Americans who actually assigned great importance to religious belief—51 percent—with the proportion that should have done so on the basis of the pattern in other countries—a mere 5 percent.[53]

The differences between European and American political orientations may be related in part to variations in religious traditions and church organizations. As emphasized earlier, European churches have been state-financed and have called on their parishioners to support the political system. They retain structures and values formed and institutionalized in medieval agrarian societies. They are hierarchical and have fostered the responsibility of the community for the welfare of its members. Thus, as with the aristocracy and gentry, the European churches, particularly the Roman Catholic, have disliked the logic of bourgeois society. Additionally, popular support for and allegiance to these institutions have declined, in part, because of their adherence to unpopular secular values: "Outside the United States, the historic association of churches with non-democratic forces, especially the aristocracy, meant that proponents of a newer, freer, more egalitarian and democratic order often had good reason to consider religious *institutions*—and by an understandable if invalid extrapolation, religious *belief*—to be their enemies."[54]

The emphasis on Americanism as a political ideology has led to a utopian orientation among American liberals and conservatives. Both seek to extend the "good society." But the religious traditions of Protestant "dissent" have called on Americans to be moralistic, to follow their conscience with an unequivocal emphasis not to be found in countries whose predominant denominations have evolved from state churches. The dissenters are "the original source both of the close intermingling of religion and politics that [has] characterized subsequent American history and of the moral passion that has powered the engines of political change in America."[55] As Robert Bellah documented: "The millennialism of the American Protestant tradition again and again spawned movements for social change and social reform."[56]

Americans are utopian moralists who press hard to institutionalize virtue, to destroy evil people, and eliminate wicked institutions and practices. A majority even tell pollsters that God is the moral guiding force of American democracy. They tend to view social and political dramas as morality plays, as battles between God and the Devil, so that compromise is virtually unthinkable. To this day, Americans, in harmony with their sectarian roots, have a stronger sense of moral absolutism than Europeans and even Canadians. Thus, when asked in the 1990 World Values Survey to choose between two statements inquiring whether "There are absolutely clear guidelines about what is good and evil. These apply to everyone, whatever the circumstances," or, "There can never be absolutely clear guidelines about what is good and evil. What is good and evil depends entirely upon the circumstances of our time," most Europeans, Canadians, and Japanese even more so, chose the second response, while Americans were more likely to respond that there are "absolute guidelines."[57] The percentages by country are listed in Table 2-2.

A sense of moral absolutism is, of course, part of what some people see as problematic about American foreign policy.[58] As Samuel Huntington has noted, Americans give to their nation and its creed "many of

**TABLE 2-2. ATTITUDES TOWARD ABSOLUTE VS.
CIRCUMSTANTIAL MORALITY** (PERCENT)

	Absolute	Neither	Circumstantial
United States	50	5	45
Britain	36	2	61.5
France	24	7	68
West Germany	26	11	64
Italy	42	6	52
Sweden	19	5	76
Canada	30.5	8	62

SOURCE: *Adapted from Ronald Inglehart, 1990 World Values Survey (Ann Arbor, MI: Institute for Social Research, 1990).*

the attributes and functions of a church. . . ."[59] These are reflected, as Bellah points out, in the American "civic religion," which has provided "a religious dimension for the whole fabric of American life, including the political sphere." The United States is seen as the new Israel. "Europe is Egypt; America the promised land. God has led his people to establish a new sort of social order that shall be a light unto all nations."[60] Everett Ladd adds: "To understand the American ideology, we need to see individualism not as a dimension of individual character but rather as a *moral* standard by which social institutions and practices are judged."[61]

The moralistic tendency generalizes beyond its sectarian origins. A distinguished French Dominican student of American religion, R. L. Bruckberger (who visited the United States in the 1950s and, deciding to stay, wound up as a professor at Notre Dame), criticized his fellow Catholics in *The Image of America* for having absorbed the American Protestant view of religion and morality. He expressed concern that American Catholics had become much more like American Baptists and Presbyterians than European or Latin American Catholics. According to him, his American co-religionists did not sound like Catholics when they spoke out on moralistic issues.[62]

The very emphasis in the Protestant sectarian tradition on the religious chosenness of the United States has meant that if the country is perceived as slipping away "from the controlling obligations of the covenant," it is on the road to Hell.[63] The need to assuage a sense of personal responsibility for such failings has made Americans particularly inclined to support movements for the elimination of evil by illegal and even violent means if necessary. A key element in the conflicts that culminated in the Civil War was the tendency of both sides to view the other as essentially sinful, as an agent of the Devil. Linked to Protestant sectarianism, conscientious objection to military service was until recently largely an American phenomenon. The resisters to the Vietnam War reenacted a two-century "Protestant" sense of personal responsibility that led the intensely committed to follow their consciences. In other Christian countries, denominations which have been state churches have called for and legitimated obedience to state authority. The American sectarians, however, have taken it as a matter of course that individuals should obey their consciences, not the state. Conscientious objection has existed in Britain, but there it stems from the 20 percent of the population who are dissenters, and consequently has been a less significant phenomenon.

An attempt to compare the extent of anti-war activity throughout American history by Sol Tax of the University of Chicago concluded that, as of 1968, the Vietnam War rated as our *fourth* "least popular" conflict with a foreign enemy.[64] Large numbers of Americans refused to support the War of 1812, the Mexican War, the Civil War, World War I, and the Korean War.[65] Conversely, those who favor American wars have seen them as moralistic crusades—to eliminate monarchical rule (the War of 1812), to defeat the Catholic forces of superstition (the Mexican War), to eliminate slavery (the Civil War), to end colonialism in the Americas (the Spanish-American War), to make the world safe for democracy (World War I), and to resist totalitarian expansionism (World War II and Korea).

Moralism is not only expressed in anti-war activity. Support for war is also moral, as too is patriotic behavior. Here again, America has been different from most other countries. The United States has insisted on the "unconditional surrender" of the enemy in various wars. The reason for this demand has been, in large part, that America, as a principled nation, must go to war for moral reasons. We set moral goals, such as "to make the world safe for democracy," as reasons to go to war. We have always fought the "evil empire." Ronald Reagan was as American as apple pie when he spoke of the evil empire as the enemy. But, if we fight the evil empire, if we fight Satan, then he must not be allowed to survive.

America's initial reaction to the expansion of communism was often one that implied no compromise. After each major communist triumph—Russia, China, North Korea, Cuba, Vietnam—the United States went through a period of refusing to "recognize" the unbearable, hopefully temporary, victory of evil. This behavior contrasts with that of Anglican conservatives such as Churchill, or Catholic rightists like de Gaulle and Franco, whose opposition to communism did not require "non-recognition." Franco's Spain dealt with Castro soon after he took power. Canada, under Conservative Party leadership, traded with Cuba and Sandinista Nicaragua, and opposed American policy in Central America. Americans have been unique in their emphasis on non-recognition of evil foreign regimes. The principle is related to the insistence that wars must end with the unconditional surrender of the Satanic enemy. Unlike church countries, the United States rarely sees itself merely defending national interests. Foreign conflicts invariably involve a battle of good versus evil. George Kennan, among others, has written perceptively of the consequences of this "utopian" approach to foreign affairs.[66]

The United States does not ally itself with Satan. If circumstances oblige it to cooperate with evil regimes, they are converted into agents of virtue. Church countries can take the opposite tack. When the Germans invaded the Soviet Union in 1941, Churchill went on the radio to welcome the Soviets as allies, and said that he was prepared to make a treaty with Satan if necessary to defeat the Nazis. The United States, however, converted Stalin into a benign, pipe-smoking "Uncle Joe." The Soviet Union was treated as a free, almost capitalist country. Eddie Rickenbacker, a right-wing conservative, described the country as operating on capitalist principles and presented Stalin in positive terms. Americans feel the need to turn the bad guys on their side into good guys.

This emphasis on moralism helps to explain American reactions to the Vietnam War. That conflict was not fought as an ideological crusade. For a curious reason, it was not defined by the government as a war against evil and Satan. President Lyndon Johnson feared that whipping up moralistic sentiment against the Communists in Vietnam would result in a new wave of McCarthyism. Ironically, until 1967 he feared an attack from forces on his right and deprecated the importance of the anti-war movement on his left. Johnson consciously attempted to restrain anti-communist moralism. The Korean War had produced McCarthyism, whose duration was co-terminous with the war, 1950 to 1954. Johnson did not want a renewal of the phenomenon. Hence, the struggle was not sold as an anti-communist crusade. The anti-war movement, therefore, had a near monopoly on morality, and ultimately was able to bring the president down and end the conflict.

The Gulf War of 1991 constitutes another example of the interaction of American moralism and military conflict. President George Bush followed the historic pattern of defining the enemy, Saddam Hussein, as the incarnation of absolute evil, frequently describing him as another Hitler. This stress should have resulted in an insistence on unconditional surrender. But for various reasons, including presumably recommendations from most area experts that the breakdown of Iraq's authority could lead to takeovers by, and conflict among, its neighbors Syria, Turkey, and Iran, the United States ended the war with Hussein still in power. One result of the failure to carry through was considerable postwar disillusionment among Americans over the outcome. Bush, like Johnson, failed to appreciate the logic of American moralism. And Clinton paid the price: lack of support for American moralistic efforts in Somalia and Haiti.

Moralistic and movement politics have remained important in the last decades of the twentieth century. Both conservatives and liberals see their domestic opponents as advocates of immoral policies. The issue which most arouses passions is abortion, which the left defines as women's right to control their bodies and personal future, and the right sees as the right of the fetus, perceived as an individual, to be born, to live. Abortion is legal in many Catholic countries in Europe, where the fact that the Church opposes it does not lead parishioners to take the kind of extreme actions their American co-religionists engage in, who, as Father Bruckberger notes, have assimilated to Protestant moralistic styles.

PHILANTHROPY

Some of the same factors which have affected or been influenced by religion appear linked to the fact that the "expansion of philanthropy . . . has gone further . . . in the United States, than in any other part of the world."[67] The greater commitment to philanthropic activities in the United States has been related historically to the rejection of a powerful central state and of a church establishment. As an English visitor to the United States in the 1830s put it: "The separation of Church and State, and other causes, have given rise to a new species of social organization, before unknown in history. . . ."[68] Many communal functions which had been handled in Europe by the state or by state-financed churches were dealt with in nineteenth-century America by voluntary associations. The lack of commitment by the state to supporting communal institutions on the scale fostered by monarchical and aristo-cratic *noblesse oblige* in Europe has meant that certain institutions have been weaker here. This is most evident in the area of high culture, where opera companies, symphonies, and museums have received much less government backing and, as a result, are in worse financial shape. Conversely, however, a variety of other private institutions, such as colleges and universities and hospitals, have been widely diffused in this country and are supported by the most extensive pattern of volun-tary contributions in the world.[69]

The considerable sums, as well as time, that are contributed to phil-anthropic works, reaching heights undreamt of elsewhere, are also a consequence of the interrelationship betweeen voluntary religion and secular achievements. The emphasis on voluntarism in both areas, reli-gious and secular, has clearly been mutually reinforcing. People have been expected to be righteous, hardworking, and ambitious. Righteous-ness is to be rewarded both in the present and the hereafter, and the successful have an obligation to engage in good works and to share the bounty they have attained. A detailed study by Merle Curti of the his-tory of American giving for overseas purposes stresses the role that "the doctrine of stewardship" played, the belief "that whatever of worldly means one has belongs to God, that the holder is only God's steward and obligated to give to the poor, the distressed, and the needy. From many diaries, letters and other evidence it is clear that this factor was a dominant one in a great deal of giving."[70]

Scholarly students of the history of philanthropy in the United States emphasize that the underlying support for private philanthropy has been sustained by American "individualistic philosophy and suspi-cion of government control."[71] Some indication of the strength of these values may be seen in the rejection by the American Red Cross, in 1931, of a proposed federal appropriation of $25 million for the relief of drought victims. The chairman of the Red Cross central committee told Congress, "All we pray for is that you let us alone and let us do the job."[72] In spite of the growth of the welfare and planning state since the 1930s, these values are not dead, even on the left of American life. In 1971, the National Taxpayers Union, a group whose board included three major New Left figures, Noam Chomsky, Marc Raskin (head of the radical think tank, the Institute for Policy Studies), and Karl Hess (former editor of the left-wing magazine *Ramparts*), together with a number of conservative free enterprise thinkers, advocated sharp cuts in the welfare responsibilities of government. To deal with the problem of "needy recipients such as welfare people," the group proposed "a sys-tem of tax credits for any individual or group that provides private support for welfare recipients." It would allow contributions to be deducted as an outright cut from taxes, rather than, as now, from gross income.[73] The fact that such a proposal could have been made in the 1970s by an organization whose leaders included some of the leading left-wing radicals in America attests to the continued vitality of the American individualist emphasis.

The Protestant ethic and the liberal emphasis on individualism and achievement combined in America, as noted earlier, to provide the values that appear most conducive for a democratic polity resting on independent secondary powers separate from the central state and, prior to the emergence of East Asian economic giants in Confucian-based societies, for economic development. The two sets of factors also helped foster the emergence of an elite which took its communal responsibilities seriously. As early as 1807, members of the Boston elite, in founding the Boston Athenaeum, stated in the founding document that, in their city, "the class of persons enjoying easy circumstances, and possessing surplus wealth, is comparatively numerous. As we are not called upon for large contributions to national purposes, we shall do well to take advantage of the exception, by taxing ourselves for those institutions, which will be attended with lasting and extensive benefit, amidst all changes of our public fortunes and political affairs."[74]

Martin Green, who has called attention to this remarkable statement, notes that "Boston merchants, and to some extent the bankers and industrialists who succeeded them, had the idea that commerce should go hand in hand with philanthropy, and even culture, and should give way to them as soon as the individual had secured himself an adequate sum."[75] In the nineteenth century, the Boston elite demonstrated the vitality of this sense of responsibility by their support for libraries, the symphony, the Perkins Institute for the Blind, the Lowell Institute, Harvard University, and the beginnings of that complex of hospitals which remains at the pinnacle of medical care in America today. The altruistic sentiments voiced by the founders of the Athenaeum were, of course, not the only reasons motivating major contributions by the wealthy. In a fund-raising letter for Harvard in 1886, Henry Lee Higginson, a leading Boston Brahmin, stated, "educate, and save ourselves and our families and our money from mobs."[76] James Buchanan Duke, the founder of the Duke Endowment, explained his concern for the expansion of health facilities in a newspaper interview in the 1920s, saying, "People ought to be healthy. If they ain't healthy they can't work, and if they don't work they ain't healthy. And if they can't work there ain't no profit in them."[77]

But though the philanthropy of the American Protestant wealthy had clear elements of self-interest, it is also true that they exhibited levels of generosity that were unmatched by the rich in other nations. John D. Rockefeller, who gave away more in his lifetime than any other individual, was frequently attacked, and with good reason, for making his contributions for public relations and political purposes, for seeking to clean the image of "tainted money." Yet it must also be noted that, from his days as a teenager on, he would give away a tenth of his earnings to charity. He was a devout Baptist who, in the words of one student of philanthropy, "apparently felt there was some divine cooperation in the construction of Standard Oil Company."

> "God gave me my money," he told an interviewer in 1915. After financing establishment of the University of Chicago; Rockefeller told a campus meeting: "The good Lord gave me the money, and how could I withhold it from Chicago?" In his later years, Rockefeller mused, his wealth was an "accident of history," possible only because of the peculiar circumstances of oil and the nineteenth century, and that he was only its trustee.[78]

The continued linkage of voluntary religion to charitable giving on a mass level may be seen in the fact that 60 percent of all individual American giving went to religious institutions in 1991.[79] Of household contributions to one or more organizations, 51 percent gave to religious charities, while health (33%), human services (28%), youth development (22%), and education (21%) followed far behind on the list.[80] One study found that "the ratio of gifts to religious organizations to discretionary receipts was remarkably constant over all the income levels."[81]

The Great Depression of the 1930s, of course, brought about a fundamental change in the role of philanthropy. The state increasingly took over responsibility for welfare functions, for hospitals, for higher education, and many other activities. Private contributions have continued to increase in absolute size, particularly since World War II, but they have become a smaller proportion of the whole, particularly in non-religious spheres. The sources of private philanthropy have also changed, to some extent. Corporate gifts have come to be recognized as excellent forms of public relations. While most of the contributions of small donors go to religious-related causes, "[e]ducation, mainly colleges and universities, is getting the largest share of corporation giving, followed closely by health and welfare agencies."[82] One student of philanthropy, Aileen Ross, contends that

> the rise in the contributions of corporations has enabled them to take over the control of raising and allotting money to many philanthropic agencies.

Management can determine the amount that will be given, and since the same men are often found on the boards of a number of the larger corporations, they have come to form an "inner circle" which can control both the gifts that are given and the selection of the top executives in the philanthropic agencies and in the more important and prestigious fund-raising campaigns, such as those for hospitals and universities.[83]

It is still true, however, that 90 percent of all giving continues to come from individuals. Seventy-two percent of American households gave charitable contributions in 1991, donating an average of $899 per household.[84] Total giving in that year stood at $122.6 billion—an amount which, in real dollars, was three times greater than the 1955 total. The historic cultural sources of support for philanthropy and voluntary associational activity in America still have vitality. Americans view charitable giving as a responsibility to the need in their community and to local social institutions. Accordingly, "[m]ore than 96 cents of every dollar given, whether by foundations, corporations or factory workers, stays in the community it came from. . . ."[85] Hospitals, however, find religious-linked contributions are less important than in earlier eras, as relatively few medical institutions are seen to serve denominational purposes. But even though the American state now provides more fully for many activities once almost totally dependent on private support, its population, as the most anti-statist people in the developed world, continues to be the most generous on a personal basis.

THE WELFARE STATE

Given this emphasis on the generosity of Americans, it is worth reiterating in David Popenoe's words that "the United States lags well behind most other advanced societies in the creation of welfare state programs. . . . [I]t is the only major industrialized nation, for example, that has no general allowance program for families with children and lacks a national insurance plan covering . . . medical expenses."[86] In fact, the United States has lagged behind the industrialized nations of Europe where many social programs are concerned. Robert T. Kudrle and Theodore R. Marmor compared the United States to five European countries (Germany, United Kingdom, Sweden, France, Italy) and found that it was consistently late in the introduction of social programs. Industrial accident insurance was introduced in Europe during the late 1880s, but was not established in the United States until 1930. Pension and unemployment insurance, both instituted in 1935 in the United States, were introduced as early as 1889 and 1905, respectively, in the European countries, and were generally in place by the end of the 1910s. To date, the United States lacks three of the six programs that the authors compare.[87]

Further detailed documentation of the lesser provisions in the United States, as compared to other developed nations, for dependent populations, particularly children and the elderly, may be found in a comprehensive work on *The Vulnerable*.[88] In discussing "various explanations . . . for this American exceptionalism," including economic and political structural factors, Stephanie Gould and John Palmer conclude that only two, "heterogeneity of population and distinctiveness of public philosophy—seem to have explanatory power." The first, they contend, makes for greater variations among subgroups in earning capacities and hence more income inequality. The second refers to "the peculiarities of the American outlook on public affairs, our extreme emphasis on individualism, our mistrust of central authority, our strong preference for public policies that promote equality of opportunity over those that promote equality of outcome."[89] These conclusions are reinforced by a variety of comparative opinion data. The World Values Surveys conducted in 1980 and 1990 found that when asked to choose between the importance of "equality of income or the freedom to live and develop without hindrance," Americans are more disposed to the latter, by 71 percent compared to an average of 59 percent in Europe in 1990.[90] Similarly, in line with their lesser support for equal economic treatment, when polled, Americans, as distinct from Europeans, show greater respect or concern for private industry and the well-to-do as opposed to the poor.

The American commitment to equality of opportunity implies that achievement should reflect ability, justifies higher differentials in reward and rejects taxing the successful to upgrade the less advantaged. Europeans reared in postfeudal societies which assumed hereditary disadvantage and *noblesse oblige* find the idea that those with higher incomes should pay larger proportions of taxes much more acceptable than do Americans. As of the early nineties, overwhelming majorities, 87 percent of West Germans and 86 percent of Italians believe in levying higher taxes on the rich to produce greater income equality, as compared to a smaller majority, only 74 percent, of Americans.[91] A more striking pattern is reflected by replies to another question indicating that a policy that reduces income discrepancies is supported by 38 percent of Americans, while favorable opinion to such action ranges from 65 percent (Great Britain) to 80 percent (Italy) in European nations.[92]

Austria is in the middle at 70 percent. Proportionately fewer Americans (56%) agree that "income differences are too large," as compared with Europeans (66–86%).[93] A review of American public opinion data over fifty years reports: "Surveys since the 1930s have shown that the explicit idea of income redistributing elicits very limited enthusiasm among the American public. . . . Redistributive fervor was not much apparent even in [the] depression era. Most Americans are content with the distributional effects of private markets."[94] Citizens of the United States have a greater tendency than others to justify income differences as judged by cross-national reactions to the statement that "[L]arge income differences are needed for the country's prosperity."[95]

The United States is an outlier (exceptional) in practice as well as belief. Its taxes amount to a much lower proportion of GDP compared to European Community countries and Japan. While America collected 31 percent of its GDP in tax revenues in 1991, other countries such as Sweden (52%), Holland (48%), Belgium (40%), France (40%), and the United Kingdom (36%) were taxed at higher levels.[96] And economic inequality as measured by the ratio of income of the richest 20 percent of households to the poorest 20 percent is greater in America (11 times) than in all the other developed OECD countries, with Japan at the other extreme with a ratio of 4. Other more egalitarian countries are Sweden, Belgium, and Holland, with ratios of 4.5 to 5.5. Britain, Canada, France, and Italy fall in between, at 6 and 7.[97] A 1995 *New York Times* review of research in this area reiterated that wealth is more concentrated in the United States than in other industrial democracies. Measuring concentration of wealth on a rising scale of zero to one, the U.S., at 0.34, outranks Italy (0.31), Canada (0.29), Germany (0.25), France (0.25), and Finland (0.21). The top-earning 20 percent of Americans control 80 percent of the national wealth, while the lowest-earning 20 percent earn only 5 percent of all income. It cites the findings of economics professor Edward N. Wolff that "We are the most unequal industrialized country in terms of wealth."[98]

Poverty estimates from the Luxembourg Income Studies, which use the economic distance approach, measuring poverty as "a fraction of the median equivalent disposable income," also find the United States has the highest rate, twice the average for all developed countries. Australia and Canada follow at one and a half times the average, and Ireland, Italy, and Britain, too, remain slightly above the average. France, Germany, and Sweden rank slightly below the average, and Austria, Belgium, Luxembourg, and the Netherlands have the lowest poverty rates.[99] And Timothy Smeeding, the director of the Project, also notes that in spite of this, the United States does less "in terms of tax and transfer policy" to reduce income differences.[100] The gap between the United States and the rest of the industrialized world in poverty rates grew during the 1980s and early 1990s. Basically, the other countries "have well-established government safety nets which more effectively moderated changes in pre-government poverty in the 1990s, muting market driven changes in poverty by substantially more than did the U.S."[101]

Opposition to redistributive policies may be linked to the greater commitment of Americans to merit pay for the most able, to unequal reward, and, of course, to laissez-faire. Compared with the citizens of four European nations (Italy, Great Britain, West Germany, and Austria), those of the United States are more opposed to government involvement in wage and price controls, in job creation, in reduction of the workweek, as well as in such non-economic forms of regulation as restrictions on smoking in public places and the requirement to wear seat belts (see Table 2-3 below).

Americans are also less likely than Europeans to believe that it should be the government's responsibility to provide a job for everyone who wants one, to provide a decent standard of living for the unemployed, and to guarantee a basic income. Table 2-4 illustrates these discrepancies, controlling by income level.

Cross-national polls continue to reveal that Americans are less favorable toward an active role for government in the economy and to large welfare programs than the citizens of Canada and European countries. Private ownership of industry is more prevalent and viewed more favorably in the United States.[102] Everett Carll Ladd, who has reviewed "thousands of the relevant survey measures" from the United States and many other industrialized democracies, reports: "These data show the American ideology manifest in the choices of the general public of today much as the historic literature, drawing on other sources, portrayed it," while "recent comparative data show that 'American values' remain distinct." He sums up his findings in definitive terms:

> [T]he survey data show that individualism is more intense, pervasive, and uncontradicted here than in other industrial democracies. As a result, support for a private-property-based economy remains strong. Americans declare themselves prepared to countenance very substantial economic inequalities, while insisting on the importance of the ideal of equal opportunity. Government has grown enormously over the past 60 years as the public has turned to it for guarantees and services, but support for limits on government are still stronger in the U.S. than in most other industrial

democracies. American policy on social welfare reflects national insistence on a large measure of individual, rather than governmental, responsibility. Americans value individual effort and achievement.[103]

CONCLUSION

The United States continues to be exceptional among developed nations in the low level of support it provides for the poor through welfare, housing, and medical care policies. As a result, though the

TABLE 2-3. ATTITUDES TOWARD VARIOUS FORMS OF GOVERNMENT ACTIVITY (PERCENT)

AGREE GOVERNMENT SHOULD . . .	United States	West Germany	Great Britain	Austria	Italy
control wages by legislation[1]	23	28	32	58	72
reduce workweek to create more jobs[2]	27	51	49	36	63
control prices[3]	19	20	48	—	67
provide health care[4]	40	57	85	—	88
finance job creation projects[5]	70	73	83	—	84
spend more on old age pensions[6]	47	53	81	—	80
reduce differences in income between those with high and low income[7]	38	66	65	70	80
AGREE/STRONGLY AGREE THAT . . .					
wearing seat belts should be required by law[8]	49	82	80	81	81
smoking in public places should be prohibited by law[9]	46	49	51	58	89

[1]International Social Survey Program of Government Survey, 1985–86. Cited in Clive Bean, "Are Australian Attitudes to Government Different? A Comparison with Five Other Nations," in Francis G. Castles, ed., *Australia Compared: People, Policies and Politics* (Sydney, Australia: Allen & Unwin, 1991), p. 84.
[2]Ibid.
[3]1990 ISSP data from Roger Jowell, et al., *International Social Attitudes: The 10th BSA Report* (Cambridge: Cambridge University Press, 1993), p. 85.
[4]Ibid.
[5]International Social Survey Program, 1990.
[6]Ibid.
[7]Ibid., 1992.
[8]Karlyn H. Keene and Everett Carll Ladd, "America: A Unique Outlook?" *The American Enterprise,* 1 (March–April 1990), pp. 113–115.
[9]Ibid.

**TABLE 2-4. GOVERNMENT'S RESPONSIBILITY IN
DIFFERENT AREAS** (PERCENT)

	AGREE STRONGLY/AGREE THE GOVERNMENT SHOULD PROVIDE A JOB FOR EVERYONE		AGREE STRONGLY/AGREE THE GOVERNMENT SHOULD PROVIDE A DECENT STANDARD OF LIVING FOR THE UNEMPLOYED		AGREE STRONGLY/AGREE THE GOVERNMENT SHOULD PROVIDE EVERYONE WITH A GUARANTEED BASIC INCOME	
	High Income	*Low Income*	*High Income*	*Low Income*	*High Income*	*Low Income*
United States	32	61	23	52	12	33
Great Britain	44	73	57	74	47	71
West Germany	77	84	61	72	45	66
Netherlands	60	82	57	68	39	58
Italy	70	93	55	76	53	80

SOURCE: *Adapted from Karlyn H. Keene and Everett Carll Ladd, "America: A Unique Outlook?" The American Enterprise, 1 (March–April 1990), p. 118.*

wealthiest country, it has the highest proportion of people living in poverty among developed nations, according to the detailed statistical analyses of the Luxembourg Income Study data, the most comprehensive available. The United States also ranks last among ten countries (six in Europe, plus Australia, Canada, and Israel) as the most unequal in comparisons of income distribution.[104] At the same time, given the fact that educational attainment, as reflected in the proportions of the relevant age groups involved in college and postgraduate study, is more equitably distributed in the United States than elsewhere, upward mobility into privileged occupations is also more common here. Thus America has more equality of opportunity into the elites and less equality of result than the rest of the developed world. And it may be argued that the two patterns are related. Given the strength of the aspiration to rise, it is not surprising that Americans are more disposed to approve of high salaries and "bonuses" for "stars" in entertainment, athletics, and the market in general—that is, for achievers at every level. Comparative survey research indicates that Americans are more approving of sizeable income differences than Europeans and Japanese.[105]

The next chapter continues the focus on the weakness of statism or the strength of laissez-faire in America by addressing the question "why no socialism?" which has engrossed analysts of American exceptionalism for over a century.

CHAPTER 3

Socialism and Unionism in the United States and Canada[1]

The United States has stood out among the industrial nations of the world in frustrating all efforts to create a mass socialist or labor party. This fact has occasioned a considerable literature seeking to explain this aspect of American exceptionalism, a term frequently used in debates on the matter in the Communist International in the 1920s.[2] In fact, for many the concept has referred primarily to the absence of strong socialist or class-conscious movements. In 1993, a new book dealing with unionism and class formation in the nineteenth century was titled *The Making of American Exceptionalism.*[3] Much earlier than these controversies, Karl Marx and Friedrich Engels grappled with the "exceptional" aspects of American society. In so doing, they presented a picture of America as a unique society, not very different from the analyses of Tocqueville and Weber.[4]

The weakness of socialism in the United States has been a major embarrassment throughout the twentieth century to Marxist theory, which assumes that the cultural superstructure, including political behavior, is a function of the economic and technological structures. The class relationships inherent in capitalism as a social system should have inevitably eventuated in a working class that would come to political consciousness and organize in a revolutionary socialist party. Logically, it followed that the most developed society should have the most advanced set of class and political relationships.[5] Since the United States has been the most advanced industrial economy for well over a century, its political system, regarded as part of its superstructure, should be more appropriate to a technologically advanced society than the systems of less developed societies elsewhere. Until the Russian Revolution, various major Marxist theorists anticipated that, following the logic of historical materialism, the United States would be the first country in which socialists would come to power.[6] They linked socialism and modernism.

Ironically, much of the efforts by Marxists and socialists to account for the failure of the prediction stressed that from sociological and political points of view, the United States was too progressive, too egalitarian, too open, and too democratic to generate massive radical or revolutionary movements on a scale comparable to those of Europe.[7] These writings tell us much about what these people, in particular the founders of communist theory, such as Lenin and Gramsci, have seen as the sources of strength and weakness, of stability and tension in the United States. A wise sociologist, W. I. Thomas, once said, "If men define situations as real, they are real in their consequences."[8]

Any effort to deal with Werner Sombart's question of "Why is there no socialism in the United States?" inherently must be comparative.[9] The myriad of writings on the subject has, therefore, contributed much to our understanding of what is exceptional about this country, as compared to the rest of the industrialized world, primarily Western Europe. In recent years, interested scholars have taken note of the fact that our northern neighbor, Canada, has had much stronger socialist and trade union movements than the United States. Since Canada has been more similar to its southern neighbor than Europe, expanding the question to why Canada differs can add much to the comparative framework. The second section of this chapter, therefore, deals with Canadian-American differences, stressing particularly the greater strength of the Canadian labor movement.

MARX AND ENGELS

The observations of Marx and Engels provide an illuminating starting point for an examination of the failure of the American socialist movement. These two radical thinkers constantly looked for signs of class-consciousness in the United States. Marx himself was initially confident that workers everywhere would form class parties because of the emergence of the American Workingmen's parties, which secured sizable numbers of votes in several eastern cities in the late 1820s and early 1830s.[10] Although the Workingmen's Party disappeared in the 1830s, Marx and Engels were to emphasize that Americans "have had, since 1829, their own social democratic school."[11] As noted, many leading Marxists believed that the working class of the most industrialized country would inevitably develop class-conscious politics and lead the world on the road to socialism.

AMERICA AS A NEW SOCIETY

In analyzing the prospects for socialism in America, Marx and Engels did not limit themselves to economic factors. Like many contemporary analysts, they considered the various unique sociological aspects of the United States, as compared to Europe. Namely, as emphasized in chapter One, America was a new nation and society, which lacked many of the institutions and traditions of previously feudal systems and as a result was the most "modern" and purely bourgeois culture. It was also the most democratic country.

The absence of a feudal past and consequent lack of a rigid status system in the United States in contrast to most of Europe was seen by the Marxist fathers, particularly Friedrich Engels, as a source of the political backwardness of the American working class. Thus, he wrote in 1890 that Americans "are born conservatives just because America is so purely bourgeois, so entirely without a feudal past and therefore proud of its purely bourgeois organization."[12] And he noted in 1892: "It is . . . quite natural, that in such a young country, which has never known feudalism and has grown up on a bourgeois basis from the first, bourgeois prejudices should also be so strongly rooted in the working class."[13] Not surprisingly, Marx and Engels, in explaining the failures of the workers' movement also pointed to other stratification variables, derived from the country's higher rates of productivity and social mobility. Among "the special American conditions" inhibiting the emergence of a workers' movement stressed by Engels in 1851 and repeated during the next four decades was "the necessarily rapid and rapidly growing prosperity of the country, which makes bourgeois conditions look like a *beau idéal* to them. . . ."[14]

SECTARIANISM

There were, of course, many other factors suggested by the Marxist fathers as inhibiting the growth of socialism in the United States.[15] It is noteworthy, for example, that they were concerned about the propensity of American radicals for political sectarianism, for treating Marxism or other radical doctrines as absolute dogmas to be applied in all situations. Engels referred to "that sectarian land America," where purists could always count on support.[16] Marx "confessed to a certain suspicion of 'Yankee socialists' as 'crotchety and sectarian.' "[17]

Why were the American socialists so sectarian? The sources of political dogmatism were linked in Marx's and Engels's minds to America's religiosity and Protestant sectarianism.[18] Marx was particularly impressed with the role of religion in American life. Following Tocqueville, he saw its vitality as a consequence of secular political institutions, the absence of an established church, and "endless fragmentation." "North America is pre-eminently the country of religiosity, as Beaumont, Tocqueville and the Englishman Hamilton unanimously assure us. . . . We find that religion not only exists, but displays a *fresh and vigorous vitality.*"[19]

In a society which has disestablished religion, "banishing it from the sphere of public law to that of private law," religion becomes

> the spirit of civil society, of the sphere of egoism, of *bellum omnium contra omnes* [war of each against all]. It is no longer the essence of *community,* but the essence of *difference.* . . . It is . . . the abstract avowal of specific perversity, *private whimsy,* and arbitrariness. The endless fragmentation of religion in North America, for example, gives it even *externally* the form of a purely individual affair.[20]

As a result, religious and political sectarianism are also certain to abound. And the most successful American radical movement, the pre–World War I Socialist Party, was more doctrinaire than others operating in democratic countries. It rejected opportunities to coalesce with trade unions in a labor party or to work with social democratic forces in the major parties, insisting on the virtue of a distinct, ideologically pure, socialist party.[21]

STRATIFICATION FACTORS

Marx and Engels cited among the "very great and peculiar difficulties for a continuous development of a workers' party" in the United States, the relative affluence of the country. Contrasting the situation in the two great English-speaking nations, Engels noted, "The native American Workingman's standard of living is considerably higher than even that of the British, and that alone suffices to place him in the rear [politically] for some time to come."[22] He also emphasized that in America, prosperity actually reached the workers, not merely the coffers of the bourgeoisie as in Russia (a class which was also experiencing growth in both countries).[23] The historian Harvey Klehr notes that in Marx's discussion of the United States economy in *Das Kapital,* he "suggests that American wages might always remain higher and satisfy more needs than those paid in Europe."[24]

Economic and population growth and an open land frontier produced high rates of social mobility, a factor also stressed by Marx in the early 1850s. He noted that "though classes, indeed, already exist, they have not yet become fixed, but continually change and interchange their elements in a constant state of flux."[25] Similarly, Engels, writing in the mid-1880s, reported that the ideal of America is a nation "without a permanent and hereditary proletariat."[26] As the post–World War II socialist theoretician Michael Harrington notes, Marx wrote that the belief of most Americans that their system assured them the opportunity to rise fostered the conviction that they lived in an equalitarian society. And Harrington, a close student of Marx's writings, concludes that he felt America therefore resembled a socialist society in value and status relations terms.[27] The argument that the socialist appeal was weak because the social content of Americanism resembled what European leftists thought socialism would provide was destined to reappear again and again through the twentieth century in the writing of socialists like Leon Samson, Sidney Hook, and Harrington.[28]

CONTEMPORARY APPROACHES

More contemporary sociological efforts to account for the political differences between the United States and Europe have necessarily focused on variations stressed by Tocqueville and Marx, the social class systems as reflected in lesser status differentials, and belief in greater opportunity to get ahead.

ACHIEVEMENT AND MERITOCRACY

Americans have never accepted the idea of rigid hereditary classes, except for the black minority, and even not for it in recent decades. Hard work, ambition, education, and ability have been regarded as more important for succeeding in life than social background. Recent opinion poll results indicate that almost three quarters of Americans believe they have a good chance of improving their standard of living, while only two fifths of Europeans display this level of optimism.[29] Americans are more disposed than Europeans to think they live in a meritocracy. They are more likely to feel that ambition is important for getting ahead in life and are less disposed to believe that "What you achieve depends largely on your family background." When asked in 1990 whether hard work or "luck and connections" are more likely to produce a better life and success, 44 percent of Americans pointed to the former as opposed to 24 percent of U.K. residents, 22 percent of the French, 29 percent of the Germans, and 20.5 percent of the Swedes.[30] A slightly different statement posed by the National Opinion Research Center (NORC) in 1993, "Some people say that people get ahead by their own hard work; others say that lucky breaks or help from other people are more important," found that 65 percent of all Americans polled replied that "hard work" was most important, 21 percent said both were important, and only 12 percent mentioned luck.

This emphasis on achievement, equality of opportunity, and meritocracy goes far back in the history of the country, underlying the support for the common school. Horace Mann, one of the most prominent of the pre-Civil War educational reformers, and his colleagues, wrote that they did not want European-type secondary-level *Gymnasia, lycées,* grammar, and English public (private) schools which educated the children of the upper 10 percent with a pre-university curriculum, while the rest went to vocational school or received little education. They noted that the European systems assumed that those who did not attend the elite high schools would become workers or peasants. The American educators advocated that everyone (except blacks) go to good public high schools, which would be common, that is, class integrated.

The strength of the early commitment to equality of opportunity may be seen in a proposal by the New York section of the Workingman's Party, which was at its height in 1828–32, that the common (class-integrated) school was not enough, would not produce equal opportunity, because the children of the poor had to go home to slum environments and to families who did not appreciate the need for education. To foster what we now call meritocracy, they proposed that all children from the age of six be required to attend state-supported boarding schools, with a uniform twenty-four hour environment.[31] This was akin to ancient suggestions by Plato and then contemporary ones by Robert Owen in England. Ironically, Newt Gingrich, speaking for congressional Republicans, has revived this idea in 1995, although only for the very poor and culturally isolated.

The continued greater American commitment to meritocracy more than a century and a half later is reflected in the findings that citizens in the United States have been more disposed than Europeans to favor greater expenditures for education. Reviewing polling data over a fifty-year span, Benjamin Page and Robert Shapiro comment that "education has long been an area in which most Americans want government to spend more money."[32] Although, as noted in chapter One, a much

higher proportion of Americans than Europeans receive higher education, many more Americans (44%) than those across the Atlantic
believe opportunities for young people to go to college should be
increased still further (compared with 29% in the U.K., 8.5% in Italy,
9.8% in West Germany, and 5.5% in Austria).[33]

The American Creed has continued its emphasis on equality of
opportunity, on meritocracy. It assumes that everyone should try to get
ahead and have the opportunity to succeed. Obviously, many Americans do not have the possibility to secure a high-status or well-paid
position. All the empirical studies of social mobility, in America as
elsewhere, demonstrate that occupational placement or achievement is
associated with social origins. Still, only 31 percent of Americans
agree/strongly agree that "what you achieve in life depends largely on
your family background," as contrasted to many more in Europe (Great
Britain 53%, Austria 51%, and Italy 63%).[34]

Americans are also less likely than Europeans, or more specifically,
the British, to think of their society as divided into two groups, the
"haves" and the "have-nots." Only one quarter, 26 percent, of Americans, compared to three quarters, or 73 percent of the citizens of Great
Britain, agreed in 1988 that their country is so divided. When asked
whether they personally belong to the haves or the have-nots, only 17
percent of Americans answered "have-nots," while over a third, 37 percent, of the British put themselves in the poorer stratum.[35]

Since early in the nineteenth century, as we saw earlier, the American road to success in large measure has been through education.
America has led the world in enrollment in the most important type of
general education which qualifies for occupational achievement, first
in the proportions graduating from public elementary school, then high
school, and more recently in the numbers going to and finishing college
and continuing with postgraduate training. Europeans generally have
been less likely to attend the kinds of schools that lead to university.
Americans, therefore, have spent a larger proportion of their government revenues on education in order to admit more *individuals* into the
race for success. On the other hand, of course, Europeans have provided proportionally more revenues for welfare, for state measures to
upgrade those at the bottom. That is, their efforts to improve the situation of the less privileged have given greater emphasis to *group* benefits, public housing, state employment, government health coverage,
unemployment benefits, family allowances, and old age pensions.
These latter policies have been supported in Europe by both the conservative and the left forces to a much greater extent than in the

United States. The welfare state was introduced in Britain and Germany by Disraeli and Bismarck, both conservatives. The organized left parties and the trade union movements subsequently pressed for a more elaborate expansion of government measures to improve the position of the lower strata. They were less insistent on opening the door to upward mobility through the expansion of universities. In America, welfare state measures have grown considerably during the Depression and postwar eras. The rates of increase, however, have declined in recent decades, and in any case the amounts spent have always been less as a proportion of the GNP and government revenues than in Europe.

Political exceptionalism, the failure of socialist parties in the United States, has been explained by numerous factors—so many that the outcome seems overdetermined. The variety of specific explanations fall into two categories. One involves emphasis on societal variables; the other focuses on factors internal to the political system. While the two sets of hypotheses are, of course, not mutually exclusive, some analysts have placed more of a stress on one dimension than the other. The various hypotheses, many of which were remarked upon by Marx and Engels, may be grouped under the following headings.

SOCIETAL FACTORS

1. America as a new society, the absence of a feudal tradition of class relations to structure politics along class lines.

2. Americanism as surrogate socialism and/or the liberal tradition as the predominant public philosophy. This approach, elaborated below, suggests Americans see their society as egalitarian and democratic and have found no need for drastic changes to attain already existing objectives.

3. The emphases in the value system on individualism and anti-statism derived from America's Protestant sectarian past and revolutionary values, which imply opposition to a strong collectivist or welfare state.

4. The impact of a steady rise in standards of living, particularly for the working class. The United States has been the wealthiest country in the developed world, at least since the post–Civil War period. Various consumer goods have been more widely distributed in America than elsewhere. As Werner Sombart argued, "all Socialist utopias came to nothing on roast beef and apple pie."[36]

5. The decline in the relative income position of the poorest fifth of the

income distribution is, as John Kenneth Galbraith has noted, concentrated in marginalized groups, such as female single heads of family, illegal immigrants, and parts of the minority populations, who tend to be politically isolated and have low voter turnout.[37]

6. Accompanying the growth in productivity and the spread of educational opportunities have been increased opportunities for upward mobility. Such opportunities have not declined; the potential for social and economic advancement in the post–World War II period has probably been greater than at any other point in American history.

7. Recent research on geographic mobility by historians and social scientists has documented the "remarkable volatility of the American working class," and reemphasized the propensity for geographic movement and the lack of stable community roots as factors inhibiting the formation of class-consciousness.

8. The consequences of being a multi-ethnic and multi-racial immigrant society.

8a. The impact of continued immigration in encouraging upward mobility by native-born whites. Census data indicate that from the second half of the nineteenth century through to the 1930s, immigrants filled the lower-status, less skilled, least well-paid jobs, enabling the children of immigrants and third- or more generation native-born to occupy more privileged positions. Since World War II, blacks, Chicanos, Puerto Ricans, and new waves of immigrants from various Third World countries have played the role once held by European immigrants. Hence, beyond the fact of greater productivity (i.e., higher standards of living) is the advantage held by native whites.

8b. Ethnic, religious, and racial differentiation have fragmented the working class and retarded the growth of class-conscious politics.

8c. The fact that a very large proportion of the working class was Catholic from the late nineteenth century on, since the Church worked actively before World War I to resist socialist appeals among workers and trade unionists.

POLITICAL FACTORS

1. The free "gift of the suffrage" emphasized by Lenin and others. As Selig Perlman noted, the masses in the United States attained the suffrage prior to efforts to organize them into class-conscious parties. In

Europe, for the most part, socialist parties appealed to the workers for support before the vote was universal. Lenin himself stressed that socialism grew through the struggle for electoral democracy. In America, the franchise predated the movement.[38]

2. The constitutional and electoral system, which results in a two-coalition party system in electing a president, since only one person can hold executive power. As noted in chapter One, it has been argued by many that in a two-coalition party system it is almost mandated by the Constitution that efforts at slowly building up third parties must fail. The spread of the primary system of nomination has strengthened this factor. Though no third party has become institutionalized, a number of independent candidates—Roosevelt in 1912, LaFollette in 1924, Wallace in 1968, Anderson in 1980, and Perot in 1992—received proportionately many more votes than socialist nominees from 1900 to the present, thus demonstrating that the electoral system was not responsible for the weakness of socialism in America.

3. The flexibility of the two-coalition party system to co-opt and/or respond to manifest evidence of pervasive discontent, often in the form of mass movements and/or third parties. This flexibility frequently has involved a major party "stealing the thunder" of the dissenters by adopting their policies. The two parties almost invariably respond to the social movements, thereby reducing social strains and the potential base for institutionalized radical parties. The primary system encourages groups to act within the two major parties, rather than against them.

4. Repression. Syndicalist, socialist, and communist movements have suffered from political repression that broke up the continuity of radical protest. It should be noted, however, that anti-radical repression was much greater in many European countries, but did not prevent the emergence of large leftist parties, some of which, like the German Social Democrats or the revolutionaries in Czarist Russia, grew greatly while being outlawed.

COMPARATIVE SOCIAL STRUCTURE

Most of the twentieth-century efforts to demonstrate the validity of particular interpretations of the exceptional character of America's socialist movement have compared conditions here with those in Europe. Some of the most influential writings—such as those espoused by the Fabian H. G. Wells, Italian Communist leader and theoretician Antonio Gramsci, American socialist writer Leon Samson, liberal political theorist Louis Hartz, and the late leader of the post–World War II American socialist movement Michael Harrington—have emphasized ways in which the special history and resultant unique social structure of the United States have negated efforts to foster class-consciousness.[39] In one of the earliest comparative efforts to explain the weakness of socialism and class-consciousness in the United States, Wells suggested that the absence of socialism and Toryism in the United States reflected the fact that two major European classes, the subservient land-bound peasants and the aristocracy, were missing from American society. The absence of the former avoided a "servile tradition," as Tocqueville noted, while the absence of the latter meant that the Tory sense of "state responsibility, which in the old European theory of society was supposed to give significance to the whole," was also missing. Louis Hartz elaborated this thesis in the 1950s.

Antonio Gramsci, perhaps the most important non-Russian theoretician of the communist movement, following a logic similar to that of Wells and Hartz, also emphasized America's unique origin and resultant value system as a source of its exceptional political and economic systems.[40] He stressed that America's special sociological background resulted in a general value system, a conception of life which he called "Americanism." It is pure rationalism, uninhibited by the traditional values of rigid social classes derived from feudalism. Americans, regardless of class, emphasize the virtues of hard work by all, of the need to exploit nature rather than people.[41] The interpretation proposed by Gramsci that Americanism represents a distinct ideology, one that is accepted by American workers, has been independently elaborated by a number of writers and social scientists in their efforts to explain the absence or weakness of socialism in America.

Hermann Keyserling, a conservative German aristocrat; Leon Samson, an American socialist intellectual; Sidney Hook, a socialist philosopher; Michael Harrington, the founder of the Democratic Socialists; and American historian Carl Degler, in writings which span the period from 1929 to the present, have all put forth or accepted the argument that socialism as a political movement is weak in the United States because the ideological content of Americanism is highly similar to socialism and hence Americans believe they already have most of what it promises.[42] As Harrington writes:

Americanism, the official ideology of the society, became a kind of "substi-
tutive socialism." The European ruling classes . . . were open in their con-
tempt for the proletariat. But in the United States equality, and even class-
lessness, the creation of wealth for all and political liberty were extolled in
the public schools. It is, of course, true that this was sincere verbiage
which concealed an ugly reality, but nonetheless it had a profound impact
upon the national consciousness. "The idea that everyone can be a capitalist," Samson wrote in a perceptive insight, "is an American concept of capitalism. It is a socialist concept of capitalism." And that, Marx had understood in 1846, was why socialism would first appear in this country in a
capitalist disguise. What he could not possibly anticipate was that this
dialectical irony would still be in force over one hundred years later. . . .
[T]he country's image of itself contained so many socialist elements that
one did not have to go to a separate movement opposed to the status quo in
order to give vent to socialist emotions.[43]

EXCEPTIONALISM IN NORTH AMERICAN
PERSPECTIVE: CANADA AND THE UNITED STATES

Canada, as noted earlier, offers those seeking to understand American
behavior and values an excellent unit for comparison.[44] The continent-
spanning neighbors, once part of the same political unit, and formed as
separate nations from the same event, have much in common culturally and structurally. Yet, they also vary in ways which have produced
different social and political systems, evident in the fact that Canada
resembles the rest of the industrial world in having socialist and trade
union movements which are much stronger than those in the United
States. The vote for Canada's national social democratic party, the
New Democrats (NDP), has varied considerably since the 1930s,
reaching 20 percent in the 1988 elections, and at times much more in
the opinion polls, sufficient to occasionally place the party in second
place. However, though still a viable electoral party, its support fell to 9
percent in a five-party contest in 1993. More strikingly, as of 1995 the
NDP has been the governing party and/or the official parliamentary
opposition in every province west of Ontario, even though its support
in the opinion polls is down. The 1991 election of social democratic
governments with overwhelming legislative majorities in the Canadian
provinces of British Columbia and Saskatchewan, following a comparable triumph in Ontario a year earlier, brought 52 percent of the nation's
population under social democratic rule. Another 25 percent have
been so governed since September 1994 by the separatist Parti Québé-

cois, a statist party which tried to affiliate to the Socialist International but was turned down because the NDP objected. The NDP was reelected in Saskatchewan, but lost power in Ontario in June 1995, and is currently the official opposition in Alberta and Manitoba.[45]

There has obviously been nothing approaching this record in the United States. The American Socialist Party's highest national vote was 6 percent in 1912. It secured 2 percent in 1932, in the depth of the Depression. Between 1936 and 1952, the party's vote fell off to under 1 percent, and it stopped running national candidates. Although the Socialist Party captured the mayoralty in many cities, particularly before 1918, it never came close to winning statewide office anywhere. Currently, the largest socialist group in America, the Democratic Socialists, has around eight thousand members and does not take part as a party in elections. The biggest third party in the United States is the Libertarian, a free market, anti-state group which secures a few hundred thousand votes, although Ross Perot, running as an independent, secured 19 percent in 1992.

The comparative story on organized labor is relatively similar. Although American unions do have millions of members, they are among the weakest in the industrialized democracies in terms of union density, the proportion eligible who belong. As of 1995, roughly 15 to 16 percent of all employed Americans belong to unions, while only 10 percent of those working in the private sector are members.

Different estimates for Canada agree that union density may have reached a peak of 40 percent in 1983 and has since fallen off to around 38 percent, still more than double the American proportion. And the record documents that except for the period 1938 to 1958—roughly the time of CIO organization—the proportion unionized in Canada has been higher than in the United States. Estimates by Huxley, Kettler and Struthers, and Bain and Price indicate that Canadian union density exceeded the American from 1918 to 1938, and again from 1958 to the present.[46] The period from the mid-1930s to the mid-1950s was one of growth by American labor organizations encouraged by New Deal government support but also, more importantly, by the Depression-stimulated social movement forces that pressed for working-class organization.

Starting in 1955, however, American unions began to decline fairly steadily from around one third of the employed labor force to less than half that proportion, while the Canadian continued to grow from the 1960s to the 1980s. The differences vary by sector, but in almost all that may be distinguished—for example, government, manufacturing, and private service in the large sectors, and various specific industry groups in the small—a greater segment is organized north of the border than south of it.[47]

Given this background, there are a number of questions to be addressed: (1) why does Canada have an electorally viable social democratic party while the United States does not? (2) why is union density in Canada so much greater than below the border? and (3) why have union movements been declining earlier and more steadily in the United States than in Canada, although as of the late 1980s to a slight extent in the north as well? Though some of these issues have been treated earlier with regard to the United States, this section addresses the American and Canadian cases from an explicitly binational comparative perspective.

Explanations for the success or failure of socialist parties in North America vary between dissimilarities in the electoral and government systems and in certain basic values. Those specific to unions also incorporate the possible effects of the different political climates, emphasizing that the nature and administration of Canadian labor legislation are more union-friendly than the American. The value differences between the two countries appear to account for the differing cross-border employee responses to union appeals, as well as for dissimilarities in worker and employer behavior, and variations in the way the two political systems treat their labor organizations.

SOCIALISM AND STATISM IN NORTH AMERICA

To look first at the sources of the variations in the position of socialism, many observers of the North American political scene have pointed to the varying effects on the prospects for third parties in the different constitutional systems. As I noted earlier, the British political model, followed in Canada, encompassing the parliamentary single-member district system, together with the disciplined legislative parties required to sustain cabinets, is favorable to a multi-party system, whereas the American division of powers with its presidential system discourages more than two. In the first, the effective election unit is the constituency. Parties which have no chance to win a national or provincial plurality can still effectively contest constituencies that are sociologically distinct—wheat farmers, coal miners, ethnic groupings, and so on. Minor ones may be major parties in some local areas. Since 1921, Canada has experienced situations in which economically or culturally distinct sections, provinces, or ethnic groups have found themselves in conflict with their traditional party allegiance, and, not wanting to go over to their major party rivals, have supported third parties, such as Progressives, United Farmers, Labor, Cooperative Commonwealth Federation, Social Credit, New Democrats, Bloc Québécois, and Reform. As of 1995, Canada has five significant parties.

The American constitutional or electoral system analysis presented earlier may account for a predominantly two-party rather than a multiparty model. But this does not help to explain its character—why social democratic tendencies have been weaker than other third-party efforts. During this century three non-socialist third presidential candidates (Theodore Roosevelt, Robert LaFollette, and Ross Perot) have been able to secure 17 or more percent of the vote, and a fourth (George Wallace) received 12 percent. Even John Anderson with his 7 percent in 1980 was stronger than any socialist nominee. To explain the political variations in North America, therefore, requires analyzing transborder value differences.[48]

As many Canadians have tried to remind us, the American Revolution produced two countries which developed distinct cultures. The United States is the country of the revolution, Canada of the counterrevolution.[49] The former is the part of British North America that successfully seceded, while Canada is the area that remained British. These diverse outcomes ultimately contributed to, among other things, very different socialist and trade union movements in the United States and Canada. The existence of an electorally viable social democratic party in Canada has been interpreted by various analysts as an outgrowth of the greater influence of the Tory-statist tradition and the stronger collectivity orientation north of the border.[50] In Canada, as in most of Europe, a common history defines the nation, while the United States, as emphasized in chapter One, is founded on an ideological creed.

Conservatism in Canada is descended from Toryism and monarchical statism; in the United States, it is derived from Whiggism, classical anti-statist liberalism. After the Revolution, about fifty thousand Tory Americans moved to Canada. Conversely, some Yankee residents of what was originally northern New England—Nova Scotia and New Brunswick—migrated to the new nation. The Revolution produced an interesting transmutation of religion. Congregationalism had been strong in Nova Scotia and New Brunswick, as in the rest of New England before the Revolution. After the Treaty of Paris in 1783, many Congregational ministers moved south.[51] Conversely, many Anglican priests went north. Hence a shift of populations in political and religious terms occurred within English-speaking North America.

Catholic Quebec, which had become a British province in 1763, remained with its conquerors in 1776 for practical reasons. Quebec was controlled by the clergy, since almost all the secular elites returned to France after the British conquest. The priesthood of the province understood that they would have much more trouble with the anti-Papist Puritan Yankees than they would with the British Anglicans. Other good reasons for staying British soon developed. The French Revolution was anti-clerical and materialistic. The Francophone clergy, including émigrés from France, deliberately sought to cut off all contact with the mother country. This made Quebec a counter-revolutionary society twice over. Canada thus became a country of two counter-revolutions: English and French Canada opposed the American Revolution, and French Canada rejected the French Revolution.[52]

In Canada, the Tory tradition has meant support for a strong state, communitarianism, group solidarity, and elitism. Most provinces continue to finance church-controlled schools. Public ownership, much of it instituted under Conservative Party administrations, is considerably more extensive than in the United States. Canadian governments spend more proportionately on welfare.[53] Canadians are more supportive of narrowing income differences, while Americans put more emphasis on equal opportunity or meritocratic competition. Conversely, the former, whether as corporations or individuals, donate much less to charitable causes than Americans.[54] The Canadian criminal justice system has resembled those of Europe, stressing crime control and the rights of the state. The American emphasis, as we have seen, is on due process and the rights of the accused.

These generalizations are sustained by opinion polls which indicate that Canadians, at both elite and mass levels, are more supportive than Americans of state intervention. Summarizing surveys of high-level civil servants and federal, state, and provincial legislators, Robert Presthus reported

> the sharp difference between the two [national] elites on "economic liberalism," defined as a preference for "big government. . . ." Only 17 percent of the American legislative elite ranks high on this disposition, compared with fully 44 percent of their Canadian peers. . . . This direction is the same among bureaucrats, only 17 percent of whom rank high among the American sample, compared with almost 30 percent among Canadians.[55]

Reflecting the other side of the Tory-social democratic tradition, a number of comparative academic surveys indicate that Canadians are more deferential than Americans to elites and institutions. Basically, the American tradition does not encourage obedience to the state and the law. Canadians, as we saw earlier, accepted the metric system when their government proclaimed it; Americans simply would not do so. Similar reactions occurred when the two governments decided to give up the dollar bill, given inflation, and to use dollar coins instead, keeping the two-dollar bill the one most in circulation. Today, there is no one-dollar bill in Canada, only a dollar coin referred to as the "loony." The two-dollar bill is the most widely used tender. In the United States, on the other hand, one can only find dollar coins in Las Vegas and Atlantic City, while the two-dollar bill is abundant in only one place, Jefferson's home, Monticello, because his picture is on it.

Canada's Tory-statist traditions are reinforced by the country's religious history. Canada's preeminent economic historian Harold Innis may have said it all when he wrote that a "counter-revolutionary tradition implies an emphasis on ecclesiasticism."[56] The majority of Canadians adhere to the Roman Catholic or Anglican Church, each of which is hierarchically organized and continued until recently to have a strong relationship to the state, while the country's sectarians largely joined together in the most successful ecumenical effort the Protestant world has seen, the United Church of Canada, which, like the Catholic Church, is politically communitarian. American sects, strikingly different in values and behavior from the American churches, as noted in chapter Two, not only have remained separate but are religiously fecund, having spawned more new denominations than any other nation. In other words, they have remained sectarian, and have continued to foster individualism and anti-statism. The American political tradition has been reinforced by the religious commitment of the majority to the "nonconformist," largely congregationally organized sects, which emphasize a personal and individualistic relation to God, one not mediated by state-supported, hierarchically organized churches.

Both Canadian cultures—secular and religious—have furthered a variant of the Tory paternalistic and statist view of the world. As the British labor union expert Henry Phelps Brown notes, the country had "no tradition or doctrine [that] inculcated an abhorrence of collectivism such as prevailed south of the border. A Tory tradition . . . stressed authority and hierarchy, but with these went solidarity and benevolence, which occupy some common ground with collectivism."[57] Seeking to explain the rise of social democracy in Quebec, Canadian political scientists William Christian and Colin Campbell suggest that it reflects the propensity for collectivism inherent in the province's values. They conclude that "Quebec's stock of [traditional] political ideas includes a strong collectivist element. . . . Quebec's collectivist past provided receptive and fruitful soil for socialist ideas once the invasion of liberal capitalism had broken the monopoly of the old conservative ideology."[58] The United States, as we have seen, has remained through the nineteenth and twentieth centuries the extreme example of a classically liberal society that rejects the assumptions of the alliance of throne and altar, of ascriptive elitism, of statism, of *noblesse oblige,* and of communitarianism.

Canadian scholars have emphasized, in the words of Herschel Hardin, that "Canada, in its essentials, is a public enterprise country, always has been, and probably always will be," while the United States has a "private enterprise culture."[59] Or as the political scientist J. T. McLeod notes, "the pervasiveness of state intervention, regulation, and the frequent appearance of public ownership" characterizes Canada, where "the State has always dominated and shaped the economy." Unlike the United States, Canada "has never experienced a period of pure unadulterated *laissez-faire* market capitalism."[60] The period from 1960 to the mid-1980s witnessed a particularly rapid expansion in the number of crown corporations; fully 70 percent of them were created in that quarter of a century.[61] Canada introduced most major social programs earlier than the United States. Some in the North cover areas not dealt with south of the border, such as family allowances and universal state-provided medical coverage. Except "when a 'crisis' more severely affects the United States than Canada or . . . major constitutional problems prevent an immediate Canadian policy response," welfare state developments have been earlier in Canada, and are usually "more advanced in terms of program development, coverage, and benefits, and are financed in a 'more egalitarian' fashion."[62] Canadians receive more than twice the proportion of their income from government transfer payments as Americans. Unemployment insurance is limited to twenty-six weeks in the United States; it can be extended to forty-two weeks in Canada. In 1994, "Canada will spend $12.6 billion on unemployment payments alone. The United States, by contrast, spends about $35 billion for a population 10 times that of Canada."[63]

In *Continental Divide,* published in 1990, I presented a myriad of aggregate and opinion poll data attesting to the varying values and opinions of Americans and Canadians. With respect to the role of the state in economic and welfare activities, they indicate, as expected, that those living in the North are much more favorable to social democratic or communitarian orientations than their neighbors to the south.[64] A more recent comparative North American study reports further congruent findings that "Canadians are more likely than Americans to favor 'the right to a publicly funded health care system available to all regardless of financial situation' (71 percent of Canadians and 52 percent of Americans) and 'the right of every individual to be guaranteed a minimum income' (62 percent and 51 percent)."[65]

Leftist collectivist, communitarian (welfare), and particularistic movements have emerged in Western society in some part in conjunction with conservative (Tory) emphases on elitism and statism. There is, of course, good reason to believe that social democratic movements are the other side of statist conservatism, that Tories and socialists are likely to be found in the same polity, while a dominant Lockean liberal (anti-statist) tradition inhibits the emergence of socialism as a political force.[66] Socialism is strong where Tory and monarchical statism have legitimated strong government, and where elitism has fostered organized counter reactions by the less privileged strata. A tradition of state paternalism fostered by national elites has served to legitimate efforts by the less privileged strata to mobilize resources to improve their position through government action. The Canadian socialist labor historian Gad Horowitz has noted that "socialism has more in common with toryism than with [classical] liberalism for liberalism is possessive individualism, while socialism and toryism are variants of collectivism."[67] The fact that the American national tradition is egalitarian, anti-elitist, individualistic, and classically liberal, has weakened efforts to mobilize workers and others on behalf of socialist and collectivist objectives, including unions. Prior to the Great Depression, the American labor movement, both in its moderate American Federation of Labor (AFL) form and radical Industrial Workers of the World (IWW) guise, opposed programs to extend the role of the state. The majority of both, like other American groupings, were suspicious of government, and therefore also rejected socialism. In a recent work dealing with law and labor unions in America, William Forbath notes that "the founders of American labor history, John Commons . . . Selig Perlman, and generations of scholars after them have sought to explain . . . [the] phenomenon, widely known as American 'exceptionalism,' " labor's " 'pragmatic,' voluntaristic perspective."[68]

Most Canadian and American trade unionists once belonged to the same international unions, part of the AFL until the CIO split in the mid-1930s, but the affiliates in the two countries have varied in ways which have reflected the divergent national traditions.[69] The dominant leaders of American workers, as noted above, were anti-statist until the New Deal and opposed a separate labor or socialist party. Canadian union officials, though not formally socialists until the 1930s, repeatedly endorsed the principle of independent labor political action from the turn of the century on, and were much more favorable to state intervention than their counterparts to the south. As Gad Horowitz notes, "The TLC [Trades and Labour Congress], though it consisted almost entirely of Canadian locals of AFL unions, and was greatly influenced by [Samuel] Gompers, never adopted the Gompers approach *in toto*. . . . [Unlike the AFL] the TLC . . . never took a stand *against* socialism. Unlike the AFL, it never adopted the phraseology of *laissez-faire* and Lockean individualism."[70]

During the 1930s, many labor activists took part in the formation of the country's first electorally viable social democratic party, the Cooperative Commonwealth Federation (CCF). The relationship became stronger over the years. A poll of labor leaders in 1958 revealed that 45 percent of the TLC (AFL) officials surveyed supported the CCF, as did an overwhelming 93 percent of the Canadian Congress of Labor (CCL-CIO) executives.[71] The two labor federations, the TLC and the CCL, merged into the Canadian Labour Congress in the mid-1950s and then went on to join with the CCF to transmute the socialist movement into the New Democratic Party (NDP) in the early 1960s. The united Canadian union movement has continued to officially support the NDP.

Although the Canadian economy has been weaker than the American, the postwar boom, involving extensive growth, an upgrading of the occupational structure, and higher income and standards of living, also occurred in Canada. But in spite of such improvements, which of course did not prevent occasional periods of recession, Canadian socialism held its own nationally, prior to the 1993 election, generally obtaining between a fifth and a quarter of the vote in English Canada. Social democracy gained a new bastion in French Canada with the rise of the Parti Québécois to major party status in the 1970s, and to government at the start of the eighties and again in 1994. And, as noted, unlike the situation in the United States, the Canadian labor movement reached new heights in membership in the early 1980s.

CROSS-BORDER UNION DENSITIES

The explanations for the cross-border differences in union strength, like those for socialism, primarily vary between emphasis on the effects of dissimilarities in values and of political structures, in this case labor representation legislation. The British labor economist Henry Phelps

Brown, cited earlier, points out that "the strong tradition of Toryism in Canada laid its stress on solidarity and against individualism and the fissiparous impact of market forces. Here it found common ground . . . with the propensity of the worker to organize for the protection of the conditions of his working life."[72]

The big anomaly in the comparison between the two countries is the greater growth in union density in the United States from the mid-1930s to the mid-1950s, which temporarily placed the American labor movement ahead of the Canadian. The same period also witnessed a change in the political and ideological behavior of much of organized labor in the United States. The American movement became involved in political action, largely in support of the Democratic Party, while the CIO and sections of the AFL adopted political programs calling for a high level of state involvement in planning the economy, as well as sharp increases in welfare and health programs.

These changes reflected the impact of the Great Depression. That unprecedented event, which undermined traditional American beliefs among large sectors of the population, led to the acceptance by a majority of the need for state action to reduce unemployment, to assist those adversely affected by the economic collapse, and to support trade unionism. Analyses of public opinion polls and election results noted that class factors had become highly differentiating variables. Samuel Lubell, who conducted in-depth interviews with many voters in the 1930s and early 1940s, concluded that the electoral support for Roosevelt and New Deal programs constituted "a class-conscious vote for the first time in American history. . . . The New Deal appears to have accomplished what the Socialists, the IWW and the Communists never could approach. It has drawn a class line across the face of American politics."[73]

This Depression-inspired development seemingly declined with the postwar prosperity that effectively lasted through to the beginning of the 1990s, though with some significant recessionary and inflationary periods. The Roosevelt New Deal electoral impact has ended; the correlations between class position and party voting have declined. From 1952 to 1988, Republicans won seven of the ten presidential elections, although the Democrats, who are more effective at local appeals to national interests and values, controlled the Congress much more often than not. Bill Clinton, the most centrist Democratic nominee since 1968, was elected in 1992, albeit with 43 percent of the vote. The third candidate, Ross Perot, appealed strongly to fiscal conservatives, and most of his fifth of the vote went over to the Republicans in

1994, giving them a strong congressional majority pledged to oppose statism and extensive welfare benefits. What the prolonged postwar prosperity did, in my judgment, was to refurbish the classic American laissez-faire, anti-statist, market-oriented, meritocratic, individualistic values; in short, the Whig tradition.

Considerable opinion poll data show Americans have strengthened their belief in opportunity for the individual.[74] They also strongly oppose government restrictions on becoming rich. When the Roper Organization repeated a question in 1992 which they had asked in 1939: "Do you think there should be a law limiting the amount of money any individual is allowed to earn in a year?" it found a large falloff, from 24 to 9 in the percentage favoring limits. The drop was even greater among those at the lowest income level, from 32 to 9. Similarly, when asked by the National Opinion Research Center to place themselves in a "social class"—middle, lower, working, or upper—the percent replying "working class" declined steadily from 60 in 1949 to 47 in 1972, changing little from then on. It was 45 percent in 1993. Conversely, those identifying themselves as "middle class" rose from one third of the population at the end of the 1940s to 45 percent in the nineties. And in tandem with such changes the majority turned against unions. The approval rating of unions in the United States in the Gallup Poll went down steadily from the mid-1950s to the 1980s, and this decline closely paralleled the falloff in union density. The bimodal correlation is high, around .75.[75]

Prosperity, however, was not associated with a decline in social democratic electoral strength or trade union membership in Canada, or in support for welfare state values, although the electoral strength of the NDP dropped considerably in the 1993 parliamentary election, which occurred during the country's worst postwar recession. The party, ironically, seemed to suffer from being in office provincially. Canadians turned overwhelmingly against the two parties, the Conservatives who then held federal power and the NDP, which governed three provinces, with a majority of the population. Unlike the situation in the United States, there has not been a postwar revival of the values of classical liberalism, since these have never been the national tradition. Canada's five significant political parties remain committed in varying degrees to an activist government, to communitarianism. The two conservative parties, the Progressive Conservatives, who headed the federal government from 1984 to 1993, and the new Reform Party, which replaced the Progressive Conservatives as the dominant force on the right in the 1993 elections, are both "social conservatives," with the

Conservative Party reflecting "humanitarian" concerns much more than Reform. In the 1988 election, Tory Prime Minister Brian Mulroney called the welfare state part of Canada's "sacred heritage."[76] His successor as prime minister and party leader in 1993, Kim Campbell, acknowledged in a private discussion that Canada has a "social democratic culture." During the 1993 election, Preston Manning, the leader of the Reformers, praised Canada's socialists, the New Democratic Party, saying at a campaign rally that "thanks largely to the NDP, the Canadian Parliament now has a social conscience that permeates every party. That's why medicare [Canada's government health plan], pensions and unemployment insurance are safe. . . ."[77]

The divergence in the trajectories of union density in the two countries reflects the undermining of the social democratic elements unleashed by the Great Depression in the South, and their continuation in the North. Labor law expert Paul Weiler concludes that "projections from current trends estimate that U.S. union density will drop below 10% by the year 2000, and will not 'stabilize' until it reaches a point somewhere under 5% by the year 2020."[78] Labor economist Leo Troy notes that the current density level in the private sector, "just under 13%[,] is about equal to unions' share of private nonfarm employment in 1929." Extrapolating trends, he anticipates that it "will slip to about 7% by the onset of the new century."[79] If union density in the United States is declining to pre-1930s levels, or possibly lower, the reversal appears partly related to the steady decay over the postwar era of the liberal or social democratic values which emerged in the 1930s.

This is not to deny that changes in the structure of the labor force have contributed to the weakening of unions, particularly in the private sector. Classic centers of union strength like mining, steel, printing, and shipbuilding—the goods production industries—have declined, while the much less unionized service sectors have increased. During the last decade, the proportion employed in union-favorable public employment positions has remained steady in Canada and declined somewhat in the United States. But these changes only explain a little of the variation between the two countries. All the recent comparative analyses agree that a small part of the gap results from "the greater extent of public employment in Canada."[80] While government employees in both countries are much more unionized than those in the private sector, those in Canada are better organized than those in the United States—66 percent of the publicly employed labor force in the former, 42 percent in the latter. But Noah Meltz points out that as of

1990, private-sector workers also are significantly more organized in the North than in the South, 21 percent to 12 percent.[81]

The differences are clearly not a function of structural variations in the two economies. As the Canadian political scientist John Richards concludes in a detailed comparative statistical analysis, "structural differences between Canada and the United States do explain a little of the union density gap—but not much."[82] His results reiterate the findings of W. Craig Riddell, who also reports that "the 'structuralist hypothesis' explains very little of the Canada-U.S. unionization differential, about 15 percent to be precise."[83] And in an even broader comparative study, the Dutch trade union authority Jelle Visser notes that "*sizeable differences* in the level of union organization across advanced capitalist democracies" occur "not only between the extremes . . . but also within the same region." Between "the United States and Canada . . . the differences in levels of unionization are much larger than warranted by differences in economic development, industrialization, social structure or public spending."[84] Analyzing cross-border changes in union density, Meltz finds that "the long term trends . . . [reveal a] virtually identical relationship between the rates of private service sector union density to that in all other sectors in both Canada and the United States . . . around a mean of 21 percent. . . ." He concludes that the "stability of the relationship and its similarity in both countries . . . suggests that the factors governing the overall relationship of union density [among industries] between Canada and the United States apply equally" to the private and public sectors.[85] This finding lends substantial weight to results reported earlier that the elements that differentiate and affect variations in union density between the two countries are not primarily structural, whether political or economic, that a large part of the answer lies in more sociological factors such as those I have stressed here.[86]

The thesis that the variations in union density reflect cross-national differences in values that result in a greater demand for unionization north of the border has been countered by comparative evidence on social attitudes. When asked directly in recent years about feelings toward trade unions, "more Canadians than Americans view unions as too powerful; more Canadians than Americans perceive labor as the greatest threat; fewer Canadians than Americans have confidence in labor as an institution; more Canadians than Americans blame unions for inflation"; and Americans are more likely to express approval of unions than Canadians.[87] These findings appear to contradict the thesis that Canadian values are more supportive of trade unionism and class organization than American. The conundrum, however, may result from the different national contexts within which the citizens of the two countries respond to *specific issues,* as compared to values. These attitudes (much like the even greater anti-union polling responses in Australia and Great Britain, whose labor organizations and Labor parties are more important and stronger than those in Canada) may be a reaction to the fact that Canadian unionism does have more power, is indeed stronger than its southern compeer.[88] They may also reflect antagonism by Canadians to the high strike rates in their country, which have been much greater during the 1970s and 1980s than those recorded south of the border.[89]

Some indication of continued cross-national differences in relevant values, as distinct from attitudes, is suggested by the variations in response to a question posed in the 1980 and 1990 World Values Surveys (see chapter Four, p. 145, for the wording). When asked to give priority to freedom or equality of position, Americans were the least likely of the citizens of seventeen developed countries to choose equality. Less than a quarter, 24 percent, did so in 1990. The corresponding figure for Canada was 34 percent, for fourteen European nations, 37 percent, and for Japan, 38 percent. The numbers were almost identical ten years earlier.

Beyond the supportive evidence from public opinion data are differences in behavior. Unions generally favor strict seniority and job security or tenure. And Canada and other more group-oriented or particularistic nations give more emphasis to seniority and job security in their public employment practices than the United States. Thus, America follows meritocratic up-or-out policies at different age levels in the military and foreign services, Canada does not. Canadian universities, like their British and Japanese counterparts, award life tenure more quickly and readily than American ones. These differences support the assumption that values congruent with trade union principles are stronger outside of the United States.

The greater expressed hostility to unions north of the border may also derive from the closer link between the Canadian labor movement and a political party, the NDP, which never secured more than 20 percent of the vote in a national election. The American trade unions, on the other hand, are less directly affiliated with a party, but are identified with the Democrats, who, until 1994, led the Republicans in party identifications, congressional elections, and control of most state governments for most of the post–World War II era, usually by a considerable margin. These national differences in popular support for the union-supported parties may affect the cross-border variations in the popularity of unions. Opponents of the NDP may carry their rejection of the party over to their feelings about the political and power position of unions, at the same time that most "Canadians perceive unions as fulfilling a legitimate role within society."[90] A survey of attitudes to unions north of the border taken in 1989 reported that "Canadians do not endorse labour's financial support for the New Democratic Party: seven in ten respondents to the 1989 poll felt that labour unions should not be involved in this activity, similar to the level of opposition toward this practice recorded two years ago."[91]

One may argue, as I have done in previous writings, that values are deep sets of feelings, much more stable than attitudes, superordinate sentiments, and are reflected in cross-national differences over beliefs about class relationships, equality and inequality, the role of the state, individualism, communitarianism, and the like. Henry Phelps Brown argues that Canada's Tory statist and particularistic history helped to generate social democratic institutions and communitarian values in the second half of the twentieth century, which facilitated the growth of unions. Conversely, the individualistic competitive values of the United States were refurbished in the postwar prosperity, thus reversing the Depression-spawned increase in collectivity orientations and reducing the constituency for trade unions.

Values and attitudes apart, many analysts attribute the much larger membership of Canadian unions to differences in the governmental environment, the fact that unions north of the border have experienced greater legal protections as compared to those operative in the United States.[92] They contend that the divergence in the trends of union density in the two countries results in large part from the fact that federal and provincial union representation legislation in Canada has encouraged labor organization. They emphasize that in contrast to Canada, "the American legal scheme *allows* rather than *encourages* [collective] bargaining, and that it also allows comparatively free play to the very considerable forces opposed to it."[93]

Reflecting populist traditions, American labor groups are seemingly handicapped by the need to win representation elections, often held months after the unions have submitted the requisite number of authorization cards, or *petitions,* signed by at least 30 percent of the employees. In 1992, unions were winning only half of all such contests, down, it should be noted, from three fifths in 1965, two thirds in 1955, and three quarters immediately after World War II. In most of Canada, on the other hand, unions are certified after demonstrating that they have enrolled a majority, 50 to 60 percent depending on jurisdiction, as *dues-paying members*. Where representation elections are required, as in Nova Scotia, they are almost invariably held within two weeks.[94] Hence, Canadian employers have little or no opportunity to try to change their employees' pre-filing decision to join a union, while American companies can and often do conduct lengthy anti-union campaigns prior to the election.

This argument is sustained by a number of American studies of the effect of employer opposition to unions in certification elections, which indicate that such activities play a major role in preventing union victories. Reviewing the literature, Richard Freeman and James Medoff conclude that "opposition, broadly defined, is a major cause of the slow strangulation of private sector unionism."[95] Canadian employers are less disposed to engage in unfair labor practices than Americans.[96] American companies, however, have had less need in recent decades to deter pro-union votes because the number of representation elections called by unions has dropped precipitously, from 7,773 in 1970 to 2,993 in 1992.[97]

Although the main focus of the discussion on the effects of the legal procedures affecting certification has been on variations in North America, it should not be forgotten that European trade unions, most of which are invariably more successful than North American ones in recruiting members, operate without the sanction of certification by a government agency. As labor law expert Derek Bok emphasizes:

> What is distinctive about our [North American] law is the active part it plays in regulating the process by which the union achieves recognition from the employer. In other countries . . . the laws create no formal machinery [certifying unions] . . . no provision has been made for representation elections, nor does the law require the selection of a union to serve as exclusive bargaining agent for any given group of employees.[98]

The British experience, typical of that in Europe, assumes "that trade unions must be allowed to operate informally, in a legal vacuum. . . . The unions of manual workers had very generally gained recognition by their ability to strike in the works of employers who refused it. . . ."[99] And except for the British, European labor organizations also secure and hold members without contractual provisions that require workers to join or remain in labor organizations, a common practice in North America. As Everett Kassalow pointed out, "formal arrangements, through collective bargaining (or other) arrangements to make union membership a condition of employment, are largely absent in continental Western Europe. Indeed, under a number of continental West European national constitutions, or in separate labor statutes, such compulsion is illegal."[100] Paul Weiler, who has emphasized the importance of the legal framework in facilitating unionization, has also questioned the extent to which legal changes can affect the situation: "One should be wary of any claim that a mere variation in legal procedure could actually influence larger trends in union organization."[101]

The stress on the explanatory power of values is congruent with the results of a National Bureau of Economic Research statistical analysis of survey and aggregate structural data for the United States and Canada by Henry Farber and Alan Krueger, which finds that "virtually all the decline in union membership in the United States between 1977 and 1991 seems to be due to decline in demand for union representation. There is no evidence that any significant part of the decline in unionization is due to increased employer resistance. . . . Additionally, very little . . . can be accounted for by structural shifts in the composition of the labor force."[102]

The thesis that dissimilarities in public policy, or, as some argue, in employer behavior, are largely responsible for the cross-border variations in union density is also challenged by the finding that the minority of employed persons who tell pollsters they would vote for a union in a representation election is lower in the United States than in Canada, and may be declining further; 39 percent so indicated in a University of Michigan Survey Research Center study taken in 1977, down to 33 and 34 percent in polls taken by the Harris Organization in 1984 and 29 percent in a National Opinion Research Center (NORC) survey in 1991.[103] A *Washington Post*/ABC News Poll conducted in 1986, using a different sample, provided an even lower estimate: 24 percent. These findings coincide with the results of union representation elections.[104] Not surprisingly, the proportion of American non-union workers who believe "that unions improve the wages and working conditions of workers . . . fell significantly from 1977 to 1984."

Survey evidence indicates that "workers who are satisfied with their jobs are significantly less likely to demand union representation."[105] Nearly three fourths of Americans surveyed by Harris Polls in December 1993 thought wages and working conditions had been improved as a result of union effort, but only 34 percent of all adults and 44 percent of adults from union households would rate overall union performance positively. Such unwillingness by non-members to support unions in the respondents' workplace and the decline of non-unionists' confidence in the efficacy of unions is presumably not affected by how labor legislation is written or enforced, or the ways American employers take advantage of these policies to defeat unions in representation elections. Rather, as noted, they may reflect to some degree the refurbishment of free market, individualistic values over the postwar decades in the United States.

Employed Canadian seemingly feel differently. The most recent Canadian polls on the subject show a higher percentage of non-union-ists in Canada expressing preference for joining unions than are willing to vote for union representation in the United States. A national Cana-dian survey conducted by Angus Reid Associates in 1989 found in response to the question, "Would you prefer to belong to a labour union or would you rather not?" that 39 percent of non-union workers said they would, compared to 29 percent among equivalent Americans polled by NORC in 1991.[106] Thus, independent of government or employer reaction to union-organizing campaigns in any given com-pany, these polls and the research of Farber and Krueger find that the demand for unionization is greater among Canadian non-union workers than among Americans, even though a much larger proportion of Cana-dians are already in unions.[107]

In any case, the fact that the legal environment is more union friendly while business is less aggressively anti-labor in Canada than in the United States only raises the conundrum one step further to the question why Canadian authorities, who have included many business-related Conservative and Social Credit governments, are seemingly more supportive or permissive with respect to unions than American ones. British Columbia, which before the election of an NDP govern-ment in 1991 had been governed for all but three of the previous thirty-eight years by what was arguably the most ideologically right-wing, laissez-faire, and anti-union-oriented government in North Amer-ica, that of the Social Credit Party, is second only to Newfoundland among Canada's ten provinces in union density.[108] Clearly, as John Calvert emphasizes, varying labor laws "do not fall from the sky; they reflect the prevailing norms and mores of the wider society."[109] Or, as Bowden notes, "it can be plausibly argued that Canadian-American dif-ferences in labor law reflect differences in underlying values."[110] The same may be said about cross-border variations in corporate behavior. Comparative studies of the opinions of federal and provincial-state leg-islators and high-level civil servants in both countries taken in the 1970s and 1980s, mentioned earlier, point up the cross-border differ-ences between political elites. These indicate that the Canadians have

been more supportive of statist-welfare (Tory-social democratic) policies than Americans, and that Canadian Conservatives have been more
liberal on such issues than American Democrats.[111] These differences
in the orientation of political elites, which show up with respect to
income-redistribution policies, are probably also reflected in attitudes
to labor union rights.

These variations tie in with the behavior of the business sector. The
Dutch student of comparative labor movements Jelle Visser reports
that "in no other advanced capitalist democracy has capital gone so far
in rejecting trade unions and collective worker representation" as in the
United States.[112] An American analyst of corporate behavior, David
Moberg, agrees, saying that "in no other advanced industrial country
. . . have corporate executives been as hostile to unions as in the
United States." He goes on to comment that the "roots of this 'American exceptionalism' on the part of management run deep, forming the
complement to . . . the much more analyzed 'exceptionalism' of American working-class consciousness." Moberg links both exceptionalisms—business as well as labor—to America's traditions and social
structure, which have "contributed to the creation of an *individualistic*
culture."[113]

The greater strength of the Canadian unions is tied to a more union-
friendly legal environment, more cooperative politicians, less hostile
employers, but more important than these, to the greater propensity of
workers to join than in the United States. As Brown notes, in Canada,
"the atmosphere of social solidarity coming down from its conservative
tradition might have been expected to let the trade unionist breathe
more freely than he could south of the border."[114] All of these factors
reflecting different political cultures and national values are interrelated. They may help to account for the results of one cross-national
comparison of the attitudes among non-unionists toward joining trade
unions: "[T]here is at least one striking difference between the two
countries. Specifically, there appears to be a higher level of latent
unionism in Canada as measured by willingness of non-unionists to
take out union membership."[115]

There is an additional important hypothesis which should be presented, that the greater retention of movement ideology, reflected in
the socialist political orientation of many Canadian unionists, has had
some effect in motivating Canadian union leaders to try harder, to see
organizing workers more in cause terms than their American compeers
do. Impressionistic evidence to this effect is based on very limited
unrepresentative cross-border contacts, although a somewhat similar

argument has been made by Donald Swartz, who points out that since the 1970s, Canadian unions have been more militant, less inclined to make concessions, than those in the United States.[116] His thesis is sustained by the cross-border variation in strike rates. Swartz emphasizes that a major reason for Canadian unions splitting away "from their American parents" in recent years is the "divergence over fundamental trade union principles." The refusal of the Canadian branch of the United Auto Workers, in 1984, to accept profit sharing in lieu of the traditional increase in base wage rates was responsible for the secession of the Canadian branch from the International and the creation in 1985 of the Canadian Auto Workers.[117] Swartz believes it is the greater capacity for struggle in the North, compared to a willingness to compromise in the South, that "underlies the expansion of the Canadian labour movement over the past two decades" and the decline in the American.[118]

In examining the American experience, it is noteworthy that the decline began at the time of the merger of the AFL and CIO in 1955. Dual unionism has always been anathema to American unionism, and the assumption at the time was that unification would strengthen the movement. It did not. It may be argued that the merger reduced an important competitive element which had motivated union officials in their organizing drives to beat out their rivals.[119] Some more recent American data which fit the assumption is the strength of teacher unionism, the National Education Association and the American Federation of Teachers, which together comprise close to 3 million members, and which have grown greatly during the period in which private-sector unionism has declined. These two groups are known for their zealous attempts to beat each other in organizing new areas.[120]

This explanation would seem to be confounded by the Canadian record, since the federations also merged north of the border. There is, however, more dual competitive unionism in Canada, national versus international unions, and competitive Quebec organizations.[121] Yet these aspects should not be exaggerated.

All these observations may be linked to the comments by Charles McDonald, assistant to the secretary-treasurer of the AFL-CIO, and socialist journalist John Judis, who in seeking to account for union membership decline in the United States, give serious emphasis to "organizing neglect" by union leaders.[122] A 1994 *New Republic* article by Judis reports on "a recent meeting of 150 local union leaders in Chicago . . . [when in response to the query] how many had participated in an organizing drive, not one hand went up."[123] Neglect of a different sort characterizes American union leaders' efforts in unfair labor practice cases. Filing such cases with the National Labor Relations Board (NLRB) constitutes an important and resource-intensive recourse for grieved workers. Canadian unions are more willing than American ones to provide legal and financial support for workers engaged in pressing unfair labor practice cases. Peter Bruce notes that in America, "while union organizers often accompany workers and play a semiactive role in section 8(a)3 hearings, the unions generally do not commit their lawyers to prosecuting. Instead, they view this as the NLRB's responsibility."[124]

CONCLUSION

In conclusion, it may be reiterated that American political exceptionalism, the absence of a socialist party, is related to trade union exceptionalism, the weakest union movement in the democratic developed world in terms of density. Canadian social democracy and unions, however, though much stronger and more militant than the American, have not done as well as their brethren in the developed Commonwealth or most of Europe. An interpretation of this difference is contained in Louis Hartz's suggestion that Canada is more like the United States than the industrialized countries across the oceans, that it is not as Tory, not as class-conscious, and more classically liberal than these other nations. In other words, as compared to Australia, Britain, and Europe, Canada is more Whig, less welfare-oriented, and less class-conscious; as contrasted to the United States, it is more group-oriented, more statist, and more communitarian. Robertson Davies, one of Canada's greatest novelists and a Tory, even argues that in spite of Canadians exhibiting a greater "decorum in the discharge of social and political affairs [than Americans] . . . beneath all of this we are a people firmly set in the socialist pattern."[125] The American social structure and values foster the free market and competitive individualism, an orientation which is not congruent with class-consciousness, support for socialist or social democratic parties, or a strong trade union movement.

The evidence drawn from political history, from studies of voting behavior, and from patterns of trade union membership, all indicates that the underprivileged and the working class in the United States are less class-conscious and less organized than in Europe, differences which, though having their ups and downs, have remained during this century.[126] This reflects (as noted) a different type of social class structure. The absence of a European aristocratic or feudal past, a relatively egalitarian-status structure, an achievement-oriented value system, comparative affluence, and a history of political democracy prior to industrialization have all operated to produce a system which remains unreceptive to proposals for class-conscious leftism.[127] The special political, sociological, and economic conditions derived from America's history remain decisive. As the political scientist Walter Dean Burnham emphasizes,

> No feudalism, no socialism: with these four words one can summarize the basic sociocultural realities that underlie American electoral politics in the industrial era. . . . There may well be much to support a theory of "American exceptionalism," a theory that emphasizes the uniqueness of the historical and cultural factors that have gone into the making of the United States. . . .[128]

EXCEPTIONS
ON THE MARGIN

Two Americas, Two Value Systems: Blacks and Whites[1]

The situation of African Americans has been qualitatively different from that of any other racial or ethnic minority in the United States. African Americans did not come willingly to this country seeking reprieve from poverty or discrimination; they were, rather, forced into the status of an underclass facing racism from the start. Being defined either de jure or de facto as a caste for most of their history, blacks, like European workers, are much more likely than whites to respond to group-related, rather than individually oriented values. They are thus the great exception to the American Creed, to American ideological exceptionalism.

TWO PEOPLES, TWO STRATIFICATION SYSTEMS

From its inception, the United States has been composed of two peoples differentiated by skin color whose values and outlook stem from radically different experiences. The dominant or majority position, as set forth in the American Creed and described by many foreign sociological observers of the country, emphasizes social egalitarianism, respect across class lines, and meritocracy, equality of opportunity. The minority situation, identified with the position of black Americans, has clearly been for most of American history a system of explicit hierarchy, of caste, of inequality related to hereditary origins. Curiously, many of the classic writings about the United States in the nineteenth century (even those written by people who were strongly abolitionist), which stressed its exceptional character as an egalitarian society, either ignored the position of blacks or cited it as a major exception that would invariably change as blacks were freed and were incorporated into the larger system.

A stress on achievement, on moving up in the class system, linked with the widespread belief in individualism and equality of opportunity, has been greater in white America than elsewhere. On the public policy level, this can be seen most clearly in the early extension of public education to all, as well as the decision to try to give everyone a *common* (equal) education. Of course this goal did not include blacks, most of whom were slaves at the time.

The strength of this early American commitment to competitive achievement may be seen in the many writings which consciously rejected the European class-differentiated education system. To foster equality of opportunity, the educational reformers, as noted earlier, held up to scorn European academic high schools, the *Gymnasia* in Germany, the *lycées* in France, the public and grammar schools in England, which only served at most the top 10 percent of the population. American educators and politicians rejected this elitist model as fostering a rigid class society. Rather, they pressed for education in a common school. These trans-Atlantic variations continued long into the twentieth century, as many European countries maintained academically high-standard schools attended by a small privileged minority, who were destined for university.

The vitality of the early stress on meritocratic values is attested to by one of the most remarkable and curious developments in American history, the emergence in the late 1820s of the first political groups in the world to be known as Workingmen's parties, mentioned briefly in chapter Three. In New York, Philadelphia, Boston, and other cities, these parties received between 10 and 15 percent of the vote in local state elections. The Workingmen were not socialists; they believed in private property, and they wanted people to strive to get ahead and become rich precisely because they favored a more open, more competitive society. The New York party, as we have seen, rejected as inadequate the idea of common schools, proposing instead the creation of state-financed boarding schools. Attending the same school for five or six hours a day would not change the basic environment of children of diverse social origins. The only way to create the proverbial level playing field, the Workingmen reasoned, was by raising the young of all classes in a common atmosphere. They clearly linked class-based cultural advantage to the perpetuation of inequality.

Not surprisingly, the Workingmen did not gain power. They were, however, able to elect members to legislatures and city councils. The fact that a party with this radical plank could get 10 to 15 percent of the vote in New York City indicates that during the first half century of the republic, at the time of slavery, there was a strong commitment to the value of equality of opportunity for whites which was associated with a belief in a competitive market economy.[2]

It cannot be stressed enough that much in contemporary attitudes and behavior may be explained by the cultural emphasis on achievement. Most Americans believe that hard work, rather than "lucky breaks or help from other people," is what enables people to move up. As noted, surveys taken by NORC from 1983 through 1992 found that around two thirds of respondents consistently agreed that "people get ahead by hard work." Much larger percentages said "ambition" is essential or very important (88%) "for getting ahead in life" than felt the same way about "coming from a wealthy family" (20%), or having well-educated parents (39%). According to a 1991 ABC poll, close to three quarters of American parents think their offspring will do better than they. As sociologist Robert K. Merton has noted, Americans have believed that everyone (which meant only white males until recently) should try to be a success, regardless of background.[3] Opinion poll data indicate that this value remains powerful, and that most white people now feel it applies to blacks and women as well. While understandably ambivalent about the promise of America, a majority of blacks also are committed to the belief that hard work and educational attainment will enable them to get ahead. A 1991 Gallup Poll found that "69 percent of whites and 68 percent of blacks say that African-Americans should focus most of their energy on improving [their] education."[4]

The strength of the achievement norm is related to another value—universalism—that should be discussed in this context. Contrary to particularism or special treatment, universalism refers to the belief that everyone should be treated similarly without reference to traits stemming from birth, class, religion, ethnicity, gender, or color.

The treatment of blacks has been the foremost deviation from the American Creed throughout the history of the republic. If we count American history as starting around 1600, blacks have been here almost from the beginning. However, they spent their first two and a half centuries as slaves. For a hundred years after 1865 they largely served as a lower-caste group working under explicit or implicit Jim Crow policies, with little opportunity to gain educational or financial resources. Caste systems, whether slavery or segregation, were much more explicitly hierarchical and hereditary than European feudalism. Blacks have only been given a claim to political equality and economic opportunity since the 1960s.

Thomas Jefferson and George Washington were concerned about the way the treatment of blacks would impact on the future of America. Reacting to slavery, Jefferson wrote in 1781 that "I tremble for my country when I reflect that God is just."[5] Anticipating in 1791 the possibility that the country might break up because it could not resolve the problem, George Washington told a friend that if this happened, "he had made up his mind to move and be of the northern."[6] Jefferson, the author of the Declaration of Independence, felt—correctly as it turned out—that its proclamation that "all men are created equal" would undermine slavery, and that the idea of equality would have a continuing effect on American politics.

In 1944, following the logic of Jefferson's observation, Gunnar Myrdal noted in *An American Dilemma* that white Americans, including most southerners, believe they believe in the Creed even though their racist practices violate it. From this assumption he concluded that if blacks would organize to vigorously defend their rights and assert that they were mistreated, the whites would give in. Once they were forced to recognize that blacks were not treated equally, they would have to change their behavior if they wanted to maintain their belief in the Creed.[7] The political successes of the civil rights movement in the 1960s showed Myrdal to be right.

The white American value system has emphasized the individual.[8] Citizens have been expected to demand and protect their rights on a personal basis. As we have seen, the exceptional emphasis on law in the United States as compared with Europe, derivative from the Constitution and the Bill of Rights, has stressed individual rights against the state and other powers. The experience of black Americans, however, has focused on group characteristics, on defining and treating people not according to their personal merits but according to their ancestry, their race, and their ethnic group. Postfeudal Europe was also organized in particularistic terms, that is, according to class background. However, Europe was less stringently stratified than the postslavery system in the United States. Thus pre–World War II America differed from Europe in two ways: (1) for its large white majority, it was much more egalitarian, individualistic, and populist; (2) for its black minority, it was much more hierarchical and particularistic, group-defined, less free, and undemocratic.

THE EUROPEAN COMPARISON

Stressing group characteristics encourages group solutions. In postfeudal Europe, the emphasis on the importance of one's station promoted class-consciousness among the lower strata and, to some extent, a Tory sense of *noblesse oblige* among the privileged. To reiterate a point made earlier, upper-class conservative leaders, such as Disraeli in Great Britain and Bismarck in Germany, favored government efforts to improve the lot of the less affluent without necessarily changing their position in the social order, beliefs which encouraged the rise of a lower-class-based social democratic left. Americans, by contrast, have always put more emphasis on expanding individual opportunity through education. Comparative public opinion research documents that they are more likely than others to approve of greater expenditures for education than for increased welfare services. Comprehensive analyses of attitudes toward public policies over the past twenty years—mainly in the OECD countries—report that "the United States is consistently at the bottom in its support for different kinds of social welfare benefits." The one issue "on which Americans fare much better—and often the best—compared with other nations . . . [is] educational opportunity, assistance and spending." And as Robert Shapiro and John Young note, these attitudes stem from "Americans' views and values concerning individualism and the equality of opportunity, as opposed to equality of outcomes for individuals."[9]

For much of this past century America has spent proportionately much more public money on education than Europe, while Europe has devoted more resources to welfare. The recent record bears out this generalization, which is discussed further in chapter Eight. As of 1981, about one fifth, 20.8 percent, of the American GDP was devoted to social expenditures, including education, as compared with over one quarter, 25.6 percent, as an average for all OECD countries. America spent 26.4 percent of its total social expenditures on education, compared with an OECD average of 22.7 percent.[10] Statistical reports for the mid-1980s reiterated this conclusion. In 1991, American educational expenditures amounted to 14.7 percent of all public spending; the average figure for the OECD countries for the same year was 11.8 percent.[11] The differences are even more striking when percentages of age cohorts who have been exposed to post-secondary education are compared.[12]

From early in the nineteenth century, the United States has led the world in the proportion of its population completing elementary and high school education. And while America also predominated in the ratio of those attending college and university, the numbers and proportions increased dramatically after World War II. In contrast to America, most European countries have devoted a much larger share of their GDP and public funds to improving the living conditions of their working classes. Since the 1930s, the European Social Democrats have had frequent opportunities to hold office and have been able to follow through on improving the situation of the working class by emphasizing group improvement policies. But, until brought to a realization of the contrast with the United States, they preserved the elite high schools and failed to focus on the expansion of university education. The pattern may be illustrated by developments in the prototypical social democratic polity, Sweden. In office from 1933 until 1991 (except for six years) and again from 1994 on, the Social Democrats in their original hold on office greatly expanded the welfare state, but failed to recognize that their policies would have little influence on the achievement orientations of working-class youth, particularly on the proportions attending university or entering the professions. The situation in Sweden did not change until the American school desegregation decision, *Brown* v. *Board of Education of Topeka, Kansas,* was announced by the Supreme Court in 1954. Up to that point, Sweden, like most other European countries, had a class-segregated high school educational system, with a privileged minority who attended the *Gymnasia* leading them to university-level education, while the majority went to vocational schools that excluded the possibility of higher education. The Swedes, the British, and others began to integrate their high school systems in reaction to developments in the United States. They adopted policies designed to facilitate individual mobility by increasing the proportion of children from poorer families going to university. The ratios, however, are still much lower than in America.

GROUP-ORIENTED SOLUTIONS IN THE UNITED STATES

In the United States, the caste-like conditions facing blacks became politically salient from the 1950s on and resulted, as in Europe, in efforts to find solutions at the group level. These have been characterized as "affirmative action." Originally used to describe early 1960s legislation, the term has had two meanings. The first, which emerged in the Kennedy-Johnson administrations, involved attempts to incorporate blacks into the meritocratic race for success. Perhaps the best statement presenting the logic of this policy was included in Lyndon Johnson's Howard University speech on June 4, 1965. He said that we want all Americans to engage in the race, but some are not able to do so because they arrive at the starting line with shackles on their legs. He called for policies to remove these chains so that they could compete equally. Soon thereafter, he issued an executive order requiring all government contractors to "take affirmative action that applicants are employed, and that employees are treated during employment, without regard to their race, creed, color, or national origin." Subsequent initiatives became the War on Poverty, including greater spending for education through programs such as Head Start, Aid to Families with Dependent Children, and other programs to strengthen the lower class, disproportionately comprised of black families. The programs were intended to increase opportunities for the poorest blacks and whites to enable them to enter integrated and better-financed schools, where they would acquire the skills needed to succeed.

These policies were reinforced by strong Fair Employment and Fair Housing legislation designed to eliminate discrimination and the effects of prejudice against blacks in the workplace, and the educational and housing markets, and eventually with respect to such caste-like barriers in social relationships as club memberships. The programs were based on the assumption that equal education and the full extension of political citizenship to blacks, which came with Voting Rights Acts and judicial decisions, meant that blacks, like whites, could press for their legal rights as individuals in the courts and administrative tribunals.[13]

The concern that these policies, particularly those designed to reduce discrimination, were not working as quickly as was hoped, and the fact that racial barriers still operated in different arenas, led to the second meaning of "affirmative action." It emphasizes equality of result for groups rather than equality of opportunity for individuals, and assumes that the best way to improve the situation of blacks is through quotas or special preferences for jobs and educational opportunities. Affirmative action quotas were first introduced in 1969 by the Nixon administration by administrative fiat. Assuming that society imposed disadvantages on blacks—educational, motivational, and social—various Nixon appointees concluded that these could only be countered by giving blacks special advantages as a group.

The implementation of these policies did not primarily derive from specific demands made by blacks or the American left. Rather, they seemed to represent an innovative effort by segments of the white elite, initially the Republicans among them, to meet the civil rights movement's drive for equality.[14] George Shultz, Nixon's first Secretary of Labor, and Leonard Garment, the president's counsel, concluded in

1969 that redress to courts and administrative agencies for anti-discrimination judgments would take too long and would not do much to open the discriminatory parts of the labor market to blacks. With the help of Labor Solicitor Lawrence Silberman, who wrote an extensive brief that racial job targets were legal exercises of presidential powers under the Fifth Amendment's due process clause, Shultz issued an administrative order which provided for hiring quotas for black apprentices, ironworkers, plumbers and pipefitters, electrical and other workers in the Philadelphia construction industry, an area in which employers and unions were cooperating to keep blacks out. The policy was soon extended to other cities.[15] Similar programs were pressed with regard to faculty and students in higher education by other Nixon officeholders, with the approval of the president.[16] In explaining the origins of the policy, Silberman, subsequently a Reagan senior judicial appointee, wrote that he and his colleagues had been disturbed by the ambiguity concerning the order issued in the Johnson administration requiring " 'affirmative action' by government contractors to redress past employment discrimination. Appalled [and] . . . uncomfortable with the image the party of Abraham Lincoln had developed, and most of all because the GOP was anxious to expand employment opportunities for blacks, we launched what I have come to see [by 1977] as a fundamentally unsound policy."[17]

Ironically, strong efforts were made to stop these policies by a Johnson appointee, Comptroller of the United States Elmer Staats, as well as by the trade union leadership, black civil rights leaders, and most congressional Democrats. They argued that the anti-discrimination clause of the 1964 Civil Rights Act, Title VII, explicitly outlawed affirmative discrimination. Staats quoted Hubert Humphrey's pledge that nothing in the Act "will give any power to the [Equal Employment Opportunity] Commission or to any court to require hiring, firing, or promotion of employees in order to meet a racial 'quota' or to achieve a racial balance," and noted that its liberal Senate floor managers agreed that there would be no "consideration of color . . . [in] the decision to hire or promote."[18] Not surprisingly, the AFL-CIO strongly opposed a quota policy, reflecting the views of "rank-and-file white workers who feared that such moves as the Philadelphia Plan would cost them jobs, and who saw themselves paying for social changes at the cost of personal and family security."[19] Unexpectedly, black civil rights leaders and Democratic congresspersons also rejected the quota plan as pitting black workers against white workers.

Congress defeated a rider to an appropriations bill which would have explicitly banned quotas. Republicans voted against the rider by 124 to 41, while Democrats supported it by 115 to 84. President Nixon and Attorney General John Mitchell actively campaigned to achieve this result.[20] Nixon proclaimed: "The Democrats are token oriented—we are job oriented."[21] On the day Congress voted, December 23, 1969, the president issued a statement emphasizing that this would be "an historic and critical civil rights vote," and threatened to veto the appropriation measure if it included a section outlawing quotas.[22] George Shultz, speaking for the Nixon administration, attacked the civil rights leaders for their unwillingness to help the struggle for quotas.[23] They, in turn, criticized the president in partisan terms.

> Clarence Mitchell, Washington lobbyist and director of the National Association for the Advancement of Colored People (NAACP), said . . . that it was a "calculated attempt coming right from the President's desk to break up the coalition between Negroes and labor unions. Most of the social progress in this country has resulted from this alliance."

> "Nixon's people are forcing employers to lay off workers and then telling them to put in a certain quota of blacks into these vacancies. It is a strategy designed to increase friction between labor and Negroes," said black Rep. Augustus F. Hawkins (D-Calif.) in November 1970.[24]

George Bush, then a Republican congressman from Texas, backed the quota system, while liberal Democrat Ralph Yarborough, who represented that state in the Senate, fought it. When Bush ran for the Senate in 1970, he stressed his vote for a fair housing bill and his support of racial quotas in employment.[25]

The Nixon and subsequent administrations applied the principle of "communal rights" to other minorities, as well as to women. This effort, designed to guarantee equal results to groups, persisted through liberal and conservative administrations, even though opinion polls have repeatedly reported that overwhelming majorities of whites—both men and women—and often more than 50 percent of blacks, said that the principle of equal opportunity should apply to individuals only, that special preferences or quota guarantees should not be accorded to members of groups underrepresented in privileged jobs or educational categories. By 1972, Nixon had publicly dropped his approval of quotas and preferences, though his administration continued to enforce them. Ronald Reagan, of course, later emphasized meritocracy, but it should be noted that as recently as 1985, a majority of Republicans in the

Senate, led by Bob Dole, wrote an open letter to President Reagan insisting on the continuation of preferences. By 1995, most of them had seemingly reversed their position. Yet segments of American elites—including conservative jurists, such as Nixon appointee Supreme Court Chief Justice Warren Burger, who faced bitter opposition from archliberal Justice William O. Douglas, and most Republican members of the Court, felt that the individualistic emphasis in the national creed should be amended to provide remedies for African Americans.[26] This concern has been extended to other groups who are perceived to lack equal rights because of ascriptive or biological traits: Hispanics, Native Americans, Asians (though the success of some of them has undermined their place), women, and the disabled.

THE CASE FOR SPECIAL PREFERENCES

During the 1960s various analysts, most notably the black scholar Harold Cruse, argued that equality of opportunity and formal integration were not enough for blacks. Given their history of oppression and continued discrimination, blacks required recognition as a unique national minority and group rights above and beyond those sought by other minorities and the non-black poor. Cruse compared the black situation to that of the Jews, and argued that although Jews had faced great discrimination, all they needed was an end to discrimination and the application of meritocratic policies to themselves. Hence, he argued, this was what Jews demanded and ultimately obtained. Jewish organizations, however, have made individual rights and meritocracy into a fetish; they continue to emphasize the need to apply the American Creed to all immigrants, women, and minorities. But blacks, Cruse argued, must demand and obtain group rights because they are handicapped in open competition with whites by the continued effects of the institutionalized racism which has marked American history.[27]

African Americans are *the* minority group in the United States. They are better able than members of any other ethnic, religious, gender, or class category, except for Native Americans, to justify a claim for preferential treatment. Beyond the general emphasis on group-oriented policies is a demand for reparations. The argument is simple: white America profited greatly from the 250 years in which blacks were held as slaves and for most of the next 100 years during the Jim Crow period, when they continued to work in lower economic and caste positions as maids, unskilled workers in the cities, and stoop laborers in the fields. Parallels are offered to the acknowledgment by Congress of the obligation to recompense Japanese Americans for being incarcerated during World War II and by the German government to pay reparations to Jews and Israel.

In the past, the special advantages given to war veterans probably have constituted the most important qualification to the emphasis on meritocracy. Veterans have been given special preference when applying for civil service jobs. Even if a veteran is clearly not equal to a non-veteran in test scores, experience, or skill, he or she may get the job. Veterans also have been given advantages with respect to higher education opportunities and obtaining home mortgages. These policies are designed to make up for the disadvantages imposed on them by their service in the military.[28]

Particularistic values operate to handicap the socially depressed in all societies. People everywhere tend to hire and to give special preference to those with whom they have ties, relatives and members of the same ethnic, religious, communal, or cultural groups they themselves belong to. To a large extent, blacks have not fitted into privileged networks.

Most institutions do not publicly acknowledge such special preferences. Universities, though meritocratic and universalistic in their explicit values, have had admission policies which provide for particularistic advantages. Many, if not most, of the private universities, including distinguished ones like Harvard, Chicago, and Stanford, have given preference (all other things being equal or, sometimes, even not close to equal) to the children of alumni, faculty, and to athletes.[29] Universities also award special scholarships and fellowships which are limited to applicants from particular regional, gender, ethnic, or religious backgrounds. Some, but not all, of these are now illegal.

In 1963, I noted: "Perhaps the most important fact to recognize about the current situation of the American Negro is that *equality is not enough to assure his movement into the larger society.*"[30] And it is important to remember that women and most other minorities have required genuine equality of opportunity, not special help; this has certainly been true for the Jews, as well as most Asian and European immigrant groups. The Jews, the "Confucian" Asians, and the East Indians have done better on average than old-stock white Americans. In any case, immigrants generally have no claim on American society for preference or special advantage. Whatever handicaps some have as a result of inadequate education, lack of skills, or lack of socialization to the ways of the cities are clearly not the fault of American society. Immigrants, including Hispanics and West Indians, are doing better economically after fifteen years in the country than persons born in the United States with the same social characteristics.[31] Although many of them were not born here, roughly 40 percent of Mexican Americans are in white-collar or higher employment positions today.[32]

Lawrence Fuchs has argued that the evaluation of proposals for preferential treatment in the occupational system should be linked to the "problem of standards," that is, the difference between jobs which require competence and those which demand special ability and training. While it is possible to recognize higher levels of performance in almost all occupations, in many, if not most, competence is what employers require. Seniority rights in business, government, and education, and legislation outlawing compulsory retirement ages are justified by assumptions about generalized competence, not superior achievement, as sufficient qualification for employment. Hence the contention that giving preference to blacks or other historically underprivileged groups is particularly relevant to competence jobs, assuming that other conditions are equal or close to equal. But it is argued that positions for which high achievement levels are necessary, such as scholarship, the arts, medicine, sports, airline pilots, and managers, should not be subject to quotas and special preference policies. A study determining the reasons for "the high rate of attrition of African-Americans training to be pilots and navigators in the armed services concluded that . . . those who graduate from college with less than a strong proficiency in verbal and quantitative skills would probably have difficulty keeping up with the rigorous curriculum and rapid pace of flight training 'whether they are blacks or whites.' " Fuchs concludes that affirmative action programs, whether for Navy flyers or ballet dancers, are "necessarily limited to special recruitment and training efforts." However, he argues, efforts to increase the number of minority workers among the less skilled such as "firefighters, machinists, computer operators, and candidates for dental school" can include numerical goals, while permitting "race to be counted as one of many factors in attempting to meet them, along with insisting on basic qualifications."[33]

Whatever the merits of the distinction between competence and achievement in occupations, those in the less privileged positions— whether firefighters, police officers, dental technicians, or assembly-line workers—do not accept inherently disparaging estimates of their worth and skills. Poll after poll finds that white workers see no reason for meritocratic standards and universalistic rules not applying to them. Conversely, it is the elite highly educated whites, whose positions and skill capital give them much more economic and status security than their lower-status racial counterparts, who are more disposed to favor or at least more willing to accept special preferences for minorities.

AMERICAN PUBLIC OPINION

Mass opinion remains invariably opposed to preferential treatment for deprived groups.[34] Whites are fairly consistently and overwhelmingly in opposition; they favor meritocracy and individual competition. Blacks, however, vary in their reaction when queried in national polls. They are invariably more supportive of group rights, quotas, or special preferences than whites, but they differ in their response pattern depending on how the question is posed. More often than not, however, a majority or plurality supports meritocratic principles, though usually by a much smaller percentage than whites. African Americans are pulled to favor group rights, but as Americans they still respond favorably to the individualistic ethos. The Gallup Poll has dealt with these issues over time more frequently than any other survey organization. It repeated the same question six times between 1977 and 1991:

> Some people say that to make up for past discrimination, women and minorities should be given preferential treatment in getting jobs and places in college. Others say that ability as determined by test scores, should be the main consideration. Which point of view comes close to how you feel on the subject?

In each survey, only 10 or 11 percent of respondents said the minorities should be given preferential treatment, while 81, 83, or 84 percent replied that ability should be the determining factor. When the 1989 answers were differentiated by the respondents' race, blacks were somewhat more supportive of preferential treatments than whites (14% to 7%), while a majority of the African Americans (56%) favored "ability, as determined in test scores." Women, it should be noted, responded in an identical way to men; 10 percent supported preferential treatment, and 85 percent ability.[35] Princeton Survey Research Associates, working for the *Times-Mirror* Center, presented the issue somewhat differently eight times between 1987 and 1994: "We should make every effort to improve the position of blacks and other minorities even if it means giving them preferential treatment." This formulation was supported more strongly than the more complex one cited earlier. In 1987, 24 percent of respondents agreed, rising to 34 percent in 1992, then falling to 29 in 1994. Blacks were more positive than whites by 62 to 25 percent in 1994. As with the other Gallup questions, there was little difference between the gender groups. The great majority of white women opposed preferences in each poll. While over four fifths of identified Republicans are against preferences, so are two thirds of the Democrats. A relatively high proportion of those who identify themselves as "strong liberals," 43 percent, "endorse preferential treatment," but they constitute only 10 percent of the total sample.[36] The same question was also put by the NBC News/*Wall Street Journal* poll eight times between May 1987 and September 1994, with comparable results. Favorable responses appear to have moved up somewhat during the 1990s, reaching a high point of 34 percent in 1993, but dropping off to 29 percent in September 1994. The gap between blacks and whites grew considerably.

Preferential treatment does somewhat better when it is justified as making up for specific past discrimination, when ability is not posed as an alternative, and when it is limited to blacks and applies only to institutions that have actually discriminated. *The New York Times*/CBS national poll has asked repeatedly since 1985: "Do you believe that where there has been job discrimination against blacks in the past, preference in hiring or promotion should be given to blacks today?" In 1985, 42 percent answered yes, 46 percent no. Most recently, in 1993 and February 1995, support sentiment had dropped to 33 percent, while 55 percent rejected justified preferences.

The opposition to preferences does not mean that whites think blacks have attained equality or that the government should not outlaw discrimination. In February 1993, Gallup found that 72 percent of all whites said society does not treat people of all races equally. In August 1994, the same organization found that 44 percent of whites agreed that "in the past few years there hasn't been much real improvement in the position of blacks in this country," down 10 percentage points from 1992. And the June 1993 NBC News/*Wall Street Journal* poll reported that 63 percent of their sample agreed that "Racial discrimination still exists and the government should pass laws to eliminate it." The majority of both whites and blacks will support a policy described as "affirmative action" if the question does not mention quotas, as the ABC News/*Wall Street Journal* poll found in July 1990. Two thirds of whites

(66%) and 84 percent of blacks responded favorably to the question: "All in all, do you favor or oppose affirmative action programs in business for blacks, provided there are no rigid quotas?" The Harris Organization reported somewhat similar results to a comparable query repeated a number of times during the 1980s, as did CNN/Gallup in January 1992 and September 1994, asking about "strengthening affirmative action laws for women, blacks and minorities" (49% in favor, 43% opposed in 1994).

PREFERENCES AND THE AMERICAN CREED

It is interesting to note that two other beneficiaries of affirmative action preferences, white women and Latinos, are less supportive of quotas as a remedy for past discrimination than blacks, women much less so. Most of the evidence for Latinos comes from surveys of Californians. These find a range of responses during the 1980s supporting special treatment or preference for minorities and women running between 55 and 67 percent among blacks and 37 and 45 percent among Latinos, with Asians at 15 to 20 percent favorable.[37] In 1995, *The Field Poll* queried Californians on how they would vote on the "California Civil Rights Initiative," a measure which respondents were told would "prohibit state and local governments from granting preferential treatment to any individual or group or using race, sex, color, ethnicity, or national origin as a criterion for hiring, promoting, granting admissions to college, or selecting public contractors." The overwhelming majority, 60 percent, said they would vote yes, while 35 percent replied no. "White men and white women responded almost identically, 65–65 percent, yes. Blacks and Hispanics also were very similar, 42 and 49 percent yes." When asked specifically about job preferences for Hispanics, the Latinos divided evenly, 46 percent for and 43 percent against.[38]

Latinos, like most Asians, seemingly see themselves as immigrants and accept the society's emphasis on opportunity for them as individuals, not as members of oppressed groups. This orientation helps explain the attitudes of Latinos toward learning and speaking English. Two-fifths, "41 percent, of California Hispanics voted in support of a successful 1986 ballot initiative amending the state's constitution to designate English the state's official language; and . . . in an opinion survey two years later, 58 percent favored 'making English the official language of California.' "[39] Upon reviewing a variety of studies, Peter

Skerry finds that "when Mexican Americans are faced with a choice between English and Spanish, or when that choice is somehow constrained, most seem to opt for English."[40]

Many of the inconsistencies in American racial attitudes point to a deep contradiction between two values that are at the core of the American Creed: individualism and egalitarianism. Americans believe strongly in both. One consequence of this dualism is that political debate often takes the form of one consensual value opposing the other. Liberals and conservatives typically do not take "alternative" positions on issues of equality and freedom. Instead, each side appeals to one or the other core value. Liberals stress the primacy of egalitarianism and the social injustice that flows through unfettered individualism. Conservatives enshrine individual freedom and the social need for mobility and achievement as values "endangered" by the collectivism inherent in liberal nostrums. Both sides treat as their natural constituency the entire American public. In this sense, liberals and conservatives are less opponents than they are competitors, like two department stores on the same block trying to draw the same customers by offering different versions of what everyone wants.

Much of the progress in the early years of the civil rights movement was made by breaking down the "compartmentalization" of the American mind and forcing the public to see that the country's attitudes and institutions fell outrageously short of our egalitarian ideals. It is the egalitarian element in the American Creed that helped to create the consensus behind the civil rights revolution of the past thirty years. But the more recent focus of the civil rights movement, with its emphasis on substantive equality and preferential treatment, has forced the country up against the individualistic, achievement-oriented element in the Creed.

The poll data reveal a "positive" pro-civil rights agreement when only egalitarian questions are at stake, but a "negative" anti-civil rights consensus when an issue also infringes on basic notions of individualism. Thus, on the central issues involving racial discrimination and Jim Crow practices, American public opinion is powerfully against discrimination. Expressed attitudes on these issues have been consistently "liberal," and even the white South has joined the national consensus. The general agreement dissolves, however, when compulsory integration and quotas are involved. Many whites deeply resent such efforts, not because they oppose racial equality, but because they feel these measures violate their individual freedom. Liberals are quick to point out the inegalitarian consequences of de facto segregation, but the data show that most whites favor individual freedom over compulsory social egalitarianism in racial matters.

Most whites, and many blacks, continue to feel that it is better for disadvantaged groups to work out their problems through individual improvement and mobility than to press collective demands for all members of the group. Most Americans approve of concrete federal programs to help the disadvantaged and combat racial discrimination. Given a choice, however, between government intervention to solve social problems and "leaving people on their own" to work out their problems for themselves, the public always chooses the latter option.[41]

Affirmative action policies have forced a sharp confrontation between egalitarian and individualistic values. Most Americans oppose the notion of special treatment for blacks, even when it does not refer to quotas or preferences, since such treatment also violates the notion of equality across racial lines. Thus in an October 1989 ABC News/*Washington Post* poll, 64 percent of whites and 44 percent of blacks disagreed with the statement: "Because of past discrimination, blacks who need it should get some help from the federal government that white people in similar economic circumstances don't get."

There has been a vast improvement in white American attitudes toward blacks, women, and other minorities since the 1950s.[42] Today, their claims to full equality are widely accepted.[43] There can be no doubt that a large majority of white Americans have come to believe that discrimination is wrong and that government should guarantee the application of the competitive merit or achievement principle to all, blacks and whites. More surprisingly, perhaps, the 1991 Gallup/*Newsweek* poll reports that "72 percent of blacks and 52 percent of whites said that they would prefer to live in a neighborhood that was racially 'half and half'—more on both sides than felt that way three years ago." Over two thirds of whites and four fifths of blacks claim to "know many members of another race well," and almost half of the former (47%) and 63 percent of the latter say they "socialize regularly with members of another race." A 1994 NBC News/*Wall Street Journal* poll finds that four fifths of blacks and seven tenths of whites say they "have a close friend whose race is different." And over four fifths of blacks and three fifths of whites answer "very often" in reply to the query, "How often do you come into contact with people of other races and ethnic groups . . . ?" Gallup indicates that almost no whites (6%) report that they would feel "uncomfortable working with members of another race" or "for a boss of another race."[44] The NBC News/*Wall Street Journal* poll reported in 1994 that 65 percent of whites, up from 61 in 1992, 45 in 1988, and 43 in 1987, agreed that "it's all right for blacks and whites to date each other." Agreement by blacks was even higher, 88 percent in 1994, up from 72 percent in 1987.

Americans make a critical distinction between compensatory action and preferential treatment. Compensatory action involves measures to help disadvantaged groups catch up to the standards of competition set by the larger society. Preferential treatment involves suspending those standards to admit or hire members of disadvantaged groups who are unable to meet the same standards as white males. Relatively few object to compensation for past deprivations in the form of special training programs such as Head Start, financial aid, and community development funds. Such programs meet with approval from the population because they are consistent with the notion that race and sex have in the past been "imperfections" in the market of free competition, that is, unjustifiable grounds for denying equality of opportunity to certain categories of individuals.[45]

To return to the image of the shackled runner, Americans are willing to do more than remove the chains. They will go along with special training programs and financial assistance for previously shackled runners, enabling them to catch up with those who have forged ahead because of unfair advantages. But most Americans draw the line at predetermining the results of the race.

Policies favoring quotas and numerical goals for integration produce a creedal response since they contradict traditional conceptions of the meaning of equality of opportunity. Americans will accept the argument that race and sex, like poverty generally, are disadvantages deserving of assistance, just as the majority of Americans approved of the New Deal as a justifiable intervention in the free market. They will accept remedial policies up to the point where it is felt that mobility resources have been roughly equalized and the initial terms of competition are once again fair. But the data show that every attempt to introduce any form of absolute preference meets with stiff and determined resistance from the vast majority of Americans, including women and, to a somewhat lesser extent, racial minorities.

In some measure, the distinction between "compensatory action" and "preferential treatment" parallels the distinction drawn between "equality of opportunity" and "equality of results." Compensatory action is probably seen as a way to enhance equality of opportunity. Because blacks have been discriminated against in the past, it is fair to give them special consideration so that they will get a better break in the future. Preferential treatment, on the other hand, probably sounds to most whites like an effort to force equality of results by predetermining the outcome of the competitive process.

The strongest support for preferential treatment seems to come from the liberal intelligentsia, the 5 to 6 percent of the population who have gone to graduate school, plus those who have studied liberal arts in college. It is also strong among the political elite, particularly Democrats, but many Republicans as well. Prior to the 1994 elections, the Democrats in Congress increasingly supported these policies, changes which may flow from the fact that the proportion of Democratic members who can be classified as liberal on the basis of their voting record has increased steadily since the 1960s.[46] Although recent court decisions have gone against the enforcement of quota policies, universities continue to press for numerical goals or special preferences. In so doing, they attest to the documented greater strength of political liberalism within them than in other institutions. And not surprisingly, the most extensive application of numerical targets in higher education can be found in the humanities and "soft" social sciences, the most left-disposed fields in academe.

BLACK PROGRESS—A CONTENTIOUS ISSUE

Government policies in the context of the largely positive economic situation since World War II have resulted in considerable improvements for blacks. Though they remain behind whites with regard to income and levels of employment, as a group they are much better off than they were before the civil rights movement of the 1960s and the adoption of various remedial programs, including affirmative action. Writing in 1994, Henry Louis Gates, Jr., head of Harvard's African American Studies Department, notes that "never before have so many blacks done so well."[47] Economist Peter Drucker sums up the post–World War II changes: "In the fifty years since the Second World War the economic position of African Americans in America has improved faster than that of any other group in American social history—or in the social history of any country. Three fifths of America's blacks rose into middle-class incomes; before the Second World War the figure was one twentieth."[48]

Awareness of such gains is not widespread, however. This is partly because the leadership of blacks, women, and Hispanics generally do not admit to significant progress. Opinion polls taken in the mid-1980s indicate that three fifths of the black leaders told pollsters that the situation of blacks was "going backward," while two thirds of a national black sample said they were "making progress."[49] In early July 1990, an NBC News/*Wall Street Journal* poll reported that 60 percent of all blacks said that, compared to ten years ago, blacks in America were "better off," while 29 percent reported they were "worse off." Not surprisingly, the 1991–92 recession led to more pessimistic views among whites and blacks. Thus, the percentage of the latter polled by *Newsweek*/Gallup who felt that "the quality of life for blacks [has] gotten worse . . . over the last 10 years" increased from 36 percent in June 1991 to 51 percent in March 1992.[50] But a March 1993 Roper survey found a considerable increase among African Americans and whites in their positive evaluations of "Conditions for black people today with regards to housing, education, job opportunities, social acceptance by whites, etc. as compared to 10 years ago." Over half, 53 percent of black and 66 percent of white respondents, said conditions are "good" or "excellent" today, as compared to 13 and 21 percent giving the same responses about ten years ago. Only 6 percent of whites and 13 percent of blacks said conditions are "poor" as of 1993, while 35 percent of the former and 45 percent of the latter felt that way about the situation a decade earlier. Both groups were much more optimistic about the way things will be ten years from now. And in the same month, the *New York Times*/CBS News Poll reported that 62 percent of blacks and 64 percent of whites agreed that "there has been significant progress toward Martin Luther King's dream of racial equality."

The refusal of some black leaders to admit improvement is understandable. The heads of groups seeking more from society and from the state justify their demands by referring to the way in which existing institutions and policies work against them. The worse things appear, and the greater the discrepancy seems between themselves and others, the more they can demand. Yet the repeated emphasis on how little progress has been made serves to sustain the argument that purposeful social action designed to benefit blacks simply does not work, that there are factors inherent in the black situation which prevent them from getting ahead. Not only most whites, but many blacks have absorbed such negative self-images. Americans believe that what determines success or failure is hard work, regardless of whether a person is black or white. Hence if blacks fail, it follows that it is largely their own fault. Reacting to the dilemma, Henry Louis Gates, Jr. writes: "We need something we do not yet have: a way of speaking about black poverty that does not falsify the reality of black achievement; a way of speaking about black advancement that does not *distort* the enduring realities of black poverty."[51]

The data are consistent in this area. NORC found that during 1985–89, 62 percent of whites and 36 percent of blacks agreed that the reason blacks on average have worse jobs, incomes, and housing than white people is that "most blacks just don't have the motivation or will power to pull themselves out of poverty." An ABC News/*Washington Post* poll taken in October 1989 found that 60 percent of whites and 60 percent of blacks agreed with the statement: "If blacks would try harder, they could be just as well off as whites." The same survey found 52 percent of blacks and 56 percent of whites accepting the view that "discrimination has unfairly held down blacks, but many of the problems blacks in this country have today are brought on by blacks themselves." A Gallup Poll conducted in December 1989 reported similar results in response to the question: "Who do you think is more to blame for the present conditions in which blacks find themselves—white people or blacks themselves?" A small majority (55%) held blacks responsible, while only 18 percent said whites, and the same percentage, 18, "feel that whites and blacks are equally to blame for their current situation. . . . However, *even among blacks it is more common to blame blacks themselves* (34 percent) *than it is to blame whites* (22 percent)."[52] In July 1993, Gallup posed the issue differently: "On average, blacks have worse jobs, income and housing than white people. Do you think this is mostly due to discrimination against blacks, or is it mostly due to something else?" Almost three quarters, 73 percent, of white respondents replied "mostly something else," but half, 49 percent, of the blacks chose the same response; only 44 percent said their deprived situation was "mostly due to discrimination."

Such beliefs have negative consequences. First, they reinforce racist attitudes and stereotypes. Whites increasingly seem to believe that they, or their officials, have done a great deal for blacks, but since the situation does not appear to be improving there must be something wrong with them. In early January 1991, NORC released the results of a survey taken in 1990. It indicated that most whites believe blacks to be less intelligent, lazier, more violence-prone, and more inclined to prefer to stay on welfare than whites and four other ethnic groups listed.

The same set of beliefs also undermines black morale and ambition. Reports of little improvement, even of retrogression, tell blacks they cannot succeed. Black youth are told that the society is against them and that there is therefore no point of trying to work hard or study.

Large numbers of blacks develop or retain the same invidious stereotypes about themselves as many whites do. These feed into feelings of
self-hatred.

The damage is compounded by the news media's relentless focus on
the social pathologies of the ghettos, which creates the impression that
most blacks live wretched existences. Stories pour out emphasizing the
disproportionate presence of blacks in urban crime and among the
homeless, as well as the considerable percentage they form of the
imprisoned, their high infant mortality, adult illness and early death
rates, and so forth. Yet social scientists estimate that the underclass,
both black and white, is small. William Julius Wilson, the social scientist most responsible for the focus on the urban underclass, now identifies the ghetto poor, a term he prefers, as those living in "areas of
extreme poverty, that is, those in which 40 percent of the people are
poor."[53] He estimates these comprise a sixth of the blacks, who are
"truly disadvantaged, a sort of destitute population."[54] The Urban Institute reaches a lower figure, noting that "if one uses multiple criteria
such as being persistently poor, living in a poor neighborhood, and
being engaged in dysfunctional behavior . . . most of the available estimates suggest the underclass [black and white] is small—probably in
the neighborhood of 2 or 3 million people in 1980."[55] About two thirds
of them are black, a fifth are Hispanic.[56] Paul Peterson also concludes
that metropolitan census tracts marked by deep poverty contained "little more than one percent of the U.S. population in 1980."[57] Still the
number living in such underclass areas is growing, even if the total
remains small.[58]

The media-driven impressions that most blacks are in the underclass
are clearly wrong, a fact acknowledged by Richard Harwood, the
ombudsman at *The Washington Post*. Recognizing that most blacks are
in "middle- and upper-income classes . . . [or] are part of the broad
working class where children, because of increasing white-collar job
opportunities, are headed for middle class lives," Harwood believes
that media bias, including that of his own influential paper, strongly
contributes to the negative picture of black America. "There is another
factor . . . our traditions of muckraking journalism, which are especially
strong at *The Post*. It looks at society from the bottom up in the hope of
reforming and changing it. . . . Of necessity, misery and failure are its
preoccupations. . . . [R]eportorial imbalance . . . creates demeaning
stereotypes of blacks as a race."[59]

To borrow Ralph Ellison's phrase, the "invisible man" of the 1990s is
the successful black working- and middle-class suburbanite, not inter-

acting with ghetto blacks and largely ignored by whites.[60] Ironically, as Richard P. Nathan writes, the identification of the black situation with the ghetto poor stems from the fact that "members of racial minority groups who are educated, talented, and motivated can assimilate in ways that a generation ago would have been thought inconceivable." Few note the blacks who "make it."[61] Yet the record is clear. "The black suburban population grew by 70 percent during the 1970's, fed primarily by an exodus from central cities. This trend has continued into the 1980's as the number of black suburbanites swelled from 5.4 million to 8.2 million. Between 1986 and 1990, 73 percent of black population growth occurred in the suburbs."[62]

Seeking a better quality of life, blacks and other minorities have moved to the suburbs as a reflection of their new middle-class status. "Minority suburbanization took off in the 1980s," University of Michigan demographer William H. Frey notes, "both as the black middle class came into its own and as more assimilated Latinos and Asians translated their moves up the socioeconomic ladder into a suburban lifestyle."[63] However, there are significant differences in migration rates between these minority groups. While the black suburban population grew by 34.4 percent from 1980 to 1990, Hispanics and Asians registered gains of 69.3 and 125.9 percent, respectively. These patterns continue to provide evidence for the long-term immigrant success story in the American experience, indicating that the divide between what I call the two Americas is largely limited to whites and blacks, not whites and people of color.

It is important to recognize that the situation of a major portion of black America was improving during the sixties and seventies. While there is a great deal of debate about the definition of poverty, census data indicate that the percentage of blacks living in poverty declined from 55 percent in 1959 to 33.5 percent in 1970. The rate has fluctuated somewhat since then, depending on the state of the economy. It moved up in the early 1980s, then fell during the Reagan prosperity, down to 30.7 percent in 1989. It then increased during the recession of the early 1990s to 33.1 percent in 1993, still much lower than during the pre–civil rights era.[64]

The stability in the poverty rate figures conceals significant changes within the African American population, which has produced a sizably better-educated and more affluent sector. The proportion of blacks ages 25 and over who are high school graduates increased from 51 percent in 1980 to 73 percent in 1994. During that same period, the white cohort reached 82 percent.[65] According to the Census, "The annual dropout rate for Blacks declined from 11 percent in 1970 to 5 percent in 1993. In 1993, there was no statistical difference in the annual high school dropout rate of Blacks and Whites."[66]

Economists James P. Smith and Finis R. Welch, analyzing changes in the situation of blacks since World War II, concluded in 1986 that "the real story of the last forty years has been the emergence of the black middle class," which "as a group . . . outnumbers the black poor."[67] These blacks are married or in stable long-term relationships. The income of married blacks is 77 percent of that of comparable whites, which is again a considerable increase from well below 60 percent two decades ago.

These drastic social and economic changes have led to growing differentiation within the black community. As a National Academy of Sciences panel, writing in the late eighties, noted:

> Conditions within the black community began to diverge sharply in the 1970s. This divergence can be seen very clearly in the experience of young men. By the early 1980s, black men aged 25–34 with at least some college, earned 80–85 percent as much as their white counterparts. They also achieved some gains in private-sector white-collar positions. In terms of education, these black men represented the top one-third of their age group. At the other end of the group were the one-quarter of black men aged 25–34 who had not finished high school and who could not compete in the stagnant 1970s economy. An increasing number dropped out of the labor force altogether. . . .[68]

The two largest groups in the black class structure, the authors say, are now "a lower class dominated by female-headed families and a middle class largely composed of families headed by a husband and wife."[69] The problem is that most black *adults* live in stable family and economic situations while most black *children* do not. They are the offspring of the large number of black women who are single mothers neither living with nor supported by a male head of household. Recent statistics indicate that well over half of all black births are out of wedlock. The proportion of black children born in female-headed households was 23 percent in 1960, 28 percent in 1969, 45 percent in 1980, and 62 percent at the start of the nineties.[70] The increase in the rate is, in large part, a function of married blacks having fewer children.[71] Middle-class married black fertility is now below the point necessary for the maintenance of the population.[72] Incomes for the black female-headed households are well under those of married blacks. "The poverty rate for two-parent black families with children was 12.5 percent in 1988, for single-parent families with children, the poverty rate was 56.3 percent."[73] Victor Fuchs's analysis of the relationship of gender to poverty demonstrates that the large proportion of women in single-parent situations accounts for much of the continued disproportionate presence of poverty among blacks.[74] Yet as Margaret Simms, the director of Research Programs for the (African-American) Joint Center for Political and Economic Studies, notes, Census Bureau data indicate that "contrary to the image of a population locked into welfare dependency, more than three-fourths of single black mothers held jobs."[75]

It is important to recognize that the magnitude of black illegitimacy is grossly exaggerated. The increase in the rate is more a function of a decline in legitimate births than of an increase in out-of-wedlock pregnancies.[76] Christopher Jencks calculates that if married black women had borne as many babies in 1987 as they did in 1960, "the proportion of black babies born out of wedlock would have risen only from 23 percent in 1960 to 29 percent by 1987."[77] And a 1994 Census Bureau Report on *Characteristics of the Black Population* indicates that "the rate of babies being born to unwed black teenagers—about 80 per 1,000 unmarried teenagers—remained virtually the same from 1970 through 1990," while that for unmarried whites increased.[78]

Whatever the causes of childhood poverty, affirmative action is no remedy for this group. Preference policies or quotas are not much help to an illegitimate black ghetto youth who grows up in poverty and receives an inferior education. "Black [young] men with less than a high school degree consistently earned the smallest proportion of their white counterparts' income."[79] Many do not have marketable skills which would enable them to be considered for well-rewarded positions. In any case, the federally enforced contract compliance program has "raised demand for black males more in highly skilled white-collar and craft jobs than in the blue-collar operative, laborer, and service occupations." Litigation efforts using the anti-discrimination section of the Civil Rights Act (Title VII) have led to considerable gains in white-collar positions, especially in professional and managerial employment.[80] Jonathan Leonard notes: "The percentage of black men in the professional and managerial occupations rose from 4 percent in 1949 to 13 percent in 1990."[81] But as William Julius Wilson has emphasized, "affirmative action programs are not designed to deal with the unique problems of the black poor—problems which have devastatingly affected the makeup of underclass families."[82] The policies are much more likely to benefit minority individuals from the most advantaged families . . . [who are] most qualified for preferred positions—such as higher-paying jobs, college admissions, promotions and so forth. Accordingly, if policies of preferential treatment for such positions are conceived not in terms of the actual disadvantages suffered by individuals but rather in terms of race or ethnic group membership, then these policies will further enhance the opportunities of the more advantaged without addressing the problems of the truly disadvantaged.[83]

Comparisons of the relationship between educational and economic attainments within each racial group indicate that the advantage of college attendance is much greater among blacks. And a study of education, occupational mobility, and earnings from 1974 and 1981 of young males (ages 18–35) also found that "black college graduates obtain more prestigious posts than their white counterparts," a result attributed by the researchers to "employer sensitivity to affirmative action requirements," as well as to the "concentration of educated blacks in the public sector."[84] O'Hare et al. report that the median income of families headed by young black college graduates is on average almost as high as for comparably educated whites, $54,400 compared to $58,800. "Average incomes for white families headed by single women who are college graduates are no higher than for black families."[85] Defining "affluence" as an income of $50,000 or more, the "number of affluent black families increased from 266,000 in 1967 to just over a million in 1989. . . ." These rates of change, however, declined during the recessions of the early eighties and nineties and the halts in the growth of government employment.[86] College-educated black women continue to do well, but equally trained males with degrees do not.

The implication that there is relatively little reverse discrimination for lower-skill positions is sustained by the result of an Urban Institute study which sent equally qualified whites and blacks to apply for general labor, service, retail, and clerical positions in Chicago and Washington, D.C., in 1990. It reported that whites were treated better in job interviews in 20 percent of the cases, compared to 7 percent for blacks, and were more likely to be hired. One finding of this research is heartening; there was no discrimination in three quarters of the interview situations. But blacks are still much more likely to suffer from racism in working-class job markets than whites are to experience reverse discrimination.[87]

POLITICAL IMPLICATIONS

As the United States approaches the twenty-first century, the debate over affirmative action continues. This phenomenon should not be surprising since the issues involve efforts to maintain or change some of the core values of the nation—individual versus group rights—and affect feelings about opportunity and security for both races.

Prior to the 1992 and 1994 elections, the arguments surrounding quotas or preferences were increasingly seen as strengthening the Republicans, who vigorously emphasized meritocratic standards.[88] Their earlier support for quotas had been forgotten. Most Democrats were uneasy as to how to deal with the issue. They were faced with a dilemma: how to respond to pressure from civil rights groups and the intelligentsia on the one hand, and on the other, how to deal with the fear that a continuing identification with quotas would alienate the party's traditional base of white working-class support. In this connection it is interesting to recall that in 1965, in private White House discussions about civil rights programs, Lyndon Johnson said: "We have to press for them as a matter of right, but we also have to recognize that by doing so we will destroy the Democratic party." He anticipated that significant sections of the white South and the white working-class in the North would defect on racial issues.[89] The record indicates that this happened, particularly in presidential elections from 1968 to 1988 and in the 1994 congressional contests. A *New York Times*/CBS News poll conducted in mid-year 1991 found that 56 percent of Americans said the Democratic Party "cares more about the needs and problems of blacks," while only 15 percent replied that the Republicans do. When asked the same question about "the needs and problems of whites," 45 percent answered the Republicans care more, only 19 percent said the Democrats do, and 14 percent said both parties care.

How salient is white concern over affirmative action? We know that in 1990 Jesse Helms won in North Carolina while using this issue, and ex-Klansman David Duke emphasized it in Louisiana and received a majority of white votes. Pete Wilson focused on Dianne Feinstein's earlier espousal of quotas in government employment and beat her for governor of California in 1990. The polling evidence suggests that the debate hurt the Democrats. Many less affluent whites responded to the argument that the number of jobs available for them declined as a result of preference for blacks.[90] Two studies undertaken in 1985 and

1987 by Stanley Greenberg, then of the Analysis Group and subsequently Clinton's pollster, commissioned by the Michigan Democratic Party to investigate white male blue-collar defections from the party, found that negative reactions to affirmative action had played a major role there. A summary of the reports notes:

> Much to the surprise and dismay of both Greenberg and his sponsors, white fury over affirmative action emerged as a top voter concern in Greenberg's 1985 report and in a second report in 1987. Quotas and minority preferences were a primary source of anti-government, anti-Democrat anger among white blue-collar voters. Democratic campaign themes such as "fairness," "equity," and "justice" had been perceived—not without justification—as code words for quotas. Therefore, white voters had become in Greenberg's terms, "de-aligned" from the Democratic Party.[91]

A Democratic pollster's study of voters in Louisiana found that racial issues played an important role in the election there. Geoff Garin writes that the response to one statement distinguished Duke voters more than anything else: "Qualified whites lose out on jobs and promotion because blacks get special preference due to affirmative action hiring goals." A majority of Duke supporters, 52 percent, said this happens "a lot," as compared to 25 percent who felt this way among those who backed his opponent.[92] National polls indicate the same concern. Two surveys, one conducted by the University of Michigan's Institute for Social Research in 1986 and the other by NORC in 1990, found large majorities of whites replying that it is "very likely" (28% in both) or "somewhat likely" (48 and 42%) "that a white person won't get a job or promotion while an equally or less qualified black person gets one instead." The 1986 study indicated that two fifths of the whites believed that they personally or someone in their family would experience job discrimination. In June 1991, the *New York Times*/CBS News poll asked a national cross section: "When preference in hiring or promotion is given to blacks, do you think in the long run this helps whites, hurts whites, or doesn't affect whites much one way or the other?" A plurality, 47 percent, replied it does not affect whites, but two fifths said it does hurt them. A March 1995 *Washington Post*/ABC News poll found that 51 percent of all Americans (57% of white males) think that "affirmative action programs giving preference to women, blacks and other minorities result in less opportunity for white men." Thirteen percent of whites reported having been denied a job or promotion for racial reasons. A report of an earlier 1991 poll sponsored by the Leadership Conference on Civil Rights also stated "that many white voters believe there is pervasive reverse discrimination in the work place and that civil rights leaders are more interested in special preferences than in equal opportunity." The Civil Rights Act of 1991, which passed in slightly modified form and was signed by President Bush after much publicized misgivings, was, according to its proponents, designed to facilitate lawsuits for remedial action by individuals claiming discrimination.

In 1992, Bill Clinton, running as a New Democrat and advised by Greenberg, rejected and even criticized the special preference or quota policies identified with his predecessors. In office, however, he seemingly returned to and extended them, by stressing racial, ethnic, and gender "diversity" in his political appointments.[93] Polls continued to reveal popular disdain for quotas, now presented by President Clinton as "diversity," attitudes which appeared to have contributed to the president's low approval ratings in 1994, particularly among men, and to the severe electoral defeats experienced by the Democrats in the midterm congressional elections. Republicans moved to a substantial majority position in both houses after four decades in the minority.

In interpreting the election, Thomas Edsall of *The Washington Post* emphasized the role which considerations of reverse discrimination played in determining the outcome. Many white males reacted to a belief that as a group they were suffering from reverse discrimination. He called attention to the votes of "White men who feel devalued and displaced everywhere from the service sector to the ranks of middle management, who see the rights revolution on behalf of women and blacks moving beyond a level playing field to a system of exclusionary favoritism and who see a future (and present) of sharply declining wages and status. White men voted Republican by a margin of 63 to 37 percent."[94]

Edsall's analysis is congruent with a variety of recent poll data which indicate that white men are particularly concerned about and opposed to special preferences for "qualified blacks" to remedy "past discrimination." Thus, Gallup found in March 1993 that only 15 percent of white males favored such policies; 83 percent were opposed, as contrasted to 24 percent supportive and 72 percent against among "others," i.e., women and minorities. The same survey inquired whether "white males are paying a fair penalty or an unfair penalty for advantages they had in the past—or don't you think white males are paying a penalty?" Almost half of the white males thought they were paying an "unfair penalty," while 29 percent replied "no penalty." Only 9 percent said they were paying a fair penalty. And a January 1995 poll taken by *Time*/CNN found that 77 percent of a national sample thought that affirmative action "sometimes or frequently discriminates against whites. Even among black respondents, 66% answered the same way."[95] In April, two-thirds of those interviewed by the *New York Times*/CBS Survey agreed preference "results in discrimination against whites."

These findings do not imply increased attitudinal backing for discrimination. Rather, as Edsall notes, Americans continue to show "strong support for basic equalitarian principles, including equality of opportunity and the obligation of employers to give everyone a fair chance." There is "strong opposition to discrimination practices based on race, gender, age or disability." However, as the Leadership Conference on Civil Rights survey indicated in 1991, "civil rights laws are seen by a substantial number of voters as creating unfair advantages, setting up rank or class privilege in the labor market."[96] Commenting on the same study, a black *Washington Post* columnist, William Raspberry, emphasized:

> White Americans . . . do not see themselves as racists, or as opponents of equal opportunity and fundamental fairness. What they oppose are efforts to provide preferential benefits for minorities. . . .
>
> They aren't buying. How could we [blacks] expect them to buy a product we have spent 400 years trying to have recalled: race-based advantages enshrined into law?[97]

Two surveys conducted by Gallup for CNN and *USA Today,* one at the start of the Clinton administration in February 1993 and the second in December 1994, provide further evidence that concerns with minority preference contributed to the Democratic debacle. Gallup inquired: "How often does it happen these days that a less qualified black person gets a job or promotion, only because of affirmative action?" White males were more disposed to reply "very often" than the sample as a whole or white women. The percentage of the entire sample who so answered increased over the twenty-two months of the Clinton administration, from 26 to 34 percent, while white men went up from 29 to 38 percent. The change was comparable to the shift in their vote from 1992 to 1994.

These findings are reinforced by changes reported by the *Los Angeles Times* and *Newsweek* polls. In a September 1991 survey by the former, 24 percent of the national sample and 32 percent of the white male respondents agreed that "affirmative action programs designed to help minorities get better jobs and education go too far these days." (Thirty-seven percent of the total and 16 percent of the white men said they "don't go far enough.") Three and a half years later, in January 1995, 39 percent of all those interviewed and fully half, 49 percent, of the white males thought affirmative action goes too far, an over-50 percent jump among the latter. *Newsweek* inquired in 1987 and 1995, "Have we gone too far in pushing equal rights in this country?" Perhaps because the sympathetic phrase "designed to help minorities" was not in the question, more whites agreed than in the *L.A. Times* poll, 54 percent in 1995, up from 42 percent in 1987.

There is also evidence to suggest that there is widespread belief that African Americans no longer need affirmative action policies. A March 1995 *Newsweek* poll found that 46 percent of the sample believe that "blacks' status in the workplace would stay about the same without affirmative action." Thirty percent thought it would get worse, and 19 percent believed it would improve.

CONCLUSION

Special racial, ethnic, and gender-based preferences have introduced a new approach to promoting equality in American life. The old approach, initially implied in the Declaration of Independence, emphasized equality for *individuals,* equality of opportunity. The new one focuses on equality for *groups,* equality of result. It is the collision of these two views on equality that has underscored the growing public controversy over affirmative action and quotas, and that is symbolic, in some ways, of the larger friction between the black situation and the American Creed. In order to understand how these perspectives fit into the American debate, this chapter has examined their origins in the diverse historical experiences of whites and blacks. It was the potentially complementary egalitarian and individualistic elements in the American Creed that created the consensus behind the civil rights revolution which began in the 1960s. But the more recent focus of the civil rights movement, with its emphasis on substantive equality and preferential treatment, explicitly conflicts with the individualistic, achievement-oriented element in the Creed.

It is important to recognize that white opposition to various forms of special governmental assistance for blacks and other minorities is in part a function of a general antagonism to statism and a preference for personal freedom in the American value system. The American Creed, as we have seen, subsumes classical liberalism, which strongly distrusts the state and emphasizes competitive meritocracy.[98]

Public opinion research indicates that the vast majority of Americans, including most blacks, believe that this is still a land of opportunity. They not only believe in meritocracy; they think that it exists. As of 1987, according to NORC, 72 percent of Americans said that they have a good chance of improving their standard of living, many more proportionately than Italians (45%), Germans (40%), British (37%), or Dutch (26%).[99] Although more Americans go to college than people in any other country, close to two thirds of Americans (65%) say that the opportunity to go to college should be increased. This figure is higher than among the British (55%), the Germans (31%), or other Europeans and Japanese. These views tie in with the greater propensity of Americans than Europeans to believe that "ambition is [essential or very important] for getting ahead in life."[100] When asked, however, how government should provide financial assistance to college students, more Americans than Europeans respond through loans (by 57 to 31%), and more Europeans favor government grants (by 51 to 31%).[101]

The findings of comparative survey research completed in the early 1980s and repeated in 1990 in the World Values Surveys, discussed briefly in chapter Three, imply that the contemporary opposition to preferential treatment for blacks or other underprivileged minorities is not primarily a result of racial prejudice. The results point to varying attitudes about equality of result in the United States, Canada, and eleven West European countries. Interviewees in each country were told:

> I'd like to relate an incident to you and ask your opinion of it. There are two secretaries, of the same age, doing practically the same job. One of the secretaries finds out that the other earns 20 dollars [100 marks, Kroner, etc.] a week more than she does. She complains to her boss. He says, quite rightly, that the other secretary is quicker, more efficient and more reliable at her job. In your opinion, is it fair or not fair that one secretary is paid more than the other?

The question is clearly and intentionally biased in favor of obtaining the reply that the more productive secretary should be paid more, and large majorities in North America and Europe answered this way. However, twice the proportion of Europeans (39% in 1981, 27% in 1990), as of Americans (18% in 1980, 15% in 1990), said that it is unfair to pay more to the more efficient and more reliable person.

Americans are clearly more likely to believe in distinguishing by merit. Canadians fall between the two; 25 percent in 1980 and 18 percent in 1990, said it was unfair.[102]

The same studies found comparable cross-national difference with respect to statements which emphasize personal liberty and individual initiative versus a reduction of class differences. Respondents were asked:

> Which of these two statements come closest to your own opinion? I find that both freedom and equality are important. But if I were to make up my mind for one or the other, I would consider personal freedom more important, that is, everyone can live in freedom and develop without hindrance.

> Certainly both freedom and equality are important. But if I were to make up my mind for one of the two, I would consider equality more important, that is, that nobody is underprivileged and that social class differences are not so strong.

Most people in the United States, 74 percent in 1981 and 71 in 1990, favored personal liberty over class equality (23 and 24%, respectively). In fourteen European countries surveyed by the World Values Survey in those two years, 56 and 58 percent favored freedom and 37 percent equality. Independent of race or ethnicity considerations, citizens of the United States are significantly less favorable to equality of income or class position than Europeans, or it may be noted Canadians, although the difference with the latter is somewhat smaller (65 to 32% and 61 to 34%).

Although Americans are less willing than Europeans to use government as an instrument of income distribution, their egalitarian values lead them to approve of programs providing more opportunities for blacks. They favor more expenditures on education, special schools, and other intensive programs such as Head Start. But opinion surveys taken in various developed countries indicate that Americans are much less prone than Europeans and Canadians to endorse measures to help the underprivileged generally. Thus, as noted in chapter Two, in 1987, only a fifth (21%) of Americans agreed that "the government should provide everyone with a guaranteed basic income," as compared with 50 percent or more in Austria, Germany, Great Britain, Italy, and the Netherlands. Comparable cross-national differences were reported with respect to statements dealing with the government's responsibility to "provide a job for everyone who wants one," and a "decent standard of living for the unemployed," and to reduce sharp income differences.[103] In 1991, the *Times-Mirror* Survey, conducted by the Gallup Poll, asked respondents in thirteen countries to react to the statement: "It is the responsibility of the state (or government in the U.S.) to take care of very poor people who can't take care of themselves." Over 60 percent of those polled in Britain, France, Italy, and Spain agreed, as did 50 percent of all Germans, as compared to but 23 percent of Americans.[104] Various questions that have been put to national samples of Americans in the eighties and early nineties concerning the responsibility of government to provide jobs and economic opportunity or "help people when they are in trouble" have found majorities opposed to government action.[105]

The interpretation that American opposition to governmental enforcement of group rights for blacks is more a reflection of general principle than of racism is reinforced by the findings of a study of attitudes toward government efforts to assure free residential choice.[106] Comparing attitudes toward enforcing rights of blacks, Japanese Americans, Jews, and Christians "to live wherever they can afford to," Howard Schuman and Lawrence Bobo found little difference in reactions to the various ethnic and religious groups. Those "who oppose enforcement of housing rights [do so] regardless of the racial or religious group affected, so that the principle of government enforcement in this area seems to be critical rather than opposition to any particular group."[107]

The recurrent conflict between different versions of equality, between emphasis on the individual and on the group, will continue in all free societies. The countries which have most thoroughly enshrined group quotas into their basic law—India, Pakistan, and Canada—are strongly organized on group lines, the first two caste, the third, separate linguistic cultures.[108] Affirmative action quotas in India for the scheduled (untouchable) castes go back to the 1920s. They were introduced in a few provinces in colonial India, and have been enlarged and expanded considerably by independent India and Pakistan. The Canadian Constitution has always contained provisions to protect linguistic and religious minorities, and has been somewhat more limited in protection of individual rights than ours. The Charter of Rights and Freedoms, which was added to the Constitution in 1982, specifically authorizes programs and activities directed to "the amelioration of conditions of disadvantaged individuals or groups including those that are disadvantaged because of race, national or ethnic origin, colour, religion, sex, age or mental or physical disability."[109] Canada and its provinces have explicitly defined more than thirty such groups as worthy of special treatment, behavior which conforms to its founding decision to emphasize the protection of groups rather than individuals.

The same logic has been used by various analysts to account for the absence of significant socialist movements and the low level of class politics in the United States and the converse patterns in Europe. As we saw in the previous chapter, the evidence and arguments suggest that the European developments reflect the influence of postfeudal relationships which explicitly structured the social hierarchy according to fixed social classes, requiring the lower-statused to show deference to their class superiors. Consequently, the emerging working class there reacted to the political world in class terms. Conversely, white America—the purest bourgeois and classically liberal society in the world—has treated class as an economic construct. Social classes have been of limited visibility compared with the situation in Europe. Hence, class-conscious politics and socialist demands for equality of results have been limited in scope.

The failures of different varieties of socialism and the greater acceptance of the market as the dynamic force underlying economic growth have led to a revival of market liberalism in Europe, emphasizing competitive meritocracy and individualism. Conversely, the increased awareness and better organization of the blacks in America have given more support here to group-linked efforts to reduce inequality.

The black situation in America is analytically comparable to that of the European underprivileged strata. The post caste situation has, in fact, been even more explicit in limiting the economic and social opportunities of the socially oppressed than the postfeudal ones. It is not surprising, therefore, that American blacks are more group-conscious than European workers, or that many support a version of the old socialist emphasis on equality of results. Ninety percent of American blacks vote Democratic, much more than any other ethnic group or trade union members. At least three of the Democratic black members of Congress are openly socialist, a phenomenon found for only one white.

Poll data support these generalizations. Blacks are much more disposed than whites to favor state intervention rather than to emphasize individual initiative as the way to improve their situation. The National Election Studies conducted every two years have posed the choice between government help to minorities and individual initiative in the following terms:

Some people feel that the government in Washington should make every possible effort to improve the social and economic position of blacks and other minority groups. Suppose these people are at one end of the scale, at point 1. Others feel that the government should not make any special effort to help minorities because they should help themselves. Suppose these people are at the other end, at point 7. And, of course, some other people have opinions somewhere in between. Where do you place yourself on this scale?[110]

The survey has found repeated and consistent differences of 35 to 50 percent between black and white respondents. The majority of African Americans say the government should "make every possible effort" to improve the "position of blacks and other minority groups." The most popular position among whites is that minorities "should help themselves."[111] Most blacks, in effect, favor a socialist group solution, most whites a laissez-faire, individualist one.

Civil rights leaders, liberals, and Democrats are faced with the negative reactions by most whites to their identification with quotas, special preferences, and reverse discrimination. Opinion polls indicate that not all blacks are favorable to these policy alternatives, a reaction that goes back more than a century. During the Reconstruction period, in 1871, the celebrated black abolitionist and civil rights leader Frederick Douglass ridiculed the idea of racial quotas suggested by African-American Union Army officer Martin Delany as "absurd as a matter of practice," noting that it implied blacks "should constitute one-eighth of the poets, statesmen, scholars, authors and philosophers." Douglass emphasized that "natural equality is a very different thing from practical equality; and . . . though men may be potentially equal, circumstances may for a time cause the most striking inequalities."[112] On another occasion, in opposing "special efforts" for black freedmen, Douglass argued that they "might 'serve to keep up very prejudices, which it is so desirable to banish' by promoting an image of blacks as privileged wards of the state."[113] One hundred years later, at the start of the 1970s, black leaders like Clarence Mitchell of the NAACP feared and opposed quotas because they anticipated these would lead to the loss of white working-class support for civil rights.

Shelby Steele, a contemporary black writer once active in Jesse Jackson's Rainbow Coalition, has concluded that "affirmative action has shown itself to be more bad than good and that blacks . . . now stand to lose more from it than they gain."[114] Like Douglass, he rejects the idea of leaping "over the hard business of developing a formerly oppressed people to the point where they can achieve proportionate representation on their own. . . ." He sees affirmative action quotas as undermining black morale, contributing to "an enlargement of self-doubt," for racial preferences imply that successful blacks have not earned their positions, that they are inferior to whites at their achievement level.[115]

The American left from Jefferson to Humphrey stood for making equality of opportunity a reality. By a supreme irony, the man most hated by contemporary Democrats, Richard Nixon, created a situation which has placed them on the wrong side of the issue from national values and electoral standpoints. The leadership of some of the party's strongest bases of support, blacks and other minorities, feminists, liberals, and the intelligentsia, all strongly endorse numerical preferences, targets, and quotas. But a considerable majority of Americans, including most Democrats, oppose them.

To rebuild the national consensus on civil rights and racial justice, affirmative action should be refocused, not discarded. It is clear, for example, that quotas or special preferences will not help the poorly educated and unskilled to secure good jobs. As the American economy undergoes a major structural transformation in eliminating a large proportion of blue-collar, less skilled jobs, the less trained and less educated of all races are pressed out of the labor market or into lowly paid positions. To succeed in postindustrial society requires good education. Extending and vastly improving education in the ghettos, from very early Head Start Programs, to financial incentives for students, teachers, and successful schools, to expanding apprentice programs that combine classroom instruction and on-the-job training, are the directions to be followed for children and school-age youth. As William Julius Wilson urges, such programs should be offered to all less privileged people, regardless of racial and ethnic origins.

The experience of blacks in the military suggests an option for young adults. Prior to the downsizing of the military following the end of the Cold War, the armed services offered blacks career training and a chance for stable employment and upward mobility. The whole society can learn from the success of this performance-oriented institution in integrating blacks and offering real incentives to succeed.[116] That record argues in favor of a large-scale national service effort, more extensive than the one enacted in 1993. If all youth are encouraged to volunteer for duty in national service, those with inadequate education and skills can be trained for positions that are in demand, while helping to rebuild publicly supported infrastructures or deliver social services. Studies of the experience of the economically disadvantaged in the military could shed much light on the subject.

Moving away from policies that emphasize special preferences need not—indeed, must not—mean abandoning the nation's commitment to guaranteeing equal opportunity for disadvantaged citizens. The concept of individual rights remains integral to the American Creed. Yet, racial injustice and castelike divisions have constituted a contradiction to the organizing principles of the nation. The American dilemma is still with us, and with it a moral obligation to ensure that race is neither a handicap nor an advantage. Until black Americans are absorbed fully into the economy and society, we should, in Jefferson's words, continue to fear a just God.

CHAPTER 5

A Unique People in an Exceptional Country[1]

If African Americans are perceived as close to the bottom of the stratification system, Jews are seen by friend and foe alike as near or at the top. Though extraordinarily successful in the meritocratic competition, they resemble blacks in their commitment to liberal social reform and in their concern over discrimination against minorities. This combination of success and leftist ideology makes them unique in the American ethnic kaleidoscope. To understand the role of Jews in American society, it is important to recognize that they are exceptional among the world's Jewries, and that their experience on this continent differs qualitatively from those of their co-religionists in other countries. Jews won acceptance as fully equal citizens earlier here than elsewhere. They have faced much less discrimination in the United States than in any other predominantly Christian nation. Although never more than 3.7 percent of the population and now 2.5 or less, they have been given one third of the religious representation. In many public ceremonies, there is one priest, one minister, and one rabbi. Strikingly, non-Jews greatly overestimate the size of the American Jewish population. A 1992 national survey conducted for the Anti-Defamation League by Marttila & Kiley found the median estimate of the percentage of Americans who are Jewish is 18. Only a tenth perceive them as less than 5 percent.

As Calvin Goldscheider and Alan Zuckerman note: "The pace of socioeconomic change and the levels [of occupation and income] attained are exceptional features of Jews compared to non-Jews."[2] A national survey of American Jews and non-Jews completed for the American Jewish Committee in 1988 by Steven M. Cohen led to the conclusion that "Jews are among the wealthiest groups in America. . . . Per capita Jewish income may actually be almost double that of non-Jews." Proportionately, more than twice as many Jewish as non-Jewish whites report household incomes in excess of $50,000. At the other end of the spectrum, almost twice as many non-Jews as Jews indicate incomes of less than $20,000.[3] The 1990 National Survey of Religious Identification (NSRI), based on a representative sample of 113,000 people, reported that Jews had the highest median annual household income ($36,700) among thirty different denominations, including agnostics and those reporting "no religion" as separate groups. Unitarians were second at $34,800, agnostics third at $33,300, and Episcopalians fourth at $33,000.[4] An analysis of the four hundred richest Americans, as reported by *Forbes* magazine, finds that two-fifths of the 160 wealthiest are Jews, as are 23 percent of the total list.[5] Jews are disproportionately present among many sections of elites, largely drawn from the college-educated. These include the leading intellectuals (45%), professors at the major universities (30%), high-level civil servants (21%), partners in the leading law firms in New York and Washington, D.C. (40%), the reporters, editors, and executives of the major print and broadcast media (26%), the directors, writers, and producers of the fifty top-grossing motion pictures from 1965 to 1982 (59%), and the same level people involved in two or more prime-time television series (58%).[6] Since the 1994 congressional election, there are twenty-four Jewish representatives and nine senators.[7] Since almost all Jews in the previous Congress were Democrats, and the latter suffered heavy losses in the mid-term contests, it is noteworthy that over three-fourths of the Jewish representatives were reelected. Many represent regions with few Jews.

These achievements are related to the extraordinary scholastic accomplishments of American Jews. At the beginning of 1990, 85 percent of college-age Jews were enrolled in higher education, as compared to two fifths for the population at large.[8] And, like the Jewish faculty, they are heavily located in the more selective schools. An American Council on Education survey of college freshmen found that those of Jewish parentage had significantly higher secondary school grades than their Gentile counterparts, in spite of the fact that a much larger proportion of all Jews than of others go on to college. Moreover, Jews seemingly perform better as undergraduates; by a considerable margin, they are disproportionately elected to Phi Beta Kappa.[9]

THE LINKAGE WITH AMERICAN VALUES

It has been argued that the ability of Jews to do so well in America reflects the fact that Jewish characteristics and values have been especially congruent with the larger national culture. Writing in the 1920s, the sociologist Robert Park "suggested that Jewish history be taught in the schools so that Americans can learn what America is. Park argued that in their energy and drive for achievement Jews were quintessentially American."[10] Evidence in support of such assumptions may be found in Weber's analysis of the relationship between the Protestant ethic and the spirit of capitalism in America, East European Jews' reaction to Benjamin Franklin, and the contemporary links between a capitalist reformer, Margaret Thatcher, and British Jews. As indicated in chapter Two, Weber, in explaining the economic success of the United States, noted that the Puritans brought the religiously derived values conducive to capitalism—rationality, hard work, savings, a strong achievement drive—to America, values ultimately expressed in the secular writings of Benjamin Franklin.[11]

Franklin's values not only appealed to Americans, they found an enthusiastic audience in Eastern Europe among Jews, to whom they also resonated as consistent with their religious beliefs and secular culture. Franklin's writings were translated into Yiddish around 1800, were read devoutly, and discussed in Talmudic discourse fashion by young Jews in Poland and Russia after they had completed their daily religious studies in yeshivas.[12] Weber recognized the "actual kinship of Puritanism [Calvinism] to Judaism," and the way it played out in America. He noted that "Puritanism always felt its similarity to Judaism. . . . The Jews who were welcomed by Puritan nations, especially the Americans . . . were at first welcomed without any ado whatsoever and are even now welcomed fairly readily. . . ."[13] Benjamin Franklin himself "subscribed to a fund for a new synagogue in Philadelphia" in 1788.[14]

The linkages of Protestant sectarian and Jewish values to the bourgeois or market ethic, and the classical laissez-faire liberalism of Americanism, are to be found in the closing decades of the twentieth century in the relationship of Margaret Thatcher to the Jews. She admires them as hardworking, self-made people who believe that "God helps those who help themselves." She chose to represent the most heavily populated Jewish district in Britain, Finchley in North London, and appointed five Jews to cabinet posts at different times. She also designated the chief rabbi, Immanuel Jakobovits, a member of the House of Lords. Various British publications have noted that she much preferred the tough-minded, self-help, work-oriented values of the chief rabbi—which also encompass commitment to personal philanthropy—to the soft Tory welfare emphases of the archbishop of Canterbury.[15]

Unlike her predecessors (or in part her successor, John Major) as leaders of the Conservative Party, Thatcher is not a Tory, which as noted earlier is an orientation once described by one of them, Harold Macmillan, as "paternalistic socialism." She is a classical liberal, that is, a supporter of the Hayek–Friedman–Reagan laissez-faire, anti-statist, meritocratic view of the world. Basically, the goal of the Thatcher revolution of the 1980s, whether consciously conceived of in these terms or not, was to create a country that resembled the United States sociologically, to get rid of the postfeudal emphasis on ascriptive status and mercantilist Tory-socialist elements, and become an achievement-oriented, bourgeois liberal society. She sees the Jews as most like the kind of people she would prefer her compatriots to be: prototypically meritocratic and competitively oriented. And unlike American Jewry, British Jewry turned conservative, reacting to the pro-Palestine position of many socialists, as well as Thatcher's overtures and enthusiastic support of Israel.

THE BACKGROUND

From its origins, America has been a universalistic culture, slavery and the black situation apart. As emphasized in previous chapters, America has been the purest example of a society which has followed capitalist market norms, relatively unhindered by values derived from feudalism. These norms assume universalism. Perceiving America in these terms implies that it emphasizes the values of meritocracy, of an open society, which is open to talent, open to the most efficient, the most competent.

As the self-conscious center of the liberal and increasingly populist revolutions (from 1776 to early in the twentieth century), the United States has been viewed by Americans and foreigners alike as open to new members. One may become an American by joining the party, accepting the Creed. Though immigrants may acquire citizenship almost everywhere, the meaning of being English, French, or German is predominantly a birthright status. And until relatively recently, citizen rights were associated with the dominant established religion—different Christian denominations in Europe and Latin America, and Islam in most of the Muslim world.

American voluntary denominationalism, as Tocqueville emphasized, encourages allegiance and participation as well as the formation of a host of mediating organizations positioned between the citizenry and the state. But no one is expected to adhere to any religious group. For the first time in the history of the Diaspora, Jews became free to partake in the polity as equals with everyone else. As sociologist Edward Tiryakian presents the unique American environment:

> At the heart of American exceptionalism concerning the Jewish experience in America, is that, while, for Jews, the United States is not and cannot be ontologically and existentially "the Land" in the way that Israel is, it has been more of a rewarding and accepting home than any other setting outside Israel itself. . . . What makes the American case different from others?
>
> Jews in America have not been marginalized as "wholly other" by virtue of their religion, there has been no historical ghetto experience, no pogroms. In fact because of a deep-structure, affinity of Calvinist-Puritanism for Judaism, it is in America that Jews have increasingly found full societal and cultural participation and acceptance in recent years of the term "Judeo-Christian."[16]

The encouragement to American Jewry to play a full role in society and the polity is endemic in George Washington's message to the Jews of Newport in 1790, that in the new United States, "all possess alike liberty of conscience and immunities of citizenship." Even more significantly, the first president emphasized that the patronizing concept of "toleration . . . of one class of people . . . [by] another" has no place in America, that Jews are as American, and on the same basis, as anyone else.[17] He recognized that tolerance denotes second-class citizenship. Jefferson and Madison also emphasized that America was different from Europe, that the discrimination against Judaism prevailing there did not exist here, where in Jefferson's words, all are "on an equal footing." Jefferson "rejoiced over the presence of Jews in the country because they would insure that religious diversity which, in his judgement, was the best protector of Liberty."[18]

The European democratic movements sought to free Jews from religious-based restrictions on their rights to citizenship and free movement. But anti-clericalism led them to denigrate Judaism as an obscurantist doctrine that should wither under the pressure of the Enlightenment. The French Revolution gave Jews all civic rights, but specifically limited their freedom to maintain an organized communal structure, explicitly denying them group rights.[19] Subsequently, Napoleon, who tore down ghetto restrictions in countries he conquered, grew concerned about the seeming desire of French Jews to remain religious and socially distinct from others. Such concerns were foreign to the Americans; they opposed church establishment, but welcomed religion.

The most dramatic indicator of the pluralistic character of religion in the first half century of American independence is evident in one of the most interesting and peculiar pieces of legislation enacted by an American Congress, the Sunday Mails Law. Passed in 1810, it authorized the Postmaster-General to sort and deliver mail on Sundays. In 1825, postmasters were ordered to keep offices open for the entire day. Some churchmen reacted by forming a General Union for Promoting the Observance of the Christian Sabbath. In answer to such protests, a Senate Committee headed by Richard Johnson, a Kentucky senator and head of a national Baptist group, wrote a Report on the Act, to be adopted by the full Senate in 1830, which explicitly said: "The Constitution regards the conscience of the Jew as sacred as that of the Christian," and concluded that the government was obligated to affirm to all its "institutions on Sunday, as well as every day of the week."[20]

The fact that leading politicians could openly advocate that the federal government consider the rights of Jews and other non-Christians indicates the extent to which many believing Protestants of the early United States were able to accept religious diversity.[21] Richard Johnson, the author of the 1830 Senate Report, was nominated for the vice presidency as Martin Van Buren's running mate on the Democratic ticket, supposedly because of his popularity stemming from the Report. The Sunday requirement lasted until the late 1880s, when it was dropped by the Postmaster-General.[22] It must be noted, however, that the situation was quite different in many states, some of which, under Sabbatherian and later trade union pressure, preserved or reenacted colonial legislation requiring Sunday closing by business. By 1868, however, fifteen states had exempted Saturday observers—Jews, Seventh Day Adventists, and Baptists—from the rule.[23]

In 1860, when Jews still could not hold office in most of Europe, the House of Representatives was opened with a prayer by a rabbi, thus acknowledging "the equal status of Judaism, with Christianity, as an American faith."[24] Congress was to reaffirm in 1861 the position that Jews were entitled to the same rights as Christians. It had passed a law concerning military chaplains, which stated that they had to be regularly ordained ministers of some Christian denomination. Objections from Jewish groups led to an amendment to allow rabbis to serve as well.

The position of the Jews in early America was not only a function of political developments, but related to the special character of American Christianity, the fact that the United States is the only Protestant sectarian country. The churches ascendant elsewhere in Christendom, as noted earlier, have been established and hierarchical, while Protestant sectarianism, which stresses the personal relationship of individuals with God, unmediated by church or hierarchy, has been dominant here. The competitive relationship of the Christian sects and churches has enabled the Jews to fit in as one out of many, rather than as the only or principal deviant group, which they have been in much of Europe. In any case, until relatively recently, most Protestant sectarians viewed Roman Catholics more negatively than the Jews. Catholicism was seen by many Americans not as a different set of religious beliefs, but as an alien conspiracy seeking to undermine the American Protestant way of life and, therefore, as outside the pale.

The American Jews adapted to the prevalent Protestant pattern. They developed a congregational style, eschewing the organized communal or hierarchical structures that once characterized Jewry in many European countries.[25] In the latter case, Jews were governed by *kehillahs,* communal organizations, which included all of them, and in a number of nations, by chief rabbis whose status resembled that of bishops or archbishops. Canadian Jewry, living in a country that places greater emphasis on the solidarity of ethnic and religious communities than the United States, is organized in one group, the Canadian Jewish Congress, which is somewhat like a European *kehillah.* American Jewry has no chief rabbis or disciplined communal bodies. An effort to form a *kehillah* in New York before World War I failed.[26] Judah Magnes, who played a major role in creating the short-lived New York *kehillah* in 1909, was to note a decade later that the "European notion of a uniform . . . all-controlling . . . *kehillah* cannot strike root in American soil . . . because it is not in consonance with the free and voluntary character of American religious, social, educational, and philanthropic enterprises. . . ."[27]

RELATIONS WITH THE LARGER SOCIETY

There were relatively few Jews in the United States before the Civil War. They totaled only fifteen thousand in 1825, increasing to fifty thousand in 1848. Some were able to reach high places in the American military and political systems, including a number of congresspersons and elected local officials. During the first quarter of the nineteenth century, Jews were elected to a variety of local and state offices, mainly in the South, including a governor of Georgia, and mayors in Richmond and Charleston. They were in the first classes at both West

Point and Annapolis.[28] Two very assimilated Jews, David Yulee of Florida and Judah P. Benjamin of Louisiana, were elected to the U.S. Senate, in 1844 and 1854, respectively. Benjamin is better known as Secretary of the Treasury and Jefferson Davis's closest adviser in the Confederacy during the Civil War.[29] The most prominent of northern Jewish politicians, Mordecai Noah, served at different times between 1813 and 1841 as U.S. Consul to Tunis, High Sheriff of New York, Surveyor of the Port of New York, Associate Judge of the New York Court of Sessions, and editor of six different New York newspapers. He also headed a number of Jewish communal organizations.[30] August Belmont, a Jewish banker who had once represented the Rothschilds, was chairman of the Democratic National Committee from 1860 to 1872. In 1860, the Commander of the Mediterranean Fleet was Uriah Levy, an affiliated Jew. There were at least four Jewish generals in the Union Army.[31]

On the other hand, there were some anti-Semitic occurrences during the Civil War. In the North, Jewish cotton speculators and traders were stigmatized as helping the South economically. The most noteworthy action against them was Ulysses S. Grant's order barring Jewish peddlers from the area under his command.[32] Abraham Lincoln promptly countermanded it. The president did not object to penalizing individuals whose actions were aiding the enemy, which, as he told Grant, presumably "was the object of your order, but . . . it is . . . [the] terms [which] proscribed an entire religious class" that were objectionable. Grant, it may be noted, was quick to indicate regret and said that the order was penned "without reflection." He informed the War Department a day later that it would never have seen the light of day had it not been telegraphed immediately after he signed it. More significantly, he told his wife that congressional censures against him had been deserved, since he "had no right to make an order against any special sect." As president, Grant "proved himself a friend of the Jews and appointed many to posts at home and abroad. He offered a Jew, Joseph Seligman, the post of Secretary of the Treasury, which he declined." Grant supported the Jews in the "controversy raised by . . . the A.S.P.C.A. (American Society for the Prevention of Cruelty to Animals) over the alleged cruelty practiced by Jews in the [kosher] slaughtering of animals."[33]

Concern for the welfare of Jews in other parts of the world has been characteristic of Western Jewry since Roman times, and American Jews have conformed to the rule. What is particularly notable about the phenomenon is the extent to which they have been able to get support from the larger political system. In 1840, the United States protested the persecution of Jews in Turkish-controlled Syria; in the 1880s, pogroms in Czarist Russia were officially condemned. In the first case, the Secretary of State wrote to the American Minister to Turkey to do what he could to mitigate the oppression. His letter noted that the United States places "upon the same footing the worshipers of God, of every faith and form, acknowledging no distinction between the Mahomedan, the Jew and the Christian."[34] The American government frequently sought to intervene on behalf of the Jews of Romania, demanding that American and native Jews be accorded equality before the law. In 1879, in writing to the American minister dealing with Romania, Secretary of State Evarts noted: "As you are aware, this government has ever felt a deep interest in the welfare of the Hebrew race in foreign countries, and has viewed with abhorrence the wrongs to which they have at various periods been subjected by followers of other creeds in the East."[35]

In the period between the Civil War and World War I, protests against anti-Jewish policies and pogroms in Czarist Russia occurred repeatedly. Some stemmed from an 1832 commercial treaty, which provided that local laws applied to nationals of each power in the other country. However, when these provisions were used by the Russians to legitimate restrictions on American Jews, the State Department and Congress objected. In 1881, President Garfield, in denouncing a pogrom, inaugurated a pattern of protests about the treatment of Russian Jews. From then through World War I, American governments often expressed sympathy with them and voiced complaint to the Czarist government. Such actions were frequent from 1903 to 1906 when over three hundred pogroms occurred, reflecting the tumultuous revolutionary times.[36] Resolutions were passed by Congress calling for the abrogation of the treaty. In 1908, the platforms of both major parties denounced it, and it was canceled in 1911.

There were limits to the willingness of the American government to intervene on behalf of Jews abroad, a fact which may convey a message for contemporary times. It is easy to win games in which you are the only major player, but you can lose against a strong opponent. In 1858, Jews in America and Europe rallied to protest the kidnapping and enforced conversion to Catholicism of an Italian Jewish youngster, Edgardo Mortara, an action which the Vatican refused to reverse. Although American Jews put as much pressure on the national administration as they could and many supportive editorials appeared in the public press, this time the State Department did not react. The failure may have reflected the weakness of President James Buchanan, but more importantly, Jewish pressure was countered by Catholic efforts. The Democratic politicians apparently did not want to alienate this large group of supporters.[37]

ANTI-SEMITISM

The seemingly philo-Jewish behavior on the part of nineteenth- and early twentieth-century American political elites did not imply the absence of hostile attitudes or behavior. Anti-Semitism, of course, existed in America, sometimes on a large scale. It is a disease endemic in the long-term competitive relationship between Judaism and its daughter religion(s). Antagonistic beliefs and negative stereotypes are part of the folk mythology of Christendom, and the original settlers and subsequent groups of immigrants brought them to the New World. The special economic skills in finance and commerce, which Jews developed in Europe to survive in societies that denied them access to ownership of land (the principal form of capital and investment), made them especially vulnerable to blame and persecution in periods of economic malaise and other severe crises.

The United States has not been an exception, even if the anti-Jewish outbreaks here have been much less virulent than in other countries. A detailed historical analysis of anti-Semitism in the United States up to the Civil War period by Frederick Jaher emphasizes "the mildness of American anti-semitism relative to that encountered by Jews in other parts of the world."[38] Comparing the phenomenon in nineteenth-century Europe and America, another scholar, Leo Ribuffo, also concludes that "Anti-Semitism in the United States was relatively less violent, less racist, and less central to the world views of those who accepted it."[39] Conversely, nativism (hostility to immigrants) was a recurrent phenomenon in America, particularly active during periods of economic and political crisis. Jews sometimes were included as a secondary target, but the most extreme forms of nativism were to be found among the more fundamentalist Protestants and took the form of anti-Romanism, of opposition to supposed conspiracies and real immigration waves that seemingly threatened the Protestant character of the country.[40]

Significant anti-Semitism showed up in the late nineteenth century, directed against the growing affluence of the German Jews, at a time when the Jews numbered about 250,000. As of 1889, "bankers, brokers, wholesalers, retail dealers, collectors, and agents accounted for 62 percent of their occupations. In addition, 17 percent were professionals."[41] In the post–Civil War period, a number of Jews of German origin developed the leading banking houses of the country. They, together with New England scions of the Puritans, dominated investment banking.[42]

These extraordinarily successful people were opposed to social separatism. Some were among the founding members of the high-status social clubs formed in many cities immediately before and after the Civil War. But as the number of the first generation or otherwise affluent Jews grew, wealthy Gentiles began to look for ways to deny them social access. Status strains endemic in a rapidly expanding and changing society upset people at different levels of the social structure. Those descended from the old wealthy of the pre–Civil War era found their claims to superior status threatened by the newly wealthy, some of whom were Jews. The Gentile *nouveaux riches,* in turn, discovered that wealth alone was not sufficient to earn them admission to high society, and sought to differentiate themselves from the Jews. There was open resistance to allowing Jews into the social elites, into their neighborhoods, into their clubs and resorts, and ultimately, there were efforts to hold down their numbers in high-ranking universities and professions.[43] But it "is important to stress the fact that this caste line was only drawn at the end of the nineteenth century, when . . . the members of the upper class were setting themselves apart in other ways."[44] As John Higham describes the background:

> At every level so many successful people clamored for admission to more prestigious circles that social climbing ceased to be a simple and modest expectation. . . . In order to protect recently acquired gains from later comers, social climbers had to strive constantly to sharpen the loose, indistinct lines of status. With a defensiveness born of insecurity, they grasped at distinctions that were more than pecuniary, through an elaborate formalization of etiquette, the compilation of social registers, the acquisition of aristocratic European culture, and the cult of genealogy.[45]

EAST EUROPEAN JEWS

The late nineteenth century also witnessed the steady mass immigration of poor Jews from Eastern Europe which, by World War I, produced a population of over 3 million, mostly concentrated in the tenement districts of the major northern cities. Although much poorer than their German-origin co-religionists, they were much better prepared for the life and economy of American cities than other immigrants. Most Jews came from urban environments. Goldscheider and Zuckerman point out that "Between 1899 and 1914, fully two-thirds of the Jews entering the United States had been engaged in manufacturing and mechanical pursuits in Europe, more than three-fourths as skilled workers." This background provided them with "an enormous structural advantage over other immigrants in the pursuit of occupational integration and social mobility."[46] Although able to obtain employment in their traditional skills, most were poor. They worked mainly in the garment industries or in trade, often initially as peddlers, the lowliest form of self-employment.[47] Living in crowded slums, in areas marked by high crime rates and red-light districts, speaking Yiddish, frequently looking unkempt and outlandish, they helped to produce new anti-Semitic stereotypes. These fed nativist prejudices. Considerable tensions developed between the Jews and other immigrant groups, which presaged some of the more serious, working-class–based, anti-Semitic movements of the 1930s.

Many East European Jews arrived as supporters of radical politics. Facing anti-Semitic regimes and societies, they could not simply enter the majority cultures. Barred from being members of conservative parties, they supported left-wing movements.[48] They came to America as socialists and tried to remain such as workers. As the foremost student of the subject, Arthur Liebman, notes: "American Jewry has provided socialist organizations and movements with a disproportionate number—at times approaching or surpassing a majority—of their leaders, activists, supporters."[49] Similar statements can be made about the supporters of subsequent other left third parties, including the LaFollette Progressive Party in 1924, the Communist-dominated Progressive Party in 1948, and the Anderson Independent candidacy in 1980.[50]

In 1914, Zionism had much less support among American Jews than socialism as an alternative political strand, with only twelve thousand members that year.[51] Jews of German descent retained their Abe Lincoln–born Republican attachments until the 1930s, but on the whole they backed the liberal or progressive Republicans who were an important force in the party. The one important genuinely conservative segment among Jews came from the Orthodox minority. Their journalists felt that in a country in which the right was not anti-Semitic, religious "conservatism in Jewish matters could best be complemented by conservatism in politics." But the circulation of their papers "was small in comparison with the [socialist] *Daily Forward.*"[52] The Orthodox opposed Zionism, believing that only God could redeem the promised land.[53]

Poverty and bad housing conditions did not stop these East European Jews from moving up. The skills and values they brought with them enabled them to quickly outdo others at their starting socioeconomic level in rates of upward social mobility. "For each wave of immigration from Russia bringing penniless and green immigrants into the slums, there was an exodus by immigrants who after five or ten years or so had managed well enough so they could leave the squalor of those slums."[54] They advanced through self-employment and education, particularly education. "Jewish children were in school longer than other immigrant groups . . . and accounted for relatively high percentages of those who attended schools and universities in the large cities of the Northeast. . . . In comparison to most other immigrant groups, as well as to native-born Americans, Jewish children were more likely to reach and finish high school and more likely to enroll in college preparatory courses."[55]

The most significant aspect of the American Jewish experience prior to the Great Depression was not its religious, organizational, and political diversity, but the improvement in its circumstances, as the children of the immigrants acquired substantial education and skills. Without going into further detail on the specific patterns of upward mobility, it should be noted that the East European Jews have been able to become, first, the best educated; then, the most middle class; and, ultimately, the most affluent ethnoreligious group in the country other than their co-religionists of German origin.[56] As Lucy Dawidowicz notes, no "other immigrant group evinced such rapid and dramatic success."[57] From a concentration in the garment and other skilled trades, East European Jews moved toward heavy involvement in the professions.

The desire to attain a first-class education at the best universities led to crises in the 1920s, as the major eastern private colleges and professional schools found the proportion of Jews among their students rising into the double-digit percentiles (40% at Columbia). Arguing that these developments were undermining the character of their institutions and professions, and that concentrations of Jews in particular places would result in anti-Semitism, they covertly or openly restricted Jewish enrollment through the use of quotas or special forms of preference, for which few Jews could qualify. Although these restrictions

kept down the number at the Ivy League and other elite private colleges, they did not stop ambitious young Jews from securing higher
education. They flooded the public institutions, such as City College
in New York.

Limited in the proportion who could become physicians, many who
could not get into the medical schools became dentists or pharmacists.
Others who were not admitted to major law schools went to less prestigious ones, or studied for other business-related professions, such as
accounting. During the 1930s, when economic adversity limited support for prolonged professional education and opportunities for
employment in private industry, many young Jews became teachers or
civil servants. Self-employment, the most traditional way for Jews to
escape restrictions, probably absorbed the greatest proportion of the
ambitious.

To analyze the sources of Jewish achievement would take this discussion too far afield. Suffice it to say that students of the subject have
stressed: (1) a religiously inspired drive for education, which, secularized, has been linked to disproportionate intellectual contributions
since the early Middle Ages; (2) the fact that Jews have been urbanites
par excellence, a background that has favored individuals in succeeding
in the centers of business, professional, and intellectual life; (3) a
greater socialization in middle-class norms and habits than any other
less privileged group, including a strong achievement drive, "the habits
of care and foresight," and the capacity to defer gratification;[58] and (4)
greater rootlessness, the ability to form new social relations in different
ecological and class environments, an ability which Jews show up as
having more than other American ethnic groups.[59] In discussing these
issues, Nathan Glazer notes:

> Judaism emphasizes the traits that businessmen and intellectuals require,
> and has done so since at least 1,500 years before Calvinism. We can trace
> Jewish Puritanism at least as far back as the triumph of the Maccabees
> over the Hellenized Jews and of the Pharisees over the Sadducees. The
> strong emphasis on learning and study can be traced that far back, too. The
> Jewish habits of foresight, care, moderation probably arose early during the
> two thousand years that the Jews have lived primarily as strangers among
> other peoples.[60]

The restrictions on Jewish entry into elite institutions, which, in
part, reflected the competitive concerns of the non-Jewish middle class
and elites, were paralleled by increasingly negative reactions among the

less affluent mass population—particularly, but not exclusively, fundamentalist and evangelical Christians in rural areas and smaller urban
centers. This religious stratum dominated the country numerically
until the start of the twentieth century, but massive non-Protestant
immigration—Catholic, Eastern Orthodox, and Jewish—and the
steady growth of metropolitan areas were undermining its cultural and
religious supremacy. American society was becoming cosmopolitan,
secular, and urban. The Census of 1920 reported that for the first time
in American history, urban dwellers were in a majority. Symbolically,
large cities had become the centers of Jewish and Catholic influence.

Evangelical Protestantism, as noted earlier, had long formed the
base for opposition to Catholic immigration, while ignoring or even
accepting the Jews for the most part. But in reaction to their massive
infusion and economic success, the largely urbanized Jewish population also became a target, starting in the second decade of this century.
In 1914, Tom Watson, a former leader of the People's Party, and subsequently intellectual Godfather of the revived Ku Klux Klan, stimulated a lynching of a Georgia Jewish businessman, Leo Frank, "for the
death of a working-class Gentile" girl, a crime of which he was inno-
cent. Watson continued a vitriolic anti-Semitic campaign for years
thereafter. The outpouring of hate against Catholics, Jews, and blacks
contained in Watson's nationally circulated newspaper took an institutionalized form in the multi-million-member Ku Klux Klan of the
1920s, although Watson himself never joined, as far as is known.[61]

The Klan, which documentably represented a form of evangelical
Protestant backlash, was supported disproportionately by lower-status
rural and small urban community white sectarians. It attacked
Catholics, blacks, Jews, radicals, and "immoral" people (divorcees,
adulterers, prostitutes, and the like). Although much less concerned
with Jews than with Catholics and personal immorality, Klan publications were replete with elaborate Jewish conspiracies. They reprinted
the *Protocols of the Elders of Zion*, which they found in another 1920s
focus of anti-Semitic agitation, Henry Ford's *Dearborn Independent*.[62]

RELIGIOUS AND POLITICAL ACTIVITY

The changing composition of American Jewry and the diverse impact
of world events led to deep divisions in the community. The older German strand adapted to their late nineteenth-century environment by
modifying their religious practice. They developed Reform Judaism,

whose practice and doctrine resembled the liberal Protestantism and Unitarianism of the non-Jewish middle to upper classes.[63] The more successful among the East Europeans—coming, if they were religious, from more Orthodox backgrounds—helped to create a more Americanized religious movement, the Conservatives. The Orthodox retained strength among the poorer and less-assimilated elements.[64]

To iterate the obvious, the period from the start of the Great Depression and the rise of Nazism has witnessed the greatest transformation in world Jewry since the destruction of the Second Temple. The prolonged economic collapse stimulated the growth of extremist movements, some of which, in Germany, the United States, and elsewhere, focused on blaming the Jews for all that went wrong. The German developments led to the Holocaust and the murder of 6 million Jews, one third of the world's Jewish population. Ironically, the chain of events set in motion by Nazism also resulted in increased emigration to Palestine, and to the rebirth of the state of Israel in 1948. Thus, the most terrible and the most triumphant moments of Jewish history since the Second Exile are intimately interlinked.

In the United States, assorted anti-Semitic right-wing movements, the most important of which was Father Coughlin's National Union for Social Justice, as well as a number of smaller ones which appealed to evangelical Protestants, gained strength. There is no reliable estimate of their support; they failed miserably at the ballot box. On the other hand, national opinion polls suggest that as much as one quarter of the population approved of the racist demagogue Charles Coughlin, who broadcast every Sunday on a national radio network. That support dropped to one seventh by 1940. Assorted surveys designed to estimate the degree of anti-Semitism among the American public by responses to various prejudicial statements about Jews, conducted by Jewish defense groups, reported, however, that roughly one out of two could be classified as anti-Jewish. This pattern lasted through World War II.[65]

Although the presence of proto-fascist movements and the increase in anti-Semitism did not have much effect on the personal or economic lives of American Jews, they clearly affected governmental policy toward Germany and the Holocaust. Franklin Roosevelt, though strongly anti-fascist and supportive of American participation in a war against Germany, consciously refrained from linking such concerns to the plight of the Jews for fear of losing popular support. America turned refugees from Europe away. Anxiety about public sentiments continued to affect American policy during the war, helping to block efforts to help Jews in extermination camps.

The Depression stimulated growth of anti-Semitism and the country's shameful response to the plight of Jewish refugees and to the Holocaust. It clearly challenges the assumption that the Jewish experience in America is qualitatively different from that in other countries, and that the United States is exceptional. All that may be said is that if the United States behaved badly, many others—such as Canada, which refused to take in any Jews—did worse. The American government and the large majority of Americans supported all that was necessary to defeat Nazism. Very few people, including the great majority of American Jews, could bring themselves to believe that the Nazis were, in fact, trying to physically annihilate the Jews of Europe. The leaders of the Zionist community in Palestine, including David Ben Gurion, who headed it, and Yitzhak Shamir, subsequently the hard-line nationalist prime minister of Israel, also refused to give priority to the rescue of Jews in Europe.

For whatever reason, the situation in America changed dramatically almost as soon as the war was over. Opinion polls documented striking drops in bigoted attitudes, not only toward Jews but to other minorities as well.[66] The United States strongly supported the creation of the state of Israel. Although most Americans lacked enough knowledge of the Middle East to voice opinions, the large majority of those who were familiar with the issue backed Israel against the Arab states that were trying to annihilate it.

On the behavioral level, dramatic changes developed as well. Almost all the restrictions against Jews, such as restrictive quotas, began to decline or disappear. This was particularly evident in academe both with respect to admission and hiring. The greater numbers of Jews trained in elite institutions were able to secure employment commensurate with their academic background. By the 1990s, it is hard to find any area of American life in which discrimination is still a problem.[67] Public opinion has changed in tandem with behavior, although a declining minority, sometimes as much as 25 percent, will still voice agreement with particular anti-Jewish statements when put to them by pollsters. Without going into a methodological discussion, it may be noted that the significance of these opinions is reduced when considered in light of reactions to the same statements about excessive power, choice of neighbors, and intermarriage posed for other groups. Viewed in comparative ethnic context, Jews do extremely well.[68] For example, in March 1993, the Roper Poll inquired how many of different ethnic groups "you would like to see living in this neighborhood?" Jews were much more popular than Hispanics, Blacks, and Asians.

They and Italians, the only other ethnic group listed, were responded to the same way: only 8 to 9 percent would not like them as neighbors.[69] There had been no change in these low figures since 1978. Tom Smith, a historian now directing the National Opinion Research Center, concluded a comprehensive review of the plethora of relevant opinion data on anti-Semitism, noting that the "available evidence indicates no reversal in its long-term decline. On most indicators anti-Jewish attitudes are at historic low" as of 1993.[70]

A telling indicator of the low level of anti-Semitism may be inferred from the fact that the country's most engaged politician, Bill Clinton, appointed two Jewish jurists, Ruth Bader Ginsburg and Steven G. Breyer, to fill his first two vacancies on the Supreme Court. Clinton is as sensitive to public opinion as any person who has occupied the White House. And to sustain his judgment, the press has almost totally ignored the religious background of the new justices. He also nominated four Jews to cabinet posts, one of whom Zoe Baird, the Attorney General-designate, withdrew during the confirmation process.

There are seven developments that appear crucially relevant to an understanding of contemporary American Jewry: (1) commitment to and activities in support of Israel; (2) Israel-Diaspora relations; (3) differentiated religious involvements; (4) demography—including extremely low birth rates and sharply increasing numbers of intermarriages; (5) continued high levels of social mobility; (6) communal organization; and (7) political participation. The concerns about and links to Israel are not treated separately; they constitute the most important underlying issues that have determined the nature of American Jewry since the formation of the state. Israel is the center of Jewish life, the cause to which more Jews are deeply dedicated than any other. The story of Jewish philanthropy and political activity on behalf of the Jewish state has been covered in a myriad of books and articles and need not be reiterated here.

Philanthropy is particularly important. According to Barry Kosmin, director of research for the New York Council of Jewish Federations, Jews contributed $3.5 billion to assorted causes in 1986.[71] Perhaps one quarter of this went to Israel, of which less than $400 million had come via the United Jewish Appeal. The results of the 1990 National Jewish Population Survey (NJPS) indicate that over three quarters of all Jewish households in 1989 contained at least one member who "contributed or gave gifts to Jewish or non-Jewish philanthropies, charities, causes or organizations."[72] Only a tenth gave only to Jewish causes, while a quarter contributed only to non-Jewish secular groups.

Two fifths donated to both.[73] In a 1992 national survey of giving and volunteering conducted by the Independent Sector, a large percentage (85%) of Jewish respondents, a close second to Presbyterians (87%), reported giving—contributing an average of 2.1 percent of household income and an average of 3.6 hours per week of volunteer time to charity.[74]

The emphasis on giving goes back to medieval Europe and has its roots in the need that the secure and prosperous help the less affluent and persecuted. This has carried over to contributions to politics as well, much more so for Democrats than Republicans, but in significant amounts to the latter also. Jews have played a particularly important role in financing recent elections.

The results of the postwar elections, as indicated in many opinion polls, confirm Milton Himmelfarb's generalization that while Jews earn more than any other ethnoreligious group for whom data exist, including Episcopalians, they are still more liberal or left in their opinions than other white groups, and vote like Hispanics. In November 1988, over 70 percent of the Jews backed Michael Dukakis. In 1992, Bill Clinton, who won a three-candidate race with 43 percent of the vote, secured 79 percent among Jews, while George Bush and Ross Perot garnered 10 percent each.[75] Republican presidential support has declined slightly, but steadily, since 1980. Close to four fifths backed Democrats for Congress, behavior repeated in 1994, a year of major GOP gains. The only identifiable subset that has been conservative and Republican at times is composed of the Orthodox (less than 10%), particularly the more extreme and less affluent among them.[76]

Blacks apart, Jews are the most favorable of all ethnoreligious groups toward policies designed to help the less fortunate, including maintenance or expansion of government welfare programs, relying on the state as an employer of last resort for the unemployed, wage and price controls in inflationary periods, and government regulations to remedy assorted ills for which business or other large organizations are held responsible. They also support activist politics with regard to various social concerns, such as the death penalty, abortion, gun control, nuclear freeze proposals, and the like.[77] National opinion data gathered by Steven M. Cohen indicated that as of 1988, in spite of their relative affluence, "more Jews than whites or blacks endorse raising taxes as a way of cutting budget deficits," and opposed reductions in domestic spending. Jews are also much more likely than others to approve of liberal and civil rights organizations such as the National Association for the Advancement of Colored People, Planned Parenthood, the

National Organization for Women, and the American Civil Liberties Union.[78]

Opinion surveys continue to find that in no area "are Jews significantly more conservative than non-Jewish whites . . . on many issues the Jewish center is well to the left of the white gentile center."[79] Black mayoralty candidates, such as Tom Bradley in Los Angeles, David Dinkins in New York, and Harold Washington in Chicago, received a much higher proportion of votes among Jews than from any other definable white group other than academics. "In 1983, the Chicago mayoral election pitted a black, Democrat Harold Washington, against a Jewish Republican. . . . [S]lightly less than half the Jews voted for Washington. But that was still two and a half times as high a percentage as other whites in Chicago gave the Democratic candidate, even though Democratic loyalty in Chicago had long seemed a fact of nature."[80] Clearly, Jews continue to be among the principal supporters of organized liberal to left tendencies in the country, giving heavily and disproportionately to liberal political candidates and various liberal to left organizations.

Most American Jews have remained adherents of the social democratic values of their parents, as evident in the results of a national telephone survey taken by the *Los Angeles Times* in 1988. When asked which among three qualities "do you consider most important to your Jewish identity," over half, 57 percent, replied "a commitment to social equality"; about a fifth chose "support for Israel" or "religious observance."[81]

The explanation for Jewish adherence to liberal left politics, despite having become astonishingly affluent, is obviously complex. Earl Raab and I have dealt with it elsewhere.[82] We suggest that the behavior is linked to the continued effect of leftist political values imported from Eastern Europe, noted above; to deep concern about anti-Semitism, still linked in the minds of many American Jews much more to the political right than to the left; and to the impact of norms underlying *tzedekah,* the obligation on the fortunate, the well-to-do to help individuals and communities in difficulty. The latter norm became general among European Jews during the Middle Ages when it was literally a condition for survival, given that some communities were generally experiencing severe persecution while others were doing well. The political values derived from *tzedekah* are communitarian, implying support for the welfare state. Beyond this, historic experience with discrimination seemingly leads many Jews to favor civil rights legislation for other minorities. Whether for these reasons or not, a plurality by 44 to 31 percent said in a 1988 opinion poll that "Jewish values, as I understand them, teach me to be politically liberal." And the 1990 National Survey of Religious Identification, the best and by far the largest sample taken of American religious affiliation, reported that 41 percent of the Jews said their usual stand on political issues was liberal, as compared to 19 percent conservative; 35 percent responded middle-of-the-road. No other denomination came close to the Jews in degree of liberal identification.[83] Surveys of the American population as a whole taken at the same time found 35 to 40 percent answering conservative, and 15 percent liberal.

Apart from the fact that Jews generally agree with most liberal positions on both domestic and foreign policy, they still have a historically based visceral feeling that they belong in the company of political liberals. They were released from the medieval ghettos by "the liberals." They were joined in the fight against Nazism by "the liberals." Anti-Semitism, religious intolerance, and immigration restrictions, in their memory, have been associated with "the conservatives." Cohen found in 1988 that, when asked what proportion of a number of groups in the United States is anti-Semitic, three times as many (20 to 7%) said that many or most Republicans are, as compared to Democrats. The replies for "few are" were 32 percent for Republican and 47 percent Democrats. The pattern was similar with conservatives and liberals, 23 to 9 percent, for "many or most are," and 32 to 51 percent for "few are."[84] The Democratic Party is perceived as the "liberal" party and the Republican Party as the "conservative" party, and thus the former is seen as more friendly. In 1991, Cohen inquired how Jewish respondents identified the attitudes of the adherents of the two major parties toward Israel. By over two to one, 58 percent to 24 percent, respondents perceived more Democrats than Republicans as "generally friendly" to the Jewish state.[85]

Jews are basically more comfortable in the Democratic Party than in the Republican Party. They are more at ease with the kinds of people they find in the Democratic Party—their fellow ethnics with whom they grew up in America—than with the white Anglo-Saxon Protestants (WASPS) still predominant in the Republican Party. As Alan Fisher comments, "Jews identify the Democrats as friends, and, by and large, they stay with their friends. The Democratic Party is home to them."[86]

Jewish liberalism may also be strengthened by the strong concern for learning, transmuted from religious tradition into an emphasis on secularized intellectuality and education. As we have seen, 85 percent of all

Jewish youth go to universities. They constitute close to one third of the professoriate at major universities and an even larger proportion of leading intellectuals.[87] In discussing "the intellectual pre-eminence of the Jews," Thorstein Veblen commented at the end of World War I on the fact that they not only contributed "a disproportionate number" of leaders of "modern science and scholarship," but that they "count particularly among the vanguard, the pioneers, the uneasy guild of pathfinders and iconoclasts, in science, scholarship, and institutional change and growth."[88]

Creative intellectuality, as Veblen and many others have recognized, includes an emphasis on innovation, on newness, on rejection of the old, of the traditional.[89] It is also linked to universalism, to reacting to knowledge independently of the background of its exponents. Secularized Jews, in their desire to be treated like others, to become part of the larger society, support a universalistic ethic, which emphasizes equality for groups and individuals. Intellectuality and universalism predispose American Jews to liberalism.

The United States has been open to Jews and the evidence clearly points to a sharp falloff in social and economic restrictions on, and prejudice toward, them since World War II.[90] Still Jews remain fearful of anti-Semitism. Only one out of seven of those responding to Cohen's questionnaires agreed that "Anti-semitism in America is currently not a serious problem for American Jews." An overwhelming majority, over three quarters (76%), replied that it is a serious problem; two thirds disagreed with the statement: "Virtually all positions of influence in America are open to Jews." The surprising fact that they feel this way contributes to an identification with the left against the right, as Cohen's survey data (noted earlier) indicate.

The reluctance of most Jews to accept evidence that anti-Semitism has declined or to shift their image as to the relative contribution of the left and the right, given the reality of their progress in American society and the strong efforts on behalf of Israel by pre-Bush Republican administrations, is striking testimony to the role of historical experience and memory. San Francisco provides strong evidence of how some Jews can totally ignore reality. Polls taken by Earl Raab among contributors to the San Francisco Jewish Community Federation have found that one third agree that a Jew cannot be elected to Congress from San Francisco. His survey reported such results in 1985 when all three members of Congress from contiguous districts in or adjacent to the city were Jewish, as were the two state senators, the mayor, and a considerable part of the city council.

The lack of confidence in the larger community goes beyond concern with anti-Semitism. A national survey taken in 1964 by NORC produced evidence that Jews are very much less trustful of others on a personal level than the members of seven other white ethnic groups—Irish, Scandinavian, Slavic, German Protestant, German Catholic, Italian, and WASP. On a scale based on answers to six questions, running from plus 4 (total trust) to minus 4 (total distrust), Jews scored on the average minus 3. No other group was in the minus range. The questions included items such as "Do you think most people can be trusted?" and "If you don't watch out, people will take advantage of you?"

But if Jews were more distrustful than others, they were more self-confident and less self-deprecatory than any of the other ethnic groups. Congruently, they were highest on the scale measuring "inner-direction," self-reliance, and lowest on "other-direction," need for approval.[91] These orientations contribute to the anti-establishment stance of the astonishingly successful Jews (i.e., their willingness to be highly participatory critics of their society) and to their upward mobility.

The obvious question with respect to these findings about Jewish attitudes and behavior is to what extent do they continue to hold for new generations, for those coming of age? The evidence from a number of national studies and analyses conducted by Steven Cohen, Alan Fisher, and William Helmreich, as well as examination of the *Los Angeles Times* April 1988 survey and election exit polls by various newspapers and networks, is consistent with respect to politics. During the 1980s younger Jews (under 30 or under 45) were more likely to vote Republican and to identify as Republicans than older cohorts, by 10 to 15 percent. Younger age is also related to lesser concern over anti-Semitism, to lower identification with Israel, and to less willingness to contribute to Jewish philanthropy. Such findings are to be expected, since these younger Jews are more distant in time from the experiences which led older generations to act as they do. It seems that success in an open society, characterized by less anti-Semitism than at any time in the twentieth century, and growing up with the state of Israel as an established fact should produce age-related increased conservatism.[92] However, as Alan Fisher notes, the lead among Jews of Democrats and liberals over Republicans and conservatives has "remained surprisingly stable over the last decade."[93] Even though more conservative behavior by young Jews has been reported over a number of elections, the next older generations (defined as over 30 or 45) repeatedly turn out to be more Democratic than they were when younger.

The lack of an identifiably more conservative group to emerge among the older cohorts suggests that as Jews move into mature adult status and sink roots in the community, some drop their more conservative youthful orientations and absorb the dominant community pattern toward American politics and Israel. New substantive issues may eventually make a difference, but it will require an emotional wrenching, or more generational difference, to eliminate the Democratic Party's advantage in Jewish voting or the overwhelming commitment to Israel. The shift to the Democrats in 1992 among all groups probably resulted from the reluctance to the Bush administration to provide loan guarantees to Israel in 1992 and the various disdainful remarks made by the president and Secretary of State James A. Baker III about the Israeli lobby in America and the Israeli government. Bill Clinton, by pursuing almost Judeophilic appointment policies and endorsing Israeli foreign policy objectives, has been reinforcing the ties. And as noted, in 1994, when the Democrats suffered a major setback among all regions, income classes and religious groups, they received 78 percent of the Jewish vote, statistically equivalent to the 79 percent reported in the 1992 exit poll.[94] In California, bitterly divided in 1994 over the effects of massive Latino immigration, Jews voted against Proposition 187, which denied illegal immigrants basic rights, by 59 to 41 percent. But the measure passed overwhelmingly, with strong support among blacks, Asians, and other whites.

CONCLUSION

Can we still speak of American exceptionalism with respect to the position of the Jews? The answer would appear to be yes. As in the nineteenth century, America has continued to give more support to Jewish causes abroad than any other nation by far. This has been evident in its extensive and often isolated political and financial support of Israel, in the liberal admission policies for Soviet Jewish émigrés, and in the financing of the latter's settlement costs in both America and Israel.

American Jews continue to do extraordinarily well in the economic, political, and social structures of the country. They not only contribute liberally to Israel, communal institutions, and politics, but to many other causes as well. "Jewish support of hospitals, museums, symphonies, and universities [as well as the United Funds] across the country now appears disproportionate not only to their numbers but also even to their proportion of the wealthy."[95]

The commitment of American Jews to their larger community is being undermined by certain positive developments, such as the decline of anti-Semitism and the movements toward peace in the Middle East. These reactions have been dealt with elsewhere by Earl Raab and myself.[96] Anti-Semitism and threats to Israel have pressed Jews to be involved. And the absence of a strong religious commitment among most Jews lessens the barriers to assimilation and intermarriage.

Ironically, Jewish success also contains within it the seeds of decline. Almost all Jewish youth attend universities, disproportionately the very best, and these institutions are liberal both politically and socially. They not only reinforce the propensity to back left causes, but press the newer generations of Jews to live by universalistic criteria, which disparage particularistic ethnic loyalties, not only with respect to dating and mating but unquestioning support of Israel as well. The very high rate of intermarriage, now 52–57 percent for new weddings between 1985 and 1990, and the extremely low birth rate (1.1 for each Jewish woman) are linked to the high achievement level.[97] Jews, it should be noted, are behaving like other American ethnic groups, only more so. With the exception of African Americans, most of the members of almost all ethnic ancestry and religious sectors are marrying across ethnoreligious lines. The melting pot is operative as never before.[98]

The fears concerning demographic decline may be counterbalanced in small part by the continued attractiveness of America to foreigners, including Jews. The United States is still by far the world's largest receiver of refugees and other immigrants. The upswing from the 1970s on has included a renewed Jewish influx, a phenomenon not generally publicized since it involves a rejection of Israel as a place to settle or live. According to HIAS (Hebrew Immigrant Aid Society) reports, the agency assisted in settling over 125,000 Jews in the United States between 1967 and 1980. HIAS records do not include the large number of Jewish immigrants from Latin America, Canada, South Africa, and Iran. Nor do they list the well over 100,000 Israelis who have come here.[99]

Clearly, the story of American and Jewish exceptionalism, closely intertwined as they are, is not over. But the tale bears telling, for it is one of the better ones in human history. Unlike the saga of black Americans, which, as reported in the previous chapter, is still one marked more by racism than universalism, and by continued hardship, that of the Jews shows the United States at its best.

CHAPTER 6

American Intellectuals—Mostly on the Left, Some Politically Incorrect[1]

In America, intellectuals, like blacks and Jews, may be described as "exceptions on the margin." They have sustained the historically marginalized left in American politics. But the left within intellectualdom is currently under attack for creating a wave of repression, comparable to previous efforts coming from the right, by insisting on "political correctness," a term referring to the efforts of advocates of left liberal politics to impose their views with respect to multiculturalism, minority rights, and feminism by limiting the free speech and job opportunities of their ideological opponents. This chapter attempts to account for the left orientation of American intellectuals, as well as the spread of a new wave of repressive moralism, to explain some of the issues involved, to specify sources of support and opposition, and to locate the moralistic behavior of American intellectuals in a comparative context, that is, in exceptional traits.

MORALISM AND THE POLITICS OF INTELLECTUALS

The concern for political correctness is the latest expression of moralism in the United States, and moralism, as United States history demonstrates, is as American as apple pie. Starting with the Alien and Sedition Acts of the 1790s, through various waves of xenophobia and of heightened nationalism (of which McCarthyism was the most recent), and including abolitionism, Prohibition, anti-war movements from 1812 through Vietnam, and most recently pro- and anti-choice advocacy and debates over the place of religion in the public schools, Americans both of the right and the left have exhibited a Protestant sectarian-bred propensity for crusades.

The sectarian emphasis on moralism is reinforced by elements derived from the fact that the United States defines its *raison d'être* ideologically. The emphasis on Americanism as a political ideology has led to a utopian and absolutist orientation among American liberals and conservatives. Both seek to impose their version of a good society. As noted previously, those who reject American values are incorrect, are un-American, and may be denied rights. In describing the political scene of the 1990s, Suzanne Garment notes that the liberals have viewed politics

> as a secular religion, prescribing damnation for ideological evildoers but absolution for the faithful.
>
> This zealotry gave Mr. [Newt] Gingrich an opening [in 1994]. He would apply to Democrats the same standards they had applied to the Republicans. . . . Mr. Gingrich thought that the "secular religion" he saw on the left could be successfully opposed only by equally moralistic rhetoric.[2]

The current efforts to impose political correctness on the polity, but particularly on the campus and intellectualdom generally, go back to the controversies of the 1960s, when the anti-war and radical university-based movements opposed the Vietnam War as immoral. This moralistic stance led them to try to prevent supporters of the war from speaking on campuses, to end all forms of collaboration by universities with the warmaking government, and to politicize discipline organizations like the Modern Language Association and the American Sociological Association.

Political correctness is not a new phenomenon in American academe. As all histories attest, private higher education largely began in church-affiliated schools. Most of these insisted that their faculty be denominationally correct, be members of the church which paid for the institution. Faculty who deviated from religious doctrine could be fired. When particular institutions changed, and became less orthodox, the churches' right wings set up new schools. Yale came into existence to counterbalance Harvard, which had moved toward Unitarianism.[3] Abolitionists lost jobs in southern schools, and sometimes in northern ones as well.

The relationship of American values and leftist political ideology to political correctness rests in the fact that this tendency mainly arose among intellectuals, the only occupational stratum in American society in which radical leftist doctrines have made significant headway. American intellectuals (those involved in creative activities), as well as major sections of the intelligentsia (those who use intellectual products), have been alienated from the mainstream of bourgeois society, and for much of the past century a goodly number turned to socialist ideas as an alternative. An anti-establishment position on the part of intellectuals is not new. As early as 1798, President John Adams concluded that "learned academies, not under the immediate inspection and control of government . . . are incompatible with social order."[4]

American intellectual arenas have been centers of opposition, of an "adversary culture."[5] Daniel Patrick Moynihan has noted that since "about 1840, the cultural elite have pretty generally rejected the values and activities of the larger society."[6] Writing in 1873, Whitelaw Reid, then editor of the *New York Tribune,* emphasized that "exceptional influences eliminated, the scholar is pretty sure to be opposed to the established. . . . Free thought is necessarily aggressive and critical. The scholar . . . is an inherent, an organic, an inevitable radical."[7] Twenty-eight years later, after observing such political tendencies at work in the campus opposition to the Spanish American War and the occupation of the Philippines, an older and more conservative Reid commented: "It is a misfortune for the colleges, and no less for the country, when the trusted instructors are out of sympathy with its history, with its development, and with the men who made the one and are guiding the other."[8] Richard Hofstadter, writing in 1963, concluded that academe had been on the left for the previous three quarters of a century.[9] Many in the smaller group of non-left intellectuals, such as Henry Adams, William James, and T. S. Eliot, were also alienated from American business and materialistic values. One of the constant patterns in American political life from the late nineteenth century on, the anti-materialistic conservation (environment) movement, has always drawn on the intelligentsia for support.

As the social sciences emerged in the latter part of the nineteenth century, trustees, alumni, and politicians found the teaching and writing of some scholars offensive. Sociology became identified with radicalism at Stanford, when E. A. Ross was fired at Mrs. Stanford's insistence in 1900 because he had attacked Leland Stanford and other railroad barons. Other California universities followed Stanford's lead in rejecting sociology. Concern that morals would be corrupted led to repression of teaching and research about sex-related issues. A celebrated University of Chicago sociologist, W. I. Thomas, was dismissed in the early twenties because of publicized relations with prostitutes, which he claimed were part of his research. Pacifists, socialists, and other opponents of the U.S. involvement in World War I were discharged by major universities, including Columbia, which let Charles Beard go. The American Association of University Professors was founded in 1915 to defend academic freedom, to protect the rights of leftists and agnostics to secure and retain faculty positions.

SOCIAL SCIENCE EVIDENCE AND ANALYSIS

The earliest surveys of faculty values (questionnaire polls of attitudes toward religion) were conducted in 1913–14 and again in 1933 by James Leuba. They attest to the validity of Hofstadter's report. Leuba found that the majority in both periods did not believe in God or immortality, with irreligion stronger in 1933. Studies of American religious behavior indicated that professors and scientists were far more likely to be agnostics or atheists than the general population, a pattern that would reappear in every subsequent survey of faculty opinion. While Leuba did not inquire directly about politics, anti-religious views have been associated with left politics. It is noteworthy that both in 1913 and 1933 the more distinguished professors were much more irreligious than their less eminent colleagues.[10] Later local and national surveys taken in the late 1930s and 1940s, which dealt with partisan orientations directly, found that faculty were much more leftist and Democratic than other occupational strata, while social scientists were disproportionately leftist within academe.[11] A late 1930s effort to account for the leftist views of the more intellectually oriented by two psychologists suggested that to be "bookish" meant to be exposed to radical thought.

> To be bookish in this era has meant to steep oneself in the disillusioned gropings of postwar thinkers, most of whom, from philosophers to lyricists, are clearly "radical." . . . The literary groups to which these men belong, the day-by-day conversations in which they train one another to think and to feel, are full of the modern doubt and disquietude, and even more frequently, of the modern challenge and rebellion. To be bookish today is to be radical.[12]

The Great Depression pressed many American intellectuals to the far left. In 1932, four hundred writers, artists, and academics, many of whom were very distinguished, issued a public statement endorsing William Z. Foster and James W. Ford, the candidates for president and vice president of the Communist Party. Postwar quantitative studies of the politics of academics have found anew that professors, particularly those in the social sciences and the humanities, have been much more disposed to support socialist or other leftist candidates than any other segment of the society for which opinion data exist.[13] This does not mean that the majority have been radicals, but that the level of such commitments among them has been far higher than among the public at large. And more important than the opinions or vote of the stratum as a whole is the fact that the survey data indicated that the more successful, the more distinguished, the more creative they are, the more likely intellectuals are to be on the left.[14]

In 1949, just before the advent of McCarthyism, Friedrich Hayek, the doyen of free market economists, then visiting at the University of Chicago, commented that as he traveled around the universities of America the dominant tone in faculty club conversation was "socialist," by which he probably meant supportive of the Keynesian planning welfare state. Hayek went on to say that the brightest academics he encountered were the most likely to be socialist. In seeking to explain the phenomenon, Hayek understandably did not hold with the hypothesis that creativity and intelligence dispose to leftism. Instead, he suggested selectivity—that the more intelligent among the young who support the status quo seek out non-intellectual occupations, while the "disaffected and dissatisfied" reject positions linked to the business system and are more inclined to find a career in the intellectual realm.[15] A national survey of 2,500 social scientists conducted in 1955 by Paul Lazarsfeld and Wagner Thielens, Jr., found that 8 percent had backed left third-party candidates in 1948, compared to 2 percent in the electorate generally. Most, 63 percent, voted for Harry Truman; only 28 percent voted for Thomas Dewey.[16] And, as Hayek suggested, those at leading universities were considerably to the left of their colleagues at other institutions. A number of opinion surveys taken in the late sixties and the seventies, some by Everett Carll Ladd and myself, found again that militancy and radicalism were strongest at the most prestigious campuses supported by the brightest students and the most distinguished faculty. In discipline terms, they had their greatest strength among the more purely academic liberal arts subjects, especially the humanities and non-quantitative social sciences.[17] And as Thorstein Veblen emphasized at the end of World War I, intellectual creativity and social and political marginality appeared to be functionally interrelated.[18]

The most recent national survey of American academe, taken by the Carnegie Foundation in 1989, found that 56 percent identified themselves as liberals, while 28 percent said they were conservatives.[19] Studies of journalists find the same pattern.[20] Conversely, most polls indicate the general population to be more conservative, about 35–40 percent, than liberal, 10–20 percent.

Hypotheses to explain findings such as these have been suggested by Thorstein Veblen, Carl Becker, Joseph Schumpeter, Paul Lazarsfeld, and C. P. Snow. They contend, in different ways, that academe and intellectualdom reward originality, innovation, a rejection of the past, of what one has been taught—ways of thinking linked to political radicalism.[21] Seeking to explain such phenomena generally, Becker commented in 1936 that the function of the intellectual "is to increase rather than preserve knowledge, to undermine rather than to stabilize custom and social authority."[22] In a similar vein, Schumpeter suggested that "from criticism of a text to the criticism of a society, the way is shorter than it seems."[23] Much earlier, Veblen made a comparable point in 1919 concerning intellectuals' inherently "skeptical frame of mind."[24] Consequently, the best and the brightest are disproportionately found among the more radical or anti-establishmentarian, usually located on the left but sometimes on the right as well, particularly in countries where the left has held longtime power. Inherent in the obligation to create is the tendency to reject the status quo, to oppose the traditional as philistine.[25]

The Lazarsfeld-Thielens study was in fact conducted to evaluate the impact of McCarthyism on social scientists. As might be expected, the overwhelming majority were strongly anti-McCarthy. What was much more surprising, given the assumption that Joseph McCarthy and other government investigations of communism were intimidating even politically moderate faculty, pressing professors to expound conformist views, was the conclusion that it was less dangerous on campus for a faculty member to be an opponent of McCarthy than to be a left-winger. Lazarsfeld and Thielens noted that overt supporters of the Wisconsin senator, of the anti-communist security program, at major universities were much more likely to be ostracized by their colleagues (and, probably, if young, to be denied tenure or promotion) than were pro-communists.[26] While some on the left were discharged or otherwise penalized, these tended to be scholars who could be formally charged with or refused to answer questions about present or past Communist Party affiliations. A number lost their jobs.[27] Other well-known radicals, including socialists, Trotskyists, and anarchists, were rarely sanctioned. Val Lorwin of the University of Oregon, whose red Socialist Party card was reported to investigators as a communist one by his landlady, is a notable exception.

POLITICIZATION AND QUIESCENCE: THE SIXTIES, SEVENTIES, AND EIGHTIES

The militant civil rights movement of the early sixties, which engaged in civil disobedience tactics, was heavily campus-based. Black and white students joined in demonstrations and sit-ins. They were backed by many of their professors, who saw in the activity of the movement revenge for the passivity and outward conformism of the early fifties. Through a process which led from civil rights sit-ins in business establishments to student takeovers of administration buildings, actions that resulted almost everywhere in the calling in of the police and produced the recurrent condemnation of campus officialdom by faculty, the American campus was politicized by the end of the decade.

The major catalytic events that gave rise to the movements of the 1960s were the civil rights and anti-war struggles. The student mass base was dedicated to the substantive issues, but radicals of diverse varieties took over the leadership in many local and national demonstrations. They became carried away with the illusion that they were creating a revolutionary mass movement. As support for authority began to weaken, a broad coterie of anti-establishment causes was added to the movement, such as gay and women's rights, environmentalism, and greater freedom in personal behavior, particularly in the realms of sexual activity and use of drugs.

The movement issues affected faculty as well. They led to the politicization of many academic organizations, particularly in the social sciences and the humanities. Election to offices that had previously been perceived as honors to be given for contributions to scholarship, much like prizes, became vigorously contested elections, with the left winning out in a number of associations. Major scholars were defeated because of their alleged conservatism. Similar issues divided campuses. Formal faculty political parties were established to contest elections for faculty senates and to affect the outcomes of faculty meetings. The formal splits continued within some of the academic organizations into the nineties; the campus-based parties have disappeared, but the lines of ideological cleavage that undermined collegial relations in departments and universities remain, to be activated when new issues dealing with matters such as multiculturalism and free speech rights arise.

The "movements" exhilarated in their seeming ability to stop the war and to reduce segregation and racially discriminatory hiring practices, but victory brought frustration. The great majority of the student protesters dropped away, once the Vietnam War and the great civil rights demonstrations ended. A political quiescence descended on the American campuses in the mid-1970s, with the end of the Vietnam conflict. Faculties became less liberal or more conservative between 1969 and 1984, according to a series of national surveys conducted for the Carnegie Corporation, although they remained far to the left of the general population. The proportion describing themselves as left or liberal fell off from 46 percent in 1969, to 41 percent in 1975, to 39 percent in 1984, still more than double those so reported among the public. Conversely, those academics identifying themselves as conservative increased from 28 percent in 1969, to 31 percent in 1975 and 33 percent in 1984.

The move to the right among faculties seemingly was reversed in the latter half of the eighties. In the most recent Carnegie poll (taken in 1989), the percentage agreeing with the statement, "I am apprehensive about the future of this country," moved up from 50 to 63 percent between 1984 and 1989. The proportion describing themselves as liberal jumped to 56 percent, considerably higher than the 39 percent in 1984.[28] Again, the data show that scholars at the most prestigious universities are to the left of those at other institutions. At the research universities, 67 percent are liberals, while only 17 percent are conservative. Conservatives are strongest at the predominantly teaching institutions, 27 percent at four-year colleges and 35 percent at two-year community colleges, although liberals predominate in these as well, 59 and 48 percent, respectively.[29]

As the eighties progressed, the intellectual world, including professors, had been moving toward the left. The "new" faculty liberalism did not reflect revived mass protest. To some degree, the change may have been a reaction to Reaganism, to the triumphs of the Republican right in the larger polity. For even while shifting away from radical left and activist views, the bulk of academe, particularly in the upper echelons, remained very much more liberal and Democratic than the general electorate and more critical of business-related institutions and values. Hence, many faculty perceived the eighties as a decade of increased materialism, and as less egalitarian.

The growth of faculty activism, particularly with respect to multiculturalism and political correctness, related but partially independent developments, appears to be a product of the increased presence of the "veterans" of the sixties, of former student radicals as well as of feminists, racial minorities, and gays in the tenured ranks. In their rejection of the "bourgeois" world, many student activists had turned to the academy. The historian John Diggins reports: "Consisting to a large extent of graduate students, the New Left entered the academic profession en masse. . . ."[30] As leading cultural critic and African-American scholar Henry Louis Gates, Jr., cited earlier, notes: "Ours was the generation that took over buildings in the late 1960s and demanded the creation of black and women's studies programs and now, like the return of the repressed, has come back to challenge the traditional curriculum."[31]

Even more than in the past, left faculty are to be found in greater numbers in the humanities and "soft" (qualitative and historical) social sciences, as well as in some of the professional schools (such as law and social work), while their relative strength in the quantitative social sciences has fallen off. Existential and class analyses linked to Marxist thought have made considerable gains in humanities departments with the emergence of deconstructionism, and in the law schools in the form of critical legal studies. In their teachings and writings today, many historians, legal scholars, English professors, and qualitative sociologists try to expose the dominant "hegemonic" culture that—in their view—legitimizes the traditional establishments of affluent white males, by deconstructing their cultural products. *New York Times* cultural correspondent Richard Bernstein has analyzed the political content of the new cultural criticism in accurate, albeit polemical terms:

> Much of what is claimed under the banner of the new is actually a stale, simpleminded, Manichaean, and imitative reformulation of that discredited nineteenth century concept called Marxism. . . .
>
> Open up almost any contemporary [humanist] academic journal and you will find phrases like "colonized bodies," "the vantage point of the subjected," the "great underground terrains of subjugated knowledge," the "marginalized other," which are in contradistinction to . . . the "socially produced meaning" of the "dominant white-male culture represented in the hegemonic curriculum." Inspired by the French philosopher Michel Foucault, the jargon represents the reformulation of basic nineteenth-century Marxist ideas that have been borrowed by generations of intellectuals bent on showing that the world as it exists is the creation (the "social construction") of the groups that hold power, their ideology (the "dominant discourse") used to maintain sway over everybody else (the "victimized subalterns").[32]

Berkeley philosopher John Searle, once an ardent supporter of student activism but more recently a champion of the more traditional canons, has sought to answer the question why "the 'cultural left' is not heavily influential outside the departments of French, English and comparative literature and a few history departments and law schools . . . [since] the study of poetry, plays and novels is hardly the ideal basis for understanding modern structures of power or the mechanisms of revolutionary change?" His tentative answers make good sense in explaining "the migration of radical politics from the social sciences to the humanities."

First, as empirical theories of society or blueprints for social change, Marxism and other such theories have been discredited by recent events. The collapse of the Soviet empire only marks officially something that most intellectuals have known quietly for a long time. The standard versions of radical leftist ideology in the form of theories of society and social change, such as Marxism, Leninism, Stalinism, Maoism, and Castroism, are all in disrepute. The most congenial home left for Marxism, now that it has been largely discredited as a theory of economics and politics, is in departments of literary criticism.

Secondly, for reasons I do not fully understand, many professors of literature no longer care about literature in the ways that seemed satisfactory to earlier generations. It seems pointless to many of them to teach literature as it was understood by such very different critics as Edmund Wilson, John Crowe Ransom, or I. A. Richards; so they teach it as a means of achieving left-wing political goals or as an occasion for exercises in deconstruction, etc. The absence of an accepted educational mission in many literary studies has created a vacuum waiting to be filled. Perhaps the original mistake was in supposing that there is a well defined academic discipline of "literary criticism"—as opposed to literary scholarship—capable of accommodating Ph.D. programs, research projects, and careers for the ambitious. When such a discipline fails to be "scientific" or rigorous, or even well defined, the field is left wide open for various fashions such as deconstruction, or for the current political enthusiasms.[33]

Observers, both on the left and the right, native and foreign, have repeatedly noted in the eighties and nineties that Marxism is alive and relatively well in American intellectualdom, even beyond the activism of the humanities. The Marxist scholars Bertell Ollmann and Edward Vernoff introduce a comprehensive work on Marxists in academe by saying, "A Marxist cultural revolution is taking place today in American universities."[34] Journalist Garry Abrams notes that "American universities may be one of the last bastions of intellectual Marxism, at least in the developed world."[35] Oxford political theorist John Gray, writing in the *Times Literary Supplement,* also concludes that "the academic institutions of capitalist America will be the last redoubt of Marxist theorizing. . . ."[36] Feminist historian Elizabeth Fox-Genovese observes that "a good case could be made that, as a group, they [conservatives] are more vulnerable to exclusion from or marginalization within the academy than even the most radical of their left-wing opponents."[37] And radical sociologist Richard Flacks, a former leader of Students for a Democratic Society (SDS), states that by the eighties, "the tradition of the left was rather well-entrenched in American academe, having come to have a taken-for-granted influence on the curriculum, on dominant outlooks of the social sciences and humanities, and the micro-politics of academic life. . . . [I]n the major universities (if nowhere else in this country), it is intellectually respectable to express an affinity with 'Marxism' and to be some kind of socialist."[38]

Journalist John Leo, reporting on the annual convention of the 32,000-member Modern Language Association, describes the major organization of American humanists as a "hard-edge, heavily politicized academic group that looks at Western literature . . . as the ideological expression of white male dominance." He comments that the central orientation at the conference, "totally dead in the real world, is Marxism. It is a vulgar Marxism . . . and it goes like this: Whether we acknowledge it or not, everything we do or say works to support our ideological interests. Realizing that all creative writing is already political, the left works to reveal literature as the expression of an elite ruling class."[39]

Gerald Marzorati, senior editor of *Harper's* magazine, emphasizes that the American academic radicals have dropped "liberalism, with its notions of tolerance" in favor of "a mix of neo-Marxism and semeiotics . . . a Continental language, precisely that [is] being abandoned" by the younger European intellectuals who have resuscitated liberalism, the emphasis on individual rights, and pragmatism. Ironically, he notes that these overseas "writers and thinkers seem to harbor none of the easy anti-Americanism of their intellectual forefathers and of America's academic radicals."[40]

Writing in the *New York Review of Books* on the attitudes and writings of American elite scientists, Cambridge University Nobel laureate M. F. Perutz indicates, "Marxism may be discredited in Eastern Europe, but it still seems to flourish at Harvard."[41] Commenting in a similar way in *The New Republic* on the differences between American and Russian literary analysts, Robert Alter, a leading student of comparative literature, points out that "Literature in our own academic circles is regularly dismissed, castigated as an instrument of ideologies of oppression. . . ." But after a trip to Moscow, he "came away with the sense that there are still people in the world for whom literature matters urgently."[42] Margo Culley, a University of Massachusetts professor of English, is not one of them. In contradistinction to Alter, she exuberantly called attention to the growth of the multicultural world view in the humanities as a kind of Copernican revolution, which has reduced the importance of materials produced by Euro-centered white males in favor of non-white, non-European, and female products. She notes that within the Modern Language Association, "the subjects of gender and race have overwhelmed the field. . . ."[43]

Leftists in other disciplines also emphasize their dominance. Richard Flacks wrote in *Critical Sociology* in 1988, "If there was an Establishment sociology twenty years ago, we helped do it in, and so, for good or ill, the field is to a great extent ours."[44] A year later, the leftist historian Jonathan Wiener noted in the *Journal of American History* that "radical history in the age of Reagan occupied the strongest position it has ever held in American universities."[45] He documented his thesis elsewhere by noting that in "the past several years an impressive number of prizes have gone to radical and feminist historians. . . . [E]specially in the crucial field of American history, radical and feminist historians have made their work the center of discussion and debate. . . . The Organization of American Historians has elected several leftists to its presidency in recent years. . . ."[46] A survey of emphases in the humanities conducted under the auspices of the Modern Language Association found Marxist approaches used in more than one quarter of all humanities departments and in over two fifths of those in major universities.[47] Self-identified radicals have been elected to office in communities with concentrations of academics and the creative intelligentsia—for example, Ann Arbor, Amherst, Austin, Berkeley, Boulder, Burlington (Vermont), Cambridge, Hyde Park (Chicago), Ithaca, Madison, the West Side of Manhattan (New York City), Santa Cruz, and Santa Monica.[48]

If American academics, particularly in the leading research universities, have remained on the left, the bulk of the intellectuals in Europe and Japan appear to have dropped their former allegiance to Marxism. Polls indicate that British intellectuals and academics have backed center-left parties, while Swedish professors have also supported nonsocialist groups. French intellectuals turned very anti-Marxist and were anti-Soviet hard-liners during the seventies and eighties.[49] Japanese academics have also moved to the right.[50] Their behavior in different countries may stem from past links to strong socialist, labor, and, in Italy and France, Communist parties.[51] Socialism as a utopia clearly has failed, both in its authoritarian and democratic forms. Many intellectuals previously involved with left politics have turned away. An analyst of Swedish society, Ron Eyerman, in explaining why European intellectuals, unlike American, have not been "an alienated stratum with an independent tradition vis a vis the state," points out that continental intellectualdom, even when on the left, "found itself at the center, rather than the margins, of society." Intellectuals there could take part in the large labor and social democratic movements. The "alienated intelligentsia that did exist was limited to the arena of high culture," not academe.[52]

The American situation has been quite different. As Richard Flacks emphasizes, "The left has had more meaning in the United States as a cultural than as a political force."[53] Leftist party politics, particularly since World War II, has been too small a matter to count, and trade unions disdain intellectuals. There has been little application of radical theory to policy. As a consequence, John Gray indicates, the American "academic class . . . uses the rhetoric and theorizing of the radical intelligentsia of Europe a decade or a generation ago to legitimate its estrangement from its own culture. . . . American academic Marxism . . . [is] politically irrelevant and marginal . . . [and] compensates for its manifest political nullity by seeking hegemony within academic institutions."[54] Leftist ideologies, therefore, have been academic in both senses of the word. They remain important in the university world and the creative culture generally, and a large and perhaps growing segment of the American intelligentsia, including the media and entertainment elite, appears more inclined to support leftist ideologies than their compeers in most European countries.[55]

Radical sentiments do not appear to affect the bulk of the students nor the majority of the faculty on most teaching-oriented campuses. But they have reached out to many in the leading universities and have received the support of many discipline leaders. As Hayek noted half a century ago, in an analysis that is even more true today, the conservative bourgeoisie control the economy while the campus anti-establishmentarians dominate intellectual life in the humanities and much of the social sciences, particularly in the elite research universities.

CONFLICTS WITHIN THE LEFT

Relative to the size of the organized left in America, ideologically purist tendencies (i.e., political sectarianism) have been stronger in this country than elsewhere in the democratic world, a phenomenon discussed earlier. Prior to 1945, Trotskyism was more influential in the United States than in Europe. Trotskyism appealed as a revolutionary ideology not corrupted by power or the need to compromise with electoral realities which undercut the social democratic appeal. *Partisan Review,* for many years the major literary magazine in America, was edited by people loosely sympathetic to Trotskyism. A significant number of intellectuals were Trotskyist fellow travelers during the 1930s. They took ultra-left positions developed in the conflicts among the intelligentsia about Marxism, socialism, the nature of the Soviet Union, the Spanish Civil War, and the like. Besides the Trotskyists, who declined numerically with the outbreak of World War II, there was a vigorous, much larger independent left which also thought of itself as revolutionary. The American Socialist Party, led by Norman Thomas, stood considerably to the left of the European affiliates of the Second International during the 1930s and 1940s, as was the larger pre–World War I party led by Eugene V. Debs. Anti-Stalinism, a sophisticated radical opposition to the Communist International, was very popular among a sizable minority of American intellectuals. Although the Communist Party was the strongest force among leftists in membership terms and general political influence during the New Deal period, it had less appeal to Marxist theory-oriented intellectuals than the Trotskyists and revolutionary socialists, in part because the Communist Popular Front supported Roosevelt and the Democrats.

The 1930s witnessed incredibly bitter fights between the communist and the anti-communist American lefts about the character of the Soviet Union.[56] Stalinism was seen by the anti-communist radicals not only as oppressive in the USSR, but as having betrayed the cause of revolutionary socialism around the world. As Gillian Peele notes, "the primary divisions in American intellectual life in the 1930s were within the far left," and resulted in "a heritage of ideas and an awareness of disputes within the communist movement which was unusual among scholars and rare among practicing politicians."[57] A generation of radicals was weaned on the interpretation that the communists were responsible for the rise of Hitler, since they had cooperated with the Nazis in strikes in 1931 and 1932, and had undermined the Social Democratic government in Prussia. Before the Nazis came to power, Stalinist communists denounced the socialists as social fascists, that is, objective allies of fascism. The anti-communist left believed that the Stalinists had sabotaged the anti-fascist struggle during the Spanish Civil War, that they had been more concerned with destroying anti-Stalinist radicals than with defeating Franco. Ultimately there was the Hitler-Stalin Pact in 1939 which made World War II possible. In 1940, Molotov, the Soviet foreign minister, visited Berlin and said that fascism was a matter of taste. Until the Soviet Union itself was invaded, communists sought to work with the German conquerors in occupied Europe. The French Communist Party, for example, applied for permission to publish *L'Humanité* in Paris in 1940. In 1941, after the Soviet entry into the war, the American communists openly supported the Roosevelt administration's indictment of the leaders of the Trotskyist Socialist Workers Party under the Smith Act, a law enacted as an anti-communist measure. The revulsion to Stalinism among the American anti-communist left affected reactions to McCarthyism in the early 1950s. Although no one who could be considered "left" openly supported Senator Joseph McCarthy, some anti-Stalinist radicals were soft on his platform. While they agreed that his methods were bad and disapproved of his tactics, they favored fighting his target: the communists. The communists themselves played into the hands of McCarthy and his allies by rarely defending their constitutional right to free speech, to agitate or organize as communists. When attacked by government or congressional investigators, they would insist they were liberals, that the investigations were designed to intimidate the Progressive movement. Although the Socialists and the Wobblies, members of the Industrial Workers of the World (IWW), had defended their civil rights as radicals when arrested during World War I, and the Trotskyists did the same in 1941, as did New Leftists during the Vietnam War, communists never stood up to McCarthy or other post–World War II investigators to proclaim their right to be revolutionaries. For the most part, they took the Fifth Amendment, either refusing to answer political questions or denying, even when under oath, that they were members of the Party. Hence, frequently at issue was whether X actually was a communist, not whether he or she had a right to be one. Under such conditions, some anti-Stalinist leftists found it difficult to speak up for people whom they regarded as committed supporters of an extremely repressive and anti-Semitic system.

The anti-Stalinist left intellectuals on the whole continued to identify themselves as socialists or liberals during the postwar period. The Cold War of the late 1940s and early 1950s was waged in the free world by liberals and social democrats, for example, Harry Truman, Clement Attlee, Ernie Bevan, Kurt Schumacher, Guy Mollet, and Haakon Lie. When Henry Wallace left Truman's cabinet and joined with the communists to set up a new dovish left third party, the Progressives, in 1948, few liberals or trade union leaders followed.

The reasons for the growth of anti-Stalinism in the immediate postwar period were rooted in events: the takeover of Czechoslovakia in 1948, the overtly anti-Semitic trials subsequently held in that country, Stalin's increasing reliance on anti-Semitism in the Soviet Union, the end of any pretense of democratic rights and the suppression of the

Socialists in Eastern Europe, the blockade of Berlin, and the Korean War. The non-communist intellectuals united for a brief period in the Congress for Cultural Freedom, an organization set up to oppose communist influence in the intellectual world. At the most important meeting of the Congress in Milan in 1955, many leaders from both the democratic left and right were present, joined in their agreement that communist totalitarianism should be opposed.

This unity dissolved in the 1960s with the Vietnam War and the subsequent rise of a radical, student-based anti-war movement which rejected the anti-communism of the anti-Stalinist left.[58] These developments led to a sharp split within the liberal and social democratic communities. In the United States, the leading New Left group, Students for a Democratic Society (SDS), emerged out of the student section of the League for Industrial Democracy (SLID). The parent organization was founded in 1905 to organize intellectuals and professionals in support for trade unions and social democratic principles generally. In the mid-1960s, as the youth affiliate turned further to the left and showed a willingness to collaborate with any radical group, including the Communists, the older socialists in the LID, led by Michael Harrington, sought to discipline their youth, telling them to stay away from the communists. The student segment rejected this advice, which they viewed as red-baiting. They broke with the SLID and, as the SDS, went out on their own. They adopted a strong anti-anti-communist stance and denounced Harrington and his political friends.

The division was not limited to the student or youth movements. A growing conflict developed within the adult left, particularly between the New Left and the old Trotskyist and social democratic segments. The bitter anti-communism of the old left continued to be the main passion of many involved in the latter two. Max Schactman, who founded a dissident revolutionary movement that broke with the official Trotskyists in 1940 over their support of the Soviet attack on Finland, opposed World War II as an imperialist war, but in the mid-1960s endorsed the American involvement in Vietnam. At the onset of American intervention, the majority of the American non-communist left supported an American role in Vietnam, viewed as support of resistance to communist aggression. South Vietnam had a labor movement with close ties to the AFL-CIO. As the war continued, the left and liberal communities became increasingly involved in the anti-war movement, and leftists who did not oppose it found themselves isolated. When the protest took on the character of a mass movement led by radicals, those who wanted to continue leftist or socialist activities were faced with a choice: oppose the war or be perceived by the new growing generation of young radicals as reactionaries. The Socialist Party, which included the former Trotskyists, split. Its left was to reorganize as the Democratic Socialists. Its right formed an organization called Social Democrats USA, which supported the Vietnam War. The left, led by Michael Harrington, opposed the war, though they rejected the pro-Hanoi–Viet Cong stance of many of the New Left radicals involved in the anti-war movement and their confrontationist tactics, frequently aimed at universities.

These struggles within the non-Communist left were paralleled in the conflicts within the Democratic Party and the liberal community. The New Deal groupings, which had been more or less united behind the strong anti-communist foreign policies of Harry Truman and John F. Kennedy, also began to divide. The New Politics wing, identified with Senators Eugene McCarthy, George McGovern, and Robert Kennedy, opposed the war and favored efforts to negotiate with the Soviets on arms control and other matters. Conversely, a number of old-line New Dealers, including Lyndon Johnson, Hubert Humphrey, and Henry Jackson, together with the major leaders of the AFL-CIO, remained strong in their opposition to communism and supported the war in Vietnam.

The left and liberal worlds were now sharply split. Some prominent intellectuals with roots in the anti-Stalinist left were dismayed by the rise of the increasingly influential New Left and New Politics tendencies, which they perceived as soft on communism. They were especially critical of the student movement, and identified many of the new single-issue movements that had developed in the 1960s as somehow linked together in undermining resistance to communism. These reactions gradually led them to concentrate on fighting the anti-anti-communist left. They continued, however, to favor welfare state policies and strong trade unions. Viewing democracy as an end in itself and strongly attached to the values of scholarship, they argued that the confrontationist attacks by the New Left and the anti-war movement on the universities and on the democratic political system were not only unwarranted, but played into the hands of anti-democratic extremists, both of the left and the right. Hence they were regarded as renegades by the New Left. To their surprise, they found a greater emotional kinship with Old Right conservatives and Republicans than with their erstwhile political colleagues, whom they considered too dovish in their foreign policy views.

LABELING AND THE EMERGENCE OF
NEOCONSERVATISM

The hard-line anti-Stalinists were, however, still perceived as within the liberal or left communities until Michael Harrington, the leader of the Democratic Socialists, one of two major groups which succeeded the Socialist Party, and his colleagues on the editorial board of *Dissent*, coined the term "neoconservatism" in the mid-1960s.[59] They argued that the right wing of the dissolved party, Social Democrats USA, and their intellectual fellow travelers among other former radicals were neoconservatives, people who are objectively conservative and allied to, if not a part of, the conservative movement. They were in effect telling the left of center world, particularly the militant New Left students who regarded self-described left social democrats like Harrington and Irving Howe as non-radicals, that there was a difference between themselves and right-wing hawkish social democrats and other pro–Vietnam War leftists.

The subsequent development of the neoconservative "movement" is a good example of the consequences of a phenomenon sociologists describe as "labeling." Labels determine reactions to those labeled, whether they are described as "psychotic," "communist," or "conservative." In the case of the neoconservatives, the label induced many of their former friends and allies, for whom "conservative" is an invidious term, to reject them. Conversely, the label led many traditional rightists, Republicans and business people, long unhappy about their limited support among intellectuals, to welcome as new allies a group of prominent writers and academics who, they were told, had come over to their side.

The term quickly became part of American political discourse. Many in the United States and elsewhere assumed that neoconservatives were hard-line right-wingers on domestic as well as foreign issues, in spite of the fact that initially almost all of them remained supportive of welfare planning state and New Deal policies. They were identified with the Hubert Humphrey, Henry Jackson, Pat Moynihan Democrats; the George Meany, Lane Kirkland trade unionists; and the Social Democrats USA led by Sidney Hook and Bayard Rustin. But this background was forgotten or ignored as the old-line conservative intellectuals, Republican politicians, and many in the business community reacted positively to being told that a group of prominent, disproportionately Jewish, intellectuals, who had once been on the left, were now conservatives.

Neoconservatives (though more social democrats than not) thus found themselves rejected by their old friends and hailed by their opponents. The latter's welcome frequently included appreciative audiences, particularly when the neoconservatives dealt with issues upon which they and the conservatives agreed, such as an anti-Soviet foreign policy and opposition to affirmative action quotas. Neoconservatives were invited to write for conservative magazines, speak to their meetings, and work for their think tanks. Since the neoconservatives' strongest passions were reserved for their opposition to the Soviets and communists and they were concerned that most American liberals had become appeasers, they welcomed an alliance with hard-line foreign policy conservatives. But their political leaders remained Humphrey, Jackson, and Moynihan.[60] The latter two were to become the co-chairs of the one organization which could be described as neoconservative, the Coalition for a Democratic Majority (CDM), founded in 1973 to rally Democrats in opposition to the New Politics McGovern liberals.

The Republicans tried hard to win over the neoconservatives. Richard Nixon appointed Moynihan as his domestic policy adviser in 1969, and subsequently made him his ambassador to India and the United Nations. He tried to recruit Henry Jackson to serve as Secretary of Defense. In 1972, the Republicans pressed the neoconservative intellectuals to endorse Nixon against the Democratic presidential nominee, George McGovern, who as an ardent foreign policy dove was anathema to them. Few, except for Irving Kristol, did so. The majority sat out the election, although Daniel Bell and Nathan Glazer, successively co-editors with Kristol of *The Public Interest,* publicly endorsed McGovern. The Social Democrats USA and the AFL-CIO under George Meany abstained.

In 1976, most of the neoconservatives backed Henry Jackson for the Democratic nomination for president, but the previously unknown Jimmy Carter won. Carter, who had supported Jackson against McGovern four years earlier, turned out to be a big disappointment to the anti-communist left. His appointments to positions below cabinet level were largely to people identified with McGovern's views on foreign policy and Ralph Nader's on domestic issues. CDM, which had backed Carter for the nomination after Jackson withdrew, submitted a list of sixty names to Carter as possible appointments. Only a few were appointed to minor posts. Among those on the list who were not appointed were Jeane Kirkpatrick, Richard Perle, Max Kampelman (until the last six months), and Nathan Glazer.

The Republicans attempted to capitalize on the frustrations of the neoconservatives with the Carter administration. Bill Brock, the chairperson of the Republican National Committee, invited neoconservative intellectuals to lunch on a one-to-one basis, but had little success in recruiting them. At his invitation, Jeane Kirkpatrick wrote an article in 1979 for *Common Sense,* a Republican magazine, explaining "Why We Are Not Republicans." She said the problem rested in the fact that the Republican Party was a WASP vehicle, and the people connected with it were corporate board, country club types who were anti-welfare and had no concern for the poor and blacks.[61]

By 1980, many of the neoconservatives had become deeply antagonistic to Jimmy Carter, whom they saw as too soft in foreign policy terms. They were personally wooed by Ronald Reagan. He asked Jeane Kirkpatrick (who together with her husband Evron had been close to Humphrey) and others among them to be on his campaign team. She was subsequently given the U.N. ambassadorship. A number of neoconservatives, such as Richard Perle (a major Jackson aide), Kirkpatrick, Carl Gershman (a leader of Social Democrats USA), Elliott Abrams (a son-in-law of Norman Podhoretz, editor of *Commentary*), and Max Kampelman (formerly Humphrey's chief of staff), were appointed to major positions in the State or Defense departments. Richard Pipes worked for the National Security Council. Others such as Podhoretz and Ben Wattenberg (previously a Johnson aide) received advisory posts in the administration's international communications apparatus. Michael Novak became ambassador to the U.N. Human Rights Commission. William Bennett served consecutively as chairman of the National Endowment for the Humanities and Secretary of Education, where he was assisted by Chester Finn and William Kristol. Gertrude Himmelfarb held a presidential appointment on the Council of the National Endowment for the Humanities. A 1987 article in *The New Republic* described these developments as a Trotskyist takeover of the Reagan administration.[62]

As should be evident from this list of Reagan's erstwhile left and Democratic appointees, their positions were almost entirely in the foreign, defense, or education and intellectual policy realms. No neoconservative was assigned to a post affecting economic or welfare policy, such as the Treasury, Commerce, Agriculture, Labor, or Health and Human Services departments. The reason is fairly clear: questions of affirmative action and meritocracy apart, almost all the neoconservatives remained liberals on most domestic policy issues, at least as of the beginning of the Reagan presidency in 1981. Although the ideological leader of the tendency, Irving Kristol, supported Nixon in 1972 and became a Republican soon after, he continued to favor a variety of welfare programs and to disagree with Friedman, Hayek, and Reagan on these issues. As he put it in a 1976 article seeking to define what it meant to be a neoconservative, "Neo-conservatism is not at all hostile to the idea of the welfare state. . . . In general, it approves of those social reforms that, while providing needed security and comfort to the individual in our dynamic, urbanized society, do so with a minimum of bureaucratic intrusion in the individual's affairs. . . . In short, while being for the welfare state, it is opposed to the paternalistic state." The reforms he approved of "would include, of course, social security, unemployment insurance, some form of national health insurance, some kind of family assistance plan, etc."[63] Two decades later, writing in the *Wall Street Journal,* Kristol reiterated this description. In comparing neoconservatives to the "sober" conservatives around William Buckley's *National Review,* he noted that while "critical of Great Society programs," the "neoconservatives" did not share *National Review*'s hostility to the New Deal or its enthusiasm for Jeffersonian individualism.[64]

Kristol noted in the 1976 article that while he was willing to accept identification as a neoconservative, "some of my friends who have been identified as fellow neo-conservatives are less complaisant about this business. Daniel Patrick Moynihan, for instance, suggests that he is a modern version of a Wilsonian progressive. Professor Daniel Bell of Harvard asserts that he is, as he always has been, a right-wing social democrat."[65] Dan Himmelfarb, assistant editor of *The Public Interest,* denied in 1988 that the neoconservatives had changed ideologically. Rather, he concluded that American liberalism had moved left. Neoconservatives, he contended, believed that the left had "usurped the liberal label, leaving real liberals to be designated neoconservatives."[66]

The wooing of neoconservatives by Reagan and Brock, and, more fundamentally, changes in the larger political scene, led a number of them to follow Kristol in becoming Republicans. This group included Elliott Abrams, William Bennett, Peter Berger, Midge Decter, Gertrude Himmelfarb, Evron and Jeane Kirkpatrick, Norman Podhoretz, and Aaron Wildavsky. While they have been well received by the Republican Party leadership, traditional American conservative intellectuals, adherents of classical liberal laissez-faire doctrines, increasingly began to criticize neoconservatives as a foreign body within their ranks, corrupting their basic values. Patrick Buchanan has described the views of the neoconservatives, which are distasteful to the "Old Right," in these terms:

Ex-Great Society liberals, almost all of them, they support the welfare state and Big Government. They are pro-civil rights and affirmative action, though anti-quota. They are pro-foreign aid, especially for Israel. They favor higher immigration quotas, and some demand open borders. Many are viscerally hostile to the Old Right, and to any America First foreign policy. They want to use America's wealth to promote "global democracy" abroad and impose "democratic values" in our public schools.

While they support Ronald Reagan against Jimmy Carter, their heroes are Woodrow Wilson and Franklin D. Roosevelt, globalists and architects of the mammoth modern state.[67]

And he tells conservatives that they are "going to have to take back their movement . . . [from] the neoconservatives . . . the ex-liberals, socialists and Trotskyists who signed on in the name of anti-communism and set the limits of permissible dissent." One of his presidential supporters, Clyde Wilson, complained that the "offensives of radicalism have driven vast herds of liberals across the borders into our territories."[68]

Buchanan's views are not idiosyncratic. John Judis summarized the criticisms that appeared in various conservative journals: "[The traditionalists] . . . charge that the neoconservatives are not really conservatives, but welfare-state liberals and Wilsonian internationalists."[69] Writing of conflicting conservative tendencies, E. J. Dionne noted the critique by "old-time conservatives" of "neoconservatives, such as Irving Kristol and Norman Podhoretz . . . , who are mainly former Democrats . . . [for] importing liberal ideas within the conservative movement and seeking to transform conservatism into something quite different: a kind of 1940s anti-Communist liberalism more suitable to Harry S. Truman than to Robert Taft or Barry M. Goldwater."[70]

Judis's and Dionne's conclusions referred to articles published in traditional conservative magazines, which have argued that "welfare-state Democrats . . . have taken over once conservative publications and institutions,"[71] that ex-Democrats like "Irving Kristol seem to want to reconstitute the Democratic party of the 1950s and early 1960s (the party of big government and anti-Communism—Senator Henry Jackson's dream)."[72] Earlier, George Gilder criticized the neoconservatives for their refusal to support the conservatives on social issues such as the Equal Rights Amendment, abortion, sex education, pornography, school prayer, and gay liberation.[73]

Although Jeane Kirkpatrick joined the GOP, in 1985, she remained on the liberal side on many domestic issues. *The National Review* explained her rejection of a presidential bid in November 1987 on the grounds that she recognized that "questions about her views on economic and social issues would have inevitably arisen." As "a portent of the battle to come," an aide to then prospective conservative candidate Jack Kemp sent a letter to the *Manchester Union Leader* listing her liberal positions on various matters.[74]

The bulk of the neoconservatives remained Democrats. Writing in 1985, the conservative sociologist Robert Nisbet noted that "only a small fraction of those who had been most prominent in *The Public Interest* and in *Commentary* voted for Reagan."[75] The one important neoconservative organization during the seventies and early eighties was the Coalition for a Democratic [Party] Majority, although it preferred to be known as neoliberal. It basically disintegrated during the 1984 election when its members differed over their role in the presidential contest. At its height, the group included four past presidents of the American Political Science Association, and many other prominent scholars, such as Nathan Glazer, Michael Novak, Martin Peretz, John P. Roche, Adam Ulam, Leon Wieseltier, and Raymond Wolfinger. The organization was supported by a number of AFL-CIO leaders, including its president, Lane Kirkland, as well as by Social Democrats USA. The CDM intellectuals and the labor movement had a mutual admiration society and cooperated strongly. In the late 1970s, the Committee for Labor Law Reform, set up on behalf of the AFL-CIO, was chaired by two prominent neoconservative political scientists and drew largely on the CDM for membership. In 1992, the Cold War over, a number of neoconservatives who had supported Reagan endorsed Bill Clinton. But they were not welcomed into the new administration, which, like Carter's, largely appointed liberals into its foreign policy posts.[76]

Although they have separated politically, Democratic and Republican neoconservatives have been able to work together. From its inception in 1965 to 1972, *The Public Interest* was co-edited by Irving Kristol, who supported Nixon in 1972 and Reagan in 1984, and Daniel Bell, who endorsed McGovern in 1972 and Mondale in 1984. In 1973, Nathan Glazer, who also had backed McGovern and Mondale (and would later support Clinton), took over Bell's position as co-editor. Its publications committee has included Republicans like Robert Nisbet and a key Democratic leader, Senator Daniel Patrick Moynihan, who is liberal on domestic issues.

THE MEANING OF NEOCONSERVATISM

Neoconservatism arose out of and is therefore defined by a specific sequence of historical events. The common link in the sources of neoconservatism is past involvement in struggles against communism as anti-Stalinists in the radical movements, or as liberal opponents of Communist-dominated factions in sections of the Democratic Party where the Communists were once strong, for example, the states of Washington, Minnesota, and New York.

While I have stressed the continuing commitment to New Deal objectives of most neoconservatives, they have, like most socialists, become more moderate in their general approach to the polity. Their experiences with the confrontationist tactics of the New Left, such as the attacks on the universities in the 1960s and early 1970s, led them and others to place a greater emphasis on public order and respect for authority. An opposition to the "adversary culture" and anti-Americanism is also an important characteristic of neoconservatives. The failure of socialism abroad and the counterproductive results of many U.S. welfare policies led to a concern for "unanticipated consequences."[77] This involved the belief that many of the social changes of the past few decades which were designed to extend equality and to upgrade the bottom have brought with them unanticipated destructive consequences for the individuals who were supposed to be helped. Hence, it is necessary for government to act with humility, caution, and recognition of complexity.

Neoconservative views remain difficult to locate ideologically precisely because the "ism" was invented in an effort to label a diverse group of political opponents. No one created a doctrine and called him-/herself a neoconservative. Daniel Bell once summed up the political views of people like himself by saying that "I am a socialist in economics, a liberal in politics, and a conservative in culture." That is, he believes in the welfare state, in meritocracy and individualism, and in employing "the principle of authority" and tradition in evaluating cultural developments.[78] Not surprisingly, Irving Kristol has referred to Bell as "the theoretician for what may be called our 'social democratic' wing."[79] Kristol, himself the Godfather of Republican neoconservatism, strongly attacked Ronald Reagan's domestic policies in 1987, late in his administration, as miserly, as typical of "Republican administrations [which] are forever denying themselves any interesting initiatives in social policy, because such initiatives always cost some money." He urged support for a variety of welfare policies, even though "they would cost money" and increase the budget deficit. Most specifically, he argued for measures to aid the elderly, such as withdrawing the restrictions on incomes earned by those who receive Social Security and, more radically, for raising stipends for all those existing below the poverty line. "Why not raise Social Security payments so that the Reagan administration can proclaim proudly that it has abolished poverty for our older citizens?"[80]

The neoconservative priority on resisting Communist expansion continued to surface into the late 1980s among veterans of the political wars of the 1960s. A 1987 article in the radical magazine *Mother Jones* described the foreign policy accomplishments of a young neoconservative Democratic "Gang of Four," three of whom, Bruce Cameron, Robert Leiken, and Bernard Aronson, were active in the anti-Vietnam and other liberal and radical movements, and one, Penn Kemble, was a leader of the Social Democrats. They were credited with playing a major role in the Washington debates over Nicaragua and helping win crucial Democratic congressional votes for aid to the contras.[81]

Neoconservatism, however, has basically ceased to exist. The term lost its meaning as commentators applied it beyond its original application to strongly anti-communist leftists. The label has since been used to describe a wide range of traditional conservatives in the United States and abroad who are classically liberal anti-statists on domestic issues and hard-liners on foreign policy, largely by non-Americans, who identifying conservatism with Tory statism, thought the neo label applied to libertarians. Political scientist Percy Lehning writes: "I have chosen the theories of Friedrich Hayek and Milton Friedman as representative of neo-conservative thought," and stresses their views on the market system.[82] The *New York Times Book Review,* in dealing with two books on the Margaret Thatcher years, called the most powerful British disciple of Milton Friedman a "neoconservative," a description the author of the review gave to Ronald Reagan as well.[83] Canadian political scientist Philip Resnick, in analyzing the right-wing, laissez-faire Social Credit government of British Columbia, categorized it as "neo-conservatism on the periphery."[84] These writers are simply wrong. Hayek, Friedman, Reagan, and Thatcher are classical liberals, libertarians, not neoconservatives. Others have erroneously applied the term to social conservatives, advocates of teaching religion in the public schools and opponents of legalized abortion, although most neoconservatives take the opposite position on these and related issues.

These varied uses of the label, as I have noted, are incorrect since almost all of the original neoconservatives have been supporters of the welfare state and most continue to reject Friedmanite free market economics. Ironically, on a philosophical level the neoconservative position is closer to classic Toryism in British or Canadian terms. But since the British Conservative Party under Margaret Thatcher moved toward classic anti-statist liberalism, the Tory position in the United Kingdom, prior to John Major's accession, was advocated by the Liberal Democrats and a Conservative minority led by Edward Heath, the so-called wets. If the neoconservatives were in Britain during the 1980s, most would have been members or supporters of the Social Democratic Party, the right-wing split from the Labour Party, which during its short life probably came closer to the positions of the American neoconservatives on most issues (except trade unionism) than any other party in the world, and which was much more strongly anti-Soviet than the Tory wets. The British Social Democrats were no longer socialists; they resembled the strongly anti-communist American New Dealers.

Evidence of the disparate orientations of the neoconservatives is illustrated by the changing perspectives (loosely defined) of a number of magazines that were at one time labeled "neoconservative." David Broder referred in the mid-1970s to the principal organs of neoconservatism as *The Public Interest, Commentary,* and *The New Republic.* The editorship of the first has been divided between a Democrat and a Republican, as are the articles which it publishes; the editors of the second were social democrats who eventually became fairly consistent supporters of Reaganite conservatism; while the third has been dominated editorially by centrist Democrats who have been hard-liners and interventionists on foreign policy and moderate liberals on domestic issues.

It is interesting to note the impact of an earlier politically influential group of formerly radical American intellectuals, those who gathered around William F. Buckley and the *National Review* in the 1950s and afterwards. They played a major role in changing the direction of American politics. As in the case of the neoconservatives, what initially drew the group together was hard-line anti-communism. Buckley, his brother-in-law Brent Bozell, and his family friend Frank Chodorov apart, almost all of the major initiators of the magazine were former leftists: ex-Communists Willi Schlamm and Frank Meyer, former Trotskyists James Burnham and Willmore Kendall, and the first managing editor, Suzanne LaFollette, who had been involved with Socialists and Progressives. As John Judis notes in his biography of Buckley, the

"*National Review*'s masthead was heavily weighted with former left-ists."[85] Over the years, former radicals, both socialists and communists, associated with it have included Tom Bethel, Whittaker Chambers, Robert Conquest, John Dos Passos, Max Eastman, Will Herberg, Eugene Lyons, Frank Meyer, Richard John Neuhaus, John P. Roche, Morris Ryskind, George Schuyler, Ralph de Toledano, Freda Utley, Karl A. Wittfogel, and a host of others. Like the neoconservatives, many are Jewish. Unlike the neoconservatives, they were never singled out for attack by leftist critics as a special new movement since they explicitly placed themselves on the right and rejected the welfare state. Together with longtime conservative intellectuals like Edward Banfield, Milton Friedman, Russell Kirk, Robert Nisbet, and William Rusher, they helped to revive American conservatism (classical laissez-faire liberalism), transform the Republican Party, and refurbish belief in the free market system. They paved the way for Reaganism.

THE EMERGENCE OF POLITICAL CORRECTNESS

The emergence of various types of "conservatism" in the main centers of intellectual life seemingly also stimulated what was left of the "movements," particularly of ethnic civil rights protesters, the blacks and the Hispanics, the feminists and the environmentalists. The traditional radicals, undermined by events in Eastern Europe and the Soviet Union, also have turned to the movements and have added a strong intolerant strain to their activity. Frustrated by the Reaganite domination of the polity, the movement radicals concentrated on the campus, raising issues about South African investment, preferential hiring and admission practices, and multicultural programs which challenged the dominance of the traditional literary canon as standards of intellectual judgments.

Conservative, even moderate, speakers, faculty, and books have become "politically incorrect." Major political spokespersons with impeccable academic credentials such as former professors Jeane Kirkpatrick, Henry Kissinger, and Daniel Patrick Moynihan have been forced to cancel lectures because of actual or threatened protest demonstrations.[86] A survey taken of a national sample of senior college and university administrators during the 1990–91 academic year indicated that "controversies over the political or cultural context of remarks made by invited speakers are reported by 1 in 10 institutions, and by 20 percent of the nation's doctoral universities." Complaints from faculty "about pressures to alter their course content [occurred] at five percent of institutions. Among doctoral universities, 12 percent reported such complaints." Similarly, 4 percent of all institutions and 10 percent of doctorate-granting ones report having "experienced significant controversy over the political or cultural content of information presented in the classroom."[87] A year earlier, in 1989, a comparable survey of college and university presidents, which questioned whether "disruptive protest demonstrations" were a problem on their campuses, found that 91 percent of all institutional chief officers replied they were not a problem, but many fewer, 60 percent of the heads of research and doctorate-granting institutions, gave this response.[88] Such variations between the research universities and others may be credited to the greater liberalism of the students at the former and/or to encouragement given to activists by a more leftist faculty.

How strong are the movements behind such efforts? Not very, if we examine the distribution of opinions among students. More powerful, if we recognize the ability of activist minorities to mobilize militant student demonstrations against "incorrect" opinion and teaching, which though including only 5 or 10 percent of the undergraduate population, means a few thousand demonstrators on large campuses. An indication of the incendiary role played by some faculty may be found in an article by a prominent professor of English and Law at Duke University, Stanley Fish, a founding leader of the left academic association Teachers for a Democratic Culture. In an essay entitled "There's No Such Thing as Free Speech and It's a Good Thing Too," Professor Fish writes:

> [A]bstract concepts like free speech do not have any "natural" content but are filled with whatever content and direction one can manage to give them. Free speech, in short, is not an independent value but a political prize, and if that prize has been captured by a politics opposed to yours, it can no longer be involved in ways that further your purposes for it is now an obstacle to those purposes. . . .
>
> [P]eople cling to the First Amendment pieties because they do not wish to face what they correctly take to be the alternative. That alternative is *politics,* the realization . . . that decisions about what is or is not protected in the realm of expression will rest not on principle or firm doctrine, but on the ability of some persons to interpret—recharacterize or rewrite—principle and doctrine in ways that lead to the protection of speech they want heard and the regulations of speech they want silenced. . . . When the First Amendment is successfully invoked the result is not a victory for free speech in the face of a challenge from politics, but a *political victory* won by

the party that has managed to wrap its agenda in the mantle of free speech.[89]

Such views are not an aberration among the American cultural left. During the sixties and early seventies, opposition to free speech had wide circulation in Herbert Marcuse's ideas about "repressive toler-ance," a critique of the free circulation of ideas as suffocating revolu-tionary approaches, which had considerable support among New Left students.[90] In 1969, Louis Kampf, professor of literature at MIT and president of the Modern Language Association, told the activist stu-dents to disrupt all establishment cultural institutions, not just the uni-versities. Speaking of the new Lincoln Center in New York City, which he said was "built upon the ruins of a low-cost residential area," he pro-posed that "Not a performance should go without disruption. The fountains should be dried with calcium chloride, the statuary pissed on, the walls smeared with shit."[91] Writing of the situation two decades later, the Berkeley sociologist and former SDS leader Todd Gitlin noted that "A bitter intolerance emanates from much of the academic left."[92] And the socialist intellectual Paul Berman observed in 1992 that "if the intolerance is bitter among some of the professors, how much worse it is in the world of their students—among the hard-pressed student leftists especially."[93]

The Marxist historian Eugene Genovese, who stands out as a defender of the rights of those with whom he disagrees, has summed up the situation in strong terms in reacting to "the repression of profes-sors and students who take unpopular stands against quotas, affirma-tive action, busing, abortion, homosexuality and the like." He sees the situation as worse for the right than it was for the left in the fifties, not-ing: "As one who saw his professors fired during the McCarthy era, and who had to fight, as a pro-Communist Marxist, for his right to teach, I fear that our conservative colleagues are today facing a new McCarthy-ism in some ways more effective and vicious than the old."[94]

The nature of the concerns for academic freedom and free speech on campus has changed particularly at the leading universities and col-leges. Complaints once came from the more liberal or left faculty and students who worried about extramural efforts—undertaken by conser-vative trustees, alumni, and state legislators as well as administra-tions—to dominate the university, to repress various forms of deviance and political radicalism. Today, the more conservative and apolitical faculty now are the most likely to report harassment by students and colleagues, as well as feelings of malaise about the behavior of adminis-trators.

Increasingly, non-scholarly, particularistic criteria, such as political views, and ethnic, religious, and gender characteristics, are affecting faculty selection.[95] Of course, they always have done so. Atheists, Catholics, Jews, women, and leftists faced discrimination before World War II. The norms, however, remained as they must, universalistic and meritocratic, even if they were violated. But they are now being challenged by demands for increased representation of women and minorities, and, less openly, for political correctness, that is, for overt discrimination in favor of those with correct attributes, even if they are less competent than other candidates.

Progress has been made with respect to gender for some time. Changes in the position of women attest to this. Jessie Bernard, an older feminist sociologist, described the considerable increase of women in academe which occurred after World War I as an outgrowth of the suffragette movement. The proportions, however, declined greatly immediately after World War II, a phenomenon described by Bernard as "the great withdrawal." What she documented was the way in which the values espoused by female leaders, including the heads of women's colleges, were revised to emphasize the creative roles of mother and wife, which were put on par with a career. They argued that denigrating child rearing, community activity, and homemaking in favor of jobs was an anti-female view. Bernard contended that the college women of the forties and fifties responded willingly, *rejecting* the greater emphasis on career of earlier cohorts. She noted a change in values, which pressed women in the years following World War II into "a headlong flight into maternity. Whether they wanted babies or not, they felt they should have them."[96] She pointed out that the dropoff in the proportion of women in the professoriate in the forties and fifties appeared to be "the result of a declining supply of women offering their services" much more than of a "declining demand. . . . The picture seems to be one not of women seeking positions and being denied but rather one of women finding alternative investments of time and emotion more rewarding."[97] The situation, of course, changed dramatically once again from the mid-sixties on as a new wave of feminists rejected the home in favor of career and demanded not just meritocratic equal opportunity, but preferential treatment to make up for past discrimination. The record shows that women, who, unlike African Americans, are distributed in the same class and formal educational attainment groups as the traditionally dominant group, white males, have been able to take advantage of such increased opportunities.[98]

The condition of blacks has, of course, been different from that of white women. They entered the affirmative action era considerably behind whites in educational attainments, as we have seen. Proportionately, relatively few were qualified (had good Ph.D.'s) for academic positions, particularly in major universities. As more have won entrance to the better institutions, they have sought to qualify for the more economically rewarding positions, rather than for academe or intellectual pursuits. Doing so is typical first-college-generation behavior among all groups. Henry Louis Gates, Jr., explains the shortage of black Ph.D.'s by the fact that "we don't have a long tradition of academic families."[99] The best and the brightest among African Americans disproportionately seek to succeed in business management, medicine, law, and the like. This pattern has continued the situation in which African Americans remain heavily underrepresented in the pool of those qualified for the professoriate. And their low presence among the faculty contributes to campus tension and activism among minority students and left-disposed faculty. It seems to confirm the belief that discrimination is still widespread in hiring in higher education.

Higher education has been severely divided between those favoring meritocratic norms and others who press for social diversity and affirmative action quotas since special preferences and quotas for minorities and women were introduced by the Nixon administration in 1969.[100] While opinion surveys of faculty indicate that significant majorities back meritocracy, administrators, members of the affected minorities, feminists, the more left-inclined academics, and activist students all press for proportional representation targets. The latter goals have become "politically correct." Political correctness also involves support for multiculturalism, the emphasis on including in the curriculum the contributions of minority and Third World cultures, while reducing or rejecting any emphasis on Western ones.[101] As John Diggins concludes: "To be PC was to denounce Western Culture. . . . [M]ulticulturalists attacked racism, sexism, and DWEMism—partiality to dead, white, European males who wrote most of the books on a course's reading list."[102] Opponents face stigmatization as racists or chauvinists and frequently fear to speak up at faculty or student meetings.

CONCLUSION

As far as I can judge, an emphasis on political correctness is much more prevalent in American universities than elsewhere in the economically affluent democracies. Such behavior is not unique to academe or to leftists, feminists, or environmentalists. Social conservatives in this country are much more aggressive in their efforts to impose their morality on the body politic with respect to issues like the right to life than their ideological compeers elsewhere, even in predominantly Catholic countries like Italy, France, or West Germany. Such repressive aspects of American culture may be related to two exceptional national characteristics discussed earlier: first, the utopian ideological context of the American Creed, which defines the country in ways that nations characterized by a common history, not an ideology, lack; and second, the predominance in the United States of Protestant sectarianism, a minority elsewhere in Christendom. As we have seen, the political emphasis on loyalty to Americanism, the defining of deviants as "un-American," and the sectarian stress on personal morality represent forms of behavior that are less prevalent in historically defined countries, where religious ethos and orientation toward personal morality reflect the values of hierarchically organized, state-related churches, which assume that humans and their institutions are inherently imperfect. American values encourage concern for "correctness," both on and off campus, by the right as well as the left. Both are more moralistic, insistent on absolute standards, than their ideological compeers elsewhere in the developed world.

A quarter of a century ago, I dealt in some detail with the efforts of the activist left to politicize the American university.[103] I will not repeat the arguments here. The debate then was almost identical to that waged today. Principles apart, I noted that "the myth of the apolitical university, though a myth, serves to protect unpopular minorities," often radicals, and I cited various prominent leftists, including Noam Chomsky, to this effect. He wrote: "One legacy of classical liberalism that we must fight to uphold with unending vigilance, in the universities and without, is the commitment to a free market place of ideas. . . . Once the principle is established that coercion is legitimate . . . it is rather clear against whom it will be used. And the principle of legitimacy of coercion would destroy the university as a serious institution. . . ."[104]

Universities must be free places; they must be open to talent, to critical ideas, to the possibility of revisionism from many sources. Censorship, even self-censorship, has no place on the campus. Repression from the left, even though drawing its legitimacy from populist values, must suffer the same fate as repression from the right once did. If it does not, it will repeat the pattern. The only policy possible in a university worthy of the name was enunciated in 1975 by the Committee on

Freedom of Expression at Yale, chaired by the historian C. Vann Woodward, who still identifies himself as a socialist.

> No member of the community with a decent respect for others should use, or encourage others to use, slurs and epithets intended to discredit another's race, ethnic group, religion, or sex. It may sometimes be necessary in a university for civility and mutual respect to be superseded by the need to guarantee free expression. The values superseded are nevertheless important and every member of the university community should consider them in exercising the fundamental right to free expression. . . . The conclusions we draw, then, are these: even when some members of the university community fail to meet their social and ethical responsibilities, the paramount obligation of the university is to protect their right to free expression. . . . If the university's overriding commitment to free expression is to be sustained, secondary social and ethical responsibilities must be left to the informal processes of suasion, example, and argument.[105]

In the following section, I return to macroscopic comparative considerations, seeking to document the way in which the sharply differing organizing principles of Japan and the United States have produced American *exceptionalism* and Japanese *uniqueness*. The two remain the outliers among the developed nations.

PACIFIC
DIVIDE

CHAPTER 7

American Exceptionalism—Japanese Uniqueness[1]

Japan and the United States are two of the foremost examples of industrial success in the contemporary world, and they took very different paths to reach that position.[2] Efforts to account for America's past success discussed earlier have emphasized that, as compared to Europe, it had fewer encrusted preindustrial traditions to overcome, and in particular, that it had never been a feudal or hierarchical state church-dominated society. All of Europe and, of course, Japan was once feudal, organized in terms of monarchy, aristocracy, and fixed hierarchy, with a value system embedded in institutions that both emphasized the virtues inherent in agrarian society and deprecated commercial activities. Japan's feudal period, moreover, did not end until the latter half of the nineteenth century.

As I indicated in chapter Three, in discussing the expansion of capitalism, nineteenth- and early twentieth-century Marxists, much like followers of Max Weber, pointed to the United States as the purest of bourgeois societies, the least feudal one, and therefore the most successful. An efficient market economy is seemingly best served by a value system which regards the individual as the equivalent of a commodity within the market.

The interpretation which identifies postfeudal structures and values as antithetical to the development of modern industrial society is challenged by the history of Japan, which boasts the most successful economy of the postwar era. Rising from a terrible military defeat and the almost total destruction of its economy, Japan experienced a level of sustained economic growth which enabled it to become, in per capita terms, one of the wealthiest countries in the world, and to compete successfully with the United States. But this postwar "miracle" continues a successful development pattern that began in the latter part of the nineteenth century, long after Northern Europe and North America began their industrial revolutions. Self-starting industrialization and modernization took place almost exclusively in a few European countries and the English-speaking overseas settler societies. Japan is the earliest non-Western country to become affluent and industrially developed. Its record, compared to that of the United States or, to some degree, of Western Europe, seems to contradict much of what economic historians and comparative social scientists generally had thought they learned from the American experience.

In this chapter, I look at the two outliers, the two developed nations which are most different from each other. They clearly have distinct organizing principles and their values, institutions, and behaviors fit into sharply different functional wholes. These variations, of course, have been written about in myriad comparative scholarly, business, and journalistic works.[3] These analyses not only tell us about Japan; they give insights into Western, particularly American, culture, which is the main concern of this book as well.

The question which now interests the West is: what is it about Japan that enabled this to happen? The Japanese themselves are fascinated with discussions of Japanese uniqueness, *Nihonron,* their counterpart to American exceptionalism.[4] The "reiterated refrain underlying the literature on Japanese identity is that of uniqueness."[5] One literature survey estimates that over two thousand works dealing with Japanese uniqueness have been published since World War II.[6] Sugimito Yoshio and Ross Mouer take note of the agreement among many Japanese that their culture is "uniquely unique" and consequently cannot be understood by Western scholars.[7] These arguments have a long history.

REVOLUTION FROM ABOVE

Japan has modernized economically while retaining many aspects of its preindustrial feudal culture. Until the mid-nineteenth century, the social structure under the Tokugawa Shogunate was still feudal; its culture still resembled that of Renaissance Europe. Japan was an extremely hierarchical society, which placed a tremendous emphasis on obligation to those higher up as well as to those down below. Inferiors were expected to show deference and give loyalty while superiors were obliged to protect and support them.

Until the mid-nineteenth century, Japan avoided a prolonged breakdown of feudalism, when the Japanese aristocratic elite decided that the country had to industrialize to escape being conquered by the imperialist West. Determined to avoid dependence on or takeover by

Western powers, this elite sought to remake the country economically along Western lines. To do so, they recognized the need to consciously remold the social structure so as to create the conditions for economic development, a dauntingly gargantuan task.[8] If individualism, egalitarianism, and liberalism (a weak state) are highly conducive to economic development, Japan has been more disadvantaged than most nations. Comparatively, it is still extremely status-conscious (the vernacular language and social relations are particularly hierarchical), politically centralized, and above all, by Western standards, collectivity-oriented and particularistic (group-centered).

Few Westerners, other than scholars, are knowledgeable about the reorganization of Japan. The record of the country's mid-nineteenth-century barons, that brilliant group of oligarchs who took over the country determined to modernize it, makes that of any group of Communist rulers seem like the work of indifferent bumblers. The changes which occurred in Japan from the 1860s on were among the most remarkable societal transformations that have ever occurred. The barons carried through a sociological transformation, using Emperor Meiji to legitimate it.[9]

Recognizing that the rapid and major changes they planned for the nation would create major social strains which could precipitate serious discontent and protest, the Meiji barons restored the prestige of the emperor, enlarged his role, and revitalized the ancient Shinto religion with its links to emperor worship and stress on loyalty to the state.[10] The concern to resist domination by the West and the continued postfeudal association of aristocratic status and military prowess led to a strong emphasis on armed strength, which continued until the end of World War II. Still, the Meiji elite were prepared to deliberately introduce an institution, the modern university, which they anticipated would be an inherently disruptive, even rebellious, force.

In 1870, Japan did not have a single institution which resembled a university when Arinori Mori, the first minister of education, prepared a memorandum stating that the country required first-rate universities. These would train people to become leaders in scientific research, engineering, and other necessary aspects of modern life. Mori wrote that a university is a place whose faculty and students must be free to read and discuss all the ideas that exist in the world. He recognized that scholarship involves innovation, the superseding of old knowledge, of tradition. In this context, he wrote, the creation of new ideas means a rejection of the past, and therefore exposure to new concepts could result in expressions of doubt about the validity of the predominant values of Japanese society. Hence, though universities are endemically sources of disloyalty, he emphasized that Japan must have them. Since they inevitably will be centers of opposition, even of sedition, they should not be allowed to influence those who teach students at lower levels of education. He proposed that teachers' colleges be separated geographically from universities, so that children in the elementary and secondary schools would not be taught by instructors who had attended a university.[11]

The Meiji planners were faced with the need to reorganize the status system. In a feudal agrarian society, banking and other commercial activities were held in low repute. This had been true in Europe where merchants, even when wealthy, were looked down upon by the feudal rulers; they were necessary, but they were not considered equals by the aristocracy. The Meiji elite realized that Japan had to encourage commerce and industry, the pursuit of profits. The populace, and the elite as well, had to regard business pursuits as important and worthy occupations. The solution was to foster the merger of aristocratic and business statuses by encouraging the lowest aristocratic stratum, the samurai (knights), to become businessmen. This was possible since the samurai had been almost functionless even before the end of feudalism.[12]

The Meiji transformation highlights the widely discrepant roles of the state in developed societies. The ideological heritage of Japan, derived from a postfeudal alliance of throne and altar, engenders a positive sense of the role of government, much as a somewhat similar background produced in most of Europe. Industrialism in Japan, as in Imperial Germany, was planned by the government, indicating Japan has been less unique in this respect than many Japanese believe.[13] Thorstein Veblen, writing in 1915, noted these developments in terms which resemble recent writings:

> It is in this unique combination of a high-wrought spirit of feudalistic fealty and chivalric honor with the material efficiency given by the modern technology that the strength of the Japanese nation lies. In this respect . . . the position of the Japanese government is *not unique* except in the eminent degree of its successful operation. The several governments of Europe are also . . . endeavoring similarly to exploit the modern state of the industrial arts by recourse to the servile patriotism of the common man.[14]

The "evolution of Japan," Emile Durkheim stressed, corresponded in many ways to European "social evolution. We have passed through almost the same phases."[15] Norman Jacobs, Carmi Schooler, and Ken'ichi Tominaga all emphasize that feudalism and consequent state centralization aided industrialization in Japan and Europe.[16] The United States developed with much less government involvement in the economy than almost all other now industrialized countries, making it truly exceptional.

The Ministry of International Trade and Industry (MITI) has continued the tradition of guidance set by the Meiji economic planners.[17] David Okimoto points out that MITI's contemporary approach is "anticipatory, preventive, and aimed at positively structuring the market in ways that improve the likelihood that industry-specific goals will be achieved." The ministry views the operations of a "pure" market economy as flawed, in part because laissez-faire ideology entails the pursuit of narrow interests, and thus a lack of attention to "collective interests . . . and . . . national goals."[18] Conversely, the classically liberal, laissez-faire, anti-statist ideology is the political tradition of the United States.[19] The American polity stands out in resisting state leadership in the economic arena.[20] In contrast to the Japanese experience, the U.S. government "tends to deal primarily with failures after they have occurred. . . . [It] suggests a preference for leaving the market alone unless there is tangible evidence of a breakdown. . . . Whereas Americans are content to let the chips fall where they may, the Japanese prefer to remove as much of the element of uncertainty from the market processes" as possible.[21] In an exaggerated sense, the Japanese economy may be described as a form of market socialism, or, as Shin-ichi Nakazawa, a popular social critic, comments: "It's as if Japan has a kind of Communistic capitalism, or state socialism without the socialism."[22] Douglas Moore Kenrick, a successful businessman and Japanologist, after thirty-five years of working in Japan, wrote a detailed analysis of the society and economy under the title *Where Communism Works.*[23] He emphasizes that Japan has developed "an advanced, bureaucratic, economic and social system that is different from, as well as similar to capitalism."[24] Chalmers Johnson also describes the system as a "different kind of capitalism," one which operates in "ways that neither Adam Smith nor Marx would recognize or understand," one which is fundamentally different from the American.[25]

The image of the Japanese economy as operating under qualitatively different rules than the American or other Western ones has frequently been challenged by Western economists.[26] Two North American economists, Richard Beason and David Weinstein, examine thirteen sectors and conclude that the Japanese bureaucrats, like Soviet ones, fail to pick winners in the economic competition. Basically, they report a negative correlation between government support and growth: the more support to an industry, the slower its growth.[27] But these findings may only demonstrate that the Japanese planners, like other "socialist" ones, seek to keep less productive sectors operative, not that they believe these will become winners.[28]

As I stated in chapter One, comparative approaches such as this can never produce absolute evaluations. It should be noted that most European countries fall in between the United States and Japan; they are more like Japan than the United States is, but more like the United States than Japan is. As Ronald Dore emphasizes in concluding a book comparing Britain and Japan: "In the dimension . . . which I have called 'individualism-collectivism,' 'individualism-groupism,' the United States and Japan stand at opposite ends, with Britain somewhere in the middle."[29]

The group or consensus model of Japanese society, and the individualistic and conflict model of American society, both of which are followed by much of the literature and are employed in this chapter, have been criticized by some scholars. They suggest that other approaches, including the structuralist, stratification, and social exchange (focusing on the emphasis on reciprocity and gifts) models, provide alternate ways to conceptualize the two nations. Harumi Befu has suggested as an alternative model for Japan a social exchange one. He notes correctly that the Japanese stress the need to repay all obligations, indebtedness to others who may have helped out or given favors of any kind; while Americans feel less impelled to act in such ways, especially when to do so may create the impression of cronyism, of special favors in return for "bribes."[30] But these are not mutually exclusive.[31] Nations develop new institutions, patterns of acting, which fit into their organizing principles. Receptivity to particular modes of behavior is a function of the larger value system. Quality circles premised on group cooperation, which were invented in the United States, took hold in Japan, not in America. Clearly, while it is possible to organize the analysis of any society along a variety of lines, it is necessary for comparative societal analysis to focus on organizing principles or values that encourage insight into sources of variation with other systems.

Societies are characterized by both aspects of analytical polarities. A society is not either group-oriented or individualistic or ascriptive or egalitarian or consensual or not.[32] All systems are marked by stratification, conflict, and consensus. There is considerable individualism in

Japan as well as particularism (group orientation) in the United States. Such concepts must be treated in a comparative context, as measured by relative rankings, that is, as more or less. Viewed in such a fashion, Japan appears to be the most group-oriented culture among developed societies; the United States is the most individualistic. Beyond the data presented in this chapter, these conclusions are documented in Tables 8-1 and 8-2 of chapter Eight (drawn from the 1990 World Values Survey led by Ronald Inglehart), which demonstrate that Americans belong to and are more active than Europeans and Canadians in voluntary organizations, while Japanese are the least involved.[33] Worldwide surveys of fifteen thousand managers conducted between 1986 and 1993 by Charles Hampden-Turner and Alfons Trompenaars on many attitude and behavioral items also produced large differences between Americans and Japanese, with the two almost invariably at opposite poles; all other nations fell between them.[34] (See Appendix, pp. 293–296.

DUTY AND OBLIGATION

A fundamental difference between Japan and the United States lies in the fact that the Japanese governing elite has made a conscious effort to merge the traditional with the modern. The Japanese have continued to uphold values and institutions which, from the perspective of Western market economics analysis, make little sense. They maintain a society in which deference and hierarchy are important, in which there is a "continuing ethos of patrimonial relations derived from Japan's feudal past. . . ."[35] In theory, the person does not exist as an individual, but only as a member of certain larger groups: family, school, community, company, nation.[36] A 1990 Japanese government study of American and Japanese high school students concluded that, unlike the situation in the United States, "child rearing in Japan, the educational system, the style of education plays against individualism. Rote learning is favored over a creative approach to study. In addition, the Japanese do not want to STAND OUT as individuals. The proverb about the nail sticking up which must be pounded down implies that the individual who behaves in an individualistic way is significantly different from the group, will be punished and not rewarded."[37]

The continuity in the American emphasis on individuality and the Japanese emphasis on conformity to the group may be seen in the cross-national variation in polls taken in 1989, which asked respondents to react to the statement: "It is boring to live like other people." Over two thirds, 69 percent, of the Americans agreed that conforming is tedious, compared to 25 percent of the Japanese.[38] The latter seek to avoid individual responsibility.

The 1990 World Values Survey asked respondents to locate themselves on a ten-point scale running from "Individuals should take more responsibility for themselves" to "The state should take more responsibility to ensure that everyone is provided for." Seventy percent of the Americans places themselves in the three highest individual responsibility categories (45% at the extreme point), in contrast to 17 percent of the Japanese (7% at the top end).[39]

Notions of duty and obligation constantly come through in conversations with Japanese.[40] They feel an obligation to each other and to the institutions of which they are a part. Individuals are indebted to their parents, teachers, employer, and state. They must repay all favors, even casual ones. Gifts are exchanged frequently as a way of maintaining social relationships, of meeting and developing obligations.

The psychologist Janet Spence, in explaining how "the Japanese character differs profoundly from the American one," notes that contrasting socialization processes result in sharp variations in ego, with individualism in the United States leading to "a sense of self with a sharp boundary that stops at one's skin and clearly demarks self from non-self." For the Japanese, the "*me* becomes merged with the we, and the reactions of others to one's behaviors gain priority over one's own evaluations." These differences are related to the varying values and institutions of the two nations. "These contrasting senses of self in the two societies are produced by and lead to differing emphases on rights versus obligations, on autonomy versus personal sacrifice, and on the priority of the individual versus that of the group—differences that have broad ramifications for the structure of political, economic, and social institutions."[41]

According to psychological studies, the development of these distinct cultural identities begins in infancy. After noting "sharply different styles of caretaking" in the two societies, William Caudill and Carmi Schooler comment: "[I]t would appear that in America the mother views her baby, at least potentially, as a separate and autonomous being who should learn to do and think for himself. . . . In Japan, in contrast to America, the mother views her baby much more as an extension of herself, and psychologically the boundaries between them are blurred."[42] A report on comparative surveys of children age 7 to 11 indicates that when questioned "whether their mothers treated them 'more like a grown-up or a baby,' 65 percent of the American children answered 'more like a grown-up,' compared to only 10 percent of the Japanese children."[43] A similar cross-national view of the parent-child relationship is found in the answers samples of fathers gave in 1986 to the question: "Do you try to treat your child like an adult as much as possible?" An overwhelming majority of American fathers, 79 percent, replied, "Yes," compared to less than half, 43 percent, of Japanese.[44] The same survey inquired of children aged 10 to 15 years: "When you and your father disagree, does he listen to your opinion?" In tandem with the responses of the fathers, the majority of American offspring, 72.5 percent, said, "Yes, he does," compared to 45 percent of the Japanese.[45] And when asked: "What does your father usually do when you do something bad?" twice the proportion, 37 percent, of the Americans chose the response, "He doesn't get upset but tries to talk to me," contrasted to 18 percent of the Japanese young people.[46] The latter were more likely than Americans ages 10 to 15 to continue the pattern when dealing with younger siblings. Only 36 percent of the Japanese, against 56 percent of the Americans, said they would allow "a younger child [who] wanted to watch some other [TV] program" to do so even when the older one would like to see another one.[47]

The strength of Japanese group allegiance is strangely and starkly illustrated by the Japanese prisoners of war who offered to engage in espionage against their homeland during World War II. "The prisoners became excellent spies. Once they had changed ingroup, having been taken prisoner against the explicit instructions of their superiors, they no longer defined the self as Japanese."[48] This behavior, when compared to the intense sense of duty and commitment of kamikaze fighter pilots, seems to indicate that motivating ideology is of secondary importance to the basic fact of group cohesion.

Ironically, the Japanese emphasis on obligation and loyalty to membership groups appears to result in a lower level of civic consciousness, a lesser willingness to help individuals or institutions to whom no obligation exists, than in the more individualistic America.[49] I have been told by Japanese that they are not supposed to assist strangers unless they are in very serious difficulty, since the person assisted will then have a new obligation which he or she does not want. Such reports are congruent with opinion poll findings. Youth surveys (ages 18–24) have been conducted in different countries by the Japanese Youth Development Office of the Department of Public Affairs. In 1977, 1983, and

1988, the Office asked: "Suppose you meet a man lost and trying to find his way. What would you do?" Over half, from 51 to 60 percent, of the Americans chose the answer "ask him if he needs help," while less than a third, 26 to 32 percent, of the Japanese gave the same response.[50] Similar cross-national differences were reported in the study of 10- to 15-year-olds in 1986. They were asked: "If you saw a person with more luggage or packages than he or she could comfortably handle, would you offer to help him or her even if you didn't know him or her?" Over three fifths, 63 percent, of the American young people said they would, while only a quarter, 26 percent, of the Japanese would do the same.[51]

American parents are much more likely than Japanese ones to report that they try to teach their children to help those in need and to follow civic rules. A 1981 comparative survey conducted for the Prime Minister's Office in Japan, based on interviews with parents of children under 15 years old, reported that over two thirds, 70 percent, of Americans were instructed to "care for the elderly and the handicapped," compared to one third, 33.5 percent, of the Japanese. The corresponding figures for "not to litter in parks and on roads" were 66 percent for Americans and 33 for Japanese; for "to wait one's turn in line," the percentages were 44 for Americans and 19 for Japanese.[52]

CHANGE AND STABILITY

A detailed review of the literature on Japanese uniqueness, inherently comparative like that on American exceptionalism, suggests major differences in structures, cultural styles, and values, variations which "are more or less identical with differences between industrial and preindustrial (feudal) civilization in the West."[53] Japanese social scientists have been monitoring their values and "national character" through survey research since the 1950s. Their findings indicate that "no change in basic values has occurred in Japan. This evidence challenges the evolutionary view which posits the Western pattern as the end point, the culmination of societal development. Alternative patterns of family and human relations appear to be enduring rather than transitional."[54] The studies stress that the "central Confucian and Samurai values such as seniority, loyalty or priority of the group are still dominant. . . ."[55] Tatsuko Suzuki concludes from reviewing the Japanese experience that in spite of "institutional changes . . . in the areas of economics and politics . . . the systems of belief in Japan owe their relative stability to the stability in the structure both of family relations and of supplementary, informal social relations."[56] These findings seemingly reiterate Veblen's, reached in 1915, that it is "only in respect of its material ways and means, its technological equipment and information, that the 'New Japan' differs from the old. . . ."[57]

Various reports on Japanese values indicate, however, that while many attitudes and values appear stable, a number have changed considerably between the 1950s and the 1990s. Some of these changes seem to involve an acceptance of Western values. For example, the proportion of Japanese who would "adopt a child to continue the family line" (traditional behavior for those without children) declined steadily over eight National Character surveys taken between 1953 and 1993, from 73 to 22 percent. Those who say the prime minister should visit the Imperial Shrine annually moved down from 50 percent in 1953 to 17 percent in 1993.[58] Asked repeatedly what sex they would choose to be if born again, the percentage of women who would prefer to be men fell off in linear fashion from 64 percent in 1958 to 29 percent in 1993. The proportion of men, however, who opt for a masculine rebirth has been constant at 90 percent from 1958 on. In three American polls taken between 1946 and 1977, the same and unchanging percentage, also around 90, of American males preferred to be born in the same sex. American women, however, have consistently shown a much greater desire to retain their gender than Japanese women, with the percentage wanting to be of the opposite one going down from 26 in 1946 to 17 in 1958 and 9 in 1977.[59]

Conversely, respondents to the National Character surveys, as well as to the youth studies, have become more traditional and less Western in their answers to many other questions. The varying patterns have been brought out in a review of the National Character studies by Japanologist Scott Flanagan of the six surveys taken between 1963 and 1988.[60] Flanagan summarized the patterns of change for seven items, classifying responses as being "traditional," "modern," or "unclassifiable." I have not used one of the items due to difficulties I have with coding which response is modern and which is traditional. The unit of measurement is the percentage difference between modern and traditional responses. In four of the six items, the change from 1963 favored the traditional response, while the remaining two items changed in the modern direction. Five of these six changes were relatively small, from 6 to 12 percent.

Flanagan's results also indicate that the few early postwar shifts toward modernity began "to halt or reverse in the 1970s, as a result of several factors":

> The 1973 Arab oil boycott sent shock waves through the Japanese econ-
> omy; the oil crisis diverted attention from the environmental, quality-of-
> life, and participation issues that had come to the forefront in the 1960s
> and refocused national attention on economic issues, leading to a resur-
> gence in conservatism. This period also coincided with a renewed interest
> in Nihonjinron (essays on what it means to be Japanese) as the Japanese
> began to reassess the enduring aspects of their culture in light of the previ-
> ous three decades of massive importation of goods, ideas, and practices
> from the West. Toward the end of the 1970s this renewed interest in the
> enduring traditions of Japanese culture was reinforced by a growing nation-
> alism and cultural self-satisfaction with Japan's new international standing
> and dramatic economic success.[61]

In Flanagan's analysis, as well as in results from other studies, I find further evidence for the continued strength of traditional values. An increasing lack of confidence in science, certainly a modern institution, appears to characterize the Japanese, while Americans retain their confidence. The belief that there is a loss in "the richness of human feelings as a result of the development of science" increased from 30 percent in 1953 to 51 percent in the National Character studies of 1993. These results are supported by the findings of 1980–81 and 1990 World Values Surveys, which asked: "In the long run, do you think that scientific advances we are making will help or harm mankind?" They both found the majority of Japanese critical or fearful of science, while most Americans reacted positively. Fifty-six percent of Americans replied in the first World Values Survey that advances would "help," increasing to 62 percent a decade later; Japanese who responded this way increased from 22 to 26 percent. Similar cross-national results with comparable magnitudes of difference in response rates were obtained to a number of questions seeking to evaluate benefits or damages from the development of science and technology in cross-national surveys conducted in 1991 by the Japanese Science and Technology Agency. For example, 83 percent of Americans, compared to 54 percent of Japanese, agreed that "Scientific development makes my daily life healthier, more safe and comfortable." The Agency also reported much higher interest in "News and Topics on Science and Technologies" in the United States in 1990 than in Japan in 1991.[62] Interest by Japanese young people in science and technology is declining. It fell from 67 to 41 percent between 1977 and 1991. Studies of the occupational aspirations of Japanese high school students found that in spite of the fact that "the employment rate for science and engineering [university] graduates is very high. . . . High school students are steering away from the science and engineering disciplines."[63]

Other responses in the National Character research also suggest a revival of traditionalism. Thus, when asked to choose the "two most important values," those answering "respect individual rights" fell off from 48 percent in 1963 to 38 percent in 1993. Those listing "filial piety," being dutiful to one's parents, increased from 61 percent to 69 percent over the same period, while "respect freedom" increased slightly from 40 percent in 1963 to 42 percent in 1993. And on "the rather delicate question of whether or not the Japanese feel they are superior to the Westerners . . . those who believe they are superior increased from 20% in 1953 to a massive 47% in 1968 . . . [and then went down somewhat to a lower 41% in 1993]. The pattern observed here indicates the renewed self-confidence of the Japanese. . . ."[64]

Perhaps the best example of the strength of traditional practices even when they appear dysfunctional for an economically developed society is the nation's refusal to adopt the system of street names and consecutive numbers on buildings that exists in the West. Japanese streets are not named or numbered in the same systematic way, and house numbers refer to the order of construction in a given district. Strangers are expected to find their way with local maps or by directions from a nearby landmark, such as a train station. The Japanese had an opportunity to change after the war when the American occupation forces assigned alphabetical or numerical names to streets. But this system, apparently so much more functional for commerce in a large city like Tokyo, was largely discarded as soon as the occupation ended.

Seemingly, in spite of the tremendous strides Japan has made toward technological modernization, higher self-esteem is leading toward a regained "confidence in tradition," to a "return to traditional values."[65] These developments in turn should enhance the differences between Japan and the United States and other Western countries. The variations which have been suggested in the literature between the Japanese and American belief systems are summed up in Table 7-1, a modified version of one presented by Peter Dale.

Many Japanese tend to agree with the stereotype that they are a less universalistic and more particularistic society than America. Thus, when asked by the Nippon Research Organization in 1990 whether Japanese are more "intolerant of other races," 40 percent said they

TABLE 7-1. DIFFERENCES BETWEEN AMERICA AND JAPAN

America	Japan
A. Society (*Gesellschaft*)	A. Community (*Gemeinschaft*)
B. Individualism	B. Groupism contextualism
C. Horizontality	C. Verticality
D. Egalitarianism	D. Hierarchy
E. Contract	E. "Kintract"
F. "Private"	F. "Public"
G. "Guilt"	G. "Shame"
H. Urban-cosmopolitan	H. Rural-exclusive
I. Rights	I. Duties
J. Independence (inner-directed)	J. Dependence (other-directed)
K. Universality	K. Particularity-uniqueness
L. Heterogeneity	L. Homogeneity
M. Absolutism	M. Relativism
N. Rupture	N. Harmony, continuity
O. Artifice	O. Nature
P. Abstraction	P. Phenomenalism, Concreteness
Q. Donative/active	Q. Receptive/reactive
R. Open	R. Closed

SOURCE: *Adapted and modified from Peter N. Dale, The Myth of Japanese Uniqueness (New York: St. Martin's Press, 1986), pp. 44, 51.*

were, while only 13 percent thought Americans were more intolerant than Japanese. A plurality of Japanese (35.5%) replied that their countrymen are more disposed to "put priority on [matters concerning] one's own country" (nationalistically self-centered), compared to 22.5 percent who believe the Americans are more nationally oriented. More Japanese, 33 percent, see themselves as "selfish," while only 12 percent identify Americans this way. In each case, Americans, answering the same questions for the NBC News/*Wall Street Journal* poll, were more likely to give the converse response, to think themselves more tolerant of other races than the Japanese (by 46 to 40%), less nationalistic (by 64 to 24%), and less selfish (by 44 to 33%). Analysis of the 1990 World Values data indicates that the belief that the Japanese are much more intolerant and xenophobic than Americans is true. Americans are more disposed than Japanese to believe it important to encourage their children to exhibit "tolerance and respect for other people," by 72 to 59.5 percent. Asked to react to various groups, as neighbors, Japanese are much more likely than Americans to reject "immigrants/foreign workers," as well as Muslims, Jews, and Hindus. They object even more strongly to homosexuals, people who have AIDS, and drug addicts. When the issue is presented in terms of employment, when "jobs are scarce," only 14 percent of the Japanese disagree with giving priority to their fellow citizens, while an astonishing 43 percent of Americans would deny such advantages.

CONFLICT AND CONSENSUS

The United States is a much more discordant society than Japan and, to a lesser extent, much of Western Europe. The combination of capitalist and Protestant sectarian values, to be found dominant only in America, encourages conflict and moralism. As the purest example of a bourgeois nation, America follows the competitive norms of the marketplace in union management and other relationships. Actors seek to win as much as they can and will ride roughshod over opponents if possible. American unions have been reluctant to cooperate with executives on management problems or to take responsibility for corporate welfare. They are described in the comparative labor literature as "adversarial," as distinct from the behavior of unions in postfeudal, more social democratic, corporatist nations.[66] The American unionists have pressed to secure as much from management as their strength permits. (In recent years, of course, their loss of membership, as detailed in chapter Three, has hampered their ability to gain concessions and they are much less militant.) Unionists among the Japanese belong to companywide labor organizations which show concern for the company's needs, not nationwide ones which include all in the same trade or industry, as in America. American unions historically have not been concerned about the welfare of specific companies. Japanese workers have been much less prone to strike than American unionists. The proportion and number of workers engaged in work stoppages have declined in both countries, but the United States remains far ahead of its trans-Pacific rival. Thus in 1980, one million work days were lost to strikes in Japan, as compared to almost 21 million in the United States. By 1991, the Japanese figure had fallen to 96,000, while the American was close to 4.6 million.[67] A "de facto incomes policy has grown organically out of a routinized set of norms, procedures, and institutions developed over years of interaction between labor and management." Okimoto points out that the cooperative and "self-regulating nature of labor-management relations has spared the Japanese government from being engulfed by the consuming task of binding up economic and social wounds following outbursts of labor unrest."[68]

Related to the emphasis on obligation (exchange relations) is the ideal of a consensual society. "The ideal solution of a conflict . . . [is] not a total victory for one side and a humiliating defeat for the other, but an accommodation by which winner and loser could co-exist without too much loss of face."[69] Labor relations reflect the more general patterns. "Japanese dispute processing structures tend to minimize adversarialness. . . . They parallel Japanese social structure in the sense that they tend to treat people as connected rather than separated, and to encourage solutions that minimize conflict and reduce the probability that relations between disputants will be permanently severed by the dispute."[70] When conflict occurs, persons and groups linked by institutional relationships seek agreement. Majorities do not simply outvote minorities in parliament. Those who can win the vote (pretend to) allow their opponents to influence the final outcome. Japanese politicians, as one once told me, deliberately introduce sections of legislation which they do not want so they can yield them in the final negotiations with the minority opposition. In American election contests, the minority is voted down. The electoral system invariably produces a recognizable winner and loser even when the difference in votes between them is small. The traditional Japanese method, on the other hand, now in the process of being modified in the mid-1990s, has encouraged minority representation by a number of parties via the election of members of parliament representing disparate groups in the same multi-member constituency. But the myth of consensus, the rituals of agreement, remain dominant.[71]

In America, as we have seen, Protestant sectarian moralism helps to produce adversarialness, since political and social controversies are more likely to be perceived as non-negotiable moral issues than as conflicts of material interests which can be compromised. Japanese religious traditions reinforce the need for consensus and compromise. They are synchronistic rather than sectarian. Many Japanese who are both Buddhists and Shintoists pray at the temples of the former and the shrines of the latter. Unlike America, "Japan never possessed a dogmatic religion which makes a sharp distinction between right and wrong. . . . None of . . . [Japan's] religions had a stern, omnipotent

God. . . . In a situation where no one fought for God or against Satan, it was easy to reach an accommodation once the fighting was over."[72]

The varying consequences of a society which stresses obligation to groups as a major virtue and one which emphasizes individual success and rights are also reflected in the sharply different rates of crime. In America, as noted, the emphasis is on winning, by fair means if possible and foul if necessary. The Japanese crime rate is much lower than the American on a per capita basis. As a result, while Americans worry about walking the streets of their cities, "Japan is one of the few major nations—perhaps the only one—where one can walk the streets of its large cities late at night and feel in no danger."[73] The serious crime rate in the United States is over four times the total crime rate of Japan. Only .98 per 100,000 of the Japanese population were murder victims in 1994, compared with 9.3 Americans; for rape, the variations were 1.5 and 42.8. The data were even more striking for robbery: 1.75 cases per 100,000 population in Japan, contrasted with 255.8 in the United States, while for larceny the differences were much less, 1,526 and 3,103.[74] As with other measures, European crime rates fall in between.[75] As Hamilton and Sanders note: "Japan and the United States occupy the opposite poles in the distribution of violent and property crimes among the major capitalist countries."[76]

The trans-Pacific rates are not converging. Between 1960 and 1995, they increased greatly in the United States for homicide and larceny, while in Japan they fell for murder and remained constant for larceny.[77] In 1995, in proportionate terms, thirteen times as many Americans were in prison as in Japan, a gap which has been growing. Japan has a much smaller police force, about 68 percent the size of America's in per capita terms, and many fewer lawyers.[78]

There is a frequent and much exaggerated reference to the enormous difference between the number of lawyers in the two countries, allegedly 13,000 in Japan and around 800,000 in the United States. The second figure is correct. America has one third of the world's practicing attorneys; but the first refers only to *bengoshi,* who are the licensed litigators (barristers) handling "only a small part of Japan's lawyering." In fact, the country has about "125,000 suppliers of legal services," including all sorts of specialized persons dealing with particular aspects of law, and "in-house corporate legal staffs filled with law graduates who never bothered to pass the bar exam."[79] Adjusting for these results shows a difference of three to one, 312 lawyers per 100,000 for the United States and 102 for Japan.[80] There are many fewer tort cases in Japan. As a result, the "tort tax" on business and the professions is much lower across the Pacific. It is estimated that "liability-loss payments in America totalled $117 billion in 1987, about 2.5% of the GNP. Japan's cost was eight times less, about 0.3%."[81]

The vast differences have been explained by variations in structures, rules, and culture, though the first two are in large part an outgrowth of the third. As a postrevolutionary new society, the United States has lacked the traditional mechanisms of social control and respect for authority that mark cultures "based on traditional obligations which were, or had been, to some extent mutual."[82] The American emphasis on individualism has therefore been associated with the universalistic cash nexus and legally enforceable contractual agreements, a pattern which in comparative terms has continued to the present. Agreements among business firms are spelled out in much less detail in Japan than in America. Contracts are not written in anticipation of possible future litigation. It is assumed that if conditions change so as to benefit one party against the other, the two will modify the agreement, including adjustments in price. The Japanese "prefer mediation. Even when suits are brought before a court, the judges prefer to use conciliation in order to avoid humiliating the loser."[83] Legal informality, rather than litigiousness, characterizes the Japanese approach to law.[84] On the other hand, the United States' legal-rational culture has resulted in a very much higher rate of litigation. Tocqueville stressed the contractual and litigious character of Americans in the 1830s, and over 150 years later, John Haley writes: "In no other industrial society is legal regulation as extensive or coercive as in the United States or as confined and as weak as in Japan."[85]

Japan has relied much more than the United States on informal mechanisms of social control—the sense of shame or loss of face, not only for individuals but for their families and other groups with which they are closely identified, including business. An Australian criminologist, John Braithwaite, explains the uniquely low rate of crime in Japan as a product of the "cultural traditions of shaming wrongdoers, including an effective coupling of shame and punishment."[86] The anthropologist George DeVos concludes that "most social evidence points toward the greater continuing influence of informal social control and social cohesion within the Japanese groups than is found within their western counterparts."[87] As a 1995 *New York Times* article notes: "The value of good behavior, of fitting into a common society, is drummed into [Japanese] children from the moment they set off to first grade in identical school uniforms." Should someone exhibit criminal behavior, the judicial system emphasizes making the offender feel remorse, fostering a societal environment where crime is not to be tolerated. In prisons, offenders are "sometimes kept in tiny, individual cells, and at times they are barred from talking to one another or even looking at one another."[88] And even after completing their sentences, paying their debt to society, Japanese criminals typically face ostracism from their families and friends. An earlier 1983 survey of the opinions of national samples of 10–15-year-olds, which inquired about various socially disapproved activities, found only 28 percent of the Japanese children admitting to such behavior, in contrast to 80 percent of the Americans.

Behavioral as well as attitudinal data show that Japanese have been much less prone to violate traditional norms with respect to marital continuity than Americans, even though the proportions voicing discontent with the relationship are similar. Opinion poll data from the 1980s show Japanese much more opposed to divorce than Americans. The cross sections of mothers of teenagers were asked whether they believed that "a man and a wife, even if they want a divorce, should consider their children's future and remain married." The question yielded overwhelming majority responses in both countries, but in opposite directions. Almost three quarters of those in Japan said they should stay married, while three fifths, 61 percent, in the United States chose the option of divorce.[89] The divorce rate, as of 1992, was much lower in Japan, 1.53 per 1,000, than in the United States, 4.80 per 1,000.[90] As William Goode emphasizes, "by Western standards, it remains low."[91]

Comparative surveys indicate that the Japanese are much more consciously committed to following the rules or customs than innovating, while Americans take the opposite tack. In 1978, cross sections interviewed for the Japanese National Character studies in both countries were asked to respond to the following question:

> If you think a thing is right, do you think you should go ahead and do it even if it is contrary to usual custom, or do you think you are less apt to make a mistake if you follow custom?
> 1. Go ahead even if contrary
> 2. Depends
> 3. Follow custom

Fully three quarters, 76 percent, of the Americans replied "go ahead" even if you have to violate traditional custom, as compared to less than one third, 30 percent, of the Japanese. Even when the issue does not involve illegitimate or socially disapproved activities, Japanese prefer to adhere to the rules, while Americans will innovate.[92]

Americans are much more likely than Japanese to say they will do anything necessary to get ahead individually. A majority of the former, 52 percent, agreed in 1989 that "I will do whatever I can in order to succeed," compared to only 14 percent of the latter. Comparable differences were reported for the responses to the statement: "I want to be successful no matter how much pain might be involved in doing so." Over three fifths, 63 percent, of the Americans and more than one third, 36.5 percent, of the Japanese agreed.[93]

WORK AND THE ECONOMY
—

Although a highly urbanized industrial nation, Japan retains many of the informal practices, norms, and client relationships of manorial societies.[94] Companies, particularly large ones, are obligated to their employees, for example, to keep them employed, and to establish pension funds, and are quite paternalistic in ways that range from arranging marriages to school placement for employee offspring. The "corporation is a social unit in which everyone has a role and a stake."[95] Ideally, boards of directors are not supposed to emphasize the maximization of profits. "Many senior Japanese managers . . . feel at least as obligated to the workers as to the owners of the corporation."[96]

Employees are expected to be loyal to their companies. And as indicated in Table 7-2, the survey evidence confirms the generalization that employees in Japan are much less prone to shift jobs than in America.[97] The comparative study of managers found that 59 percent of Japanese and only *one* percent of Americans agreed that if they applied for a job with a company, "I will most certainly work there for the rest of my life."[98] These cross-national variations have also held up among the three samples of youth, with no change occurring between 1977 and 1988. Close to three quarters, 72 percent, of the Japanese said they were still on their first job, a reply given by only one quarter, 24 percent, of the Americans. Almost a third of the Americans reported having held four or more positions; only one percent of the Japanese did the same.[99]

Some analysts challenge the belief that prolonged employment and low separation rates in Japan have cultural components by the contention "that life-time employment is only a large-firm phenomenon."

TABLE 7-2. ESTIMATES OF THE NUMBER OF JOBS HELD BY MALES OVER A LIFETIME IN JAPAN AND THE UNITED STATES

	ALL JOBS			
	OECD		HASHIMOTO-RAISIAN	
	JAPAN	UNITED STATES	JAPAN	UNITED STATES
Age Group	1977	1981	1977	1978
16–19	0.54	1.07	0.72	2.00
20–24	1.19	2.54	2.06	4.40
25–29	1.54	3.69	2.71	6.15
30–34	1.75	4.57	3.11	7.40
35–39	1.92	5.35	3.46	8.30
40–44	2.05	5.98	4.21	10.25
45–49	2.15	6.45	4.91	10.95
50–54	2.26	6.90	—	11.15
55–64	2.62	7.50	—	11.16

Source: OECD Employment Outlook, September 1984, p. 63. Masanori Hashimoto and John Raisian, "Employment Tenure and Earning Profiles in Japan and the United States," American Economic Review, 75 (September 1985), p. 724, as reprinted in Masahiko Aoki, Information, Incentives and Bargaining in the Japanese Economy (Cambridge: Cambridge University Press, 1988), p. 61.

In fact, however, research by Masanori Hashimoto and John Raisian and also by Robert Cole indicates that although job tenure "is longer in large Japanese firms, it is quite long even in the tiny and small firms," and much longer in all size groups than in American ones.[100] And although mandatory retirement age is 60, the age at which guaranteed job security ends, many Japanese workers continue to work for the same employer—but often with fewer benefits and responsibilities.[101] International comparisons of the labor force participation rate by age show that at age "65 and over," Japanese participation (at 38%) far exceeds the United States rate (16%).[102]

The recession of the early 1990s forced many Japanese companies to tighten their belts. The unemployment rate of 3.5 percent in 1995 is the highest since the post-war growth cycle began, up from 2.2 in 1992, 1.9 in 1975 and 2.6 in 1985.[103] Thus far (1995) they have not broken the obligation to retain long-term employees, but they have cut back sharply on hiring new potential executive talent and have laid off female employees, many of whom have always been looked on as "temporary," until they married.

Japanese clearly exhibit much stronger ties to their employers than

Americans do. Cross-national interviews with samples of male workers in 1960 and 1976 found that the proportions who said that they thought of their company as "the central concern in my life and of greater importance than my personal life," or as "a part of my life at least equal in importance to my personal life," were much greater in Japan than in the United States in both years and increased in absolute terms in Japan. The combined percentages for the company commitment responses, in surveys taken sixteen years apart, were 65 moving up to 73 percent for Japanese workers, compared to 29 declining to 21 percent for the Americans. The Americans were much more likely to choose other categories defining their relations to their employers in instrumental terms, that is, as less important than their personal lives. Seemingly, the Japanese changed toward favoring a deeper involvement with their company, while the Americans became even less enamored of such a stance over the decade and a half between the two surveys.[104]

Varying emphases toward particularism in economic life are evident in the responses to 1978 surveys in both countries, which indicated that Japanese were much more likely than Americans to prefer a work supervisor who "looks after you personally in matters not connected with work," by 87 to 50 percent. The alternative formulation, favoring someone who "never does anything for you personally in matters not connected with work," was endorsed by 10 percent of the Japanese and 47 percent of the Americans.[105] The difference in particularistic expectations about the role of supervisors is brought out most strongly in the responses by samples of male workers in 1960 and again in 1976 to the question, "when a worker wishes to marry, I think his (her) supervisor should [pick from four alternatives]." Close to three quarters, 71–74 percent, of the Americans chose the category, "not to be involved in such a personal matter," as contrasted to 7 going down to 5 percent of the Japanese. The dominant answer of the latter, 66 percent moving up to 80, was "offer personal advice to the worker if requested," an answer given by 20 percent descending to 15 of the Americans.[106] Similar cross-national differences are reported by the World Youth Surveys when they inquired in 1972, 1983, and 1988: "Suppose you work under a superior, do you think it is a good idea to have social contact with him after hours?" The percentage replying, "No" changed slightly from 25.5 to 28 among the Japanese, a response given by a much larger segment of Americans, 42 to 46 percent.[107] Japanese workers are in fact much more likely to socialize "outside of work" with their supervisors and managers, as well as with co-workers.[108]

The continued Japanese preference for particularistic relations is also exhibited in the reactions to a question posed in 1973 and 1978 asking them to choose between working for a firm which "paid good wages, but where they did nothing like organizing outings and sports days for the employees' recreation" and a "firm with a family-like atmosphere which organized outings and sports days, even if the wages were a little bit less." The Japanese respondents to both surveys over-whelmingly chose the particularistic alternative, even if it involved less pay, by 74 percent in 1973 and 78 percent in 1978.[109] Japanese executives (50%) were much more likely than Americans (21%) to feel that in determining compensations, "a company should take into account the size of the employee's family," as compared to believing that "an employee should be paid on the basis of the work he is doing for the company ... [which] does not have to take into account the employee's family."[110]

The Japanese, to reiterate, are more loyal to their employers than are Americans.[111] A review of the relevant behavioral evidence of the early eighties documented the generalization that "Japanese workers put in more time on the job per week than American workers ... unexcused absenteeism is generally so low as to seem nonexistent; strike activity is lower in Japan than in the U.S. . . . and unions cooperate with management in achieving corporate goals and in carrying out company pro-grams. . . ."[112] Since 1992, however, the workweek differential has van-ished as American industry has become "leaner" to be competitive, although the other generalizations still held up.[113]

Studies of leisure and family involvements, both attitudinal and behavioral, agree that the Japanese devote less time than Americans to leisure pursuits and are more disposed to emphasize work over leisure or home life generally. Thus James Lincoln and Arne Kalleberg found "only 35 percent of our Japanese sample (vs. 70 percent of the Ameri-cans) rate family life as more important than work responsibilities."[114] The Japanese (49%) were also more likely than Americans (28%) to agree with the statement: "Employees shouldn't take time off when things are busy, even though they have a right to take time off."[115] A 1980 NHK (the public broadcasting system) survey found more than a quarter, 27 percent, of Americans gave the highest priority to leisure activities, while 18 percent of Japanese did. The World Youth Survey reported that when asked in 1977, 1983, and 1988, "Which do you find more worthwhile, work or something else?" two thirds, 67–71 per-cent, in the United States replied something other than work, as com-pared to around half, 49–57 percent, of those in Japan.[116]

A survey-based comparison by the Leisure Development Center of Japan in 1989 of work and leisure in seven developed nations noted that the Japanese work the most and have the least time off. Two out of three Japanese employees worked more than 45 hours a week; in every other country surveyed, the majority of workers spent less than 45 hours per week at their jobs. "The American figure [for more] is 42.5 percent. As for weekend holidays, the most common pattern in Japan is one day off, and less than 20% of workers have two-day weekends every week. On the other hand . . . 68% of Americans are assured two-day weekends every week."[117] Not surprisingly, "leisure participation is comparatively low in Japan. Japan was last in 23—or more than half—of the [42 leisure activity] categories."[118]

The United States is not an outlier in these respects. In 1994, *The Economist* reported that behaviorally, Americans are now close to the Japanese pattern and well ahead of the citizens of the European Union in average number of working hours per year, 1,945 for the United States, 2,017 for Japan, and 1,771 for the European Union.[119] Americans appear significantly more work-oriented than Europeans for every country, still reflecting their Protestant sectarian origins.

Although Japanese groups and firms are intensely competitive, individuals within them are not expected to be—nor do they want to be—in overt rivalries with colleagues in seeking to get ahead. Promotion and salary increases within Japanese firms tend much more to be a function of seniority than in American ones, even among white-collar employees and executives.[120] Seniority is even more important and strictly respected within the civil service, where political appointees do not intervene in personnel matters.[121] Chie Nakane points out: "In the West, merit is given considerable importance, while in Japan the balance goes the other way. In other words, in Japan in contrast to other societies, the provisions for the recognition of merit are somewhat weaker, and the social order is institutionalized largely by means of seniority."[122] When national cross sections of employed young adults (18 to 24 years of age) were asked in 1977, 1983, and 1988 for their preferred basis for promotions and pay increases, an average of 80 percent of the Americans favored giving more weight to performance than seniority, compared to 36 percent of the Japanese. Preference for seniority basically stayed constant from 1977 to 1988 at 46 to 44 percent among the Japanese and 16 to 15 percent for the American youth.[123]

The two World Values Surveys conducted in 1981–82 and 1990–91 also found that Americans are much more likely than Japanese to believe in merit pay; more of the latter are inclined to pay the same to all in a given type of work. Thus in the first survey, as noted in chapter Four, when asked whether a secretary who "is quicker, more efficient and more reliable at her job" should be paid more than one of the same age who does less, over four fifths of the Americans, 82 percent, said pay the more useful one more, compared to 68 percent of the Japanese.[124] The American support for merit basically stayed the same a decade later, while the Japanese actually fell to 48 percent. A second question, presented in 1990, asked respondents whether "there should be greater incentives for individual effort," or should "incomes be made more equal." As in the response to the earlier query, the Americans favor greater emphasis on "incentives" by 59 percent to 29 for the Japanese (top four categories). Not surprisingly, business executives in the two countries differed in a similar fashion. Thus, when asked to express a preference between "Jobs in which no one is singled out for personal honor, but in which every one works together" or "Jobs in which personal initiatives are encouraged and individual initiatives are achieved," almost every American (97%) opted for "individual initiatives," compared to 49 percent of the Japanese.[125]

Individualistic expectations of the American worker, in contrast to the Japanese, are reflected in a comparison of job satisfaction measures taken in 1991 using the "Worldwide Office Environment Index." In response to a question about things workers look for in a job, a large number of U.S. workers said it was very or somewhat true that "I can contribute significantly to my company" (92%), "My job is challenging" (92%), "Management recognizes my contributions" (84%), and "Employees at all levels are encouraged to participate in problem-solving" (78%). The concomitant percentages of Japanese workers who responded similarly were 69 percent, 73 percent, 63 percent, and 51 percent.[126]

Ronald Dore accounts for the conundrum of greater emphasis on equality of result in the more elitist society by suggesting that in Japan, "egalitarianism is a matter of the equal rights of all members of the family to consideration *granted* by the responsible head—viz, in modern terms, responsible elite," in other words, Tories. In America, on the other hand, "egalitarianism is based on the notion of equal rights of free-standing, rights-*asserting* individuals."[127] The difference may also be linked to the greater stress on individualism and competitiveness in the United States (see Appendix pp. 293–296).

Economists and culturally oriented social scientists debate to what extent the much higher savings rate of the Japanese (15% in 1991) compared to Americans (4.9% in 1992) is a function of variations in corporate structures and tax policies or of values.[128] Without trying to challenge the effect of economic and political policies on savings patterns, it may be noted that in the 1990 World Values Survey, the Japanese were more likely than Americans to say that it is especially important that parents should encourage or teach children about "thrift, saving money and things"—by 40 to 28 percent.

Some, though not all, of the comparative survey results dealing with economy-related attitudes appear contradictory. On a subjective verbal level, a number of surveys have found that Japanese are less work-oriented, less satisfied with their jobs, and less positive in feelings about their companies than Americans.[129] James Lincoln and Arne Kalleberg, who have commented on these inconsistencies between behavioral and survey findings, note—correctly, I believe—that there are "cultural biases operating to generate overly positive assessments of work life on the part of American employees and understatements by the Japanese. . . ."[130]

The cultural biases are in part an "apparent manifestation of Japanese collectivism and Western individualism . . . [as in] the tendency for Japanese respondents to give average or non-committal answers, while Anglo-American respondents are somewhat more prone to take strong, even extreme stands on issues. . . ."[131] Ronald Dore suggests that variations in "average personality" also affect cross-national attitudes, such as "a difference on a dimension which has cheerfulness and good-humored complacency at one pole and a worried earnestness and anxious questing for self-improvement on the other." He believes this affects varying propensities to express job satisfaction.[132] Answers to questions about job satisfaction or working hard or ratings of employers are also relative, are affected by conceptions of what hard work means, of expectations about a job or organization, by perceptions about fellow workers or supervisors. It has been argued that it is "precisely because the Japanese subscribe to a strong work ethic that they are less likely to feel that their expectations have been met."[133]

If the Japanese are more reluctant than the Americans to speak in favorable terms to interviewers about their work role and environment, the positive feelings of the former may show up in their response to another question posed in the 1990 World Values Survey as to qualities which it is especially important to impress on children. Almost three fifths, 59 percent, of the Japanese mention "determination, perseverance," compared to 36 percent of the Americans. But it must be noted that the Americans lead in emphasizing "hard work," 48.5 to 31 percent, a response pattern which reiterates the curious reluctance of Japanese to speak in approving terms of work.

Cultural dispositions clearly affect differences in verbal responses. Japanese are not disposed to boasting, to expressing positive judgments about themselves, a trait which extends to groups of which they are part, such as pride in country, an item on which they rank close to the bottom in international comparisons. Kiyoshi Ando, in explaining why "Americans start speeches by cracking jokes, [while] the Japanese do so by apologizing for their lack of information and their inability to live up to the expectations of the audience," notes that the difference reflects the fact that in Japan, "to be modest is considered desirable and to boast of one's accomplishments is regarded as negative." He refers to research which shows that the more advanced elementary school students are, the more likely they are to consider "humble pride or modesty as the hall-mark of a capable person."[134] Americans, conversely, are almost uninhibited in such terms. They lead the world in positive expressions about their own country.[135] In 1991, 77 percent told Gallup, "I am very proud to be an American," and 19 percent said, "quite proud." Only 4 percent responded negatively. Americans also show up as among the most optimistic people in Gallup Polls conducted in thirty countries, while the Japanese are among the least. Polls taken annually near the end of each year from 1959 to 1987, and again in 1990, posed the following question: "So far as you are concerned, do you think [next year] will be better or worse than [last year]?"[136] Even in December 1990, after the recession began, the United States still led, with 48 percent of Americans, compared to only 23 percent of the Japanese, who had not yet entered a recession, replying next year will be better. At the end of 1992, Americans were even more optimistic (61%), while the Japanese were unchanged; 24 percent thought 1993 would be better.

Individualism may also press Americans to give positive responses about satisfaction with job and company, while embeddedness in strong group allegiances reduces the propensity of the Japanese to answer in comparable terms. Since Americans believe in personal choice of jobs, schools, and mates, a response that one does not like his/her situation raises the question: what is wrong with the individual?[137] Why does he/she not quit? Japanese, in contrast, do not have the option to break from a group relationship. If the individual does not like the spouse or company, there is no implication that there is something wrong with the respondent. Hence, Japanese can be much more outspoken about voicing negative feelings than Americans.

In this case, individualism constrains speech; group allegiances liberate it.

Group-oriented commitments are weak in the United States, where the religious tradition, linked to its Puritan origins, emphasizes individualism and personal rights. Bourgeois norms enjoin the same behavior. Americans do not feel obligations, other than familial, if these conflict with the requirements of efficiency or income. They are more disposed than other people to expect individuals to do their best for themselves, not for others.

STATUS PATTERNS

The dominant stratification orientations of the two societies are also quite different. America, as noted, stresses equality of opportunity and equality of respect, but not of income. Tocqueville suggested that Americans believe individuals should give and receive respect because they are human beings. Everyone recognizes that inequality exists, but it is impolite to emphasize it in dealing with others.

In Japan, as the industrialized society most recently derivative from feudalism, hierarchy remains important in defining social relations. Edwin Reischauer has written that no other people place a greater emphasis on status differentiation in social relationships than the Japanese.[138] Living in a relatively collectivist society, Japanese "show much more status consciousness and accept [social] inequality to a greater extent than individualists," such as Americans.[139] Each person and institution has a place in the prestige order. It is generally recognized that medicine everywhere is the most status-conscious occupation. Physicians demand and receive more deference than those in other professions, perhaps because of the concern about health and the consequent need to respect and obey doctors.[140] But the comparative evidence indicates that the Japanese again are outliers in this respect. Stephen Anderson reports that more than in other "advanced industrial societies, physicians in Japan make treatment decisions with little consultation with their patients. Compared to client behavior in the United States, clients in Japan seldom question a physician and are less likely to file cases of malpractice to challenge errors in medical judgment."[141] Conversely, Americans are the most prone to do so.

This concern for status also shows up with respect to education. The comparative surveys of youth aged 18–24 conducted in 1977,

1983, and 1988 found, in response to the questions concerning the factors valued about a college education, that the Japanese were much more likely than their trans-Pacific counterparts to say that "having gone to a top ranking college" should be valued, by an average margin of 25 to 16 percent, while Americans put much more emphasis than Japanese on "school performance and school record," by 39 to 10 percent.[142] The results of a detailed study of the relationship of college status and occupational attainment in Japan and the United States on a mass level challenges the thesis that educational credentialism is greater in Japan than in the United States. However, "when we focus on the process of elite formation, a different picture emerges. *The linkage between the summit of educational stratification and top of the corporate managerial [and civil service] hierarchy appears to be much stronger in Japan than in the United States.*"[143] And Ronald Dore notes that in Japan, the "examination-selected official still has higher prestige than the elected politician."[144] Douglas Kenrick states that Americans "think of civil servants as wielders of red-tape which clogs private enterprise. The Japanese think of them as functionaries who make and implement the rules which make for communal harmony."[145]

Hierarchy is particularly evident in the Japanese use of words, many of which are laden with social-status connotations. Japanese employ different terms in conversations with superiors, equals, and inferiors. In this way, their language is one in which status determines how people talk to each other. When two people meet, they must be able to place one another in order to determine how to interact, although for a brief meeting persons who are unacquainted may use status-neutral terms. A friend of mine, an anthropologist at Stanford, tells of an experience during his stay in Japan as a visiting professor. He invited two Japanese colleagues, who did not know one another, to dinner. They devoted considerable time trying to place each other hierarchically. Not only would this determine the language they used to each other, but even who would walk through the door to the dining room first. My friend could not get them to move to go in to dinner. At last, acting like a hungry, uncouth American, he literally shoved them into the dining room. To those who may think this story is unrepresentative, I submit the observation by Chie Nakane: "In everyday affairs a man who is not aware of relative ranking is not able to speak or even to sit or eat. When speaking, he is always expected to be ready with differentiated, delicate degrees of honorific expressions appropriate to the rank order between himself and the person he is addressing. The English language is inadequate to supply appropriate equivalents in such contexts."[146]

Although both countries are political democracies, the Japanese are more respectful of political leaders, of persons in positions of authority, and less likely to favor protest activities. Americans, on the other hand, tend to be more anti-elitist and suspicious of those in power. George DeVos notes that in Japan, "[a]uthority figures—political, administrative, and familial—are for the most part, granted a degree of respect rare in the United States. . . ."[147] These generalizations are borne out by comparative survey research which indicates that Japanese are more likely than Americans to agree that "if we get outstanding political leaders, the best way to improve the country is for people to leave everything to them, rather than for the people to discuss things among themselves." Both, however, express a low level of "confidence" in their current (1995) crop of politicians. Japanese respect for authority is also evident in the finding that a much greater percentage of them than of Americans feel that parents should support teachers by denying to their child the validity of a story "that his teacher had done something to get himself in trouble," even if the rumor is true.[148]

The Japanese are also less disposed to give verbal support to extra-parliamentary activism, although the behavior of their students during the sixties may have contradicted such statements. The youth surveys conducted in 1972, 1977, 1983, and 1988 found that the Japanese were the least likely among persons aged 18 to 24 in six countries (France, Sweden, the United Kingdom, the United States, and West Germany) to say that if they "are not satisfied with the society," they would "engage in active actions as far as they are legal" to change things—21 percent in 1988, down from 37 in 1972—while the Americans were the most disposed among the six to favor activism, 55 percent falling off from 62. The modal response (39 to 41%) for the Japanese was, "I will use my voting rights but nothing more."[149] A somewhat similar question was posed in the 1990 World Values Survey with comparable cross-national findings. Over three fifths, 61 percent, of the Japanese said they would never take part in a demonstration, while only 38 percent of the Americans would commit themselves not to do so. The latter were consistently more likely to indicate a greater willingness than their trans-Pacific peers to engage in various forms of more militant or even illegal political action. Here is further evidence of the different attitudes of Americans and Japanese (as well as Europeans) to conformity.

GENDER RELATIONS

Gender-linked behavior presents another area in which the United States and Japan continue to vary along the traditional-modern axis, with Japan continuing to maintain its historic values and behavior. Mary Brinton emphasizes that Japan is "a persistent outlier among industrial societies, demonstrating a greater male-female wage differential and more pronounced sex segregation across a range of indicators, including employment status and occupation. . . ."[150] The United States differs from Japan on all of these variables.[151]

Before the recession of the early 1990s, structural changes in the economy forced the Japanese to choose between admitting large numbers of foreign workers, thereby upsetting their traditional aversion to accepting outsiders, or allowing a sizable increase in employed married female labor, thereby undermining the norms defining the relations between the sexes. The Japanese chose to do the latter, although they remained far behind the United States and almost all other industrialized nations in participation by women in the employed labor force.[152] The recession, however, led to a great erosion of the job gains Japanese women had made during the eighties. This reaction could have been anticipated from the findings of the 1990 World Values Survey, which asked respondents to react to the statement: "When jobs are scarce, men have more right to a job than women." The great majority of Americans, 70 percent, disagreed, a sentiment shared by only 23 percent of the Japanese. A 1993 Labor Ministry survey of one thousand companies "found that more than half said they were cutting back in the hiring of women so they could keep hiring male students. . . ." *The New York Times* reported in May 1994 that Japanese "corporate executives said . . . they were not inclined to . . . comply with the country's eight-year old Equal Employment Opportunity Law. . . ." The behavior of Japanese employers during a recession demonstrates that their previous willingness to hire women "had far less to do with a change in national values than with a shortage of workers."[153] Essentially, Japan responded to the economic downswing of the early nineties by cutting back sharply on female employment. Many companies stopped hiring women college graduates.[154]

Japanese values, of course, do change. This is particularly evident in the almost 40 percent decline in the marriage rate in Japan over the past two decades, while the increase in the average age of newlyweds has been greater than in any other society. Marriage rates have changed little in America in recent years, hovering around 15 per 1,000 population, aged 15 to 64, between 1960 and 1991, while dropping from 14.5 to 6 per 1,000 in Japan in the same period.[155] The age of marriage in Japan is the highest in the world.[156] And not surprisingly, the changes in behavior have been paralleled by shifts in attitude. The proportion of Japanese females agreeing with the statement: "Women had better marry because women's happiness lies in marriage," declined from 40 percent in 1972 to 14 percent in 1990.[157] Marriage rates apart, traditional values concerning cross-sex relations and the behavior of single women remain much stronger in Japan. Mary Brinton points out: "Rates of cohabitation [with an unmarried person of the opposite sex] have . . . increased dramatically in the United States, but this trend is scarcely visible in Japan."[158]

Gender relations remain much more traditionally hierarchical, more asymmetrical in Japan than in Western nations, particularly the United States.[159] The traditional male-dominant family is much more characteristic of Japan. Comparative survey data gathered by NHK in 1980 indicate that three fifths of the Japanese think males "have higher analytical ability" than women; most Americans, 72 percent, believe that "by nature there are no differences between men and women." The same NHK study reports that 80 percent of Japanese men and 74 percent of the women say the "husband should have the final deciding voice" in the family, compared to 40 percent of American men and 34 percent of the women. When asked how the household chores should be divided when the husband and wife both work, 90 percent of the Americans said equally between the spouses, a position taken by only slightly over half of the Japanese, including 54 percent of the women.[160] That these cross-national variations in opinions correspond to behavioral differences is evident in Table 7-3 below. In Japan between 1965 and 1990, an unchanging nine tenths or more of the time spent on household chores is spent by women, compared to 79 percent declining to 64 percent in the United States.

Given these cross-national differences, it is not surprising that the Prime Minister's Office multinational Survey of parents of children, which inquired in 1981 whether women should have jobs after marriage or "after childbirth," found that a majority of Americans, 52.5 percent, replied, "Yes, at any time," in contrast to 30 percent of the Japanese.[161] Similarly, the 1990 World Values Survey reports that Japanese are more likely than Americans to agree that "A pre-school child is likely to suffer if his or her mother works," by 70 to 51 percent. The

TABLE 7-3. DISTRIBUTION BETWEEN WOMEN AND MEN OF AVERAGE TIME SPENT PER WEEK IN HOUSEWORK AND CHILD CARE: JAPAN, 1965–90, AND THE UNITED STATES, 1965–86 (PERCENT)

COUNTRY	YEAR	PERCENT SHARE OF:		
		Women	*Men*	*Total*
Japan	1965	92	8	100
	1970	92	8	100
	1975	91	9	100
	1980	91	9	100
	1985	92	8	100
	1990	90	10	100
United States	1965	79	21	100
	1975	75	25	100
	1986	64	36	100

Source: Noriko O. Tsuya, "Work and Family Life in Japan: Changes and Continuities." Unpublished paper, Department of Sociology, Nihon University, Tokyo, 1992, Table 4.

Japanese-conducted international youth surveys reported cross-national differences running in the same direction when they asked respondents to react to the more general statement: "Men should go out to work while women stay home and take care of the house." In each year (1977, 1983, and 1988), the large majority of Americans disagreed by 71, 81, and 81 percent, compared to minorities, albeit increasing ones, of Japanese, 32, 35, and 44 percent, who felt the same way.[162] The Prime Minister's Office also reported that American spouses are much more likely to socialize together than Japanese. The percentages for "eating out" are 48 American, 17 Japanese; for "films and theaters," 40 percent and 7; for "social parties," 37 and 5; and for "travel," 33 and 5.[163]

Polls conducted in 1990 by the Roper Organization and the Dentsu Institute for the Virginia Slims Company in both nations supply further evidence of continued Japanese traditionalism in gender relations.[164] Working females were asked whether "the men you work with really look on you as an equal or not?" American women replied by 59 to 29 percent that they are viewed as equals. The Japanese response pattern was diametrically opposite, with 55 percent of the women saying they are not looked upon as equals and only 31 percent thinking they are. Asked whether women's opportunities are the same as those of men in various job-related areas, American women are much more likely than

Japanese women to perceive equality for salaries—65 to 24 percent; for responsibility—74 to 37 percent; for promotion—60 to 18 percent; and for becoming an executive—49 to 15 percent. These perception differences correspond to variations in national behavioral patterns. In 1990, two fifths, 40 percent, of administrative and managerial positions in the United States were filled by women, up from 27.5 in 1981, as compared to only 7.9 percent in Japan, up from 5.3 in 1981.[165] Clearly, women are gaining more rapidly in America than across the Pacific in the attainment of executive positions. And a report by the Japanese Ministry of Labor shows that "women made up just 1.2 percent of company division managers in 1991, not significantly higher than the figure of 0.8 percent recorded in 1981."[166]

A 1991 survey of mothers of junior high school students in Japan and America found again that women in Japan are much more traditional than their trans-Pacific peers with respect to gender roles of adults and their treatment and expectations for their offspring. Thus over half, 53 percent, of the Japanese mothers agree that "Husbands should work outside and wives should take care of the family," in contrast to 39 percent of the Americans. Similarly, over three fifths, 61 percent, of the American mothers disagree with the statement: "Men are supposed to play a central role and women are supposed to support them," a point of view rejected by less than half, 44 percent, of the Japanese mothers.

Japanese mothers are more disposed than Americans to vary their treatment of siblings according to gender. Just over half the former, in contrast to 38 percent of the latter, say "boys and girls should be raised differently." More specifically, when asked: "What education level do you want your child to achieve?", Americans do not differentiate their expectations for sons and daughters; 83 percent want both to graduate from university. Japanese mothers, on the other hand, vary anticipations according to the sex of their children. Sixty-seven percent want their male offspring to go to university, while only 35 percent wish the same for females.[167]

Cross-national attitudinal and behavioral differences are linked closely. Of the 38 percent of Japanese males who continue their education beyond high school, fully 95 percent attend four-year universities; among the one third of females who are in post-high school studies, "nearly two-thirds . . . go on to junior colleges and the rest enroll in four-year universities."[168] The situation is reversed in the United States, where a larger proportion of college-age women (64%) than of men (55%) are enrolled in tertiary institutions, more or less proportionally distributed by gender in different types of higher education.[169]

Basically, as Mary Brinton has stressed, "a central purpose of women's education in contemporary Japan is preparation for family roles." More education does not lead to "a stronger career orientation." University graduates are less likely to take a job upon graduation than junior college or high school graduates. Conversely, "the primary reason stated for enrollment in higher education among American women in 1980 was job preparation."[170]

The distinctive gender-linked attitudes and behaviors in Japan and America appear to be supported by friendship patterns. Both younger (18–24) and older (65 plus) Japanese are much more likely than comparably aged Americans to say that all of their close friends are of their sex. Among the youth, the ratio of Japanese to Americans to so report is 51 to 10 percent; among the aged, it is 57 to 32 percent. The dropoff between the generations in traditional behavior is clearly much greater in the United States. Over four fifths of American youth report having friends of both genders in 1977, 1983, and 1988; less than half of the Japanese do so, although the percentage has been increasing from 32 percent in 1977 to 49 percent in 1988.[171]

FAMILY RELATIONSHIPS

The family has been an area of considerable change as societies have moved from predominantly rural and small-town environments to industrial and metropolitan ones. There has been a shift everywhere from single-household, multi-generational, stem families to nuclear ones; fertility rates have declined greatly; and the role of parents in arranging marriages has been replaced by an emphasis on love. The United States has been in the forefront of such developments; Japan has been a laggard among industrialized nations, although it too has moved considerably.[172]

Familial relations seemingly reflect the continuity of traditional elements in Japan. In spite of the strains of adjusting to the rapid social change encompassed by the pace of industrialization and urbanization in postwar Japan, the family is more secure there than in the United States. As Nathan Glazer emphasizes, "The Japanese family is undoubtedly changing; but for a developed country it still maintains a remarkable stability, which underlies the stability of the value patterns. . . ."[173] Divorce rates, as noted earlier, are much lower in Japan. Aged parents are more likely to live with or near their off-spring and to receive deference and assistance from them. A 1980 international study of "human values" found 89 percent of a national cross-section of Japanese in favor of adult children living with their parents and older parents residing with a married son or daughter, a position taken by only 25 percent of a comparable sample of Americans. Surveys of the elderly, 65 and older, taken in 1981, 1986, and 1991, found that the majority of the Japanese in each year (59, 58, and 54%) said they wished to always "live together" with their children and grandchildren, compared to very few Americans (6.5, 2.7, and 3.4%).[174] Cross-sections of mothers of teenagers in the two societies, when interviewed in 1983, also varied in their responses to a question concerning their desired relationship with their children in old age. The overwhelming majority of Americans, 87 percent, said they would like to dwell apart from their offspring; 56 percent of the Japanese preferred to be with them. These attitudes correspond to behavior. In the 1980s, three fifths of Japanese 65 years or older were living with relatives, compared to one seventh of similarly aged Americans. The 1981, 1986, and 1991 studies of people aged 65 and over found that in the United States, about four fifths of the "elderly were either living alone or were living alone as couples. In Japan, about 50 percent of the elderly interviewed were living with children. . . ." Even more strikingly, the data showed that "roughly 35 percent of the Japanese are living in three [adult] generation households against [almost] no Americans."[175] Conversely, during the 1980s, 30.4 percent of Americans 65 years of age or older were living by themselves, as contrasted to 8.6 percent of elderly Japanese. Comparative research finds that "except in Japan, the one-person household has shown the most rapid growth of all household types since 1960."[176]

These findings reinforce the conclusion put forth in 1992 by Junko Matsubara that Japanese society basically "recognizes families as basic social units and disregards individualists who desire to live alone." An unmarried freelance writer in her mid-forties, Matsubara was told by landlords she was unqualified to rent an apartment by herself.[177] Grown children among the Japanese are more disposed to remain with their parents in the (physically small) family households than Americans, who generally live in much larger dwelling units. Surveys of 18- to 24-year-old Japanese youth report that from 79 percent in 1977 to 83 percent in 1988 were residing with parents, compared to 59 percent to 62 percent of the same age group of Americans.[178] The differences are particularly strong for women, in spite of the great changes in Japanese marital patterns.[179]

THE PERPETUATION OF TRADITION

The argument has frequently been made that to develop economically, less developed countries must become modern, individualistic, and meritocratic. In other words, they must come to resemble America. Even Marxists, writing in a period when the United States was perceived as the great capitalist success (not yet the great capitalist villain), saw America as the equivalent of modernity.

The Japanese elites were able to employ the country's traditions in ways that made industrialization possible. They were able to use religion, since pre-Meiji beliefs contained elements that encouraged rationally oriented work and economic behavior. Robert Bellah concludes that Japanese economic development was causally linked to its Buddhist and Confucian heritages.[180] Shinto, one of the country's two major faiths, is older than most Western religions and helped to legitimate the Meiji transformation. Traveling around Japan, one can see business people enter Shinto shrines and clap to get the attention of the local god, the god of a river, of aviation, of a district. They are practicing a form of the same animist or shamanist religion that existed in the pagan Western past and persists today in tribal societies.[181]

Religion everywhere tends to institutionalize values and practices from previous eras. As Weber emphasized, traditionalism in the form of religion helped to modernize America and facilitated the development of a competitive capitalist society. The same Protestant sects which fostered individualism and rational market behavior also sustained many values and beliefs derived from the preindustrial history of Western societies. Americans form the most devout population in the West, as we saw in chapter Two.

The Japanese, of course, not being Christians, cannot be expected to accept biblical teachings, but in any case they are much less religious than Americans. The three youth surveys report that, over an eleven-year period, more than 90 percent of Americans said they believe religion should be important in their life (41–47% "very important," 45–46 "somewhat"), contrasted to around two fifths of Japanese (6–10 percent "very," 31–35 "somewhat").[182] The 1990 World Values Survey found 79 percent of Americans and only 17 percent of Japanese reporting religion as an important value. It is interesting to note that similar differences showed up when the responses of a national cross-section of Japanese were compared with those of a sample of Japanese Americans in Hawaii, both taken at the beginning of the 1970s. For example, only 31 percent of the Japanese said they had a personal religious faith, compared to 71 percent of the Hawaiian Japanese.[183]

The lesser religiosity of the Japanese may explain the poll findings that they are more permissive or liberal with respect to sexuality-related issues. Americans are more likely than Japanese to say that married people should never have an affair, by 79 to 57 percent.[184] They are 10 percent less likely than Americans to believe that "pre-marital sexual intercourse is immoral," and 14 percent more disposed to agree that "legal abortions should be available to women who choose to have them."[185] Even more strikingly and logically, the Japanese are more likely to believe that "what is good and evil depends entirely on the circumstances of our time" than European and American Christians (see chapter Two, Table 2-2), who give more emphasis to guidelines, with Americans showing the greatest differences.

Various students of American values cited in chapter One have concluded that, as in Japan, there has been little change over time in the key characteristics of American culture. For the most part, this judgment is premised on the assumption that the United States was "born modern"; that values like universalism, egalitarianism, individualism, and an emphasis on meritocracy were present from the beginning of the republic.[186] However, the European postfeudal societies, with their earlier stress on hierarchy, particularism, and ascription (hereditary status), while remaining different from America, changed greatly to meet what some believe are the functional requirements of industrial society. But Japan, as we have seen, has modernized economically while retaining many traditional ways which have declined in most of postfeudal Europe.

The United States, like Japan, contradicts the assumption that the emergence of a developed urban economy necessarily undermines tradition. Most Americans still adhere to pre-modern religious beliefs. In some ways, therefore, as Alan Wolfe has emphasized, America is a more traditional society than Western Europe, or even Japan.[187] Public opinion studies conducted since World War II in the United States attest to the strength of ancient sacred traditions, which are much stronger in America than in almost all other Christian countries.

The supposedly greater commitment of the Japanese to traditional ways of life, such as choosing to live in small towns, also did not appear when samples in both countries were asked in the late 1970s by Gallup

International about preferences for community of residence. The Americans turned out to be more wedded to older models. Close to three fifths (56%) of those interviewed in the United States stated they would like to live in rural areas or in a small town of up to ten thousand persons, as compared to only a quarter (27%) of the Japanese. Although the Japanese are closer in time (generations) to residence in small communities and although many now have to live in highly congested urban conditions, 36 percent said they would prefer to live in a large city, while only 13 percent of the Americans expressed the same choice.

Antagonism to big cities in America has been linked for many decades to an image of these communities as centers of moral corruption, sin, and irreligion, an image held by fundamentalists and evangelical Protestants. As Earl Raab and I documented, such views have given rise to anti-modernist and anti-urban movements from the Anti-Masonic Party of the 1820s and 1830s through the Know-Nothing American Party movement of the 1850s, the Ku Klux Klan of the 1920s, and the more recent right-wing religious linked groups, of whom the most publicized have been the Moral Majority of the 1970s and 1980s and the Christian Coalition of the 1990s.[188]

On a completely secular level, the American refusal, discussed in chapter Three, to give up the ancient systems of measurement in favor of the metric system is another illustration of an American attachment to established ways. By the criterion of measurement units, America (and Britain) are more traditional than Japan. But the latter, as noted earlier, insists on retaining an equally dysfunctional approach to street names and numbers.

Another major pattern in the United States which involves the perpetuation, even the extension, of traditional behavior is ethnicity. Until recently, most scholars of this topic agreed that ethnicity reflected the conditions of traditional society, in which people lived in small communities isolated from one another and mass communications and transportation were limited or nonexistent. They expected that industrialization, urbanization, and the spread of education would reduce ethnic consciousness, that universalism would replace particularism.

But as we have seen in chapter Four, this generalization is still problematic in the United States, not to speak of various European countries. However, the image of the universalistic American "melting pot" would appear to be validated by intermarriage statistics, which indicate that majorities of Catholics, Jews, Italians, Irish, and Japanese Americans marry out of their ancestral groups. But the rise of minority ethnic and racial consciousness has resulted in a deprecation of the melting pot as the image of the future of American ethnicity, particularly by intellectuals and the ideological left, in favor of the goal of an ethnically pluralist society that seeks to preserve various national origin groups—blacks, Asian Americans, Hispanics, Jews, and so on.[189] The emphasis on universalism has declined in political discourse, while particularism—described by some as multiculturalism—has become more important. But these discussions and proposals have little impact on mass behavior. The "melting pot" remains as appropriate an image as ever. Japan clearly is much more particularistic and race-conscious.

MODERNITY AND CONSERVATISM

The belief that Japan is a peculiar exception to the assumption that economic development necessitates a shift from tradition to modernity, because it retains major aspects of the value systems associated with feudalism, is clearly invalid. Every industrial country is a combination of tradition and modernity. As Weber, Reischauer, and Bellah have suggested, development in the Western sense is an outgrowth of certain traditions that fostered rational economic behavior, elements present more strongly in Northern Europe, North America, Japan, and Confucian East Asia than in other parts of the world. The new is introduced as an outgrowth of the right combination of the old. The strains of social change, of adjusting to new forms of behavior, of rejecting the old, can only be reduced if societies are able to link the new with the old, if they maintain considerable elements from previous stages of development. Not all cultures, however, have equally usable cultural elements.

Tatsuzo Suzuki draws conclusions from examining the responses to five Japanese National Character surveys conducted over a quarter of a century which apply to some degree to the United States and other developed countries.

> First, the processes of social change did not bring about a total disappearance of a "traditional" outlook, to be replaced by a "modern" outlook. Despite all the changes in the postwar era, the systems of values in Japan have continued to provide culturally legitimate and meaningful outlets for different ideas.
>
> Second, large-scale institutional changes may occur without drastic

shifts in the systems of attitudes. In fact, in view of the Japanese experience, we are inclined to argue that it is precisely the relative stability in the systems of beliefs which allows institutional changes to take place, for example in the areas of economics and politics, without major social dislocations.[190]

The Japanese differ from Americans and most Western Europeans in having done much more to plan their economic development. One of the reasons they were able to do this was that they were latecomers on the industrial scene and were pushed into modernizing by the desire to prevent being colonized. The Meiji elite sought to maintain what was truly Japanese, to restore the status of the emperor, and at the same time to become an industrial power. The United States was fortunate in having the right combination of a different set of traditional values to make efficient use of its economic resources. It is important to note that the great Japanese postwar reforms (e.g., land reform, democratization, demilitarization, the elimination of the peerage) were legitimated by the same mechanism as in the Meiji Restoration, the emperor's approval. Those most upset by the changes were the most bound to the emperor. General MacArthur played out the classic role of a controlling shogun standing behind the emperor, but by doing so he helped preserve much of the older traditions. More than a quarter of a century earlier Winston Churchill had urged a similar role for the German Kaiser, arguing that by retaining him the Allies would avoid the alienation of the right wing and the military from the new German democracy.

From a perspective of the diverse indicators of "traditionalism" discussed here, Japan and America appear more traditional than most West European and Australasian cultures, despite being as or more modern or developed technologically. If the ability to maintain traditionalism is linked to or identified with conservatism, then both are also conservative cultures.

"Conservatism" tends to be a political term, and from a political perspective both are conservative. As we have seen, America is exceptional in its lack of an important labor or socialist party. Japan does have a viable socialist party, which as of 1995 is part of a governing coalition with the much larger Liberal Democrats. The prime minister, Tomiichi Murayama, is a Socialist. In 1985, the Socialists explicitly gave up adherence to Marxism and the doctrine of class struggle, a change typical of many of the world's left parties, a position they have enlarged in the mid-nineties. Class solidarity, as reflected in trade union strength as of 1995, is also weaker in both countries than else-where, albeit with a much smaller percentage of the non-agricultural labor force organized in the United States, 16, than in Japan, 25.[191] Membership is declining in both. In recent years, commentators have been wont to emphasize the fact that 90 percent of the Japanese iden-tify themselves as "middle class," rather than "upper" or "lower," as evi-dence that the country has become uniquely classless. The interpreta-tion is wrong. Americans and Europeans distribute themselves similarly when responding to this question. All these answers mean is that few people will choose to say they are sufficiently privileged to be in the upper class, or that they belong to the invidiously labeled "lower class." When faced with further choices which include "working class," 53 percent select this option in Japan, compared to 45 percent in the United States; only 29 percent of the former put themselves in the "middle," again less than the 38 percent of Americans who do the same.[192]

The meaning of "conservatism," of course, is quite different in the two societies. In America, it involves support of laissez-faire, anti-sta-tist doctrines, which correspond to bourgeois-linked classical liberal-ism. In Jefferson's words, "that government governs best which governs least." In Japan, as in postfeudal Europe, conservatives have been asso-ciated with the defense of the alliance between state and religion (i.e., throne and altar), the maintenance of elitist values, and extensive reliance on government to further economic and social purposes. Aris-tocratic monarchical conservatives (Tories) have favored a strong state. From Meiji onwards, this meant a powerful state bureaucracy and politicians who consciously planned the use of national resources to enhance growth and, in prewar times, military power. The business community, insofar as it took independent stances, was more classi-cally liberal, more supportive of laissez-faire, and less militaristic than the aristocracy, but it was weak politically.

In Europe, aristocratic, agrarian-based conservatism, which favored a strong state, fostered the *noblesse oblige* communitarian values of the nobility, disliked the competitive, materialistic values and behavior of the capitalists, and introduced the welfare state into Germany and Britain. The socialists, when they emerged, also favored a powerful state and extensive welfare programs, as well as democratization of the polity. In Japan, the conservative postfeudal impulse led, as we have seen, to state guidance of the economy; but, unlike Europe, the emphasis on *noblesse oblige* and communitarianism has been expressed more within the confines of private institutions, in the obligations of firms for their employees (lifetime employment, company-provided annuity payments), what Ronald Dore calls "welfare corporatism," than in state institutions.[193] Hence, direct state payments for welfare have been lower in Japan than anywhere else in the developed world.

America and Japan have made important moves in the extension of the welfare benefits, but they remain at the bottom on the international list of Organization for Economic Development (OECD) nations for levels of taxation generally and spending for welfare purposes particularly. In 1992, Japan and the United States ranked last in a six-nation comparison of ratios of social security benefits (medical care, pensions, other) to national income: Japan (15%), United States (16.6%), United Kingdom (21.9%), West Germany (27.5%), France (34.1%), and Sweden (46.5%).[194] It should be noted that Japan uses the private sector in ways that do not occur in the United States, for example, to provide universal health insurance or benefit packages. Hence, there is much more private communitarianism in Japan than in America, even though a comparison of public welfare supports would suggest otherwise. Still, when presented in 1990 by the World Values Survey with a choice between the classical liberal or Tory-socialist positions in the form of a ten-point scale, running from "Individuals should take more responsibility for providing for themselves" to "The state should take more responsibility to ensure that everyone is provided for," the two countries were outliers among the developed countries. Over half, 55 percent, of the Japanese placed themselves on the Tory-statist side of the scale, while only 17 percent chose individual responsibility. Conversely, fully 70 percent of the Americans, inheritors of an anti-statist, individualistic value system, favored individualism, while 14 percent answered that the state should be responsible. Although both countries have private insurance rather than state coverage for health care, their employee benefit systems differ greatly, reflecting these differences in national values. As Tomoni Kodama of the Japanese Ministry of Health notes:

> The U.S. structure of employee benefits seems to be based on diversity and individualism. Companies have a real choice in selecting and planning their employee benefit system. . . .
>
> [T]he structure of Japanese employee benefits is equity and uniformity for everyone. The Japanese priority has been to assure equal access to benefits for everyone. . . . [I]n order to provide equal access to all employees, health insurance is strictly regulated across the board by Japanese government. In other words, employees of a small company on the verge of bank-

ruptcy are provided basically the same coverage as employees of a well-known big company such as Honda or Toyota. . . . The same type of equity and uniformity is more or less a common feature among other Japanese employee benefits such as pension plans and health care.

As a result . . . it is not the companies but the central government that has consistently taken the key role in planning and implementing the employee benefit system.[195]

Until 1993, Japan had a conservative government throughout its postwar decades of economic growth and prosperity, one, however, whose business-related Liberal Democratic administration responded quite differently to the recession of the early nineties than the American Republican one under George Bush. The former tried to improve the economy by Keynesian pump-priming policies, including "more public investments to boost the economy . . . public works and housing. . . . [A]n additional ¥1.12 trillion will be allocated to public funds for investment in stocks. This is separated from the ¥10.7 trillion stimulus . . . [most of which] will be spent on public works and housing. . . . Economic Planning Agency officials [announced] . . . 'the package will fill the gap between demand and supply in the economy. . . .' "[196] The Republican regimes of the 1980s and early 1990s, and even the subsequent Democratic Clinton administration, would oppose comparable policies for the United States as too leftist. As of 1995, the Japanese government remains centralized; its bureaucracy and politicians continue, as under Meiji, to strongly influence general economic policies, although its new Socialist-led but predominantly LDP coalition government has announced it will relax controls a bit. The American rejects proposals for a state-coordinated "industrial policy," although the Clinton Democrats use the term in suggesting a much more moderate version than the Japanese one. In Japan, the big business sector is still trying to adhere to a *noblesse oblige* sense of obligation to employees, but the recession of the early nineties forced companies to press employees to take early retirement. Feudal or postfeudal values continue to penetrate Japanese life and economy in ways that are largely absent from the American.

Japan has a relatively strong Socialist Party, a much weaker, more moderate (social democratic) Democratic Socialist Party, and a fairly radical small Communist Party. Their combined vote has ranged up and down between 36 percent in 1958 and 32 percent in 1990, while such tendencies have almost no electoral support in the United States.

Further evidence that the variations in political orientation and social policies between Japan and America are linked to basic differences in orientation toward individualism and equality, which occur even when class position is held constant, may be found in the first 1981–82 World Values Survey, which asked respondents to choose between two statements:

Q—Here are two opinions about conditions existing in our country. Which one do you happen to agree with?

A—There is too much emphasis upon the principle of equality. People should be given the opportunity to choose their own economic and social life according to their individual abilities.

B—Too much liberalism has been producing increasingly wide differences in people's economic and social life. People should live more equally.

The Japanese have been very much more disposed to favor equality than individual competition, as reiterated by the data reported in Table 7-4. Commitment to meritocracy presumes a competitive race for position and great reward for the successful.

The second World Values Survey did not include the individualism-equality question, but it repeated one requesting respondents to choose between statements emphasizing freedom or equality. As might be expected, in both years Americans were more likely than Japanese to opt for freedom over equality.[197]

TABLE 7-4. ATTITUDES TOWARD INDIVIDUALISM AND EQUALITY IN JAPAN AND THE UNITED STATES (PERCENT)

	JAPAN		AMERICA	
	Individualism	*Equality*	*Individualism*	*Equality*
TOTAL	25	71	56	32
SOCIAL CLASS				
High	47	53	62	33
Upper middle	38	59	61	26
Middle	25	72	58	31
Lower middle	22	75	49	43
Low	13	80	56	20

Source: Adapted from Elizabeth H. Hastings and Philip K. Hastings, eds., Index to International Public Opinion, 1980–1981 (Westport, CT: Greenwood Press, 1982), p. 519; "Survey in Thirteen Countries of Human Values," Leisure Development Center, Tokyo, October 1–5, 1980.

TABLE 7-5. ATTITUDES TOWARD FREEDOM AND EQUALITY IN JAPAN AND THE UNITED STATES (PERCENT)

	JAPAN		AMERICA	
	1980–81	*1990–91*	*1980–81*	*1990–91*
Agree with Freedom	44	46	74	70.5
Agree with Equality	39	38	23	24

Source: Adapted from Ronald Inglehart, 1991 World Values Survey (Ann Arbor, MI: Institute for Social Research, 1991).

The data in Table 7-5 point up the greater emphasis in American culture than in Japanese on individual freedom. Seemingly there was little change in Japan over the decade of the eighties, while the very high commitment in the United States for the "freedom" choice may have moved down slightly, though it remained the opinion of the large majority.

CONCLUSION

The United States and Japan follow different organizing principles. National traditions continue to inform the cultures, economies, and the politics of both countries in very dissimilar ways. One, the United States, follows the individualistic essence of bourgeois liberalism and evangelical sectarian Christianity; the other, Japan, reflects the group-oriented norms of the postfeudal, aristocratic Meiji era. The former still stresses equal respect across stratification lines; the latter still emphasizes hierarchy in interpersonal relations. The United States continues to suspect the state; Japan places heavy reliance on its directing role. They are both among the world's most successful societies as measured by levels of productivity. Clearly, nations which have reached the same high point of technological development and economic success can still be very different culturally and can continue to be anomalies, outliers, among the developed countries, exceptional or unique compared to most others.

But while American economic patterns have been exceptional, Japanese patterns resemble those in Europe, particularly Northern Europe. Japanese and European corporations have shown a propensity to cooperate with each other and with the government. Americans rank low with respect to both orientations.[198] Efforts to introduce quality circles and worker involvement in industrial production have succeeded in Japan, Sweden, and other Northern European countries. They have failed in the United States.[199]

There is a body of literature which concludes that Japan will do better than the United States in the future, considerations of industrial policy apart, because its group-oriented culture is better suited to the economic structure of a postindustrial society. The argument is that engineering innovations, the key to economic growth, are more successfully fostered by groups, while scientific discoveries, yet-to-be-applied basic research, are more likely to occur in societies that stress *individual* initiative. The latter lead to Nobel prizes, but the contention is that they are less likely to have a direct impact in the postindustrial marketplace. This hypothesis is far from the only one presented to account for Japanese economic success. Others stress the impact of group-solidarity values on the willingness of Japanese, including corporate business executives, stockholders, and employees, to earn less than comparably placed Americans or Europeans, while the gap between those who run companies and ordinary workers is also much smaller in Japan.[200] Sony Corporation chairman Akio Morita has "described in detail the corporate management style of Japan—thin profit margins, low dividends to stockholders, overwork [by and low pay to] . . . employees, seizing market share above all. . . ."[201]

The comparative evidence indicates that

> [T]he employees of the Japanese company share more equally in the cash benefits available from the company than is the case in other countries [particularly the United States]. . . . Surveys of executive attitudes indicate that Japanese executive pay levels are set with a conscious awareness of the need to stay within reasonable ranges with regard to other levels of compensation. . . . Organizational pressures work to limit executive pay at least as much as do self-sacrificing impulses by the executives themselves.[202]

Survey data bear out the generalization that Japanese executives place the goal of increasing market shares, one which benefits workers, ahead of profits and short-term gains for stockholders. A 1980 cross-national poll of 291 Japanese and 227 American top corporate executives found the Americans giving first and second place to return on investment and increasing the value of company shares, while the Japanese put enlarging market shares first, and placed enhancing the worth of shares at the bottom, ninth.[203] The Hampden-Turner and Trompenaars worldwide study of managers conducted in the late eighties and early nineties asked them to choose between two statements:

(a) "The only real goal of a company is making profit," and (b) "A company, besides making profit, has a goal of attaining the well-being of various stakeholders, such as employees, customers, etc." Only 8 percent of the Japanese executives replied, "profit only," compared to 40 percent of the Americans.[204]

The answers to various other questions posed in this survey reiterated the differences presented in the qualitative and case study literature. The Japanese reported close relationships with "distributors, customers, suppliers, and subcontractors," and "somewhat cooperative relationships with competitors," while the Americans noted "remote relationships" and "rivalry" with the two groups. The Americans followed a pattern of "head-on competition stressing cost efficiency," while the Japanese emphasized "coexistence with competitors stressing 'niche' and differentiation." The Japanese sought "information-oriented leadership" and generalists; the American preference was for "task-oriented leadership" and specialists. The American executives were inclined "toward innovation and risk-taking," the Japanese toward "interpersonal skills." The responses indicated that American managers were disposed to handle "conflict resolution by confrontation . . . [and] decision-making [by] stressing individual initiative," while the Japanese engaged in "group-oriented consensual decision-making."[205]

The Japanese postwar success, when contrasted to the much slower growth rate and the loss or decline in markets in major industries by American business, led various analysts prior to the recession of the nineties to argue that the United States should adopt comparable policies to those followed across the Pacific. Assuming that various specific Japanese ways were responsible for higher productivity increases, the fact remains that these developed in a very different context. "The literature on Japanese development is generally pessimistic regarding the transfer of Japanese organization. It suggests that Japanese organizations derive from cultural factors such as homogeneity, familism, and group loyalty. . . ."[206] Yet a comprehensive study by Richard Florida and Martin Kenney of Japanese "transplants" in the automobile industry in America indicates both that they have done well economically and that they "have been successful in implanting the Japanese system of work organization in the U.S. environment. The basic form of Japanese work organization has been transferred with little if any modifications."[207] These do not involve major practices like lifetime employment or the emphasis on seniority, but include a very much lower number of job classifications, more job rotation, greater emphasis on worker initiative, and quality circles. Seemingly, Japanese management can secure an acceptance of practices that failed when sponsored by Americans. (Quality circles, as noted earlier, were originally an American idea, which ironically did not take hold in their native land.)

The Japanese are bound together by a common history, by a long-time desire to remain distinct from foreign culture. From the start of the seventeenth century to the mid-nineteenth, they maintained barriers against contact with other societies and economies. They had to be forced by Commodore Perry and the American Navy to recognize the greater power of the West and to open the door to outside influences.

But even though open to intellectual, commercial, and physical contact with the rest of the world, they have insisted on preserving their separateness. As a nation, Japan emphasizes ancestral purity. As James Fallows notes: "Rather than talking about race . . . the Japanese talk about 'purity.' Their society is different from others in being pure. . . ." The system is closed, unlike the United States, where "in theory anyone can become an American. A place in Japanese society is given only to those who are born Japanese."[208] Legal immigration is close to impossible. The more than a half million Koreans, left over from the period when Korea was ruled by Japan, do not have citizenship even though most of them were born in Japan. For a long time, the Japanese government refused to accept a quota of Vietnamese boat people on the grounds that the Japanese people would not treat them well. It finally reluctantly agreed to take in ten thousand. The traditional concern for "purity" has not declined. If anything, the "discrimination against the Korean, Chinese, and other minority people who permanently reside in Japan" has been increasing rather than decreasing since the seventies.[209] The protectionist zeal of the country, the barriers to the import of foreign goods, is a related form of behavior.

The United States, on the other hand, has welcomed foreigners to enter and join up. It is an immigrant, multicultural, multi-racial society. From a comparative, particularly Japanese, perspective, the United States has been an open society, to imports as well as people. The 1980s witnessed more newcomers to the United States than during any past decade. And the immigrants now are overwhelmingly from the Third World, not from Europe. As during other downturns, the recession of the 1990s has produced xenophobic immigration-restriction reactions. Still, it may be reiterated that as of 1990, the World Values Survey data indicate that only 12 percent of Japanese disagreed with the statement: "When jobs are scarce, employers should give priority to Japanese." A much larger percentage of Americans, 42 percent, rejected the statement as applied to their society.

The American emphasis on individualism and competition has, as noted in chapter Two, resulted in a "star" system in all areas of American life with enormous rewards to those on top—business executives, scholars, professionals, entertainers, athletes. The income spread from the top to the bottom is much higher in the United States than elsewhere in the developed world, particularly Japan.

Indeed, wage and income distribution in the United States is not as equitable as found in other nations; the difference between high and low wage earners is larger. Comparisons of male workers show that those whose earnings fall into the lowest decile of earnings distribution earn only 38 percent of the median in the United States, 61 percent in Japan, 68 percent in Europe; at the top of the earnings range, in the highest decile, workers in the United States earn 214 percent of the median, while in Japan it is 173 percent, and in Europe it is 178 percent.[210] This is true in spite of the fact that formal hierarchical distinctions and family background are of greater importance in Japan and to a lesser extent in other postfeudal nations as well. In Japan, the emphasis is on the group winning, on the individual, whether athlete, executive, or worker, subordinating his/her concerns to those of the larger unit. Such behavior even occurs at the summit of politics. Prime ministers tend to be prosaic figures who hold office for two years, very occasionally a year or two more.[211] This pattern stands in sharp contrast to the American system, where elections focus on the individual rather than the party, and emphasize the role of the president, even though he must rely on influence, not authority, when dealing with Congress. Eamonn Fingleton suggests the key to Japan's economic future lies with the Ministry of Finance, a low-profile agency that centrally controls fiscal policy and growth—with power that extends far beyond that of elected officials and is analogous to the combined powers of all U.S. taxing, spending, and defense agencies.[212]

My stress here on the continued distinctions between the two most economically powerful Pacific Rim societies is not intended to deny that both have changed greatly. Obviously, as they moved from being primarily agrarian societies to industrial giants, with the bulk of their populations living in cities, they changed greatly in norms and behaviors. Their family systems are now nuclear, their birth rates are low, they are more meritocratic than in their nineteenth-century formats. Both have become more postindustrial or postmaterialist, to use Daniel Bell's or Ronald Inglehart's terms (they do not mean the same). Reflecting worldwide changes in the developed nations, their young people are more permissive with respect to traditional morality. They are more concerned about protecting the environment, they are more interested in the "quality" of life. But their organizing principles remain different. They vary from each other in much the same way as they did a century ago. The value and behavioral differences reported here are much greater than have been found in any other comparison of industrialized nations. Each maintains much of its unique or exceptional character. To adapt an analogy I first used in discussing Canada and the United States: the two are like ships that have sailed thousands of miles along parallel routes. They are far from where they started, but they are still separated.[213]

American individualism won the major international competitions in the twentieth century. Will it continue to be number one in the twenty-first? The American economy is still the more productive of the two, as documented in chapter Two. "Japan's per capita income was still only 83 percent of the United States" as of 1992.[214] Prior to the recession of the nineties, the Japanese had moved ahead, to become seemingly more efficient than the United States in industrial organization in major areas such as automobile and electronics production. As a result, some observers contended that their systems—which are leaner in the scope of management, more egalitarian in economic reward, and place more emphasis on worker participation in quality control—are more "modern" than the American, that the United States should modernize, learn from a more efficient system, much as the Japanese did for a century. But much of American industry responded to Japanese competition and the recession by becoming "leaner" and "meaner." And faced with evidence that the United States is doing better, the Japanese have taken to reading books about American business. *Reengineering Capitalism* (1994) by Michael Hammer and James Champy has been a best-seller in Tokyo, Osaka, and Kobe.

Cross-national analyses now place American economic efficiency as equal to or ahead of Japan's. In October 1994, *The Economist* noted:

A new survey of 594 manufacturing companies in Europe, the United States and Japan . . . [c]onducted jointly by Insead, a European business school, Boston University and Waseda University . . . shows that Europeans and Americans have closed or eliminated the managerial gap in areas once seen as quintessentially "Japanese."

The companies to emerge best from the survey are American. They excel at the act of mixing production with services. . . . Surprisingly, perhaps, they were also found to think further ahead than most of their competitors on matters such as investing in human capital . . . [and] focusing on quality, service and reliability. . . . [The Japanese, conversely,] are concentrating on forcing down costs. . . .[215]

Similarly, in September 1994, *Time* magazine reported that the Swiss-based World Economic Forum, which comes close to proclaiming a world champion in the business world every year, "made the announcement: after eight years of Japanese domination, the U.S. in 1993 had the world's most competitive industrial economy." American business was now beating its "Japanese, German, South Korean, Taiwanese . . . rivals . . . in products like autos, machine tools, and computer chips."[216] At the end of 1994, the economist Paul Krugman also reports that "the era of miraculous Japanese growth now lies well in the past . . . that the Japanese economists generally believe that their country's rate of growth of potential output . . . is now no more than three percent. . . . When one takes into account the growing evidence of at least a modest acceleration of U.S. productivity growth in the last few years, one ends up with the probable conclusion that Japanese efficiency is gaining on that of the United States at a snail's pace, if at all, and there is the distinct possibility that per capita income in Japan may never overtake that in America."[217]

Findings recently reported by economists Jerry Jasinowski and Robert Hamrin in *Making It in America* support the World Economic Forum's conclusions. In that book, they describe as "sunrise for manufacturing," the gains the American manufacturing sector has made in the past decade. In dispelling the myth of American deindustrialization, the authors cite industrial productivity increases of 3 percent plus in the 1980s and the creation of 5.5 million new jobs between 1992 and mid-1994. Jasinowski and Hamrin also report that "U.S. manufacturing exports from 1985 to 1993 grew at nearly 9 percent annually compared with a 2.3 percent rate for Japan and 1.7 percent for Germany."[218]

Finally, *The Economist* has sought to quantify the answer to the question: "Which industrial countries are best placed to respond to the coming challenge of a new international division of labour?" as various major Third World countries move into competitive positions. The magazine ranks "the six biggest industrial economies on the basis of five factors": labor market flexibility, proportion employed in manufacturing (lower is better), percent with upper secondary education, strength in high-tech exports, and pension fund assets. The United

States comes out far in the lead at 10, Japan and Britain have a score of 6, and Germany, France, and Italy are "a long way behind."[219]

Although public opinion will obviously not determine which country turns out to be world leader, the results of an international poll conducted for CNN by a Canadian pollster, Angus Reid, in 1992 are worth reporting here. The citizens of 16 countries were asked: "Thinking of all countries, including your own this time, which one country do you think will be known as the world leader at the end of the century?" The United States led all others with a weighted country average of 42 percent. Japan was second at 20 percent, while Germany was third with but 8 percent. America led within all nations, except among Koreans, who alone placed Japan first. Close to three-fifths of the Japanese chose the United States; only 31 percent said Japan would lead. The American results were almost identical with the Japanese, 57 percent placed their country in the lead, while 20 percent said Japan.

The issue of which system will come out ahead economically is still unresolved, but in the mid-1990s, the prospects for the United States look good. In any case, with highly disparate value systems both it and Japan have done well as cultural outliers. Their records demonstrate that such varied societies can still absorb and/or develop comparable technological systems.

CONCLUSION

CHAPTER 8

A Double-Edged Sword[1]

The belief that the traditional values which underlie American exceptionalism will continue to determine American behavior at the end of the twentieth century has been challenged by those who call for a fundamental change in our national values to stop a moral decline. These critics do not see that what they find fault with is the dark side of American exceptionalism; developments which, like many of the positive features, derive from the country's organizing principles. These include rising crime rates, increased drug use, the dissolution of the traditional family, sexual promiscuity, and excessive litigiousness.

Public opinion data over the past thirty years reveal a consistently pessimistic outlook regarding the ethical stock of America. The Gallup organization has measured this sentiment in polls over three decades. Even in 1963, only 34 percent responded affirmatively to the question whether they were "satisfied with the honesty and standards of behavior of people in the country today?" while 59 percent were dissatisfied. In 1973, 22 percent were satisfied and 72 percent were not; by 1992, the gap widened to 20 percent and 78 percent.[2] Americans have always yearned for the "good old days." Yet, as the statistics show, the trend over the past few decades is toward great pessimism about the country.[3] People are more negative with regard to moral prospects than before. In mid-1994, three quarters of Americans told pollsters that the country is in moral and spiritual decline. Over two thirds believe it is seriously off track.[4]

Though some of these social trends are recent and disturbing, others have surprisingly longstanding roots in American society. The critics have exaggerated many of the problems in the quest to demonstrate decay. There is, however, no denying that the impression of a change in basic values exists, and to dismiss public perception as somehow wrong or misinformed is to deny the reality of individual experience. The most forceful and well-intentioned attempts to address these perceptions have sought to hold the emphasis on individualism and competitiveness as being responsible for the rending of the nation's social and political fabric, and the corresponding decline in adherence to traditional norms.[5] And to be sure, as I have noted throughout this book, these values are significant forces in American culture, with widespread impact on Americans' views of their social obligations.

American values are quite complex, particularly because of paradoxes within our culture that permit pernicious and beneficial social phenomena to arise simultaneously from the same basic beliefs. The American Creed is something of a double-edged sword: it fosters a high sense of personal responsibility, independent initiative, and voluntarism even as it also encourages self-serving behavior, atomism, and a disregard for communal good. More specifically, its emphasis on individualism threatens traditional forms of community morality, and thus has historically promoted a particularly virulent strain of greedy behavior. At the same time, it represents a tremendous asset, encouraging the self-reflection necessary for responsible judgment, for fostering the strength of voluntary communal and civic bonds, for principled opposition to wars, and for patriotism.

MORAL DECLINE, OR MORE OF THE SAME

To some degree, perceptions of American moral decline result from a persistent value strain within our culture that, as I have emphasized, leads Americans to evaluate their nation and society according to pure ideals. No country could ever measure up to our ideological and religious standards. The combination of revolutionary ideology and sectarian beliefs implying the perfectibility of humanity has forged a continuing national search for utopia. Flooded with reports of rapid social, economic, and political changes, we seek an overarching explanation for the failure to live up to our own goals.

Though historically ideological, America's egalitarian and meritocratic foundations tend to undercut just those institutions that sustain the values that so concern us. The United States, as we know, was born out of a revolution that sharply weakened the hierarchically rooted community values of the European Old World, and enormously strengthened individualistic, egalitarian, and anti-statist ones. In the Old World, an aristocratic upper class dictated social and economic norms to the lower classes. America, however, has not had a stable ruling class to promote such standards of moral conduct and fair play. Social problems have, therefore, been ascribed to the lack of stable ethical standards. Consider that 18 percent of the respondents to a

July 1993 Gallup Poll believed the midwestern floods of that year to be an admonishment by God for the sins of the people who live along the Mississippi. The readiness of Americans to cite a spiritual or moral explanation for a natural disaster is similar in many ways to ascribing the perceived dissolution of the social fabric to moral decline. A number of trends seem to provide evidence of this dissolution.

THE MORALITY OF CRIME AND WORK

Rising crime rates are frequently implicated in the so-called decline of morality. Louise Shelley's detailed study of comparative crime rates in developed countries, presented earlier, states that "rates for all categories of crime are approximately three times higher [in America] than in other developed nations." Between 1960 and 1992, homicides per 100,000 of the American population rose from 5.1 to 10.5, while larcenies increased from 1,726 to 3,103 per 100,000.[6] Charles Derber posits the cyclical recurrence of periods of what he terms "wilding," in which lawlessness, disorder, and immorality threaten the stability of society. According to Derber, "Wilding is American individualism running amok."[7] In recent years, Americans' perceptions of increasing lawlessness have fed fears that civil society is collapsing.

High crime rates, as I have noted, are a problem to which distinctive American cultural traits have certainly contributed.[8] The increased rates of crime in post–World War II America can be seen in part as a result of the refurbishment of classical liberal values during this period, including individualism and achievement orientation. Interestingly, though the United States is anomalous in its quantity of crime, it is similar to other developed countries in terms of the types of crime committed. That is, violent offenses (homicide, rape, robbery, and aggravated assault) comprise 10 percent of the crimes perpetrated in the United States, while 90 percent are property crimes, a pattern consistent with other industrialized societies. Thus, crime is comparatively widespread in America, but the impression that it is a society of exceptional brutality and violence is misleading. Though crime has recently burgeoned, it is important to understand the full relationship of crime, morality, and individualism in the American context. As Robert Merton and Daniel Bell have both stressed, the country's cultural values from its inception have pressed people to succeed "by fair means if possible and by foul means if necessary."[9]

Paradoxically, though various forms of illegality thrive in this country, America remains a society profoundly rooted in law. A potent orientation toward individual rights continues to shape the attitudes of the population. The complaint that Americans go to court at the drop of a hat has become commonplace, and the American eagerness for legal settlements to disputes has led many to question the reliance on litigation as "our basic form of government."[10] As noted, the country has more lawyers per capita, more malpractice, and more environmental and occupational safety suits than anywhere else in the world. Is this excessive litigiousness indicative of our inability to deliberate and form amicable agreements among ourselves?

As with crime, however, if American legal habits represent a crisis of morality, it is one we have been experiencing for over two hundred years. Tocqueville noted the contractual and litigious character of Americans in the 1830s, as have countless other observers throughout history.

To describe the tendency to commit illegal acts for socioeconomic advancement as, in Merton's words, a "moral mandate" is seemingly oxymoronic. But in America, work and economic success have been heavily imbued with such themes. The concept of work in America is enshrined in the country's Protestant traditions. The myths surrounding the "Protestant work ethic" demonstrate the conjunction of the concepts of work and morality.[11] Alan Wolfe sums up this foundational belief: "In making things, they [Americans] came to believe, people made themselves."[12] Concern about a reduction in moral standards is directly tied to questions about the supposed economic decline of the United States. The latter involves a lessening of America's lead over other industrial nations, not its absolute level of production, which continues to increase. The problem is seen as a lack of saving and investment, which, in value terms, means an unwillingness to forgo consumption, a refusal to adopt an ethic of self-denial, and an aversion to hard work and risk taking. These assessments are drawn directly from the classic mold of the Protestant work ethic. Thus, when the American economy is suffering, widespread immorality is ascribed as both the cause and the effect of the downturn; a decline in morality is a cause of economic stagnation due to individual failings such as indolence, but it is also an effect of recession because people who do not work become morally depraved. Paradoxically, morality is also perceived to be threatened during prosperous times when wealth is increasing and Americans are overworking. The prosperity of the 1980s has become infamous as the decade of greed.

ILLEGALITY IN A LEGAL SOCIETY

Drug use is another social and, in some cases, criminal problem that many attribute to moral failure, but which, in different forms, has extensive historical roots in the American experience. Daniel Patrick Moynihan has noted that the second law passed by the first U.S. Congress was a tariff on Jamaican rum, an act intended to promote consumption of American whiskey. Moynihan points out, "[d]istilled spirits in early America appeared as a font of national unity, easy money, manly strength, and all-round good cheer. ... It became routine to drink whiskey at breakfast and to go on drinking all day."[13] The historical record bears out this observation. Annual per capita consumption of distilled spirits was five gallons in 1830—almost five times what the average American consumes today. This pattern and the consequent social ills accompanying it eventually encouraged the temperance movement of 1820 to 1850, reducing the per capita consumption rate to two gallons by 1840.[14] More surprising is the testimony of St. John de Crèvecoeur, who, in his *Letters from an American Farmer* (1782) remarks on the adoption by the women of Nantucket of "the Asiatic custom of taking a dose of opium every morning."[15] In fact, between 1840 and 1870 opium imports to the United States increased seven times faster than the population growth.[16] Reminiscent of the role of the media today in raising public concern about drug use, in the 1870s and 1880s the press shocked the public with exposés on the widespread use of opiates and other narcotics for both medicinal and recreational purposes.

Americans' inclination to use drugs is historically and, in part, culturally based. As technology gives modern society more sophisticated and different narcotics—from morphine during the Civil War to cocaine in the late nineteenth century to "free-base" cocaine in the 1980s—some Americans have always used them. There is no doubt that the connection between crime and the ever more violent drug trade presents serious social problems for the country, particularly in urban centers, but whether these depressing developments indicate a declining state of societal morality is questionable. Rather, current patterns of drug use reflect new manifestations of cultural strains brought on by the development of new and sometimes pernicious technologies. I am not denying the importance or urgency of this societal problem. My argument is merely that its basic roots do not lie in any recent change in values.

The moral state of young Americans, as evidenced by media reports of spreading drug abuse in the nation's schools, particularly in inner cities, has been of especial concern, and a recent study shows that the proportion of today's youth who report using illicit drugs appears to be increasing. National survey data on drug use by eighth, tenth, and twelfth graders from 1975 to 1994 gathered by the Institute for Social Research at the University of Michigan reveal that marijuana use is on the rise after a period of decline beginning in the late 1970s. The percentage of twelfth graders who said they had used any illicit drug, which had dropped steadily from a peak of 66 percent in 1981 to 41 percent in 1992, went back up to 50 percent in 1994. However, alcohol consumption by high school seniors is on a downward slope, with daily use falling from 4.8 percent in 1987 to 3.4 percent in 1992, and down to 2.9 percent in 1994.[17]

The common stereotype of American youth as lacking a moral compass is contradicted not only by the lower proportion trying drugs but also by the increased disapproval high schoolers express toward virtually all types of drug use. These trends are even more striking because they shatter common misconceptions about race and drugs—by almost every measure (use of marijuana, cocaine, LSD, stimulants, barbiturates, crack, alcohol, and cigarettes), blacks are consistently less prone to use illicit substances than either whites or Hispanics. And strikingly, their usage has continued to fall off in 1992 and 1993, while white rates have started to increase.[18]

Similar results are reported with respect to cheating on school exams. The percentage reporting that "not very much" cheating goes on has increased from 18 percent in 1959 to 44 percent in 1992. The numbers for reporting that they themselves "have cheated" have fallen from 62 percent in 1978 to 46 percent in 1992.[19] The latter number may require more careful examination, since "not very much" could have meant something different in 1959 than in 1992.

THE FAMILY AND SEX

The family has been regarded as a vital source of morality in traditional and modern societies alike. James Q. Wilson argues that it is "a continuous locus of reciprocal obligations that constitute an unending school for moral instruction."[20] However, the United States, as we have seen, is exceptional in its high rates of divorce and the prevalence of single-parent families. But familial fragmentation in America is not a recent development in comparative terms. The lead of the United States in divorce rates goes back to the nineteenth century.[21] This may not only reflect the power of individualism but the phenomenon discussed earlier of the greater propensity of white American Protestants to marry when a pregnancy occurs, and to separate and remarry with a different spouse later.

The so-called crisis of the family is not historically unusual, nor is it comparatively atypical in terms of the pattern of these changes. As David Popenoe has noted, "The general direction of family change in contemporary America . . . seems little different from what it is in other wealthy nations."[22] In Britain, for instance, "[u]nmarried mothers are by far the fastest growing group of one-parent families. . . ."[23] Catholic Quebec has experienced "a profound social shift." Nearly half, "48 percent of all first-born Quebec children are born to unmarried parents. . . ."[24] In Sweden, the numbers are comparable.[25] Why? In almost every advanced industrial society, marriage occurs less frequently and later in life, and cohabitation among unmarried couples is increasing. America has been similar in the *rates* of the growth of these social trends.

Not surprisingly, warnings of the extinction of the traditional family have been widespread. Yet the cherished 1950s-style nuclear family has not been as pervasive throughout history as many believe. In reviewing the current literature on the American family, Ann Hulbert argues that alternatives to the traditional family have always existed. But though they are important, she notes, they "have never beckoned for long as a competing ideal."[26] She states that "The two-parent nuclear family norm, alternately revered and distrusted as a homogeneous standard, is not ready for replacement. . . . [T]he two-parent family continues to prevail, though neither widely nor simply."[27]

Though voluminous and often confusing, the data support this assessment. In 1993, 82 percent of white families, 69 percent of Hispanic units, and almost half of all black families, 48 percent, were headed by married couples.[28] Statistics on the state of the black family have been especially misleading. For instance, as I noted in chapter Four, Christopher Jencks has shown that the startling growth of illegitimate births as a percentage of all black births—from one fifth in the early 1960s to over three fifths in the 1990s—is not so much a function of a growth in births among the unmarried as a great decline among the married, a point reiterated in a 1995 Census Bureau report. Only 8.1 percent of all African-American teenage women are single mothers.[29]

For both black and white America, the family structure remains relatively traditional. Compared to citizens of other developed countries, Americans are considerably more likely to marry at some point in their lives, tend to wed at earlier ages, and have larger families. They are also more prone to divorce or separate, and then remarry. Recent changes to the modern American family have not so much threatened its dissolution as they have shaped its internal dynamics, which are now defined by the fact of two working parents. The nuclear family remains intact even as it undergoes fundamental and complex internal change.

The high divorce and illegitimacy rates have led to an exaggerated concern about the "disintegration of the family." Similar cries were heard earlier in American history. A declining birth rate, a rising divorce rate, and evidence that younger women were no longer content to remain in the domestic sphere—all of these repeatedly contributed to perceptions of societal crisis in the century before the Great Depression. Between 1870 and 1920, the birth rate fell 40 percent overall, even more sharply among the middle class. The divorce rate jumped from 0.5 per 1,000 population in 1887 to 1.6 in 1920; by 1940 there were 2.0 couples divorced per 1,000 population.[30] The 1950s brought a respite from such developments. In reaction to the stresses of the Great Depression and World War II, the divorce rate slowed, birth rates increased, and couples married earlier. Yet the evidence suggests that this idealized period was an anomaly in the context of the country's long-term modernization trend, and not—as popular imagination would have it—the way America always was.

Related to concerns over the family as a value anchor in our society are worries over the loosening of sexual mores. Those who believe in a current moral decline view the sexual revolution of the 1960s and 1970s as a nightmare of teen pregnancies and lascivious sexual practices. This perception is much exaggerated, as a definitive new national study documents.[31] In critically reviewing new research, Andrew Greeley cites survey data that argue against notions of waning sexual morality. The National Opinion Research Center reports *no change* in the overwhelming rejection of marital infidelity since it first started polling on the subject in the early seventies. Still three quarters of respondents believe that most Americans engage in extramarital affairs, but an almost unbelievable six out of seven married Americans tell the pollsters that they "have been faithful to their spouse(s)."[32] Greeley concludes that "Americans think that sexual behavior has in general turned permissive, even though they . . . generally engage in behavior which is in most respects not incompatible with traditional morality."[33]

INDIVIDUALISM, AWARENESS, AND MORALITY
—

The standard evidence marshaled to argue that America is experiencing a value crisis is unconvincing. However, it is difficult to make the opposite case that morality in America is waxing. There is indeed a widespread perception that traditional values are threatened by recent social, political, and economic developments. In some respects this view is heightened precisely because of moral advances of recent decades, such as the recognition that throughout American history women, homosexuals, and minorities have faced political, economic, and social inequalities. Americanism has clearly not weakened, but the issues that it must address in a modern pluralist society are recognizably more difficult. It is no solution to explain away the real concerns of citizens as mere "hyper-sensitization." The fact that we have strong moral frameworks, rooted in ideals of equality and liberty, around which certain new issues of race, gender, sexual orientation, and the older and continuing concern for the impoverished have coalesced, presents a challenge to American society. Some observers have suggested that an emphasis on communitarian norms is the best way to meet this challenge. This may be true for Canada, Japan, or Europe. The American tradition, however, calls for a different alternative, which may be described as "moral individualism." An emphasis on individual morality is an elemental component of the American polity. As political theorist James Rutherford notes: "The free and equal individual with moral responsibility is the basis of communal solidarity."[34] This is an important assertion—that community in democratic pluralistic America is grounded in the individual as a thinking, moral actor, not in group solidarity.

Oftentimes, the idea of a normative community is contrasted with self-interested atomism (read individualism). But to reiterate individualism is not necessarily a force grinding against the bonds of morality; it is, rather, an integral part of American values. Our national ideology—Americanism—is not merely a context, an environment that bounds or guides individual action; it is a set of values that requires reasoning and reflection in order to produce responsible consequences. The idea that we can be better moral agents by passively soaking up the values of the social context in which we find ourselves is antithetical to the principles of our democratic culture. In the modern environment of individual mobility and societal pluralism, the stability that marked traditional communal contexts is rare. Individuals need to be capable of retaining their ideological engagements even as the world around them changes. A morality grounded in a recognition of individual autonomy is therefore vitally flexible.[35]

INDIVIDUALS IN CIVIL SOCIETY

The moral content of Americanism is only meaningful insofar as it is expressed within a social context, and that context is civil society. Commentaries, derived from Tocqueville, on the importance of civil associations permeate classically liberal (i.e., libertarian) treatments of democratic life, which argue that an idealized individualism is more attractive and more readily attainable than any idealized collectivism.

Central to this American conception of individualism is the importance of civil society and voluntary associations. Zbigniew Rau comments: "Civil society is an association of rational agents who decide for themselves whether to join it and how to act in it. . . . Therefore, the creation of and participation in civil society is caused by and further promotes the reassertion of its members as fully rational and moral agents."[36] These associations—including churches, civic organizations, school boards, and philanthropic volunteer groups—are lifelong training grounds of citizenship and leadership, and create communication networks, conclusions Tocqueville drew from American practice. They strengthen moral bonds and facilitate the understanding of democracy.

But taking part in civil society does not simply mean belonging to collective entities and thereby embedding oneself within a social identity. Rather, it is a dynamic and sometimes problematic process of engagement between the individual and associations linked to interests and ideas. Nor is civil society a gentle, comfortable sphere of activity. It can be rough and challenging. From a critical perspective, David Popenoe correctly analyzes this dimension of civil society: "Outside the moral realm of the family is the world of voluntary friendships, a sphere governed by a marketplace for acceptance. In this outside world, acceptance is a scarce commodity that is allocated through competition; it must be strived for, earned, and maintained, and, hence, is highly conditional." Yet, Popenoe's analogy of civil society to a market is not entirely appropriate. There is nothing inherently common in these two spheres of liberal society, and it is a mistake to ascribe market forces to anything that requires effort and sacrifice, such as voluntarism or church membership.[37]

Alasdair MacIntyre's notion of civil society as "simply an arena in which individuals each pursue their own self-chosen conception of the good life" hardly seems capable of providing a moral context for democracy.[38] Surprisingly, however, the evidence regarding contemporary America suggests that it is. Individuals continue to take an active role in their local religious communities and to do volunteer work, while seven out of ten give money to charity. Though the impression of a narcissistic and materialistic society has been promoted by many commentators, Aileen Ross's assessment, discussed earlier, that philanthropy is more extensive in America "than in any other part of the world" helps discount such a view.[39]

It is important to recognize that in America, individualism *strengthens* the bonds of civil society rather than weakens them. In his book *Acts of Compassion,* Robert Wuthnow examines national survey data and reports that they reveal a *"positive* relationship between self-oriented values and placing importance on charitable activities. In other words, people who were the most individualistic were also the most likely to value doing things to help others."[40] This conclusion is significant in light of Gallup surveys taken between 1977 and 1994 which show an increase from 27 to 48 percent in the proportion of respondents reporting having been "involved in any charity or social service activities, such as helping the poor, the sick or the elderly."[41]

Other students of American society have argued, as Tocqueville did, that individualism is related to the continuing vitality of religion and religious organizations. Since most of the country's sects are congregational, not hierarchical, they have fostered individualistic, egalitarian, and populist values, the moral order. And voluntary religion fostered the myriad of voluntary associations in America that so impressed Tocqueville, Bryce, Weber, and other foreign observers. These associations of what has come to be known as civil society create networks of communication among people with common positions and interests helping to sustain the moral order, political parties, and participation. Americans not only remain the most religious and most devout people in Christendom; they also are still the most participatory, the most disposed to belong to and be active in voluntary associations.

The nature and sources of the difference have been summed up by Peter Drucker:

In the United States, where there is a long volunteer tradition because of the old independence of the churches, almost every other adult in the 1990s is working at least three—and others five—hours a week as a volunteer in a social-sector organization. Outside the English-speaking countries there is not much of a voluntary tradition. In fact, the modern state in Europe and Japan has been openly hostile to anything that smacks of voluntarism.[42]

The 1990 World Values Survey, which examined membership and degree of activity in fifteen categories of voluntary organizations, plus "other groups," found that 82 percent of Americans belong to at least one organization. Japan, together with Italy, rank at the bottom among the league of developed countries, with 64 percent of their survey respondents saying they do not belong to any such groups. France is close to them at 61 percent; while Great Britain, Canada and West Germany are in the middle (see Table 8-1). The United States leads also in the proportion who are active in, do unpaid work for, voluntary associations. Fully three fifths of Americans report so doing, compared

TABLE 8-1. MEMBERSHIP IN VOLUNTARY ORGANIZATIONS (PERCENT)

	U.S.A.	Canada	France	West Germany	Great Britain	Italy	Japan
None	18	35	61	32	47	64	64
Social Welfare services	9	8	7	7	7	4	2
Religious, churchs, organizations	49	25	6	16	17	8	7
Education, cultural activities	20	18	9	12	9	5	6
Trade unions	9	12	5	16	14	6	7
Political parties	14	7	3	8	5	5	2
Local community action	5	5	3	2	3	2	0
Third World, human rights	2	5	3	2	2	1	0
Conservation, the environment	8	8	2	5	5	3	1
Professional associations	15	16	5	9	10	4	4
Youth work	13	10	3	4	5	4	1
Sports or recreation	20	23	16	32	17	11	9
Women's groups	8	7	1	6	5	0	3
Peace movement	2	2	0	2	1	1	1
Animal rights	6	3	2	5	2	2	0
Health organizations	7	9	3	4	4	3	1
Other groups	11	13	5	9	7	2	5

SOURCE: *Tables 8-1 and 8-2 are computed from the data tapes of the 1990 World Values Survey. I am indebted to Ronald Inglehart for access to these materials.*

to one quarter, 26–27 percent, of British, Italians, and Japanese (see Table 8-2). Americans are ahead in most categories—religious organizations, political parties or groups, social welfare services, education and culture, environment, youth groups, women's associations, and animal rights. They are close to the top in all others, except for trade unions.[43]

TABLE 8-2. DOING UNPAID WORK FOR VOLUNTARY ORGANIZATIONS (PERCENT)

	U.S.A.	Canada	France	West Germany	Great Britain	Italy	Japan
None	40	53	65	69	74	73	73
Social Welfare services	6	6	5	3	5	3	2
Religious, churchs, organizations	29	15	5	7	6	6	2
Education, cultural activities	10	9	5	4	3	3	3
Trade unions	2	4	2	2	1	3	1
Political parties	5	4	2	3	2	3	1
Local community action	3	4	3	1	1	1	0
Third World, human rights	1	3	1	1	1	1	0
Conservation, the environment	3	3	1	1	2	2	1
Professional associations	5	5	3	2	2	1	1
Youth work	10	7	2	2	4	3	1
Sports or recreation	8	12	6	11	3	7	3
Women's groups	4	4	1	3	2	0	1
Peace movement	1	2	0	1	0	1	1
Animal rights	2	1	1	2	0	1	0
Health organizations	5	7	2	1	3	2	1
Other groups	6	9	4	4	4	2	4

The strength of American religion shows no sign of diminishing. Polls by Gallup and others, as we saw earlier, indicate that Americans are the most churchgoing in Protestantism and the most fundamentalist in Christendom. Commenting on the continuity of religious practice in America as revealed in opinion surveys, the political scientist William Mayer concludes that "[w]hen the late 1980s are compared with the late 1930s, church membership may have declined by about five percent, while church attendance may actually be *higher* today than it was fifty years ago."[44] In 1991, 68 percent of the adult population belonged to a church and 42 percent attended services weekly, much higher ratios than in any other industrialized nation.[45] Americans still bear out Tocqueville's observation that they are among the most devout people in Christendom.

THE DECLINE OF CIVIC ENGAGEMENT

Although civil society, association life, is, as Tocqueville also noted, stronger here than elsewhere, the American data, much of which has been assembled by Robert Putnam, indicate that "civic engagement," to use his term, and political commitment have declined in the past three decades. He notes that "participation in many types of civic associations from religious groups to labor unions, from women's clubs to fraternal clubs and from neighborhood gatherings to bowling leagues has fallen off."[46]

Most, but not all, of the available evidence bears out these generalizations. A Roper survey taken in August 1993 indicates that the percentage of people who have "attended a public meeting on town or school affairs" has dropped by more than a third, from 23 percent in 1973 to 16 percent in 1993. NORC data indicate that the proportion who attended a political rally or speech, who served on a committee, or who were officers of a club or organization also fell off over this twenty-year period. All told, those reporting involvement in at least one of six civic activities declined from 50 to 43 percent.

One of the most critical forms of community participation in the United States has been in parent-teacher associations (PTA), reflecting Americans' high commitment to education. Putnam reports a very significant dropoff in membership in the PTA from the 1960s to the present, from 12 million in 1964 to 5 million in 1982, though there is some indication that membership may have rebounded somewhat to 7 million in recent years.[47] Survey data gathered by NORC from 1974 to 1993 indicate that fraternal organizations have experienced a steady decline.

There are some contradictory trends. As noted above, Gallup Polls find that the proportion of people indicating that they have volunteered for charitable, "social service," or "non-profit" organizations has doubled between 1977 and the 1990s. Ethnic organizations have increased their total membership in percentage terms. And Putnam reports a type of civic organization that has grown in membership in recent years, groups like the National Organization of Women, the Sierra

Club, and the American Association of Retired People (AARP).[48] The latter increased from 400,000 dues-paying members in 1960 to 33 million in 1993. But these Putnam sees as essentially checkbook organizations, which do not promote "civic engagement." Their members pay dues, but rarely attend any meetings and seldom, if ever, knowingly encounter other members. They are not mechanisms for communication or the learning of politically relevant skills. In any case, looking at the international data, Putnam reaffirms the conclusion that Americans are "more trusting and civicly engaged than most other people in the world."[49]

Putnam discusses various possible causes for the falloff in activity, including the movement of women into the labor force, the decline in the size and stability of the family, and high rates of geographic mobility, and finds good reason to reject these hypotheses. He notes the importance of television in helping to individualize the use of leisure time and points to various time-budget studies documenting the steady increase in time devoted to television, which has "dwarfed all of the changes in the way Americans spend their days and nights." NORC finds that the percentage of the population who watch television for only an hour a day or less decreased from 37 in 1964, to 27 in 1978, to 22 in 1989, and then went up to 25 in 1993. Those looking at the tube for four hours or more a day climbed from 19 percent in 1964 to 28 percent in 1993. Conversely, the proportion reading newspapers every day fell from 73 percent in 1967 to 46 percent in 1993. Other technological developments have had similar effects. For example, the growth in the technology for listening to music—the cassette tape, compact disc, and the Walkman—has helped privatize Americans and reduced their interpersonal contacts outside work.

THE GROWTH OF CYNICISM

Popular involvement in civil society apart, the evidence has been growing that all is not well with the American polity. Over the past three decades, opinion polls show that the citizenry is increasingly distrustful of its political leaders and institutions. When asked about their "confidence" in government, large majorities, here as in almost every country, report that they have "none," "little," or "a fair amount" of trust in the president and the legislative bodies. Those who are strongly positive are minorities, usually small ones.

The United States provides a striking example of this breakdown of respect for authority. Confidence in all United States institutions inquired about in the opinion surveys declined precipitously and steadily from the mid-1960s, though the greatest part of the fall occurred early in that decade. The Louis Harris Poll, which has investigated the subject since 1966, reported in 1994 the lowest level of confidence in government institutions ever. Those expressing a "great deal" of confidence in the executive branch of government constituted only 12 percent of a national sample in 1994, as compared to 24 percent in 1981, and 41 percent in 1966. Trust in Congress was even lower—8 percent in 1994, contrasted with 16 percent in 1981, and 42 percent in 1966. Daniel Yankelovich reports a drastic shift for the worse in response to the question, "How much of the time can you trust the government to do what's right?" In 1964, 76 percent said "always" or "most of the time." The proportion so answering fell to 44 percent in 1984, and then to an all-time low of 19 percent in 1994, a finding reported in the latest Luntz Poll for the Hudson Institute as well.

The University of Michigan Survey Research Center's national election study has been asking: "Would you say the government is pretty much run by a few big interests looking out for themselves or that it is run for the benefit of all the people?" In 1964, 29 percent said it was run for a few big interests. By 1980, the proportion so replying had moved up to 70 percent; in 1992, fully four fifths, 80 percent, expressed this cynical view. A Gallup Poll conducted for the *Times-Mirror* organization in 1994 found that 66 percent of a national sample agreed that the "Government is almost always wasteful and inefficient." A similar percentage said that "most elected officials don't care what people like me think." Again, the data show steady increases in disdain for officeholders. In response to this question, just under half, 47 percent, agreed in 1987, compared to 33 percent in the 1960s.

These doubts manifest themselves in numerous ways, including a decline in voter participation and erosion of the two-party system. The United States, which could once boast that the overwhelming majority of eligible voters cast their ballots, lost that record after 1914 and is experiencing a new pattern of decline. In fact, a much smaller proportion take part in American national elections than in any of the other older democracies, except Switzerland. The percentage voting has fallen from a postwar high point of around two thirds at the beginning of the 1960s to little more than one half in presidential elections today. Considerably fewer take part in lower-level contests, state and city elections, and even the presidential primaries. In reporting on the mid-term primaries in 1994, the Committee for the Study of the American Electorate noted that only 18 percent of the voting age population cast ballots, compared to 24 percent in 1974 and 33 percent in 1966. The November election produced a turnout of 39 percent, up 2 percent from 1990, but still among the lowest reported.

The lack of faith in the traditional American political system also is strikingly revealed by declining regard for the two-party system. In 1994, for the first time in polling history, a majority of those interviewed, 53 percent, told Gallup that they would like to see a third major party, up to 60 percent in 1995. Evidence that this sentiment is not simply symbolic is provided by the support which Ross Perot obtained in the 1992 election and continues to receive in opinion polls in 1994–95. Perot secured the highest percentage of the vote ever attained by a third-party candidate, with the limited exception of Theodore Roosevelt in 1912. Roosevelt, however, was a dissident Republican preferred in the twelve primaries of that year by most of his party's supporters. The 1995 opinion polls show that Perot continues to be endorsed by a fifth of the electorate. And the 1994 election results, like the 1992 ones, are seemingly the consequence of this distrust. The Perot voters, who disliked Bush the incumbent more than Clinton the outsider, turned in overwhelming numbers to support Republican congressional and state candidates in 1994. But the *Times-Mirror* Poll reports continued distrust of Congress and both parties, as of the fall of 1995.

THE LEGACY OF THE 1960S

This erosion of trust in American government is troubling. President Jimmy Carter characterized it in a July 1979 television address to the American people as a "fundamental threat to American democracy." That threat, he said, was a "crisis of confidence . . . that strikes at the very heart and soul and spirit of our national will." He pointed to "a growing disrespect for government and for churches and for schools, the news media and other institutions," and emphasized that "the gap between our citizens and our government has never been so wide."[50] If anything, that gap has now widened. In a report on a 1994 poll evaluating "The New Political Landscape," the *Times-Mirror* Center finds that "Voters' frustration with the political system continues to grow, as does animosity toward the media. . . . The Clinton Administration and the economic recovery have failed to stem the tide of political cynicism.

The discontent with Washington that gained momentum in the late 1980s is even greater now than it was in 1992."[51]

Other opinion polls, cited above, indicate that this severe decline in confidence began even earlier, during the mid-1960s, a period characterized by widespread protest, and has continued to the present. The catalysts for this dramatic loss of faith in institutions are a combination of reactions to the Vietnam War and the discontent represented by various social movements, initially linked to the anti-war struggles, which severely criticized America for not living up to its democratic and egalitarian promise. These were primarily concerned with race relations, the status of women, and the environment. Previously, alienation or organized protest in Western democratic society had been based largely on the traditionally underprivileged strata; but the movements of the 1960s stemmed mostly from the more affluent classes, university students, professionals, and middle-class women. The one important protest wave that reflected the problems of the underprivileged was, of course, the civil rights campaigns led by Martin Luther King, Jr.

Mass protest declined, seemingly almost vanished, with the end of the Vietnam War and the passage of important civil rights legislation, but as noted, public opinion research and electoral behavior indicated that a large percentage of Americans continued to feel frustrated with their political leaders and institutions. Events in the next decade, including the economic downswing of the early 1970s and the Watergate scandal, intensified the disdain for political leadership. The Carter years, marked by economic stagnation, high rates of inflation and unemployment, and finally the Iran hostage crisis, did not help.

A partial hiatus in the falloff in public confidence occurred in the 1980s. Ironically, given his antagonism to government, Ronald Reagan's administration produced an increase in confidence in government in reaction to economic growth and prosperity during most of his term in office. This improvement, however, was relatively minor and did not affect attitudes toward other major institutions, such as business and labor. Frustration continued to dominate. In any case, the Reagan blip ended with the Iran-Contra scandal in November 1986. The basically downward trend has continued under Presidents Bush and Clinton, although there was an upswing that proved to be very short-lived after the Gulf War in early 1991. By the summer, it was gone.

TELEVISION'S DISTORTING PICTURE

Why is there so much malaise, so much unrest about the workings of American democracy? The discontent generated in the 1960s does not explain why these feelings have continued or what has sustained them. Politicians tend to blame the media for the lack of trust. I suspect that to some degree they are right. American presidents since George Washington have complained about the way the press covered them. Thomas Jefferson, Andrew Jackson, Abraham Lincoln, and Franklin Roosevelt all felt, correctly, that much of the press was antagonistic. Those on the left, from Jefferson to Roosevelt and Truman, felt that the owners of the press were conservatives and controlled the way their papers wrote about them. Since Lyndon Johnson, presidents have identified media bias as reflecting the views of journalists, not owners, and as leftist or liberal. There can be little doubt that the predominantly left views of reporters affect the way the news is presented. But the political views or interests of those who dominate the media are not the main sources of their emphasis on the failings of elites and institutions. The fact is that good news is not news; bad news is. Planes that land do not constitute a story; planes that crash do. Politicians characterized by honesty, personal integrity, and a good family life are dull; sexually promiscuous, corrupt political figures are interesting. The press looks for failings. The desire to locate and exaggerate scandals among the political, social, and economic elites has always characterized open democratic societies.

The effect of the media is illustrated by the public's concern over the increased risk of criminal victim rates when, "according to the most reliable measure available, total levels of crime in America have fallen, not risen, over the past two decades."[52] A comprehensive review by *The Economist* of the problems involved in evaluating crime statistics dealing with many countries indicates that police reports "often quoted by politicians and given prominence in the media" considerably exaggerate the extent of crime reported in crime-victimization surveys. In polls conducted regularly by Gallup since 1971, "some 50% of Americans have usually thought crime to have risen in the preceding year in their area. Only around 15% believed—often correctly, in all probability— that crime had fallen locally."[53]

There has been a change in the nature of the media, which I think is responsible for perpetuating and extending the loss in trust: the shift

286 American Exceptionalism

from print to television as the major source of news. Television presents the news, conveys the message, in much stronger terms, in much more convincing fashion than newspapers or magazines. The massive transition from print to televised media occurred during the 1960s. The Vietnam War was the first televised war; for the first time, the public could watch the spilling of blood from their living rooms. The impact of the prolonged war on American opinion was to a considerable extent a function of pictorial reportage. And the domination of the camera has continued to grow. All problems of society now reach people almost immediately and in what appears to be an unbiased manner, because the viewer thinks he sees what is happening for himself. And in 1994, the United States led the ownership of television sets, with 81 for every 100 people. The corresponding figure for the European Union was 44, while for Japan it was 62.[54]

There have been other notable changes as well. Norman Ornstein has noted that the increase in reportage on scandals and corruption in government and other institutions is linked to greater disclosure. Sweeping reform of the political process has resulted in a drastic increase in information made possible by the computer, which has been grist for investigative journalism. As important in undermining trust in leaders has been the enormous growth in "prosecutorial zeal," flowing in part from "the reform-era creation of a Public Integrity Section in the Justice Department, which defines its success by the volume of prosecution of public officials." As a result, Ornstein reports, between 1975 and 1989 "the number of federal officials indicted on charges of public corruption increased by a staggering 1,211 percent, whereas the number of non-federal public officials indicted doubled during the same period."[55] There has clearly been more bad news to report about politics, as well as a more effective medium to transmit it.

Paradoxically, the increase in the malaise about politics and the disdain for government may also reflect the growth of dependence on government since the 1930s. Most people in the West, even those in the less statist United States, have come to rely on the state to solve most problems and to provide jobs, security for the aged, and medical care, as well as good schools. Socialism and communism may have collapsed, but heavy reliance on what Robert Dahl describes as an increasingly complex and incomprehensible government has not. We expect much from the state, and we turn against elected officials because of their failure to accomplish what we want them to do. Ironically, the decline in confidence in government in a nation which suspects government, which does not want to rely on it, makes it more difficult for the political leaders to enact new programs and deal with problems that the public would like to see resolved, such as health care.

THE SURVIVAL OF THE AMERICAN DREAM

Given the anger about politics in the United States, what accounts for the continued stability of the American system? Why do we not witness grievous forms of mass unrest? Why is the major protest movement, led by Ross Perot, basically centrist, even conservative with respect to economic and social policy? Part of the answer to the conundrum is that most Americans are not unhappy about their personal lives or prospects; if anything, the opposite is true. They still view the United States as a country that rewards personal integrity and hard work, as one that, government and politics apart, still works. The American Dream is still alive, even if the government and other institutions are seen as corrupt and inefficient. A 1994 survey-based study of "The American Dream" conducted for the Hudson Institute finds that over four fifths, 81 percent, agree with the statement, "I am optimistic about my personal future," while about two thirds, 64 percent, are "optimistic about America's future." Three quarters, 74 percent, agreed that "In America, if you work hard, you can be anything you want to be." And almost 72 percent felt that "As Americans, we can always find a way to solve our problems and get what we want." And not surprisingly, when asked to choose between "having the opportunity to succeed and having security from failing," over three quarters, 76 percent, opt for the former; only a fifth, 20 percent, prefer the security option.[56]

Gallup polling for *Times-Mirror* in 1994 presents similar results. Over two thirds, 67 percent, expect their financial situation to improve a lot or some; only 14 percent say it will get worse. Large majorities reject the statement that "Success in life is pretty much determined by forces outside our control." Most affirm the traditional American laissez-faire ideology, with its emphasis on individualism, with 88 percent agreeing with the statement, "I admire people who get rich by working hard," and 85 percent agreeing that "Poor people have become too dependent on government assistance programs." More significantly, perhaps, 78 percent endorse the view: "The strength of this country today is mostly based on the success of American business."

The American political system, though distrusted and ineffective in dealing with major social issues, is clearly not in danger. Most Americans remain highly patriotic and religious, believe they are living in the best society in the world, and think that their country and economy, in spite of problems, still offer them opportunity and economic security. Although the depression of the 1930s was worse here than in most of Europe, America came out of it with its party system, state institutions, and material values intact. The country will probably do the same today, although it must be acknowledged that the major parties appear somewhat more vulnerable than at any time since the Civil War.

CONCLUSION

To what extent is it still possible to speak of American exceptionalism? It is obvious that America and the rest of the Western world have changed greatly over the past two centuries. From a nation of thirteen states hugging the Atlantic seaboard with a population of 4 million, America has grown to a continent-spanning federation of fifty states and, as of the 1990 Census, 250 million people. Close to 30 million live in California, a state nonexistent in 1789. The country began as an overwhelmingly agrarian society, with more than 90 percent of its work force on the land, many as subsistence farmers. As the country approaches the twenty-first century, only 2 percent are farmers, and the great majority of the population live in sprawling metropolitan regions. From an underdeveloped rural economy which largely relied on Britain for its manufactured goods, it became in the latter decades of the nineteenth century the most prosperous power on earth. In real consumer income terms, it still holds this position, although the emergence of other industrial countries and the reexpansion of Europe has reduced its proportion of the world's production from two fifths after World War II to a quarter in the nineties. The character of its labor force has changed, first with the decline of agriculture and the expansion of industry, and more recently with the decrease in manual jobs and the growth of high-tech and scientific activities accompanied by an increase in white-collar and service jobs and in positions requiring college education. The resultant gap in demand for the growing population of well-educated people and the declining need for unskilled people is producing a sizable income difference, with the share going to the lowest strata falling. Other Western nations have also changed, becoming industrialized, urbanized, better educated. The postfeudal elements that characterized many European countries have declined enormously, although Britain, while also changing, still contains more

of these elements than others. In social-structural terms, these countries are becoming Americanized.[57]

The changes that have occurred around the developed world, however, still leave many differences. In comparative terms, the United
States remains more religious, more patriotic, more populist and anti-
elitist (the number of elective positions increased between 1987 and
1992 by over ten thousand, while direct involvement of the electorate
in the candidate nomination process continues to grow), more committed to higher education for the majority, hence to meritocracy, more
socially egalitarian, more prone to divorce, less law-abiding, wealthier
in real income (purchasing power) terms, markedly more job-creating,
and significantly less disposed to save, than other developed countries.
To reiterate, the United States is a "welfare laggard." It remains the
least statist Western nation in terms of public effort, benefits, and
employment.[58] It is "[t]he reluctant bride of the welfare state, institut-
ing national programs later than most countries . . . and spending a
lower share of its national income on social welfare than most. . . ."[59]
According to the OECD, the United States provides single-parent families with a much lower level of income support, 37 percent of the average production worker's wage, than any of seven other countries listed
in a recent report—Sweden (82%), Canada (69%), Finland (67%), Holland (68%), Austria (53%), Britain (53%), and Australia (52%).[60] Conversely, Americans show a marked preference for private efforts in welfare as in business; they lead the world in philanthropic giving. As
Nathan Glazer reports, "non-public resources in American welfare are
greater than is found in any other major nation."[61]

However, major changes have occurred which have modified the
original American Creed, with its suspicion of the state and its emphasis on individual rights.[62] These include the introduction of a planning–welfare state emphasis in the 1930s, accompanied initially by
greater class-consciousness and trade union growth, and the focus on
ethnic, racial, and gender group rights which emerged in the 1960s.
The first has had a continuing impact in the form of a much expanded
government that remains committed to many welfare and regulatory
objectives. But, as I noted earlier, the increase has been slowed, in
some aspects reversed. Popular sentiment in the mid-1990s seeks to
limit welfare and opposes some types of state involvement in the economy that once had considerable support. Election results from 1968 to
1994 indicate Americans want to reduce the role of the state. The
Republicans are the most anti-statist major party in the West, but the
Clinton New Democrats are not far behind. Trade union membership,

as we have seen, has fallen greatly as a share of the labor force, and the significance of class as a variable related to partisan support is much reduced. The economic role of government remains weaker in the United States than in any other industrialized economy. On the other hand, the focus on non-class forms of group rights which came to a head in the 1960s, though still a dynamic force, is under sharper criticism than any time since the Johnson era. These developments appear to be reaffirming the basic emphases on individual success, on equality of opportunity rather than of results.

Finally, it is worth reiterating that various seemingly contradictory aspects of American society are intimately related. The lack of respect for authority, anti-elitism, and populism contribute to higher crime rates, school indiscipline, and low electoral turnouts. The emphasis on achievement, on meritocracy, is also tied to higher levels of deviant behavior and less support for the underprivileged. Intense religiosity is linked to less reliance on contraception in premarital sexual relationships by young people. The same moralistic factors which make for patriotism help to produce opposition to war. Concern for the legal rights of accused persons and civil liberties in general is tied to opposition to gun control and difficulty in applying crime-control measures. The stress on individualism both weakens social control mechanisms, which rely on strong ties to groups, and facilitates diverse forms of deviant behavior.

I would like to conclude with some thoughts derived from an American political scientist, Samuel Huntington; a Canadian scholar who was named after two executed Italian American anarchists, Sacvan Bercovitch; and a communist theorist, Antonio Gramsci. Huntington and Bercovitch both note that an emphasis on a national consensus, a national myth, which some mistakenly see as the meaning of exceptionalism, is not an alternative to a stress on conflict.[63] The consensual myth fosters bitter controversy. Huntington notes periods of creedal passion in American history, intense conflicts seeking to bring "institutions and practices in accord with these values and beliefs. . . . In a political system produced by a major revolution . . . efforts may be made from time to time to renew or reaffirm revolutionary values." Such conflicts and patterns of change can only occur "in a society with an overwhelming *consensus*" on "values." They could not occur "in societies with traditional ideological pluralism, such as most of those of western Europe" and Canada.[64]

Americans fight each other in their efforts to defend or expand the American Creed. Pre–Civil War leaders of the anti-slavery struggle, such as Frederick Douglass and William Lloyd Garrison, or the founder of American feminism, Elizabeth Cady Stanton, like mid-twentieth-century American radicals, demanded changes in order, in Douglass's words, to live up to "the genius of American institutions, to help fulfill its [the nation's] sacred mission."[65] Bercovitch, who cites these radical exponents of the Creed, first entered the United States during the conflict-ridden 1960s. Expressing his reaction to the creedal passions of the era, he wrote:

> My first encounter with American consensus was in the late sixties, when I crossed the border into the United States and found myself inside the myth of America. Not of North America, for the myth stopped short of the Canadian and Mexican borders, but of a country that despite its arbitrary frontiers, despite its bewildering mix of race and creed, could believe in something called the True America, and could invest that patent fiction with all the moral and emotional appeal of a religious symbol. . . . Here was the Jewish anarchist Paul Goodman berating the Midwest for abandoning the promise; here, the descendant of American slaves, Martin Luther King, denouncing injustice as a violation of the American way; here, an endless debate about national destiny . . . conservatives scavenging for un-Americans, New Left historians recalling the country to its sacred mission.
>
> Nothing in my Canadian background had prepared me for that spectacle. . . . It gave me something of an anthropologist's sense of wonder at the symbol of the tribe. . . . To a Canadian skeptic, a gentile in God's country . . . [here was] a pluralistic, pragmatic people . . . bound together by an ideological consensus.
>
> Let me repeat that mundane phrase: *ideological consensus.* For it wasn't the idea of exceptionalism that I discovered in '68. . . . It was a hundred sects and factions, each apparently different from the others, yet all celebrating the same mission. . . .[66]

Gramsci, who also believed that America has a national ideology, wrote in the 1920s that before Italy could become socialist, it had to Americanize socially as well as economically, a development he viewed positively. Like earlier Marxists, he saw the United States as the epitome of a bourgeois democratic society, one that lacked the traditional precapitalist elements which were still to be found in Italy and other European cultures.[67] Of course, the industrialized European countries have begun to resemble the United States economically, as more affluent, and socially, as less status-conscious. In the process, their socialist movements (and the Italian Communist Party, now renamed the Party of the Democratic Left) have redefined their objectives. Not only do their conservatives, like Margaret Thatcher, increasingly advocate classical (Jeffersonian/Jacksonian) liberal doctrines, but as I have documented elsewhere, this ideology is also strongly affecting their left.[68] In line with Marx's anticipation in *Das Kapital* that "the more developed country shows the less developed the image of their future," the United States is less exceptional as other nations develop and "Americanize." But, given the structural convergences in economy and ecology, the extent to which it is still unique is astonishing.

Appendix: Individualism and Group Obligation

*Responses of 15,000 Managers and Executives, 1986–1993 (percent)**

"While you are talking and sharing a bottle of beer with a friend who was officially on duty as a safety controller in the company you both work for, an accident occurs, injuring a shift worker. An investigation is launched by the national safety commission and you are asked for your evidence. There are no other witnesses. What right has your friend to expect you to protect him?"

(a) A definite right?	(b) Some right?	(c) No right?

(C) No Right	USA	CAN	UK	GER	FRA	JAP
	94	91	82	90	53	66

"You run a department of a division of a large company. One of your subordinates, whom you know has trouble at home, is frequently coming in significantly late. What right has this colleague to be protected by you from others in the department?"

(a) A definite right?	(b) Some right?	(c) No right?

(C) No Right	USA	CAN	UK	GER	FRA	JAP
	95	81	84	94	43	56

The Dilemmas Methodology:

(a) "A company is a system designed to perform functions and tasks in an efficient way. People are hired to fulfill these functions with the help of machines and other equipment. They are paid for the tasks they perform."

*Source: Data taken from Charles Hampden-Turner and Alfons Trompenaars, *The Seven Cultures of Capitalism* (New York: Doubleday, 1993), pp. 22, 23, 31–32, 56–57, 60, 71, 90, 111, 165, and 279–280.

(b) "A company is a group of people working together. The people have social relations with other people and with the organization. The functioning is dependent on these relations."

(A) COMPANY AS A SYSTEM

USA	CAN	UK	GER	FRA	JAP
74	69	55	41	35	29

Proper Goals of a Company:

(a) "The only real goal of a company is making profit."

(b) "A company, besides making profit, has a goal of attaining the well-being of various stakeholders, such as employees, stakeholders, etc."

(A) Profit Only	USA	CAN	UK	GER	FRA	JAP
	40	34	33	24	16	8

"Suppose you, as a manager, are in the process of hiring a new employee to work in your department. Which of the two following considerations are more important to you:

(a) The new employee must fit into the group or team in which he/she is to work.

(b) The new employee must have the skills, the knowledge, and a record to success in a previous job."

(B) Individual Capacity	USA	CAN	UK	GER	FRA	JAP
	92	91	71	87	57	49

Preferences for Two Different Kinds of Jobs:

(a) "Jobs in which no one is singled out for personal honor, but in which everyone works together."

(b) "Jobs in which personal initiatives are encouraged and individual initiatives are achieved."

(B) Personal Initiatives Encouraged	USA	CAN	UK	GER	FRA	JAP
	97	96	90	84	69	49

Limited Commitment to Organizations:

"If I apply for a job in a company,

(a) I will most certainly work there for the rest of my life.

(b) I am almost sure that the relationship will have a limited duration."

(B) Limited Duration	USA	CAN	UK	GER	FRA	JAP
	99	96	84	83	79	41

Competition as Antidote to Collusion:

"Two friends were discussing the way businesses interact.

One said: 'If you allow businesses to cooperate with each other, they will usually collude against consumers and the larger society by agreeing to raise prices and/or restrain trade. They will do this for the obvious reason that it is in their self-interests to do so. Competition and still more competition is the only answer to this tendency.'

The other said: 'If you allow businesses to cooperate with each other they will usually pass on to their customers any enhanced effectiveness and economies of operations in the form of expanded trade. They will do this for the obvious reason that it is in their own and their customers group interests for this to happen. Cooperating in order to compete with the wider world is the only answer.'"

	USA	CAN	UK	GER	FRA	JAP
Competition and still more Competition	68	64	65	41	45	24

Pro-achievement, Anti-ascription (Based on Age):

"Becoming successful and respected is a matter of hard work. It is important for a manager to be older than his subordinates. Older people should be more respected than younger people."

	USA	CAN	UK	GER	FRA	JAP
Status by Hard Work	63	61.5	60	58	57	42

"Does job skill or power legitimize the boss?"

	USA	CAN	UK	GER	FRA	JAP
Job skill	78.5	68.7	64.2	79.7	75.2	26.7

"A man had a fire in his shop and lost most of his merchandise. His store was partly destroyed by the fire. He and his family had to have some help from someone to rebuild the shop as fast as possible. There are different ways of getting help.

(a) It would be best if he depended mostly on his brothers and sisters, or other relatives, to help him.

(b) It would be best to borrow some money *on his own* in order to get some construction people to rebuild his store."

	USA	CAN	UK	GER	FRA	JAP
(B) On one's own	79	80	74	67	68	50

Consensual vs. Adversarial Democracy:

(a) "It is better that all people meet and discuss things until almost everyone agrees on the same person."

(b) "It is better that all people meet, names be put up, a vote be taken, and then the person who gets the majority of the votes sent, even if there are several people who are still against this person."

(A) *Extended*	USA	CAN	UK	GER	FRA	JAP
Discussions	37.7	—	58.7	69.0	61.9	84.6

Notes

FOREWORD (pp. 13–15)

1. No one needs to elaborate on the roles of Lincoln and Roosevelt. Washington is their equal, as I tried to document in *The First New Nation: The United States in Historical and Comparative Perspective* (New York: Basic Books, 1963; expanded ed., W. W. Norton, 1979).
2. Seymour Martin Lipset, *Agrarian Socialism* (Berkeley, CA: University of California Press, 1950; Garden City, NY: Doubleday-Anchor, 1968; rev. and expanded ed., Berkeley, CA: University of California Press, 1971).
3. Seymour Martin Lipset, "Why No Socialism in the United States?" in S. Bialer and S. Sluzar, eds., *Sources of Contemporary Radicalism*, I (Boulder, CO: Westview Press, 1977), pp. 30–149 and 346–363.
4. Seymour Martin Lipset and Reinhard Bendix, *Social Mobility in Industrial Society* (Berkeley, CA: University of California Press, 1961; expanded ed., New Brunswick, NJ: Transaction Books, 1991).
5. See Lipset, *The First New Nation.*
6. Seymour Martin Lipset, *Continental Divide: The Values and Institutions of the United States and Canada* (New York: Routledge, 1990).
7. Seymour Martin Lipset and Earl Raab, *Jews and the New American Scene* (Cambridge, MA: Harvard University Press, 1995).
8. Seymour Martin Lipset, *Political Man: The Social Bases of Politics* (Baltimore: Johns Hopkins University Press, expanded ed. 1981).

INTRODUCTION (pp. 17–28)

1. Alexis de Tocqueville, *Democracy in America.* Vols. I and II (New York: Alfred A. Knopf, 1948).
2. Ibid., II, pp. 36–37. For a sophisticated critique which emphasizes external influences on America, see Ian Tyrell, "American Exceptionalism in an Age of International History," *American Historical Review*, 96 (October 1991), pp. 1031–1055. For a detailed reply, see Michael McGerr, "The Price of the 'New Transnational History,'" *American Historical Review*, 98 (October 1991), pp. 1056–1067.
3. George Wilson Pierson, *Tocqueville and Beaumont in America* (Gloucester, MA: Peter Smith, 1969).
4. Quoted in Michael Kazin, "The Right's Unsung Prophet," *The Nation*, 248 (February 20, 1989), p. 242.
5. For a brilliant analysis of the religious background of the United States, see David Fischer, *Albion's Seed. Four British Folkways in America* (New York: Oxford University Press, 1989).
6. See Seymour Martin Lipset, *Rebellion in the University* (Chicago: University of Chicago Press, 1971), pp. 12–14.
7. See Fischer, *Albion's Seed,* passim.
8. Charles Hampden-Turner and Alfons Trompenaars, *The Seven Cultures of Capitalism* (New York: Doubleday, 1993), p. 245.

9. "The European Union," *The Economist,* October 22, 1994, Survey, p. 4.

10. Mary Ann Glendon, "Rights in Twentieth Century Constitutions," in Geoffrey R. Stone, Richard A. Epstein, and Cass R. Sunstein, eds., *The Bill of Rights in the Modern State* (Chicago: University of Chicago Press, 1992), p. 521.

11. Ibid., pp. 524–525. See also Gerhard Casper, "Changing Concepts of Constitutionalism: 18th to 20th Century," *Supreme Court Review,* 311 (1989), pp. 318–319.

12. Max Weber, *The Methodology of the Social Sciences* (Glencoe, IL: The Free Press, 1949), pp. 182–185.

13. See Frank Underhill, *The Image of Confederation* (Toronto: Canadian Broadcasting Corporation, 1964), passim.

14. Hampden-Turner and Trompenaars, *Seven Cultures,* p. 48.

15. See Seymour Martin Lipset, *Consensus and Conflict: Essays in Political Sociology* (New Brunswick, NJ: Transaction Books, 1985).

16. Robert K. Merton, *Social Theory and Social Structure* (Glencoe, IL: The Free Press, 1957), pp. 168–170.

17. See Tables 8-1 and 8-2 in chapter Eight, pp. 00–00.

18. Suzanne Garment, "Newt's Law," *The New York Times,* November 20, 1994, p. 15.

1. Ideology, Politics, and Deviance *(pp. 31–52)*

1. For an earlier version of chapters One and Two, see S. M. Lipset, "American Exceptionalism Reaffirmed," in Byron E. Shafer, ed., *Is America Different? A New Look at American Exceptionalism* (London: Oxford University Press, 1991), pp. 1–45. For a more elaborate effort to place American exceptionalism in theoretical and historical perspectives, see S. M. Lipset, *The First New Nation: The United States in Historical and Comparative Perspective* (New York: Basic Books, 1963; expanded paperback ed., New York: W. W. Norton, 1979).

2. G. K. Chesterton, *What I Saw in America* (New York: Dodd, Mead & Co., 1922), p. 7.

3. See Louis Hartz, *The Liberal Tradition in America,* (New York: Harcourt, Brace & World, 1955), pp. 6, 234. The word "liberal," it should be noted, did not come into existence until the early nineteenth century and probably did not take on this meaning until the middle of that century. See Giovanni Sartori, *The Theory of Democracy Revisited, Part Two: The Classical Issue* (Chatham, NJ: Chatham House Publishers, 1987), pp. 370–371.

4. H. G. Wells, *The Future in America* (New York: Harper & Brothers, 1906), pp. 72–76. For an excellent analysis of liberal party politics in Britain, Canada, and the United States, see Robert Kelley, *The Transatlantic Persuasion: The Liberal-Democratic Mind in the Age of Gladstone* (New York: Alfred A. Knopf, 1969).

5. See Lipset, *The First New Nation,* pp. 249–252, 257–259.

6. For a critique of this focus, see Sean Wilentz, "Against Exceptionalism: Class Consciousness and the American Labor Movement, 1790–1940," *International Labor and Working Class History,* 26 (Fall 1984), pp. 1–24. Also see Richard Oestreicher, "Urban Working-Class Political Behavior and Theories of American Electoral Politics," *Journal of American History,* 74 (March 1988), pp. 1257–1286; Aristide R. Zolberg, "How Many Exceptionalisms?" in Ira Katznelson and Aristide R. Zolberg, eds., *Working-Class Formation. Nineteenth Century Patterns in Western Europe and the United States* (Princeton, NJ: Princeton University Press, 1986), pp. 397–455; and Kim Voss, *The Making of American Exceptionalism* (Ithaca, NY: Cornell University Press, 1993).

7. See "Unpublished Letters of Karl Marx and Friedrich Engels to Americans," *Science and Society,* 2 (1938), pp. 368, 375; Karl Marx, Friedrich Engels, and Alexander Trachtenberg, *Karl Marx and Frederick Engels: Letters to Americans, 1848–1895* (New York: International Publishers, 1953), p. 239; Karl Marx and Frederick Engels, *Selected Correspondence, 1846–1895,* trans. Donna Torr (New York: International Publishers, 1942), p. 449.

8. Werner Sombart, *Why Is There No Socialism in the United States?* (White Plains, NY: International Arts & Sciences Press, 1976; first published in German in 1906).

9. Wells, *The Future in America.*

10. Karl Marx, *Capital,* I (Moscow: Foreign Languages Publishing House, 1958), pp. 8–9.

11. For a discussion of the problems this question poses, see Carl N. Degler, "In Pursuit of American History," *American Historical Review,* 92 (February 1987), pp. 1–12.

12. For an analysis of nineteenth-century academic writing, see Dorothy Ross, "Historical Consciousness in Nineteenth-Century America," *American Historical Review,* 89 (October 1984), pp. 909–928.

13. Edmund Burke, *Selected Works* (Oxford: Clarendon Press, 1904), pp. 180–181.

14. J. Hector St. John Crèvecoeur, *Letters from an American Farmer* (New York: Dolphin Books, 1963), pp. 46–47.

15. Alexis de Tocqueville, *Democracy in America,* II, (New York: Alfred A. Knopf, 1948), pp. 104, 113, 129–135.

16. See, among others, C. Vann Woodward, *The Old World's New World* (New York: Oxford University Press, 1991); Max Berger, *The British Traveller in America, 1836–1860* (New York: Columbia University Press, 1943); Oscar Handlin, ed., *This Was America* (Cambridge: Harvard University Press, 1949); Henry Steele Commager, *America in Perspective* (New York: Random House, 1947); J. G. Brooks, *As Others See Us* (New York: Macmillan, 1908); Jane L. Mesick, *The English Traveller in America, 1785–1835* (New York: Columbia University Press, 1922); Robert W. Smuts, *European Impressions of the American Worker* (New York: King's Crown Press, 1953); Frances Trollope, *Domestic Manners of the Americans* (London: Whitaker, Treacher, 1832); Anthony Trollope, *North America* (New York: Alfred A. Knopf, 1951); James Bryce, *The American Commonwealth* (New York: Macmillan, 1912); Lipset, *The First New Nation,* pp. 101–137; Lee Coleman, "What Is America? A Study of Alleged American Traits," *Social Forces,* 19 (May 1941), pp. 492–499; and Everett Carll Ladd, *The American Ideology. An Exploration of the Origins, Meaning, and Role of American Political Ideas* (Storrs, CT: The Roper Center for Public Opinion Research, 1994), pp. 18–21.

17. Cited in George Wilson Pierson, *Tocqueville and Beaumont in America* (Gloucester, MA: Peter Smith, 1969), p. 271.

18. Harriet Martineau, *Society in America* (New Brunswick, NJ: Transaction Books, 1981).

19. For documentation, see Lipset, *The First New Nation,* pp. 101–137; Coleman, "What Is America?" pp. 492–499.

20. See S. M. Lipset, *Continental Divide: The Values and Institutions of the United States and Canada* (New York: Routledge, 1990), and Seymour Martin Lipset, "Historical Traditions and National Characteristics: A Comparative Analysis of Canada and the United States," *Canadian Journal of Sociology,* 11 (Summer 1986), pp. 113–155.

21. Seymour Martin Lipset, "Anglo-American Society," in David Sills, ed., *International Encyclopedia of the Social Sciences,* I (New York: Macmillan, 1968), pp. 289–302.

22. Lipset, *The First New Nation,* pp. 248–273.

23. See Louis Hartz, *The Founding of New Societies* (New York: Harcourt, Brace & World, 1964).

24. Private conversation.

25. Max Beloff, "Of Lords, Senators, & Plain Misters," *Encounter,* 68 (April 1987), pp. 69–71; "An Exchange Between Max Beloff and Irving Kristol," *Encounter,* 69 (June 1987), pp. 69–71.

26. George Grant, *Lament for a Nation* (Princeton, NJ: D. Van Nostrand, 1965), pp. 64–65.

27. See, e.g., Michael Elliott, "What's Left?" *Newsweek,* International ed., October 10, 1994, pp. 10–15; Allan Winkler, "Centre of Attention," *The Times* (London), April 15, 1994; Amitai Etzioni, "Who Should Pay for Care?" *Sunday Times* (London), October 9, 1994, p. 7; "The Ties That Bind," *The Economist,* October 8, 1994, p. 58.

28. Richard Hofstadter, *The Age of Reform: From Bryan to F.D.R.* (New York: Alfred A. Knopf, 1972), p. 308.

29. Grant McConnell, *Private Power and American Democracy* (New York: Random House, 1966), p. 38.

30. Quoted in Hofstadter, *The Age of Reform,* p. 308.

31. Seymour Martin Lipset, "Roosevelt and the Protest of the 1930's," *Minnesota Law Review,* 68 (December 1983), pp. 173–198.

32. Samuel Lubell, *The Future of American Politics* (New York: Harper & Row, 3rd ed., 1965), pp. 55–68.

33. Karlyn H. Keene and Everett Carll Ladd, "America: A Unique Outlook?" *The American Enterprise*, 1 (March–April 1990), p. 120.

34. Leo Strauss, *Thoughts on Machiavelli* (Glencoe, IL: The Free Press, 1958), p. 13.

35. For background, see Richard Hofstadter, *The American Political Tradition and the Men Who Made It* (New York: Alfred A. Knopf, 1964), pp. 8–15.

36. J. P. Nettl, "The State as a Conceptual Variable," *World Politics*, 20 (July 1968), pp. 561, 574, 585.

37. E. E. Schattschneider, *Party Government* (New York: Rinehart & Co., 1942), pp. 65–98.

38. See Daniel Bell, *Marxian Socialism in the United States* (Princeton, NJ: Princeton University Press, 1967), p. 116; Seymour Martin Lipset, "Socialism in America," in Paul Kurtz, ed., *Sidney Hook: Philosopher of Democracy and Humanism* (Buffalo, NY: Prometheus Books, 1983), pp. 55–59.

39. Allan Gotlieb, *I'll Be With You in a Minute, Mr. Ambassador* (Toronto: University of Toronto Press, 1991).

40. Sven Steinmo, "Rethinking American Exceptionalism." Unpublished paper, Department of Political Science, University of Colorado, 1992.

41. Byron Shafer, " 'Exceptionalism' in American Politics?" *PS*, 22 (September 1989), pp. 588–594; Seymour Martin Lipset and William Schneider, *The Confidence Gap: Business, Labor, and Government in the Public Mind* (Baltimore: Johns Hopkins University Press, expanded and updated ed., 1987), pp. 379–380.

42. U.S. Bureau of the Census, *Census of Government: Popularly Elected Officials* (Washington, D.C.: U.S. Department of Commerce, 1994); U.S. Bureau of the Census, *Statistical Abstract of the United States, 1994* (Washington, D.C.: U.S. Department of Commerce, 1994), p. 287.

43. Austin Ranney, "Referendums," *Public Opinion*, 11 (January–February 1989), p. 15. For similar comments, see Ivor Crewe, "Electoral Participation," in David Butler, Howard Penniman, and Austin Ranney, eds., *Democracy at the Polls: A Comparative Study of Competitive National Elections* (Washington, D.C.: American Enterprise Institute, 1981), p. 232, and Robert W. Jackman and Ross A. Miller, "Voter Turnout in the Industrial Democracies During the 1980s," *Comparative Political Studies*, 27 (January 1995), pp. 482–483.

44. Edward C. Banfield and James Q. Wilson, *City Politics* (Cambridge, MA: Harvard University Press and MIT Press, 1963), p. 1.

45. Actually, the percentage should be 1–2 points higher if aliens are excluded from the base; see Walter Dean Burnham, "The 1980 Earthquake: Realignment, Reaction, or What?" in Thomas Ferguson and Joel Rogers, eds., *The Hidden Election* (New York: Pantheon Books, 1981), p. 101.

46. Walter Dean Burnham, "The Appearance and Disappearance of the American Voter," in Richard Rose, ed., *Electoral Participation: A Comparative Analysis* (Beverly Hills, CA: Sage Publications, 1980), pp. 35–73.

47. B. F. Skinner, *Walden Two* (New York: Macmillan, 1976), p. 188; Seymour Martin Lipset, "Why Americans Refuse to Vote," in *Insight*, 10 (February 7, 1994), pp. 24–26.

48. See Raymond E. Wolfinger and Steven Rosenstone, *Who Votes?* (New Haven, CT: Yale University Press, 1980), and Francis Fox Piven and Richard A. Cloward, *Why Americans Don't Vote* (New York: Pantheon, 1988).

49. Louise I. Shelley, "American Crime: An International Anomaly?" *Comparative Social Research*, 8 (1985), p. 81; see also Leon Radzinowicz and Joan King, *The Growth of Crime: The International Experience* (New York: Basic Books, 1977), pp. 6–7.

50. Shelley, "American Crime," pp. 81, 88–89.

51. "The European Union," *The Economist*, October 22, 1994, Survey, p. 4.

52. Steven A. Holmes, "Ranks of Inmates Reach One Million in a 2-Decade Rise," *New York Times*, October 28, 1994, p. A1.

53. Shelley, "American Crime," p. 91.
54. I have drawn here on my earlier discussion in *The First New Nation*, pp. 173–177.
55. Robert K. Merton, *Social Theory and Social Structure* (Glencoe, IL: The Free Press, 1957), pp. 167–169. Merton reports considerable evidence documenting the thesis that pecuniary success is the dominant American value.
56. Ibid.
57. Daniel Bell, *The End of Ideology* (Glencoe, IL: The Free Press, 1960), pp. 116–117. A sophisticated discussion of the "malignant forms of 'achievement,'" with reference to science as well as business, may be found in Janet T. Spence, "Achievement American Style. The Rewards and Costs of Individualism," *The American Psychologist*, 40 (December 1985), pp. 1291–1292.
58. For a somewhat different critical analysis of dysfunctional consequences of the American emphasis on individual rights, its lack of concern for the needs of others, see Mary Ann Glendon, *Rights Talk: The Impoverishment of Political Discourse*, discussed and summarized in Ladd, *The American Ideology*, pp. 21–22.
59. Herbert Packer, "Two Models of the Criminal Process," *University of Pennsylvania Law Review*, 113 (November 1964), pp. 1–68.
60. Stephen Cole, "Crime as the Cost of American Creativity," *Newsday*, August 24, 1983, Viewpoint Section.
61. Fred Barbash, "Alarmed by Crime Surge, Britain Narrows Rights," *The Washington Post*, November 11, 1994, pp. 1, 41.
62. Alan F. Westin, "The United States Bill of Rights and the Canadian Charter: A Socio-Political Analysis," in William R. McKercher, ed., *The U.S. Bill of Rights and the Canadian Charter of Rights and Freedoms* (Toronto: Ontario Economic Council, 1983), p. 33.
63. David Popenoe, *Disturbing the Nest: Family Change and Decline in Modern Societies* (New York: Aldine de Gruyter, 1988), p. 287.
64. William J. Goode, *The World Changes in Divorce Patterns* (New Haven, CT: Yale University Press, 1993), p. 153. For recent statistics, see U.S. Bureau of the Census, *Statistical Abstract of the United States, 1994*, p. 858.
65. Goode, *The World Changes in Divorce Patterns*, p. 154.
66. Ibid., p. 156.
67. Popenoe, *Disturbing the Nest*, p. 288.
68. Ibid., p. 289; Robert N. Bellah, et al., *Habits of the Heart* (Berkeley, CA: University of California Press, 1985), pp. 32–35, 48–50, 89, 101–102.
69. Elise F. Jones, *Teenage Pregnancy in Industrialized Countries* (New Haven, CT: Yale University Press, 1986), pp. 36, 8–11.
70. Ibid., pp. 89, 223.
71. Richard Rose, "National Pride in Cross-National Perspective," *International Social Science Journal*, 37/1 (1985), pp. 86, 93–95; Russell V. Dalton, *Citizen Politics in Western Democracies* (Chatham, NJ: Chatham House Publishers, 1988), p. 237; Marjorie Hyer, "Poll Finds Americans Most Proud," *International Herald Tribune*, May 20, 1982, p. 3.
72. Elizabeth Hawn Hastings and Phillip K. Hastings, *Index to International Public Opinion, 1988–89* (New York: Greenwood Press, 1990), p. 612.
73. Ibid.
74. Alex C. Michalos, "Optimism in Thirty Countries Over a Decade," *Social Indicators Research*, 20 (1988), pp. 178–179.

2. Economy, Religion, and Welfare (pp. 53–76)

1. Alexis de Tocqueville, *Democracy in America*, I (New York: Alfred A. Knopf, 1948), p. 51.
2. Analyzing America in the 1880s, James Bryce reiterated Tocqueville's description. Bryce, *The American Commonwealth*, II (New York: Macmillan, 1912), pp. 817–818, 873.
3. Everett Carll Ladd, *The American Ideology: An Exploration of the Origins, Meaning, and Role*

of American Political Ideas (Storrs, CT: Roper Center for Public Opinion Research, 1994), p. 10. See also Douglas Southall Freeman, *George Washington* (New York: Charles Scribner's Sons, 1954), p. 186.

4. Martin Trow, "American Higher Education: Past, Present and Future", *Educational Researcher*, 17 (April 1988), p. 15.

5. Henry Rosovsky, *The University: An Owner's Manual* (New York: W. W. Norton, 1990), pp. 31–32.

6. Samuel Huntington, "The U.S.—Decline or Renewal?," *Foreign Affairs*, 67 (Winter 1988–89), p. 89.

7. Philip Schaff, *America: A Sketch of the Political, Social, and Religious Character of the United States of North America* (New York: C. Scribner, 1855), p. 259.

8. For Engels, see Engels to Sorge (February 8, 1890) in Karl Marx and Frederick Engels, *Selected Correspondence, 1846–1895*, trans. Donna Torr (New York: International Publishers, 1942), p. 467.

9. Max Weber, *The Protestant Ethic and the Spirit of Capitalism* (New York: Scribner's, 1935; first published in German, 1905), pp. 55ff.

10. Antonio Gramsci, *Selections from the Prison Notebooks* (New York: International Publishers, 1971), pp. 21–22, 272, 318.

11. Weber, *The Protestant Ethic*, pp. 155–183, and Max Weber, "The Protestant Sects and the Spirit of Capitalism," in *Essays in Sociology*, trans. by Hans Gerth and C. W. Mills (New York: Oxford University Press, 1946), pp. 309, 313.

12. U.S. Bureau of the Census, *Statistical Abstract of the United States, 1994* (Washington, D.C.: U.S. Department of Commerce, 1994), p. 864.

13. Quoted in ibid. For documentation, see Alan Heston and Robert Summers, "What We Have Learned about Prices and Quantities from International Comparisons: 1987," *American Economic Review*, 78 (May 1988), pp. 467–473.

14. Daniel Bell, *The Coming of Post-Industrial Society* (New York: Basic Books, 1973); Peter Drucker, *Post-Capitalist Society* (New York: Harper Business, 1993). For an earlier statement, see Nelson Foote and Paul Hatt, "Social Mobility and Economic Advancement," *American Economic Review*, S43 (May 1953), pp. 364–378.

15. Richard Freeman, "Labor Studies," *NBER Reporter* (Fall 1994), p. 2.

16. For a detailed early analysis of these shifts, see Colin Clark, *The Conditions of Economic Progress* (London: Macmillan and Co., 1940).

17. See Louis Uchitelle, "Election Placing Focus on the Issue of Jobs vs. Wages," *The New York Times*, September 4, 1988, pp. 1, 14; Joanna Moy, "Recent Trends in Unemployment and the Labor Force, 10 Countries," *Monthly Labor Review*, 108 (August 1985), p. 11.

18. Huntington, "The U.S.—Decline or Renewal?," pp. 82–83; Karen Elliot House, "The 90's and Beyond: For All Its Difficulties, U.S. Stands to Retain Its Global Leadership," *Wall Street Journal*, January 23, 1989, p. A8.

19. Peter T. Kilborn, "A Fight to Win the Middle Class," *The New York Times*, September 4, 1988, p. 5, Business Section.

20. "Business Outlook," *BusinessWeek*, August 22, 1994, p. 21.

21. Paul Blustein, "The Great Jobs Debate," *The Washington Post National Weekly Edition*, September 5–11, 1988, p. 20; M. W. Horrigan and S. E. Haugen, "The Declining Middle-Class Thesis: A Sensitivity Analysis," *Monthly Labor Review*, 111 (May 1988), pp. 3–13.

22. Sylvia Nasar, "Statistics Reveal Bulk of New Jobs Pay Over Average," *New York Times*, October 17, 1994, p. A1.

23. Paul Krugman, "Technology's Revenge," *The Wilson Quarterly*, 18 (Autumn 1994), pp. 56–64.

24. Nasar, "Statistics Reveal Bulk . . . ," p. D4.

25. Robert J. Samuelson, "Psycho-Facts Revisited," *The Washington Post*, June 8, 1994, p. A23.

26. *Statistical Abstract, 1994*, pp. 103, 91, 87.

27. Robert S. Reich, *The Work of Nations. Preparing Ourselves for 21st-Century Capitalism* (New York: Alfred A. Knopf, 1991), pp. 34–35.

28. See, e.g., Michael L. Dertouzos, Richard K. Lester, Robert M. Solow, and the MIT Commission on Industrial Productivity, *Made in America: Regaining the Productive Edge* (New York: HarperCollins, 1990), p. 26.

29. Richard Rosecrance, *America's Economic Resurgence. A Bold New Strategy* (New York: Harper & Row, 1990), pp. 44–45.

30. *Statistical Abstract, 1994*, p. 801; James J. Cramer, "Heavy Metal," *The New Republic,* April 27, 1992, pp. 23–27. See also various short articles in "Is America on the Way Down? (Round Two)," *Commentary,* 93 (May 1992), pp. 19–29, and "Trade Gap Narrowest in 9 Years," *The Washington Post,* April 17, 1992, p. D1.

31. Cramer, "Heavy Metal," pp. 23–27.

32. Reported in George V. Church, "And It Hurts," *Time,* October 24, 1994, p. 51.

33. "The Fading of Japanophobia," *The Economist,* August 6, 1994, p. 21.

34. See chapter One, p. 33. For an elaboration, see Robert N. Bellah, *The Broken Covenant: American Civil Religion in Time of Trial* (New York: Seabury Press, 1975), pp. 36–60, and Robert N. Bellah, et al., *Habits of the Heart* (Berkeley, CA: University of California Press, 1985), pp. 28–41, 219–225.

35. Edmund Burke, *Selected Works* (Oxford: Clarendon Press, 1904), pp. 180–181.

36. See Weber, "The Protestant Sects and The Spirit of Capitalism."

37. Weber, *The Protestant Ethic,* p. 175.

38. Ibid., pp. 55–56.

39. Ibid., pp. 48–50.

40. "Workaholics Anonymous," *The Economist,* October 22, 1994, p. 20.

41. Linda Bell and Richard Freeman, *Why Do Americans and Germans Work Differing Hours?* Working Paper No. 4808 (Cambridge, MA: National Bureau of Economic Research, 1994), pp. 2, 14–15.

42. Tocqueville, *Democracy in America,* I, p. 36.

43. Ladd, *The American Ideology,* pp. 12–15.

44. *Code of 1650, Being a Compilation of the Earliest Laws and Orders of the General Court of Connecticut* (Hartford, CT: S. Andrus and Son, c. 1822), pp. 90–91. Cited in Ladd, *The American Ideology,* pp. 12–13. Ladd continues: "The *Code* goes on [to] require the establishment of schools in every township 'after the Lord hath increased them to the number of fifty howshoulders' and obliges the inhabitants of each township to support them."

45. For comparative efforts, see David Popenoe, *Disturbing the Nest: Family Change and Decline in Modern Societies* (New York: Aldine de Gruyter, 1988), p. 284, and Ronald Inglehart and David Apple, "The Rise of Post-Materialist Values and Changing Religious Orientations, Gender Roles and Sexual Norms," *International Journal of Public Opinion Research,* 1 (Spring 1989), pp. 45–75. See also Ladd, *The American Ideology,* pp. 71–73.

46. Andrew Greeley, *Religion Around the World: A Preliminary Report* (Chicago: National Opinion Research Center, 1991), p. 39.

47. Ibid., p. 38.

48. Ronald Inglehart, *1990 World Values Survey* (Ann Arbor, MI: Institute for Social Research, 1990), question 37 D.

49. Ibid., question 3 F.

50. Roger Finke and Rodney Stark, *The Churching of America, 1776–1990: Winners and Losers in Our Religious Economy* (New Brunswick, NJ: Rutgers University Press, 1992), pp. 15–16.

51. Tocqueville, *Democracy in America,* I, p. 314. For an excellent current overview, see Edward A. Tiryakian, "American Religious Exceptionalism: A Reconsideration," *Annals of the American Academy of Political and Social Science,* 527 (May 1993), pp. 40–54.

52. Kenneth D. Wald, *Religion and Politics in the United States* (New York: St. Martin's Press, 1987), p. 6. For comparable findings, see Walter Dean Burnham, "The 1980 Earthquake: Realignment, Reaction, or What?" in Thomas Ferguson and Joel Rogers, eds., *The Hidden Election* (New York: Pantheon Books, 1981), p. 132.

53. Wald, *Religion and Politics,* pp. 6–7; see also pp. 8–12.

54. Ladd, *The American Ideology,* p. 15 (emphasis in original).

55. Samuel Huntington, *American Politics: The Promise of Disharmony* (Cambridge, MA: Belknap Press, 1981), p. 154. For documentation, see pp. 8, 31–32, 84–104.

56. Bellah, *The Broken Covenant,* p. 48. See also Sacvan Bercovitch, *The American Jeremiad* (Madison, WI: University of Wisconsin Press, 1978), pp. 20, 94.

57. See also chapter Seven, p. 226–7.

58. See George Kennan, *Realities of American Foreign Policy* (New York: W. W. Norton, 1966), pp. 3–50; Robert Bellah, *Beyond Belief* (New York: Harper & Row, 1970), pp. 182–183.

59. Huntington, *American Politics,* pp. 158–159.

60. Bellah, *Beyond Belief,* p. 175; Wald, *Religion and Politics,* pp. 48–55.

61. Ladd, *The American Ideology,* p. 5 (emphasis added).

62. R.L. Bruckberger, "The American Catholics as a Minority," in Thomas T. McAvoy, ed., *Roman Catholicism and the American Way of Life* (Notre Dame, IN: University of Notre Dame Press, 1960), pp. 45–47. See also Bruckberger, *Image of America* (New York: Viking Press, 1959).

63. Bellah, *The Broken Covenant,* p. 60.

64. Sol Tax, "War and the Draft," in Morton Fried, Marvin Harris, and Robert Francis Murphy, eds., *War* (Garden City, NY: Doubleday/Natural History Press, 1968), pp. 199–203.

65. See, for example, Samuel Eliot Morison, "Dissent in the War of 1812," in Morison, Frederick Merk, and Frank Freidel, *Dissent in Three American Wars* (Cambridge, MA: Harvard University Press, 1970), pp. 3–31; Alice Felt Tyler, *Freedom's Ferment* (New York: Harper, Torchbooks, 1962), p. 407; Frederick Merk, "Dissent in the Mexican War," in Morison, et al., *Dissent in Three American Wars,* pp. 33–63; Edward S. Wallace, "Notes and Comment—Deserters in the Mexican War," *Hispanic American Historical Review,* 15 (1935), p. 374; David Donald, "Died of Democracy," in David Donald, ed., *Why the North Won the Civil War* (Baton Rouge, LA: Louisiana State University Press, 1960), pp. 85–89; James McCague, *The Second Rebellion: The Story of The New York City Draft Riots of 1863* (New York: Dial, 1968); Basil L. Lee, *Discontent in New York City, 1861–65* (Washington, D.C.: Catholic University of America Press, 1943); Frank Freidel, "Dissent in the Spanish-American War and the Philippine Insurrection," in Morison, et al, *Dissent in Three American Wars,* pp. 65–95, esp. p. 77; and H. C. Peterson and Gilbert C. Fite, *Opponents of War, 1917–1918* (Seattle: University of Washington Press, 1957), pp. 39, 123–135, 234.

66. See Kennan, *Realities of American Foreign Policy.*

67. Aileen D. Ross, "Philanthropy," in David L. Sills, ed., *International Encyclopedia of the Social Sciences,* XII (New York: Macmillan and the Free Press, 1968), p. 76.

68. "An American Gentleman" (Calvin Colton), *A Voice from America to England* (London: Henry Colburn, 1839), pp. 87–88.

69. Arnoud C. Marts, *The Generosity of Americans: Its Source, Its Achievements* (Englewood Cliffs, NJ: Prentice-Hall, 1966), pp. 4–82.

70. Merle Curti, *American Philanthropy Abroad: A History* (New Brunswick, NJ: Rutgers University Press, 1963), p. 625.

71. Ross, "Philanthropy," p. 76. See essays in Teresa Odendahl, ed., *America's Wealthy and the Future of Foundations* (Washington, D.C.: Foundation Center, 1987).

72. Quoted in Robert H. Bremner, *American Philanthropy* (Chicago: University of Chicago Press, 1988), p. 138.

73. David Deitch, "Libertarians Unite in Drive to Reduce Tax Burdens," *Boston Globe,* April 10, 1971, p. 7. See also "What's This?" *Dissent,* 18 (August 1971), p. 395.

74. Cited in Martin Green, *The Problem of Boston* (New York: W. W. Norton, 1966), p. 4.

75. Ibid., p. 56.

76. Ben Whitaker, *The Foundations: An Anatomy of Philanthropy and Society* (London: Eyre Methuen, 1974), p. 53.

77. Quoted in Joseph C. Goulden, *The Money Givers* (New York: Random House, 1971), p. 47.

78. Ibid., p. 28. See also Whitaker, *The Foundations,* pp. 64–66; Bremner, *American Philanthropy,* p. 106.

79. *Giving and Volunteering in the United States: Findings from A National Survey* (Washington, D.C.: Independent Sector, 1992), p. 29.
80. Ibid., p. 40. See also Edward C. Jenkins, *Philanthropy in America* (New York: Association Press, 1950), p. 91; William S. Vickrey, "One Economist's View of Philanthropy," in Frank Dickinson, ed., *Philanthropy and Public Policy* (New York: National Bureau of Economic Research, 1962), p. 33; George G. Kirstein, *Better Giving* (Boston: Houghton Mifflin, 1975), pp. 59–71. For detailed statistics, see the annual reports, *Giving USA*, published each year by the American Association of Fund-Raising Counsel, Inc., begun in 1954.
81. Vickrey, "One Economist's View of Philanthropy," p. 45.
82. Merrimon Cuninggim, *Private Money and Public Service* (New York: McGraw-Hill, 1972), pp. 169–170.
83. Ross, "Philanthropy," p. 78.
84. *Giving and Volunteering in the United States*, p. 36.
85. Barringer, "In the Worst of Times," p. E6. Data are from Independent Sector, a Washington-based group representing the nation's non-profit institutions, and *Giving USA*.
86. Popenoe, *Disturbing the Nest*, p. 285.
87. Robert T. Kudrle and Theodore R. Marmor, "The Development of Welfare States in North America," in P. Flora and A. J. Heidenheimer, eds., *The Development of Welfare States in Europe and North America* (New Brunswick, NJ: Transaction Books, 1984), p. 83.
88. J. Palmer, T. Smeeding, and B. B. Torrey, eds., *The Vulnerable* (Washington, D.C.: Urban Institute, 1988).
89. See Stephanie G. Gould and John L. Palmer, "Outcomes, Interpretations, and Policy Implications," in ibid., p. 428.
90. Inglehart, *1990 World Values Survey*.
91. International Social Survey Program (ISSP) (Chicago: NORC, biannual, 1990, 1992).
92. Ibid., 1992.
93. Ibid.
94. Ibid. See also Benjamin I. Page and Robert Y. Shapiro, *The Rational Public: Fifty Years of Trends in Americans' Policy Preferences* (Chicago: University of Chicago Press, 1992), p. 128.
95. Tomás Kolosi, "Beliefs About Inequality in Cross-National Perspective." Paper prepared for 1987 conference on "The Welfare State in Transition," p. 33.
96. Alvin Rabushka, *Ten Myths About Higher Taxes* (Stanford, CA: Hoover Institution Working Paper, 1993), p. 15.
97. "Inequality for Richer, for Poorer," *The Economist*, November 5, 1994, pp. 19–20. The magazine presents a chart constructed for thirteen OECD countries from data drawn from diverse sources.
98. Keith Bradsher, "Gap in Wealth in U.S. Called Widest in West," *New York Times*, April 17, 1995, p. A1, D4.
99. Michael F. Förster, *Comparing Poverty in 13 OECD Countries—Traditional and Synthetic Approaches*, Luxembourg Income Study Working Paper No. 100 (Syracuse, NY: Maxwell School, Syracuse University, 1994), pp. 61–63.
100. Bradsher, "Gap in Wealth," p. D4.
101. Timothy M. Smeeding and John Coder, *Income Inequality in Rich Countries During the 1980s.* Luxembourg Income Study Working Paper No. 88 (Syracuse, NY: Maxwell School, Syracuse University, 1993), pp. 1–2, 10–12.
102. Anthony King, "Ideas, Institutions and the Policies of Governments: A Comparative Analysis: Parts I and II," *British Journal of Political Science*, 3 (July 1973), p. 300.
103. Ladd, *The American Ideology*, p. 35.
104. Brigitte Buhmann, et al., "Equivalence Scales, Well Being, Inequality, and Poverty: Sensitivity Estimates Across Ten Countries Using the Luxembourg Income Study (LIS) Database," *Review of Income and Wealth*, 34 (June 1988), pp. 126–133; Timothy M. Smeeding and Barbara Boyld Torrey, "Poor Children in Rich Countries," *Science*, 242 (November 11, 1988), pp. 873–877.

105. Sidney Verba et al., *Elites and the Idea of Equality* (Cambridge: Harvard University Press, 1987).

3. SOCIALISM AND UNIONISM IN THE UNITED STATES AND CANADA (*pp. 77–109*)

1. My most detailed analysis of the weakness of Socialist parties in America is "Why No Socialism in the United States?" in S. Bialer and S. Sluzar, eds., *Sources of Contemporary Radicalism*, I (Boulder, CO: Westview Press, 1977), pp. 31–149 and 346–363. A discussion of the decline of the American trade union movement which has been subsumed in this chapter is "Trade Union Exceptionalism: The United States and Canada," *Annals of the American Academy of Political and Social Sciences*, 538 (March 1995), pp. 115–130.

2. See, for example, Theodore Draper, *American Communism and Soviet Russia* (New York: Viking Press, 1960), pp. 268–272; Michael Shalev and Walter Korpi, "Working Class Mobilization and American Exceptionalism," *Economic and Industrial Democracy*, 1 (February 1990), pp. 31–61; and Alan Wolfe, "Cultural Sources of the Reagan Revolution: The Antimodern Legacy," in B. B. Kymlicka and Jean V. Matthews, eds., *The Reagan Revolution?* (Chicago: The Dorsey Press, 1988).

3. Kim Voss, *The Making of American Exceptionalism* (Ithaca, NY: Cornell University Press, 1993).

4. For comments and references, see Lipset, "Why No Socialism in the United States?", pp. 31–149 and 346–363.

5. Karl Marx, *Capital*, I (Moscow: Foreign Languages Publishing House, 1958), pp. 8–9.

6. Lipset, "Why No Socialism in the United States?", pp. 32–33.

7. See ibid., pp. 45–61, for references.

8. David L. Sills and Robert King Merton, eds., *International Encyclopedia of the Social Sciences: Social Science Quotations* (New York: Macmillan, 1991), p. 229.

9. Werner Sombart, *Why Is There No Socialism in the United States?* (White Plains, NY: International Arts and Sciences Press, 1976).

10. On Marx's views, see Lewis S. Feuer, *Marx and the Intellectuals* (Garden City, NY: Doubleday-Anchor Books, 1969), pp. 198–209. On the Workingmen's parties, see Nathan Fine, *Labor and Farmer Parties in the United States, 1828–1928* (New York: Rand School of Social Science, 1928), pp. 13–14; Edward Pessen, *Most Uncommon Jacksonians* (Albany, NY: State University of New York Press, 1967), pp. 183–189; Walter Hugins, *Jacksonian Democracy and the Working Class* (Stanford, CA: Stanford University Press, 1960), pp. 13, 18–20, 132–134.

11. Karl Marx and Friedrich Engels, *The German Ideology* (New York: International Publishers, 1960), p. 123.

12. Engels to Sorge, February 8, 1890, in Karl Marx and Frederick Engels, *Selected Correspondence, 1846–1895*, trans. Donna Torr (New York: International Publishers, 1942), p. 467.

13. Engels to Sorge, December 31, 1892, in ibid., p. 501.

14. Engels to Weydemeyer, August 7, 1851, in Karl Marx, Friedrich Engels, and Alexander Trachtenberg, *Karl Marx and Frederick Engels: Letters to Americans, 1848–1895* (New York: International Publishers, 1953), p. 26.

15. See Lipset, "Why No Socialism in the United States?", pp. 32–47.

16. Engels to Sorge, June 29, 1883, "Unpublished Letters of Karl Marx and Friedrich Engels to Americans," *Science and Society*, 2 (1938), p. 231.

17. Quoted in Sidney Hook, *Marx and the Marxists* (New York: D. Van Nostrand, 1955), p. 64.

18. Engels to Sorge, September 16, 1886, "Unpublished Letters," p. 358.

19. Karl Marx, "On the Jewish Question," in Karl Marx and Friedrich Engels, *Collected Works*. Vol. III (London: Lawrence & Wishart, 1975), p. 151 (emphasis in original).

20. Ibid., p. 155 (emphases in original).

21. See Daniel Bell, "The Background and Development of Marxian Socialism in the United States," in Donald D. Egbert and Stow Persons, eds., *Socialism and American Life*, I (Princeton: Princeton University Press, 1952); Martin Diamond, "The Problems of the Socialist Party: After World War One," in John H. M. Laslett and Seymour Martin Lipset, eds., *Fail-*

ure of a Dream? Essays in the History of American Socialism (Garden City, NY: Doubleday-Anchor Books, 1974), pp. 362–379; Bernard Johnpoll, *Pacifist's Progress* (Chicago: Quadrangle Books, 1970); R. Laurence Moore, *European Socialists and the American Promised Land* (New York: Oxford University Press, 1970); David A. Shannon, *The Socialist Party of America* (Chicago: Quadrangle Books, 1967).

22. Engels to Sorge, October 24, 1891, in *Letters to Americans*, p. 237.

23. Engels to Sorge, December 2, 1893, "Unpublished Letters," p. 375.

24. Harvey Klehr, "Marxist Theory in Search of America," *The Journal of Politics*, 35 (1973), p. 319.

25. Karl Marx, "The Eighteenth Brumaire of Louis Bonaparte," in Karl Marx and Friedrich Engels, *Selected Works*. Vol. II (Moscow: Cooperative Publishing Society of Foreign Workers in the USSR, 1936), p. 324.

26. Engels to Florence Kelley Wischnewetsky, June 3, 1886, in *Selected Correspondence, 1846–1895*, p. 449.

27. See Marx as quoted in Michael Harrington, *Socialism* (New York: Saturday Review Press, 1972), p. 115.

28. For a discussion of the writings of later socialists on the subject, see Lipset, "Why No Socialism in the United States?", pp. 75–83.

29. Karlyn H. Keene and Everett Carll Ladd, "America: A Unique Outlook?" *The American Enterprise*, 1 (March–April 1990), p. 118.

30. Ronald Inglehart, *1990 World Values Survey* (data reports).

31. See Pessen, *Most Uncommon Jacksonians*, pp. 183–189; and Hugins, *Jacksonian Democracy*, pp. 13, 18–20, 132–134.

32. Benjamin I. Page and Robert Y. Shapiro, *The Rational Public: Fifty Years of Trends in Americans' Policy Preferences* (Chicago: University of Chicago Press, 1992), p. 128.

33. Tom W. Smith, "Social Inequality in Cross-National Perspective," in J. W. Becker, et al., eds., *Attitudes to Inequality and the Role of Government* (Rijswijk, The Netherlands: The Social and Cultural Bureau, 1990), p. 24.

34. Keene and Ladd, "America: A Unique Outlook?," p. 117.

35. *The American Enterprise*, 4:3 (May–June), p. 85.

36. Sombart, *Why Is There No Socialism in the United States?*, p. 106.

37. John Kenneth Galbraith, *The Affluent Society* (New York: NAL/Dutton, 1963); see also Galbraith, *The Culture of Contentment* (Boston: Houghton Mifflin, 1992).

38. Selig Perlman, *Theory of the Labor Movement* (New York: Augustus M. Kelley, 1949), p. 167.

39. See Leon Samson, *Toward a United Front* (New York: Farrar & Rinehart, 1935); H. G. Wells, *The Future in America* (New York: Harper & Bros., 1906), pp. 72–76; Louis Hartz, *The Liberal Tradition in America* (New York: Harcourt, Brace & World, 1955); Louis Hartz, *The Founding of New Societies* (New York: Harcourt, Brace & World, 1964); and Harrington, *Socialism*.

40. Antonio Gramsci, "The Intellectuals," in *Selections from the Prison Notebooks* (New York: International Publishers, 1971), pp. 21–22.

41. Ibid., pp. 281, 285, 305.

42. See Hermann Keyserling, *America Set Free* (New York: Harper & Brothers, 1929), pp. 237–239, 244–252; Samson, *Toward a United Front*, pp. 1–90; Sidney Hook, "The Philosophical Basis of Marxian Socialism in the United States," in Egbert and Persons, eds., *Socialism and American Life*, I, pp. 450–451; Harrington, *Socialism*; Carl N. Degler, *Out of Our Past* (New York: Harper & Brothers, 1959), pp. 271–272.

43. Harrington, *Socialism*, p. 118.

44. For my previous efforts, see Seymour Martin Lipset, *Continental Divide: The Values and Institutions of the United States and Canada* (New York: Routledge, 1990); see also Lipset, *The First New Nation: The United States in Historical and Comparative Perspective* (New York: W. W. Norton, 1979).

45. It is not generally known that the Parti Québécois applied for membership in the Socialist International, but was rejected because the NDP would not agree.

46. Christopher Huxley, David Kettler, and James Struthers, "Is Canada's Experience 'Especially Instructive?'" in Seymour Martin Lipset, ed., *Unions in Transition: Entering the Second Century* (San Francisco: ICS Press, 1986), pp. 113–133; George Sayers Bain and Robert Price, *Profiles of Union Growth: A Comparative Statistical Portrait of Eight Countries* (Oxford: Basil Blackwell, 1980).

47. Noah M. Meltz, *Unionism in the Private Service Sector: A Canada-U.S. Comparison* (Toronto: Centre for Industrial Relations, University of Toronto, 1990).

48. For analysis and bibliography, see Lipset, *Continental Divide*; see also Lipset, *The First New Nation.*

49. Lipset, *Continental Divide*, pp. 1–18; Seymour Martin Lipset, *Revolution and Counterrevolution* (New Brunswick, NJ: Transaction Books, revised ed., 1988), pp. 37–75; Lipset, "Historical Traditions and National Characteristics: A Comparative Analysis of Canada and the United States," *Canadian Journal of Sociology*, 11 (Summer 1986), pp. 114–115, 117–118.

50. Gad Horowitz, *Canadian Labour in Politics* (Toronto: University of Toronto Press, 1968), pp. 6–9.

51. Lipset, *The First New Nation*, pp. 88, 160.

52. Northrop Frye, *Divisions on a Ground: Essays on Canadian Culture* (Toronto: Anansi, 1982), p. 66.

53. Robert Kudrle and Theodore Marmor, "The Development of Welfare States in North America," in Peter Flora and Arnold Heidenheimer, eds., *The Development of Welfare States in Europe and America* (New Brunswick, NJ: Transaction Books, 1981), pp. 91–93; Lipset, *Continental Divide*, pp. 128–134.

54. Ibid., pp. 142–149.

55. Robert Presthus, *Elites in the Policy Process* (London: Cambridge University Press, 1974), p. 463.

56. Harold Innis, *Essays in Canadian Economic History* (Toronto: University of Toronto Press, 1956), p. 385.

57. Henry Phelps Brown, *The Origins of Union Power* (Oxford: Clarendon Press, 1983), p. 249.

58. William Christian and Colin Campbell, *Political Parties and Ideologies in Canada* (Toronto: McGraw-Hill Ryerson, 1983), p. 36.

59. Herschel Hardin, *A Nation Unaware. The Canadian Economic Culture* (Vancouver, BC: J. J. Douglas, 1974), pp. 62, 140.

60. J. T. McLeod, "The Free Enterprise Dodo Is No Phoenix," *The Canadian Forum*, 56 (August 1976), pp. 6, 9.

61. Marsha A. Chandler, "The Politics of Public Enterprise," in J. Robert S. Pritchard, ed., *Crown Corporations in Canada* (Toronto: Butterworth, 1983), p. 187.

62. Kudrle and Marmor, "The Development of Welfare States," p. 110.

63. Anne Swardson, "Canada Weighs Political, Financial Costs of Welfare Reform," *The Washington Post*, October 27, 1994, p. A20.

64. See Lipset, *Continental Divide.*

65. Jeffrey G. Reitz and Raymond Breton, *The Illusion of Differences. Realities of Ethnicity in Canada and the United States* (Toronto: C. D. Howe Institute, 1994), p. 33.

66. Wells, *The Future in America*, pp. 72–76; Hartz, *The Founding of New Societies*, p. 35; Horowitz, *Canadian Labour in Politics*, p. 52; Brown, *The Origins of Union Power*, p. 240.

67. Gad Horowitz, "Tories, Socialists and the Demise of Canada," *Canadian Dimension*, 2 (May–June 1956), p. 2.

68. William E. Forbath, *Law and the Shaping of the American Labor Movement* (Cambridge, MA: Harvard University Press, 1991), p. 10.

69. Mark A. Thompson and Albert H. Blum, "International Unionism in Canada: The Move to Local Control," *Industrial Relations*, 22 (Winter 1983), p. 83.

70. Horowitz, *Canadian Labour in Politics*, p. 59.

71. Ibid., p. 184.

72. Brown, *The Origins of Union Power*, p. 240.

73. Samuel Lubell, "Post-Mortem: Who Elected Roosevelt?" *Saturday Evening Post*, January 25, 1941, p. 9.

74. Seymour Martin Lipset and William Schneider, *The Confidence Gap: Business, Labor and Government in the Public Mind* (Baltimore: Johns Hopkins University Press, 1987), pp. 134–135, 149–150, 386, 410–411.

75. Seymour Martin Lipset, "North American Labor Movements: A Comparative Perspective," in Lipset, ed., *Unions in Transition*, pp. 438–442.

76. See Lipset, *Continental Divide*, p. 140.

77. Brian Bergman, "The Crusader," *Maclean's*, October 25, 1993, p. 15.

78. Paul Weiler, *The Representation Gap in the North American Workplace* (Toronto: Woodsworth College, University of Toronto, 1989), p. 7.

79. Leo Troy, "The Futures of American Unions," *Forum for Applied Research and Public Policy*, 5 (Winter 1990) pp.37–45.

80. Ibid, p. 26.; John Richards, "A Tangled Tale: Unions in Canada and the United States," in David Thomas, ed., *Canada and the United States: Differences That Count* (Peterborough, Ont: Broadview Press, 1993), p. 68.

81. Noah Meltz, "Developments in Industrial Relations and Human Resource Policies in Canada," in Richard Locke, Thomas Kochan, and Michael Piore, eds., *Employment Relations in a Changing Economy* (Cambridge, MA: MIT Press, 1995).

82. Richards, "A Tangled Tale," p. 68.

83. W. Craig Riddell, *Unionization in Canada and the United States: A Tale of Two Countries*. Working Paper Series QPIR 1993-1 (Kingston, Ont.: Industrial Relations Center, Queen's University, 1993), p. 26.

84. Jelle Visser, "The Strength of Union Movements in Advanced Capitalist Democracies: Social and Organizational Variations," in Marino Regini, ed., *The Future of Labour Movements* (London: Sage, 1992), p. 18 (emphasis in original).

85. Noah M. Meltz, "Unionism in the Private Sector: A Canada-U.S. Comparison," in Jane Jensen and Rianne Mahon, eds., *Canadian and American Labor Respond: Economic Restructuring and Union Strategies* (Philadelphia: Temple University Press, 1993), pp. 207–225.

86. For evidence relevant to a critique of the political and employer policy arguments, see Lipset, "North American Labor Movements," pp. 427–438.

87. Gary Bowden, "Labor Unions in the Public Mind: The Canadian Case," *Canadian Review of Sociology and Anthropology*, 26/5 (1989), pp. 735–739; Lipset, *Continental Divide*, p. 69.

88. In line with this hypothesis, I would note that in October 1975, when the Labour Party was in power in Britain, and there were 11 million union members, MORI (Market Opinion Research International) found that three quarters, 75 percent, of a national sample agreed with the statement: "Trade Unions have too much power in Britain today." Opinion seemed to be anti-union, but by the late eighties and early nineties after the Conservatives had held power for a decade or more, and union membership had fallen to 7 million, the percentage holding such views had declined to around two fifths, 38 to 41 percent. Those disagreeing had risen from one seventh, 16–17 percent in the seventies, to around half, 45 to 54 percent, in the beginning of the nineties.

89. International Labour Office, *Year Book of Labour Statistics* (Geneva: ILO, 1988), pp. 1048, 1050.

90. Bowden, "Labor Unions in the Public Mind," p. 734.

91. "Canadian Public Opinion Regarding the Organized Labour Movement: A Tracking Feature," *The Reid Report*, 4 (June 1989), p. 1.

92. Bowden, "Labor Unions in the Public Mind," p. 43.; Peter Bruce, "Political Parties and the Evolution of Labor Law in Canada and the United States." Ph.D. Dissertation, Department of Political Science, MIT, 1988; Weiler, *The Representation Gap*.

93. Huxley, Kettler, and Struthers, "Is Canada's Experience 'Especially Instructive'?", p. 131 (emphases in original).

94. Unlike the situation in the United States, labor relations are largely under provincial juris-

diction in Canada. Between 1984 and 1992, a vote was required in British Columbia for certification. This provision was abolished by the NDP government in January 1993. The Conservative government elected in Ontario in 1995 is committed to requiring elections.

95. Richard B. Freeman and James L. Medoff, *What Do Unions Do?* (New York: Basic Books, 1984), p. 239. For an earlier comprehensive review, see Herbert G. Heneman III and Marcus H. Sandver, "Predicting the Outcome of Union Certification Elections: A Review of the Literature," *Industrial and Labor Relations Review*, 36 (July 1983), pp. 537–559; see also William T. Dickens, "The Effect of Company Campaigns on Certification Elections: Law and Reality Once Again," *Industrial and Labor Relations Review*, 36 (July 1983), pp. 560–575.

96. Paul Weiler, "Promises to Keep: Securing Worker's Rights to Self-Organization Under the NLRA," *Harvard Law Review*, 96 (June 1983), pp. 1769–1827; "Striking a New Balance: Freedom of Contract and Prospects for Union Representation," *Harvard Law Review*, 98 (December 1984), pp. 351–420; and *Governing the Workplace. The Future of Labor and Employment Law* (Cambridge, MA: Harvard University Press, 1990), pp. 254–255. Peter Bruce, "Political Parties and Labor Legislation in Canada and the U.S.," *Industrial Relations*, 28 (Spring 1989), pp. 115–141.

97. "Transformation: Declining and Shifting Union Membership," *The Public Perspective*, 4 (July/August 1994), p. 9.

98. Derek Bok, "Reflections on the Distinctive Character of American Labor Laws," *Harvard Law Review*, 84 (April 1971), p. 1426.

99. Brown, *The Origins of Union Power*, p. 215.

100. Everett Kassalow, "The Closed and Union Shop in Western Europe: An American Perspective," *Journal of Labor Research*, 1 (Fall 1980), p. 328.

101. Weiler, "Promises to Keep," p. 1820.

102. Henry S. Farber and Alan B. Krueger, *Union Membership in the United States: The Decline Continues*. Working Paper No. 4216 (Cambridge, MA: National Bureau of Economic Research, 1992), pp. 17–18 and 32.

103. Ibid., Table 1.

104. Henry S. Farber, "The Decline of Unionization in the United States: What Can Be Learned from Recent Experience?" *Journal of Labor Economics*, 8, no. 1 (1990), pp. S97, S94–S95.

105. Ibid., p. S100.

106. "Canadian Public Opinion," p. 15. A survey by Gallup Canada Inc. on attitudes toward unionization among non-union private sector employees in Montreal and Toronto indicates that 40 percent of the non-managerial employees would like to be unionized. Jean-Guy Bergeron, "Unionization in the Private Sector." Ph.D. Thesis, Centre for Industrial Relations, University of Toronto, 1993, pp. 101–102.

107. See Farber and Krueger, "Union Membership" and Riddell, "Unionization in Canada and the United States," pp. 28–30.

108. Noah M. Meltz, "Inter-State versus Inter-Provincial Differences in Union Density," *Industrial Relations*, 28 (Spring 1989), p. 149.

109. John Calvert, "The Divergent Paths of the Canadian and American Labour Movements," *The Round Table*, 303 (July 1987), p. 383.

110. Bowden, "Labor Unions in the Public Mind," p. 740.

111. Lipset, *Continental Divide*, pp. 140–141.

112. Visser, "The Strength of Union Movements," p. 40.

113. David Moberg, "Union Busting, Past and Present," *Dissent*, 39 (Winter 1992), pp. 73–74 (emphasis in the original). Moberg draws heavily on the more detailed and documented article by Sanford M. Jacoby, "American Exceptionalism Revisited: The Importance of Management," in Jacoby, ed., *Masters to Managers. Historical and Comparative Perspectives on American Employers* (New York: Columbia University Press, 1991), pp. 173–200.

114. Brown, *The Origins of Union Power*, p. 235.

115. Harvey Krahn and Graham S. Lowe, "Public Attitudes Towards Unions: Some Canadian Evidence," *Journal of Labor Research*, 5 (Spring 1984), pp. 160–161.

116. Donald Swartz, "Capitalist Restructuring and the Canadian Labour Movement." Unpublished paper, School of Public Administration, Carleton University, Ottawa, 1989.

117. Harry C. Katz and Noah M. Meltz, "Profit Sharing and Auto Workers' Earnings. The United States vs. Canada," *Relations industrielles*, 46, no. 3 (1991), pp. 515–530.

118. Swartz, "Capitalist Restructuring."

119. Richard B. Freeman, "What Does the Future Hold for U.S. Unionism?" *Relations industrielles*, 44, no 1 (1989), pp. 40–41.

120. For a discussion and reference to the literature, see Lipset, *Continental Divide*, pp. 140–141.

121. Meltz, "Labor Movements in Canada and the United States," in Thomas A. Kochan, ed., *Challenges and Choices Facing American Labor* (Cambridge, MA: MIT Press, 1985), pp. 327–328.

122. Charles McDonald, "U.S. Union Membership in Future Decades: A Trade Unionist's Perspective," *Industrial Relations*, 31 (Winter 1992), pp. 19–23; John Judis, "Can Labor Come Back?" *The New Republic*, May 23, 1994, p. 32.

123. Judis "Can Labor Come Back?" p. 32.

124. Peter G. Bruce, "Unfair Labor Practice Cases," in Jane Jenson and Rianne Mahon, eds., *The Challenge of Restructuring: North American Labor Movements Respond* (Philadelphia: Temple University Press, 1993), p. 192.

125. Robertson Davies, "Dark Hamlet with the Features of Horatio: Canada's Myths and Realities," in Judith Webster, ed., *Voices of Canada. An Introduction to Canadian Culture* (Burlington, VT: Association for Canadian Studies in the United States, 1977), p. 43.

126. Support for the idea of socialism in the opinion polls, membership in trade unions, and the correlations between class position and voting all declined greatly during the period of postwar prosperity and increased social mobility that lasted through most of the 1970s. See Lipset and Schneider, *The Confidence Gap*, pp. 282–284, 353; Seymour Martin Lipset, *Political Man: The Social Bases of Politics* (Baltimore: Johns Hopkins University Press, expanded ed., 1981), pp. 503–521; and "The Re-Unionization of America," *The Economist*, October 29, 1993, p. 71.

127. For a discussion which seeks to apply some of these factors to an explanation of the different patterns of working-class politics in Europe and Australasia, see Seymour Martin Lipset, *Consensus and Conflict: Essays in Political Sociology* (New Brunswick, NJ: Transaction Books, 1985), pp. 219–253.

128. Walter Dean Burnham, "The United States: The Politics of Heterogeneity," in Richard Rose, ed., *Electoral Behavior* (New York: The Free Press, 1974), pp. 718–719.

4. Two Americas, Two Value Systems: Blacks and Whites *(pp. 113–150)*

1. I have written a number of papers on this subject. The most recent, much of which is incorporated here, is "Two Americas, Two Value Systems: Blacks and Whites," *The Tocqueville Review*, 13, no. 1 (1992), pp. 137–177.

2. Edward Pessen, *Most Uncommon Jacksonians: The Radical Leaders of the Early Labor Movement* (Albany, NY: State University of New York Press, 1967), pp. 183–189; and Walter Hugins, *Jacksonian Democracy and the Working Class: A Study of the New York Workingman's Movement 1829–1837* (Stanford, CA: Stanford University Press, 1960), pp. 13, 18–20, 132–134.

3. Robert K. Merton, *Social Theory and Social Structure* (Glencoe, IL: The Free Press, 1957), p. 169.

4. Mark Whitaker, et al., "A Crisis of Shattered Dreams," *Newsweek*, May 6, 1991, pp. 28–31.

5. Thomas Jefferson, *Notes on the State of Virginia* (New York: Harper Torchbooks, 1964), p. 156.

6. James Thomas Flexner, *Washington: The Indispensable Man* (New York: New American Library, 1984), pp. 389–390.

7. Gunnar Myrdal, *An American Dilemma* (New York: Harper & Row, 1962), pp. 462–466.

8. Generalizations such as these are inherently comparative, in this case with other countries, and are clearly not meant as absolute judgments. Obviously, Americans have distinguished and discriminated by group characteristics, as is evident in nativist anti-immigrant policies, quota restrictions against Jews, and the like. But, as compared to others, they have been more individualistic.

9. Robert Y. Shapiro and John T. Young, "Public Opinion and the Welfare State: The United States in Comparative Perspective," *Political Science Quarterly*, 104 (Spring 1989), pp. 59–89.

10. Organization for Economic Cooperation and Development, *Social Expenditure 1960–1990* (Paris: OECD, 1985), pp. 21, 24.

11. Centre for Educational Research and Innovation, *Education at a Glance: OECD Indicators* (Paris: OECD, 1993), p. 69.

12. National Center for Education Statistics, *Digest of Education Statistics 1990* (Washington, D.C.: Department of Education, Office of Educational Research and Improvements, 1991), p. 380.

13. Lawrence H. Fuchs, *The American Kaleidoscope: Race, Ethnicity and the Civic Culture* (Hanover, NH: Wesleyan University Press, 1990), pp. 165–168.

14. It should be noted that proposals for special preference or equality of results actually surfaced among blacks as early as 1871, soon after emancipation, when black leader Martin Delany argued that the way to counter discrimination was to establish quotas for blacks, mulattoes, and other minorities. See Martin Delany, *Homes for the Freedman* (Charleston, SC, 1871); Dorothy Sterling, *The Making of an Afro-American: Martin Robinson Delany* (Garden City, NY: Doubleday, 1971), pp. 288–290; and Frederick Douglass, "Letter to Major Delany," in Philip S. Foner, ed., *The Life and Writings of Frederick Douglass*, IV (New York: International Publishers, 1955), pp. 280–281.

   Debates over the need for "special efforts" and welfare programs for blacks occurred during the Reconstruction period. Many of the current arguments criticizing " 'class legislation'—singling out one group of citizens for special government favors,"—and their supposed invidious effect on black morale and encouragement of dependency were made then by Frederick Douglass and other black leaders. See Eric Foner, *Reconstruction: America's Unfinished Revolution 1863–1877* (New York: Harper & Row, 1988), pp. 67–68, 237, 308–309. For a detailed recent account by two Republicans of the GOP role, see Paul Craig Roberts and Lawrence M. Stratton, Jr., "Color Code," *National Review*, March 20, 1995, especially p. 48.

15. Gary C. Bryner, "Affirmative Action Minority Rights or Reverse Discrimination?" in Raymond Tatalovich and Byron W. Daynes, eds., *Social Regulatory Policy: Moral Controversies in American Politics* (Boulder, CO: Westview Press, 1988), pp. 159–160.

16. Hugh David Graham, *The Civil Rights Era: Origins and Development of National Policy* (New York: Oxford University Press, 1990), pp. 326–331. Tom Wicker, *One of Us: Richard Nixon and the American Dream* (New York: Random House, 1991), pp. 522–523.

17. Lawrence H. Silberman, "The Road to Racial Quotas," *Wall Street Journal*, August 11, 1977, p. 14.

18. Graham, *The Civil Rights Era*, p. 331.

19. Congressional Quarterly, *Congress and the Nation*, III (Washington, D.C.: Congressional Quarterly, 1973), p. 711.

20. David E. Rosenbaum, "Shultz Appeals to House on Jobs," *The New York Times*, December 21, 1969, p. 39.

21. Graham, *The Civil Rights Era*, pp. 339–340.

22. Congressional Quarterly, *Congress and the Nation*, p. 711.

23. Rosenbaum, "Shultz Appeals to House," p. 39.

24. Congressional Quarterly, *Congress and the Nation*, p. 711.

25. Jefferson Morley, "Bush and the Blacks: An Unknown Story," *New York Review of Books*, January 16, 1992, p. 25.

26. Robert Lerner, Althea K. Nagai, and Stanley Rothman, "Elite Dissensus and Its Origins,"

Journal of Political and Military Sociology, 18 (Summer 1990), pp. 25–39. See also Roberts and Stratton, "Color Code," pp. 45–46.

27. Harold Cruse, *The Crisis of the Negro Intellectual* (New York: William Morrow, 1967), pp. 3–10.

28. There have, of course, been many examples of state support for group economic objectives, e.g., protective tariffs, guaranteed farm prices, and minimum wages.

29. Connie Leslie, "A Rich Legacy of Preference: Alumni Kids Get a Big Break on Admissions," *Newsweek,* June 24, 1991, p. 59.

30. Seymour Martin Lipset, *The First New Nation: The United States in Historical and Comparative Perspective* (New York: Basic Books, 1963; expanded paperback ed., New York: W. W. Norton, 1979), p. 331 (emphasis in original).

31. Barry R. Chiswick, "Is the New Immigration Less Skilled Than the Old?" *Journal of Labor Economics,* 9 (April 1986) pp. 168–192.

32. Benjamin J. Wattenberg, *The First Universal Nation: Leading Indicators and Ideas About the Surge of America in the 1990s* (New York: The Free Press, 1991), pp. 59–61.

33. Fuchs, *The American Kaleidoscope,* pp. 451–452.

34. For reviews of findings, see James R. Kluegel and Eliot R. Smith, *Beliefs About Inequality: American's Views of What Is and What Ought to Be* (New York: Aldine de Gruyter, 1986), pp. 200–203; John H. Bunzel, "Affirmative Re-actions," *Public Opinion,* 9 (February–March, 1989), pp. 45–49; Frederick R. Lynch, *The Invisible Victims: White Males and the Crisis of Affirmative Action* (New York: Greenwood Press, 1989), pp. 17–20; and Everett Carll Ladd, *The American Ideology: An Exploration of the Origins, Meanings, and Role of American Political Ideas* (Storrs, CT: Roper Center for Public Opinion Research, 1994), pp. 56–58.

35. Gallup Poll, *Gallup Poll Monthly,* no. 291 (December 1989), p. 18.

36. These breakdowns are from the 1987 sample. The 1990 results are similar.

37. Peter Skerry, *Mexican Americans. The Ambivalent Minority* (New York: The Free Press, 1993), pp. 288–293.

38. See "Proposed Anti-Affirmative Action Initiative Generating High Awareness and Initial Support," *The Field Poll,* March 7, 1995, pp. 1–2.

39. Skerry, *Mexican Americans,* p. 285.

40. Ibid., p. 287.

41. For poll data bearing on these points, see Bryner, "Affirmative Action Minority Rights," pp. 173–174.

42. Howard Schuman, Charlotte Steeh, and Lawrence Bobo, *Racial Attitudes in America* (Cambridge, MA: Harvard University Press, 1985).

43. The General Social Survey of the National Opinion Research Center, taken every two years since 1972, indicates steady improvement on attitudes toward racial equality in many areas through 1993.

44. Whitaker, et al., "A Crisis of Shattered Dreams," pp. 30–31.

45. Seymour Martin Lipset and William Schneider, "The Bakke Case: How Would It Be Decided at the Bar of Public Opinion?" *Public Opinion,* 1 (March–April 1978), pp. 38–44.

46. See Seymour Martin Lipset, "No Third Way: A Comparative Perspective on the Left," in Daniel Chirot, ed., *The Crisis of Leninism and the Decline of the Left* (Seattle: University of Washington Press, 1991), pp. 205–207.

47. Henry Louis Gates, Jr., "The Black Leadership Myth," *The New Yorker,* October 24, 1994, pp. 7–8.

48. Peter F. Drucker, "The Age of Social Transformation," *Atlantic Monthly,* 274 (November 1994), p. 62.

49. Linda S. Lichter, "Who Speaks for Black America?" *Public Opinion,* 8 (August–September, 1985), pp. 41–44, 58.

50. Tom Morganthau, "Losing Ground," *Newsweek,* April 6, 1992, p. 21.

51. Gates, 'The Black Leadership Myth," p. 8 (emphasis S.M.L.).

52. Diane Colasanto, "Public Wants Civil Rights Widened for Some Groups, Not for Others," *Gallup Poll Monthly,* no. 291 (December 1989), p. 15 (emphasis SML).

53. William J. Wilson, "Public Policy Research and the Truly Disadvantaged," in Christopher Jencks and Paul E. Peterson, eds., *The Urban Underclass* (Washington, D.C.: Brookings Institution, 1991), pp. 463–464.

54. William J. Wilson, "The Poor Image of Black Men," *New Perspectives Quarterly,* 8 (Summer 1991), pp. 26–29.

55. Ronald B. Mincy, Isabel V. Sawhill, and Douglas A. Wolf, "The Underclass: Definition and Measurement," *Science,* 248 (April 27, 1990), p. 451.

56. Paul A. Jargowsky and Mary Jo Bane, "Ghetto Poverty in the United States," in Jencks and Peterson, eds., *The Urban Underclass,* p. 252.

57. Paul E. Peterson, "The Urban Underclass and the Poverty Paradox," in Jencks and Peterson, eds., *The Urban Underclass,* p. 22.

58. Isabel V. Sawhill, "The Underclass: An Overview," *The Public Interest,* 96 (Summer 1989), pp. 6–11.

59. Richard Harwood, "The Focus on Blacks," *The Washington Post,* March 8, 1992, p. C6.

60. William J. Wilson, *The Truly Disadvantaged: The Inner City, The Underclass, and Public Policy* (Chicago: University of Chicago Press, 1987), pp. 8–10; William J. Wilson, "Studying Inner-City Social Dislocations: The Challenge of Public Agenda Research," *American Sociological Review,* 56 (February 1991), pp. 8–10.

61. Richard P. Nathan, "Will the Underclass Always Be With Us?" *Society,* 24 (March–April 1987), p. 58.

62. William P. O'Hare, et al., "African Americans in the 1990s," *Population Review,* 46 (June 1991), p. 8.

63. Quoted in Karen De Witt, "Wave of Suburban Growth Is Being Fed by Minorities," *The New York Times,* August 15, 1994, pp. A1, 12.

64. U.S. Bureau of the Census, *The Black Population in the United States: March 1994 and 1993* (Washington, D.C.: U.S. Department of Commerce, Economics, and Statistical Administration, 1994), p. 9.

65. U.S. Bureau of the Census, Statistical Brief for Congress, *Black Children in America: 1993* (Washington, D.C.: U.S. Department of Commerce, Economics, and Statistical Administration, 1994), p. 3.

66. U.S. Bureau of the Census, *The Black Population in the United States,* p. 9. Between the years 1980 and 1994, the percentage of college-educated blacks increased from 8 to 13 percent, while the proportion of whites grew from 18 to 23 percent (see note 64).

67. James P. Smith and Finis R. Welch, *Closing the Gap: Forty Years of Economic Progress for Blacks* (Santa Monica, CA: Rand, 1986), p. ix.

68. Gerald D. Jaynes and Robin M. Williams, Jr., eds., *A Common Destiny: Blacks in American Society* (Washington, D.C.: National Academy Press, 1989), p. 275.

69. Ibid., pp. 275–276.

70. William J. Wilson, "Race, Class and Public Policy," *The American Sociologist,* 16 (1981), pp. 126–127; Jaynes and Williams, *A Common Destiny,* pp. 279–286.

71. Jaynes and Williams, *A Common Destiny,* p. 87; James P. Scanlan, "The Perils of Provocative Statistics," *The Public Interest,* 102 (Winter 1991), pp. 5–8.

72. Wattenberg, *The Birth Dearth,* p. 77; Nicholas Lemann, *The Promised Land: The Great Black Migration and How It Changed America* (New York: Alfred A. Knopf, 1991), p. 203; O'Hare, et al., "African Americans in the 1990s," p. 11.

73. David Ellwood, and Jonathan Crane, "Family Change Among Black Americans: What Do We Know?" *Journal of Economic Perspectives,* 4 (Fall 1990), p. 70.

74. Victor R. Fuchs, *The Feminization of Poverty?* (Cambridge, MA: National Bureau of Economic Research, 1986), pp. 10–11.

75. Quoted in Steven A. Holmes, "Income Gap Persists for Blacks and Whites," *New York Times,* February 23, 1995, p. A21.

76. Ibid. See also U.S. Bureau of the Census, *The Black Population in the United States.*

77. Jencks, "Is the American Underclass Growing?" in Jencks and Peterson, eds., *The Urban Underclass,* pp. 86–89.

78. Holmes, "Income Gap Persists for Blacks and Whites," p. A21. See also *The Black Population in the United States.*

79. Soo In Son, Suzanne W. Model, and Gene A. Fisher, "Polarization and Progress in the Black Community: Earnings and Status Gains for Young Black Males in the Era of Affirmative Action," *Sociological Forum,* 4 (Winter 1989), p. 323. Jencks, "Is the American Underclass Growing?", pp. 53–55.

80. Similar class differences have been reported with respect to the effects of affirmative action on women's opportunities in James P. Smith and Michael Wood, "Women in the Labor Market and the Family," *Journal of Economic Perspectives,* 3 (Winter 1989), pp. 9–23.

81. Jonathan S. Leonard, "The Impact of Affirmative Action Regulation and Equal Employment Law on Black Employment," *Journal of Economic Perspectives,* 4 (Fall 1990) pp. 53, 60. O'Hare, et al., "African Americans in the 1990s," p. 24.

82. William Julius Wilson, "Race, Class and Public Policy," pp. 127, 129.

83. Wilson, *The Truly Disadvantaged,* p. 115; William J. Wilson, *The Declining Significance of Race: Blacks and Changing American Institution* (Chicago: University of Chicago Press, 1978), pp. 18–19, 152–153. See also James Fishkin, *Justice, Equal Opportunity and the Family* (New Haven, CT: Yale University Press, 1983), p. 92.

84. In Son, et al., "Polarization and Progress," p. 323; Fuchs, *The American Kaleidoscope,* pp. 442–444; Leonard, "The Impact of Affirmative Action Regulation," pp. 50, 52, 61.

85. O'Hare, et al., "African Americans in the 1990s," p. 28.

86. Henry Aaron, "Symposium on the Economic Status of African Americans," *Journal of Economic Perspectives,* 4 (Fall 1990), p. 5.

87. Margery Turner, Michael Fix, and Raymond Struik, *Opportunities Denied, Opportunities Diminished: Discrimination in Hiring* (Washington, D.C.: Urban Institute, 1991). See also Michael Fix and Raymond J. Struyk, eds., *Clear and Convincing Evidence* (Washington, D.C.: Urban Institute Press, 1993), and Joleen Kirschenman and Katherine Neckerman, "We'd Love to Hire Them, But . . . : The Meaning of Race for Employers," in Christopher Jencks and Paul E. Peterson, eds., *The Urban Underclass* (Washington, D.C.: The Brookings Institution, 1991).

88. For an excellent review of the changing issues and partisan stances surrounding affirmative action, see William A. Gamson and Andre Modigliani, "The Changing Culture of Affirmative Action," *Research in Political Science,* 3 (1987), pp. 137–177.

89. Lemann, *The Promised Land,* p. 183.

90. For reports of studies and an excellent analysis, see Thomas B. Edsall, "In Louisiana, Whites Often Feel Ignored," *The Washington Post,* March 12, 1991, p. A5; and "Rights Drive Said to Lose Underpinnings," *The Washington Post,* March 9, 1991, p. A6.

91. Lynch, *The Invisible Victims,* p. 3.

92. Cited in Edsall, "In Louisiana Whites Often Feel Ignored."

93. See John Judis, "The Old Democrat," *New Republic,* February 22, 1993, pp. 18–21.

94. Thomas B. Edsall, "Revolt of the Discontented," *The Washington Post,* November 11, 1994, p. A31. See also "Affirmative Action, Welfare, and the Individual," *The Public Perspective,* 6 (June/July 1995), especially pp. 31–39.

95. Richard Lucayo, "A New Push for Blind Justice," *Time,* February 20, 1995, p. 39.

96. Edsall, "Revolt of the Discontented," p. A31.

97. William Raspberry, "Why Civil Rights Isn't Selling," *The Washington Post,* March 13, 1991, p. A17.

98. See Louis Hartz, *The Liberal Tradition in America* (New York: Harcourt, Brace & World, 1964).

99. Ladd, *The American Ideology,* p. 76.

100. Tom Smith, "Social Inequality in Cross-National Perspective," in J. W. Becker, James A. Davis, Paul Ester, and Peter B. Mohles, eds., *Attitudes to Inequality and the Role of Government* (The Hague: CIP Gegevens Koninklije Bibliotheek, 1990).

101. Ibid., p. 24.

102. From the results of the World Values Survey 1981–82, 1990, supplied by Ronald Inglehart.

316 Notes (pp. 146–152)

For U.S.-Canada comparisons, see Seymour Martin Lipset, *Continental Divide: The Values and Institutions of the United States and Canada* (New York: Routledge, 1990), p. 157.

103. The International Social Survey Program coordinated by the National Opinion Research Center. For published reports, see Smith, "Social Inequality in Cross-National Perspective," and Ladd, *The American Ideology*, pp. 75–76. See also "Affirmative Action, Welfare, and the Individual," pp. 28–29.

104. Ladd, *The American Ideology*, p. 79.

105. Ibid., pp. 61–62.

106. Howard Schuman and Lawrence Bobo, "Survey-Based Experiments on White Racial Attitudes Toward Residential Integration," *American Journal of Sociology*, 94 (September 1988), pp. 283–289.

107. Ibid. The question about Christians referred to their right to "move into a house in an all-Jewish neighborhood."

108. For a discussion of the various multi-ethnic countries which give preference to deprived groups, sometimes to underprivileged majorities, see Thomas Sowell, "Affirmative Action': A Worldwide Disaster," *Commentary*, 88 (December 1989), pp. 21–44.

109. Lipset, *Continental Divide*, p. 181.

110. Bryner, "Affirmative Action Minority Rights," p. 173.

111. Ibid.

112. Frederick Douglass, "Letter to Major Delany," pp. 280–281.

113. Foner, *Reconstruction*, pp. 67–68.

114. Shelby Steele, *The Content of Our Character* (New York: St. Martin's Press, 1990), p. 13.

115. Ibid., pp. 115–118.

116. Charles Moskos, "How Do They Do It?" *The New Republic*, August 5, 1991, pp. 16–20.

5. A UNIQUE PEOPLE IN AN EXCEPTIONAL COUNTRY (pp. 151–175)

1. This chapter draws on Seymour Martin Lipset and Earl Raab, *Jews and the New American Scene* (Cambridge, MA: Harvard University Press, 1995). See also S. M. Lipset, "A Unique People in an Exceptional Country," in Lipset, ed., *American Pluralism and the Jewish Community* (New Brunswick, NJ: Transaction Publishers, 1989).

2. Calvin Goldscheider and Alan S. Zuckerman, *The Transformation of the Jews* (Chicago: University of Chicago Press, 1986), p. 183.

3. Steven M. Cohen, *The Dimensions of American Jewish Liberalism* (New York: American Jewish Committee, 1989); Andrew M. Greeley, *Ethnicity, Denomination and Inequality* (Beverly Hills, CA: Sage Publications, 1976), p. 39.

4. Barry A. Kosmin and Seymour P. Lachman, *One Nation Under God. Religion in Contemporary American Society* (New York: Harmony Books, 1993), p. 260.

5. Data from Gerald Bubis as reported in Barry A. Kosmin, "The Dimensions of Contemporary Jewish Philanthropy," in Kosmin and Paul Ritterband, eds., *Contemporary Jewish Philanthropy in America* (Lanham, MD: Rowman & Littlefield, 1991), p. 24.

6. The data for leading intellectuals are from Charles Kadushin, *The American Intellectual Elite* (Boston: Little, Brown, 1974), pp. 23–24, 35–36. Those for professors are from Seymour Martin Lipset and Everett Carll Ladd, Jr., "Jewish Academics in the United States: Their Achievements, Culture and Politics," *American Jewish Year Book*, 72 (New York: American Jewish Committee, 1971), pp. 89–128. For the other elite groups, see Stanley Rothman, Robert Lichter, and Linda Lichter, *Elites in Conflict: Social Change in America Today* (forthcoming).

7. In 1987, close to two fifths of the Jewish House members served on the Middle East Subcommittee of the Foreign Affairs Committee. Peter Y. Medding, *The Transformation of American Jewish Politics* (New York: American Jewish Committee, 1989); Michael Kahan, "Election '94: The Great Realignment," *Congress Monthly*, 62 (January–February 1995), pp. 3–5.

8. Jewish data are from the 1990 National Jewish Population Study. For the United States gen-

erally, see Mark S. Hoffman, ed., *World Almanac and Book of Facts 1992* (New York: Pharos Books 1991), p. 218.

9. The references for these findings are in Lipset and Ladd, "Jewish Academics in the United States," p. 99.

10. Park quoted in Henry L. Feingold, *A Midrash on American Jewish History* (Albany, NY: State University of New York Press, 1982), p. 189. For excellent discussions of this congruence, see Arnold M. Eisen, *The Chosen People in America: A Study in Jewish Religion Ideology* (Bloomington, IN: Indiana University Press, 1983), pp. 25–52, and Joseph L. Blau, *Judaism in America from Curiosity to Third Faith* (Chicago: University of Chicago Press, 1976), pp. 7–20.

11. Max Weber, *The Protestant Ethic and the Spirit of Capitalism* (London: George Allen & Unwin, 1930; Cambridge, MA: Unwin Hyman, 1990), pp. 48–50, 54–55.

12. Hillel Levine, personal communication. Anita Libman Lebeson, *Pilgrim People* (New York: Minerva Press, 1975), p. 178; Blau, *Judaism in America*, p. 113; Nissan Waxman, "A Neglected Book," (Hebrew) in *Shana Beshana: Yearbook of Heichal Shlomo* (Jerusalem: 1969), pp. 303–315.

13. Max Weber, *Economy and Society,* I (Berkeley, CA: University of California Press, 1978), pp. 622–623. For an elaboration of the links between Puritanism and Judaism, particularly in America, see Edward A. Tiryakian, "American Religious Exceptionalism: A Reconsideration," *Annals of the American Academy of Political Science,* 527 (May 1993), pp. 51–52.

14. Frederick Cople Jaher, *A Scapegoat in the New Wilderness* (Cambridge, MA: Harvard University Press, 1994), p. 24. For a general discussion of the acceptance of Jews, see pp. 119–129.

15. See Anthony Blond, "The Jews and Mrs. Thatcher," *Sunday Telegraph,* December 11, 1988, pp. 14–15.

16. Tiryakian, "American Religious Exceptionalism," pp. 51–52.

17. "Washington's Reply to the Hebrew Congregation in Newport, Rhode Island," *Publications of the American Jewish Historical Society,* 3 (1895), pp. 91–92.

18. Quoted in John A. Hardon, *American Judaism* (Chicago: Loyola University Press, 1971), pp. 32–33.

19. See Lucy S. Dawidowicz, *On Equal Terms: Jews in America 1881–1981* (New York: Holt, Rinehart & Winston, 1982), pp. 68–69; Arthur Hertzberg, *The French Enlightenment and The Jews* (New York: Columbia University, 1968), p. 360; Charles E. Silberman, *A Certain People: American Jews and Their Lives Today* (New York: Summit Books, 1985), pp. 39–41.

20. Seymour Martin Lipset, *The First New Nation: The United States in Historical and Comparative Perspective* (2nd ed., New York: W. W. Norton, 1979), pp. 164–165; for the report, see Richard Mentor Johnson, "Sunday Observance and the Mail," in George E. Probst, ed., *The Happy Republic* (Gloucester, MA: Peter Smith, 1968), pp. 247–255.

21. James R. Rohrer, "The Sunday Mails and the Church-State Theme in Jacksonian America," *Journal of the Early Republic,* 7 (Spring 1987), pp. 53–115.

22. Herbert A. Gibbon, *John Wanamaker,* I (New York: Harper & Brothers, 1926), p. 321.

23. Manfred Jones, "The American Sabbath in the Gilded Age," in *Jahrbuch fuer Amerika Studien,* 6 (Heidelberg: Karl Winter Universitaetsverlag, 1961), pp. 89–114.

24. Bertram Wallace Korn, *Eventful Years and Experiences: Studies in Nineteenth Century American Jewish History* (Cincinnati: American Jewish Archives, 1954), pp. 98–99.

25. Seymour Martin Lipset, *Revolution and Counterrevolution, Change and Persistence in Social Structures,* 3rd ed. (New Brunswick, NJ: Transaction Books, 1988), pp. 141–153; Blau, *Judaism in America,* pp. 51–72.

26. See Arthur A. Goren, *New York Jews and the Quest for Community. The Kehillah Experiment, 1908–1922* (New York: Columbia University, 1970).

27. Quoted in ibid., p. 252.

28. Jaher, *A Scapegoat,* p. 122.

29. Henry L. Feingold, *Zion in America* (New York: Hippocrene Books, 1974), pp. 89–90.

30. Peter Wiernik, *History of the Jews in America,* 3rd ed. (New York: Hermon Press, 1972), pp. 128–134.

31. Ibid., pp. 229–240.
32. Joakim Isaacs, "Ulysses S. Grant and the Jews," in Jonathan D. Sarna, ed., *The American Jewish Experience* (New York: Holmes & Meier, 1986), pp. 62–64; Leonard Dinnerstein, *Antisemitism in America* (New York: Oxford University Press, 1994), p. 32.
33. Wiernik, *History of the Jews*, pp. 270–271.
34. "Our State Department and the Damascus Affair," cited in Morris U. Schappes, ed., *A Documentary History of Jews in the United States, 1654–1875* (New York: Schocken Books, 1971), p. 209.
35. Quoted in Wiernik, *History of the Jews*, pp. 345–346. For a detailed account of such interventions, see Cyrus Adler and Aaron M. Margalith, *American Intercession on Behalf of Jews in the Diplomatic Correspondence of the United States 1840–1938* (New York: American Jewish Historical Society, 1943).
36. Feingold, *Zion in America*, pp. 239–249.
37. David Biale, *Power and Powerlessness in Jewish History* (New York: Schocken Books, 1986), p. 124. Bertram W. Korn, *The American Reaction to the Montara Case 1858–1859* (Cincinnati: American Jewish Archives, 1957), pp. 88–92.
38. Jaher, *A Scapegoat*, pp. 1, 243–245; see also Dinnerstein, *Antisemitism*, p. xxviii.
39. Leo P. Ribuffo, "Henry Ford and the International Jew," *American Jewish History*, 69 (June 1980), p. 437. For a review of the historical literature, see Leonard Dinnerstein, "The Historiography of American Antisemitism," in his *Uneasy at Home: Antisemitism and The American Jewish Experience* (New York: Columbia University Press, 1987), pp. 257–267.
40. Seymour Martin Lipset and Earl Raab, *The Politics of Unreason: Right Wing Extremism in America, 1790–1977*, 2nd ed. (Chicago: University of Chicago Press, 1978), pp. 47–48, 89–90; Jaher, *A Scapegoat*, p. 246.
41. Goldscheider and Zuckerman, *The Transformation*, p. 166. For details, see Nathan Glazer, "Social Characteristics of American Jews, 1654–1954," *American Jewish Year Book*, 56 (New York: American Jewish Committee, 1955), pp. 9–10; Arthur A. Goren, *The American Jews* (Cambridge, MA: Belknap Press, 1982), pp. 34–36.
42. Barry E. Supple, "A Business Elite: German-Jewish Financiers in Nineteenth Century New York," *Business History Review*, 31 (Summer 1957), pp. 143–178. Vincent P. Carosso, "A Financial Elite: New York's German-Jewish Investment Bankers," *American Jewish Historical Quarterly*, 66 (September 1976), pp. 67–87.
43. Lipset and Raab, *The Politics of Unreason*, pp. 92–95.
44. E. Digby Baltzell, *The Protestant Establishment* (New York: Random House, 1964), p. 138.
45. John Higham, "Social Discrimination Against Jews in America, 1830–1930," *American Jewish Historical Society*, 47 (1957), p. 10; "Anti-Semitism in the Gilded Age: A Reinterpretation," *Mississippi Valley Historical Review*, 43 (1957), p. 566. For these and other essays, see Higham, *Send These to Me: Immigrants in Urban America* (Baltimore: Johns Hopkins University Press, 1984).
46. Goldscheider and Zuckerman, *The Transformation*, pp. 166–167.
47. Chaim I. Waxman, *America's Jews in Transition* (Philadelphia: Temple University Press, 1983), pp. 49–51.
48. Werner Cohn, "The Politics of American Jews," in Marshall Sklare, ed., *The Jews: Social Patterns of an American Group* (Glencoe, IL: The Free Press, 1958), pp. 615–618.
49. Arthur Liebman, *Jews and the Left* (New York: John Wiley & Sons, 1979), p. 1, see also pp. 20–33; Irving Howe, *World of Our Fathers* (New York: Harcourt Brace Jovanovich, 1976), pp. 287–324.
50. Stephen E. Isaacs, *Jews and American Politics*, (Garden City, NY: Doubleday, 1974), pp. 151–152; Lawrence H. Fuchs, *The Political Behavior of American Jews* (Glencoe, IL: Free Press, 1956), pp. 151–169. On the heavily disproportionate support which the American Communist Party drew from Jews, see Nathan Glazer, *The Social Basis of American Communism* (New York: Harcourt, Brace & World, 1961), pp. 130–168.
51. Nathan Glazer, *American Judaism*, 2nd ed. (Chicago: University of Chicago Press, 1972), p. 71; Howe, *World of Our Fathers*, pp. 204–208.

52. Cohn, "The Politics of American Jews," p. 621.
53. Glazer, *American Judaism*, p. 71; Gorey, *The American Jews*, pp. 57–59.
54. Dawidowicz, *On Equal Terms* p. 51. See also Silberman, *A Certain People* pp. 125–127, 132–134, and Dinnerstein, *Uneasy at Home*, pp. 15–40.
55. Goldscheider and Zuckerman, *The Transformation*, p. 168.
56. Nathan Reich, "The Role of the Jews in the American Economy," *YIVO Annual*, 5 (1950), pp. 197–205; Nathan Glazer, "The American Jew and the Attainment of Middle-Class Rank: Some Trends and Explanations," in Sklare, ed., *The Jews*, pp. 138–146; Sidney Goldstein, "Socioeconomic Differentials Among Religious Groups in the United States," *American Journal of Sociology*, 74 (May 1969), pp. 612–631; Simon Kuznets, *Economic Structure of the Jews* (Jerusalem: Institute of Contemporary Jewry, Hebrew University, 1972); Marshall H. Medoff, "Note: Some Differences Between the Jewish and General White Male Population in the United States," *Jewish Social Studies*, 43 (Winter 1981), pp. 75–80.
57. Dawidowicz, *On Equal Terms*, p. 51. See also Goren, *The American Jews*, pp. 73–76.
58. Glazer, "Social Characteristics of American Jews," pp. 30–31. See also Silberman, *A Certain People*, pp. 137–138.
59. Fred L. Strodtbeck, "Family Interaction, Values and Achievement," in Sklare, ed., *The Jews*, pp. 162–163; Lipset and Ladd, "Jewish Academics," pp. 96–106.
60. Glazer, "Social Characteristics," p. 31. See also Blau, *Judaism in America*, pp. 112–115.
61. Lipset and Raab, *The Politics of Unreason*, pp. 97–99.
62. See ibid, pp. 110–140, esp. p. 139, for a discussion of anti-Semitism.
63. Moshe Davis, *The Emergence of Conservative Judaism. The Historical School in 19th Century America* (New York: Jewish Publication Society of America, 1963), pp. 149–228.
64. Marshall Sklare, *Conservative Judaism: An American Religious Movement* (New York: Schocken Books, 1972), pp. 43–82; Hardon, *American Judaism*, p. 119.
65. Lipset and Raab, *The Politics of Unreason*, pp. 171–189. For a detailed review of opinion polls about Jews from the 1930s to the 1960s, see Charles H. Stember, et al., *Jews in the Mind of America* (New York: Basic Books, 1966), pp. 60–76, 82–85, 116–162.
66. Lipset and Raab, *The Politics of Unreason*, pp. 493–496.
67. Dawidowicz, *On Equal Terms*, pp. 131–132.
68. Seymour Martin Lipset, "Blacks and Jews: How Much Bias?" *Public Opinion*, 9 (July–August 1987), pp. 4–5, 57–58. For a review of findings on attitudes and behavior, see Leonard Dinnerstein, "Antisemitism in the United States Today," *Patterns of Prejudice*, 22 (Autumn 1988), pp. 3–14.
69. *Roper Reports*, 4–1993, p. 11.
70. Tom W. Smith, *What Do Americans Think About Jews?* (New York: American Jewish Committee, 1991), p. 26.
71. Kosmin, "Jewish Philanthropy," p. 28.
72. Ariela Keysar, "Patterns of Philanthropy: New York Versus Non-New York Jewry in 1990." Paper for the Mandell Berman Institute—North American Jewish Data Bank, Graduate School and University Center, CUNY, New York, 1992, p. 6.
73. Ibid., chart 1.
74. Virginia Hodgkinson and Murray S. Weitzman, *Giving and Volunteering in the United States* (Washington, D.C.: Independent Sector, 1992), pp. 76–77.
75. Table, "Portrait of the Electorate," *The New York Times*, November 5, 1992, p. B9.
76. Martin Hochbaum, *The Jewish Vote in the 1984 Presidential Election* (New York: American Jewish Congress, 1985), p. 6.
77. Alan Fisher, "The Myth of the Rightward Turn," *Moment*, 8, no. 10 (1983), p. 25.
78. Cohen, *The Dimensions of American Jewish Liberalism*, pp. 42, 44.
79. Ibid., p. 34.
80. Fisher, "The Myth of the Rightward Turn," p. 26.
81. In their study of Jewish elites, Robert Lerner, Althea K. Nagai, and Stanley Rothman find "a distinctive political tradition that Jewish parents pass down to their offspring . . . a tradition

of political liberalism." "Marginality and Liberals Among Jewish Elites," *Public Opinion Quarterly,* 53 (Fall 1989), p. 348.

82. Lipset and Raab, *Jews and the New American Scene,* pp. 12–13, 22–23. See also Stephen D. Isaacs, *Jews and American Politics* (Garden City, NY: Doubleday, 1974), pp. 149–159, 196–197; Milton Himmelfarb, *The Jews of Modernity* (New York: Basic Books, 1973), pp. 65–116; Charles S. Liebman, *The Ambivalent American Jew* (Philadelphia: Jewish Publication Society of America, 1973), pp. 135–173; Leonard Fein, *Where Are We? The Inner Life of America's Jews* (New York: Harper & Row, 1988), pp. 227–235; Stephen J. Whitfield, *Voices of Jacob, Hands of Esau. Jews in American Life and Thought* (Hamden, CT: Archon Books, 1984), pp. 73–112; Silberman, *American Jews,* pp. 345–356; Fuchs, *The Political Behavior of American Jews,* pp. 149–159, 196–197; and Cohn, "The Politics of American Jews," pp. 614–626.

83. Kosmin and Lachman, *One Nation Under God,* p. 196.

84. Cohen, *The Dimensions of American Jewish Liberalism,* p. 41.

85. Ibid.

86. Fisher, "The Myth of the Rightward Turn," p. 26.

87. Lipset and Ladd, "Jewish Academics," and Kadushin, *The American Intellectual Elite.*

88. Thorstein Veblen, *Essays in Our Changing Order* (New York: Viking Press, 1934), pp. 221, 223–234. The essay on the Jews was first published in 1919.

89. For a review of the literature and an application of this type of analysis to the politics of intellectuals, see Seymour Martin Lipset and Richard B. Dobson, "The Intellectual as Critic and Rebel," *Daedalus,* 101 (Summer 1972), pp. 137–198.

90. Tom W. Smith, *Anti-Semitism in Contemporary America* (New York: American Jewish Committee, 1994), p. 84.

91. Andrew M. Greeley, *That Most Distressful Nation. The Taming of the American Irish* (Chicago: Quadrangle Books, 1972), pp. 149–155. The original data were collected by Melvin Kohn and reported on in his book, *Class and Conformity* (Homewood, IL: Dorsey Press, 1969). See especially pp. 61–65. For other data on Jewish self-confidence and mental health, see Silberman, *American Jews,* pp. 140–142.

92. For the most detailed analysis by age, see Alan M. Fisher, "Where the Jewish Vote Is Going," *Moment,* 14 (March 1989), pp. 41–43. See also Lipset and Raab, *Jews and the New American Scene.*

93. Fisher, "Where the Jewish Vote Is Going," p. 42.

94. "Portrait of the Electorate: Who Voted for Whom in the House," *The New York Times,* November 13, 1994, p. 24.

95. Kosmin, "The Dimensions of Contemporary Jewish Philanthropy," p. 16.

96. This is elaborated in Lipset and Raab, *Jews and the New American Scene.*

97. Kosmin and Lachman, *One Nation Under God,* pp. 232, 248. Avis Miller, Janet Marder, and Steven Bayme, *Approaches to Intermarriage: Areas of Consensus* (New York: American Jewish Committee, 1993).

98. See Mary Waters, *Ethnic Options: Choosing Identities in America* (Berkeley, CA: University of California Press, 1990).

99. Drora Kass and Seymour Martin Lipset, "Jewish Immigration to the United States from 1967 to the Present," in Marshall Sklare, ed., *Understanding American Jewry* (New Brunswick, NJ: Transaction Books, 1982), pp. 272–294.

6. AMERICAN INTELLECTUALS—MOSTLY ON THE LEFT, SOME POLITICALLY INCORRECT (*pp. 176–208*)

1. This chapter subsumes "Neoconservatism: Myth and Reality," *Society* (July–August 1988), pp. 29–37, and "The Sources of Political Correctness on American Campuses," in Howard Dickman, ed., *The Imperiled Academy* (New Brunswick, NJ: Transaction Books, 1993), pp. 71–96.

2. Suzanne Garment, "Newt's Law," *The New York Times,* November 20, 1994, p. E15.

3. Seymour Martin Lipset, "Political Controversies at Harvard, 1636 to 1974," in Lipset and David Riesman, *Education and Politics at Harvard* (New York: McGraw-Hill, 1975), p. 29.
4. Charles Francis Adams, ed., *The Works of John Adams,* VII (Boston: Little, Brown, 1853), p. 596.
5. Lionel Trilling, *Beyond Culture* (New York: Viking Press, 1965), pp. xii–xiii.
6. "Text of a Pre-inauguration Memo from Moynihan on Problems Nixon Would Face," *The New York Times,* March 11, 1970.
7. Whitelaw Reid, "The Scholar in Politics," *Scribner's Monthly,* 6 (1873), pp. 613–614.
8. Whitelaw Reid, *American and English Studies,* I (New York: Scribner's, 1913), pp. 241–242.
9. Richard Hofstadter, *Anti-Intellectualism in American Life* (New York: Alfred A. Knopf, 1963), p. 39. See also Richard Flacks, *Making History: The American Left and the American Mind* (New York: Columbia University Press, 1988), pp. 116–117.
10. James Leuba, *The Belief in God and Immortality* (Chicago: Open Court Publishing Co., 1921), pp. 219–287; and Leuba, *The Reformation of the Church* (Boston: Beacon Press, 1950), pp. 50–54.
11. Everett Carll Ladd, Jr., and Seymour Martin Lipset, *The Divided Academy: Professors and Politics* (New York: W. W. Norton, 1976), pp. 27–28.
12. Gardner Murphy and Rensis Lickert, *Public Opinion and the Individual* (New York: Harper & Brothers, 1938), pp. 107–108.
13. Seymour Martin Lipset and Richard Dobson, "The Intellectual as Critic and Rebel: With Special Reference to the United States and the Soviet Union," in *Daedalus,* 101 (Summer 1972), pp. 146–147.
14. Ladd and Lipset, *The Divided Academy,* pp. 132–146.
15. Friedrich A. Hayek, "The Intellectuals and Socialism," *University of Chicago Law Review,* 16 (Spring 1949), pp. 426–427.
16. Paul Lazarsfeld and Wagner Thielens, Jr., *The Academic Mind* (Glencoe, IL: The Free Press, 1958), pp. 14–17, 95, 104.
17. Ladd and Lipset, *The Divided Academy,* pp. 125–148.
18. Thorstein Veblen, *Essays in Our Changing Order* (New York: Viking Press, 1934), pp. 226–227.
19. *The Conditions of the Professoriate. Attitudes and Trends 1989* (Princeton, NJ: Carnegie Foundation for the Advancement of Teaching, 1989), pp. 143–144.
20. S. Robert Lichter, Stanley Rothman, and Linda S. Lichter, *The Media Elite* (Bethesda, MD: Adler & Adler, 1986), pp. 28–33.
21. Joseph Schumpeter, *Capitalism, Socialism, and Democracy* (New York: Harper & Row, 1962), p. 148; C. P. Snow, *The New Men* (London: Macmillan, 1954), p. 176; Lazarsfeld and Thielens, *The Academic Mind,* p. 149.
22. Carl Becker, *Progress and Power* (Stanford, CA: Stanford University Press, 1936), p. 3.
23. Schumpeter, *Capitalism, Socialism, and Democracy,* p. 148.
24. Veblen, *Essays in Our Changing Order,* pp. 226–227.
25. For an elaboration of the argument and presentation of research findings, see Seymour Martin Lipset, "The Academic Mind at the Top: The Political Behavior and Values of Faculty Elites," *Public Opinion Quarterly,* 46 (Summer 1982), pp. 143–168.
26. Lazarsfeld and Thielens, *The Academic Mind,* p. 104.
27. Ellen Schrecker, *The Age of McCarthyism: A Brief History with Documents* (Boston: Bedford Books of St. Martin's Press, 1994); *No Ivory Tower: McCarthyism and the Universities* (New York: Oxford University Press, 1986).
28. From files of the Roper Data Center at the University of Connecticut.
29. *The Condition of the Professoriate,* pp. 143–144.
30. John Patrick Diggins, *The Rise and Fail of the American Left* (New York: W. W. Norton, 1992), p. 289; see pp. 288–306 and *passim* for the role and influence of the academic left. See also Paul Hollander, *Anti-Americanism: Critiques at Home and Abroad, 1965–1990* (New York: Oxford University Press, 1992), pp. 151–155.
31. Henry Louis Gates, Jr., "Whose Lawn Is It, Anyway?" in Paul Berman, ed., *Debating P.C.: The Controversy Over Political Correctness on College Campuses* (New York: Dell, 1992), p.

193. See also Flacks, *Making History,* pp. 185–186, and Roger Kimbell, *Tenured Radicals* (New York: Harper & Row, 1990), pp. xiv–xv.
32. Richard Bernstein, *Dictatorship of Virtue. Multiculturalism and the Battle for America's Future* (New York: Alfred A. Knopf, 1994), pp. 226–227.
33. John Searle, "The Storm Over the University," in Berman, ed., *Debating P.C.,* pp. 105–106.
34. Bertell Ollmann and Edward Vernoff, eds., *The Left Academy—Marxist Scholarship on American Campuses,* I (New York: McGraw-Hill, 1982), p. 1. See this volume and Vol. II, which has a different publisher (New York: Praeger, 1984), for documentation on different disciplines.
35. Garry Abrams, "After the Wall: As New Era Emerges U.S. Political Thinkers Ponder Fate of Marxism," *Los Angeles Times,* December 6, 1989, pp. E1, E6; Tony Judt, "The Rediscovery of Central Europe," *Daedalus,* 119 (Winter 1990), p. 34; Diggins, *The Rise and Fall of the American Left,* pp. 296–297. For conservative views, see Peter Shaw, *The War Against the Intellect: Episodes in the Decline of Discourse* (Iowa City: University of Iowa Press, 1989); Paul Hollander, *The Survival of the Adversary Culture* (New Brunswick, NJ: Transaction Books, 1988); and Roger Kimball, *Tenured Radicals: How Politics Has Corrupted Higher Education* (New York: Harper & Row, 1990). For radical ones, see Ollmann and Vernoff, eds., *The Left Academy;* Jonathan M. Wiener, "Radical Historians and the Crisis in American History, 1959–1980," *Journal of American History,* 76 (September 1989), pp. 399–434; Michael Burawoy, "Introduction: The Resurgence of Marxism in American Sociology," *American Journal of Sociology,* 88 (Supplement 1982), pp. S1–S30; Michael Denning, " 'The Special American Conditions': Marxism and American Studies," *American Quarterly,* 38, no. 3 (1986), pp. 356–380; and Flacks, *Making History,* pp. 185–186, 190–191.
36. John Gray, "Fashion, Fantasy or Fiasco?" *Times Literary Supplement,* February 24–March 2, 1989, p. 183.
37. Elizabeth Fox-Genovese, *Feminism Without Illusions: A Critique of Individualism* (Chapel Hill, NC: University of North Carolina Press, 1991), p. 150.
38. Flacks, *Making History,* p. 185.
39. John Leo, "The Professors of Dogmatism," *U.S. News and World Report,* January 18, 1993, p. 25.
40. Gerald Marzorati, "Europe Is Reclaiming the Language of Liberalism," *International Herald Tribune,* July 11, 1990, p. 4.
41. M. F. Perutz, "High on Science," *New York Review of Books,* August 16, 1990, p. 15.
42. Robert Alter, "Tyrants and Butterflies," *The New Republic,* October 15, 1990, p. 43.
43. Quoted in Bernstein, *Dictatorship of Virtue,* pp. 224–225. For a description of an MLA convention, see Leo, "The Professors of Dogmatism," p. 25.
44. Richard Flacks, "The Sociology Liberation Movement: Some Legacies and Lessons," *Critical Sociology,* 15 (Summer 1988), p. 17.
45. Wiener, "Radical Historians and the Crisis in American History," p. 434.
46. Jon Wiener, *Professors, Politics and Pop* (New York: Verso, 1991), pp. 117–118.
47. Carolyn J. Mooney, "Study Finds Professors Are Still Teaching the Classics, Sometimes in New Ways," *Chronicle of Higher Education,* November 6, 1991, p. A20.
48. Hollander, *The Survival of the Adversary Cultures,* pp. 16–18.
49. For a description of the way the latter change occurred, see Tony Judt, *Marxism and the French Left* (New York: Oxford University Press, 1986). See also Mark Kesselman, "Lyrical Illusions or a Socialism of Governance: Whither French Socialism?" in Ralph Miliband, John Saville, Marcel Liebman, and Leo Panitch, eds. *Social Register 1985/86* (London: Merlin Press, 1986), pp. 240–242.
50. Masakazu Yamazaki, "The Intellectual Community of the Showa Era," *Daedalus,* 117 (Summer 1990), pp. 260–262.
51. Diggins, *The Rise and Fall of the American Left,* p. 294. Diggins classifies English academe with American as arenas where Marxism is still strong. This is true in some fields, but on the whole radicalism is weaker in British universities than American.

52. Ron Eyerman, "Intellectuals and the State: A Framework for Analysis, with Special Reference to the United States and Sweden." Unpublished paper, University of Lund, Sweden, 1990, p. 18.

53. Flacks, *Making History,* p. 189.

54. Gray, "Fashion, Fantasy, or Fiasco?" pp. 183–184.

55. A striking example is John Kenneth Galbraith who, at a conference in July 1990 on economic reforms in East Europe, railed against the "primitive ideology" of the rapid movement toward market economics. He made "a veiled attack on the privitisation programmes planned by some east European governments. . . ." "East Europe Warned Over Fast Economic Change," *Financial Times,* July 6, 1990, p. 2. See also Galbraith's critique of developments in Eastern Europe in "The Rush to Capitalism," *New York Review of Books,* October 25, 1990, pp. 51–52.

56. See Alan Weld, *The Rise and Decline of the Anti-Stalinist Left from the 1930s to the 1980s* (Chapel Hill, NC: University of North Carolina Press, 1987); William O'Neill, *The Great Schism: Stalinism and the American Intellectuals* (New York: Simon & Schuster, 1982).

57. Gillian Peele, *Revival and Reaction: The Right in Contemporary America* (New York: Oxford University Press, 1984), p. 23.

58. See Michael Wrezsin, *A Rebel in Defense of Tradition: The Life and Politics of Dwight Macdonald* (New York: Basic Books, 1994), pp. 412–458.

59. Harrington for a long time denied that he had done this. In 1989, however, in a polemical exchange, he acknowledged that the term was "in common use among *Dissent* editors and other associates of mine," though he wrote that "I don't have the least idea who was the first to use it." See Ronald Radosh and Michael Harrington, "An Exchange," *Partisan Review,* 55, no. 1 (1989), p. 82.

60. Still, it should be noted that the neoconservatives and the traditional conservatives differed considerably in the content of their anti-Communist ideology. As Dan Himmelfarb noted: "Neoconservatives are anti-Communist because Communism is the enemy of freedom and democracy, paleoconservatives [Old Right] because it is the enemy of religion, tradition and hierarchy. For neoconservatives the relevant distinction between East and West is not the distinction between atheism and belief (as it is for paleoconservatives), nor is it the distinction between socialism and capitalism (as it is for certain libertarians). The fundamental difference, rather, is that between totalitarianism and freedom." Himmelfarb, "Conservative Splits," *Commentary,* 85 (May 1988), p. 57.

61. Jeane Kirkpatrick, "Why We Are Not Republicans," *Common Sense,* 2, no. 3 (Fall 1979), pp. 27–35.

62. Michael Massing, "Trotsky's Orphans: From Bolshevism to Reaganism," *The New Republic,* June 22, 1987, pp. 18–22.

63. Irving Kristol, "What Is a Neo-Conservative?" *Newsweek,* January 19, 1976, p. 17.

64. Irving Kristol, "America's 'Exceptional' Conservatism," *The Wall Street Journal,* April 18, 1995, p. A-20.

65. Kristol, "What Is a Neo-Conservative?"

66. Himmelfarb, "Conservative Splits," p. 58.

67. Patrick Buchanan, "Crackup of the Conservatives," *The Washington Times,* May 1, 1991, pp. G1, G4.

68. Quoted in David Frum, *Dead Right* (New York: Basic Books, 1994), p. 125.

69. John Judis, "The Conservative Wars," *The New Republic,* August 11 and 18, 1986, pp. 15–18; and "The Conservative Crackup," *The American Prospect,* 3 (Fall 1990), p. 3.

70. E. J. Dionne, "High Tide for Conservatives, But Some Fear What Follows," *The New York Times,* October 13, 1987, p. A33. See also John Ehrman, *The Rise of Neoconservatism* (New Haven: Yale University Press, 1995), pp. 186–188.

71. Paul Gottfried, "A View of Contemporary Conservatism," *The Intercollegiate Review,* 21 (Spring 1986), p. 19; and "Scrambling for Funds," *Rothbard-Rockwell Report* (March 1991), pp. 9–15.

72. Tom Bethell, "Capitol Ideas/I'm Back," *The American Spectator,* 20 (October 1987), p. 15.

73. George Gilder, "Why I am Not a Neoconservative," *The National Review*, March 5, 1982, pp. 218–220. Also see Paul Gottfried and Thomas Fleming, *The Conservative Movement* (Boston: Twayne Publishers, 1988).

74. "Farewell, and Hail," *The National Review*, November 20, 1987, pp. 20–21.

75. Robert Nisbet, "The Conservative Renaissance in Perspective," *The Public Interest*, 81 (Fall 1985), p. 137.

76. Ehrman, *The Rise of Neoconservatism*, pp. 197–204. Michael Kelly, " 'New Democrats' Say Clinton Has Veered Left and Left Them," *New York Times*, May 23, 1993, p. A20.

77. The concept was first advanced in Robert K. Merton, "The Unanticipated Consequences of Purposive Social Action," *American Sociological Review*, 1 (1936), pp. 894–904. Merton, however, had a very different approach, rejecting the notion that "unanticipated consequences" justified conservative reactions. On this, see Benjamin DeMott, "Rediscovering Complexity," *The Atlantic*, 262 (September 1988), pp. 67–74.

78. Quoted in Peter Steinfels, *The Neoconservatives: The Men Who Are Changing America's Politics* (New York: Simon & Schuster, 1979), p. 165.

79. Irving Kristol, *Reflections of a Neoconservative: Looking Back, Looking Ahead* (New York: Basic Books, 1983), p. 76.

80. Irving Kristol, "The Missing Social Agenda," *Wall Street Journal*, January 26, 1987, p. 20.

81. Michael Massing, "Contra Aides," *Mother Jones*, 12 (October 1987), pp. 23–26, 40–43.

82. Percy B. Lehning, "Neo-Conservatism and the Welfare State; Justice and Retrenchment in the Eighties: A Dutch Example," in Rob Kroes, ed., *Neo-Conservatism: Its Emergence in the USA and Europe* (Amsterdam: Free University Press, 1984), p. 37. A number of articles in this book make the same mistake.

83. Peter A. Hall, "The Smack of Firm Government," *New York Times Book Review*, October 2, 1988, p. 14.

84. Philip Resnick, "Neo-Conservatism on the Periphery: The Lessons from B.C.," *B.C. Studies*, 75 (Autumn, 1987), p. 3.

85. John Judis, *William F. Buckley, Jr.: Patron Saint of the Conservatives* (New York: Simon & Schuster, 1988), p. 130.

86. See Hollander, *Anti-Americanism*, pp. 159–166.

87. Elaine El-Khawo, *Campus Trends, 1991* (Washington, D.C.: American Council on Education, 1991), pp. 17, 40.

88. *Campus Life in Search of Community* (Princeton, NJ: Carnegie Foundation for the Advancement of Teaching, 1990), Table A-2.

89. Stanley Fish, "There's No Such Thing as Free Speech and It's a Good Thing Too," *Boston Review*, 17 (February 1992), pp. 3, 25 (emphases in original).

90. Herbert Marcuse, "Repressive Tolerance," in Robert Paul Wolff, Barrington Moore, Jr., and Herbert Marcuse, eds., *A Critique of Pure Tolerance* (Boston: Beacon Press, 1965), pp. 81–117. See also Marcuse, *One Dimensional Man* (Boston: Beacon Press, 1964), pp. 7, 9, and *passim*.

91. Louis Kampf, "Notes Toward a Radical Culture," in Priscilla Long, ed., *The New Left* (Boston: Porter Sargent, 1969), p. 426.

92. Cited in Paul Berman, "Introduction: The Debate and Its Origins," in Berman, ed., *Debating P.C.*, p. 22.

93. Ibid.

94. Eugene D. Genovese, "Heresy, Yes—Sensitivity, No," *The New Republic*, April 15, 1991, p. 30.

95. Abigail Thernstrom, "Permaffirm Action," *The New Republic*, July 31, 1989, pp. 17–19.

96. Jessie Bernard, *Academic Women* (University Park, Pa.: Pennsylvania State University Press, 1964), p. 62. See also Mabel Newcomer, *A Century of Higher Education for American Women* (New York: Harper's, 1959), p. 204.

97. Bernard, *Academic Women*, p. 67.

98. Seymour Martin Lipset and Everett C. Ladd, Jr., "The Changing Social Origins of American Academics," in Robert K. Merton, James S. Coleman, and Peter H. Rossi, eds. *Qualitative*

and Quantitative Research: Papers in Honor of Paul F. Lazarsfeld (New York: The Free Press, 1979), pp. 329–336.

99. Quoted in Dinesh D'Souza, *Illiberal Education: The Politics of Race and Sex on Campus* (New York: The Free Press, 1991), p. 171.

100. See chapter Four, pp. 00–00.

101. Bernstein, *Dictatorship of Virtue*, pp. 245–250.

102. Diggins, *The Rise and Fall of the American Left*, p. 297.

103. See Seymour Martin Lipset, *Rebellion in the University*, 3rd ed. (New Brunswick, NJ: Transaction Books, 1993), pp. 201–218.

104. Noam Chomsky, "The Function of the University in a Time of Crisis," in Robert M. Hutchins and Mortimer J. Adler, eds., *The Great Ideas Today: 1969* (Chicago: Encyclopedia Britannica, 1969), p. 59.

105. As quoted in *Campus Life*, p. 21.

7. AMERICAN EXCEPTIONALISM—JAPANESE UNIQUENESS (pp. 211–263)

1. For an earlier version of the arguments presented in this chapter, see "American Exceptionalism—Japanese Uniqueness," in Mattei Dogan and Ali Kazancigil, eds., *Comparing Nations: Concepts, Strategies, Substance* (Oxford, UK, and Cambridge, MA: Blackwell's, 1994), pp. 153–212.

2. On the reasons for comparing these two countries, see V. Lee Hamilton and Joseph Sanders, *Everyday Justice: Responsibility and the Individual in Japan and the United States* (New Haven, CT: Yale University Press, 1992), pp. 1–3. On the serious difficulties faced by foreigners who seek to understand Japan, see Joseph M. Kitagawa, *On Understanding Japanese Religion* (Princeton, NJ: Princeton University Press, 1987), pp. 294–296.

3. For good examples of the first, see Ezra Vogel, *Japan as Number One* (Cambridge, MA: Harvard University Press, 1979); Ronald Dore, *Taking Japan Seriously: A Confucian Perspective on Leading Economic Issues* (Stanford, CA: Stanford University Press, 1987); of the second, Clyde V. Prestowitz, Jr., *Trading Places: How We Are Giving Our Future to Japan and How to Reclaim It* (New York: Basic Books, 1989); and of the third, James Fallows, *More Like Us: Making America Great Again* (Boston: Houghton Mifflin, 1989), esp. pp. 28–47. See also Hugh Patrick and Henry Rosovsky, eds., *Asia's New Giant: How the Japanese Economy Works* (Washington, D.C.: Brookings Institution, 1976), particularly the article by Nathan Glazer, "Social and Cultural Factors in Japanese Economic Growth," pp. 813–896; Shumpei Kumon and Henry Rosovsky, eds., *The Political Economy of Japan*, Vol. 3: *Cultural and Social Dynamics* (Stanford, CA: Stanford University Press, 1992), especially Robert J. Smith, "The Cultural Context of the Japanese Political Economy," pp. 13–31; and Subhash Durlabhji and Norton E. Marks, eds., *Japanese Business: Cultural Perspectives* (Albany, NY: State University of New York Press, 1993).

4. See James Fallows, "The Japanese Are Different from You and Me," *Atlantic Monthly*, 258 (September 1986), pp. 38–39; Chalmers Johnson, "The People Who Invented the Mechanical Nightingale," *Daedalus*, 119 (Summer 1990), p. 73.

5. Peter N. Dale, *The Myth of Japanese Uniqueness* (New York: St. Martin's Press, 1986), p. 25. For an analysis of the background of *Nihonron*, see Harumi Befu, "Civilization and Culture: Japan in Search of Identity," *Senri Ethnological Studies*, 16 (1984), pp. 66–74. Dale and Befu believe the emphasis on uniqueness is exaggerated, as does Anthony Woodiwiss, *Law, Labour and Society in Japan* (London: Routledge, 1992), pp. 4–5. For a more recent presentation of the issue on personality level, see Kiyoshi Ando, "Japanese View of Self—Is it Unique?" *Japan Labour Bulletin*, 33 (March 1994), pp. 6–8.

6. Tamotsu Aoki, *Nihon-Bunka-ron no Henyo (Evolutionary Japanology)* (Tokyo: Chuo-Koron Sha, 1990), p. 24.

7. Yoshio Sugimito and Ross Mouer, *Images of Japanese Society* (London: Routledge, 1986), p. 11.

8. Yohio Sakata, "The Beginning of Modernization in Japan," in Ardath W. Burks, ed., *The Modernizers* (Boulder, CO: Westview Press, 1985), pp. 69–83. See also Marius B. Jansen,

ed., *Changing Japanese Attitudes Toward Modernization* (Princeton, NJ: Princeton University Press, 1965); William W. Lockwood, ed., *The State and Economic Enterprise in Japan* (Princeton, NJ: Princeton University Press, 1965); Ronald P. Dore, ed., *Aspects of Social Change in Modern Japan* (Princeton, NJ: Princeton University Press, 1967); Robert E. Ward, ed., *Political Development In Modern Japan* (Princeton, NJ: Princeton University Press, 1968); Donald Shively, ed., *Tradition and Modernization in Japanese Culture* (Princeton, NJ: Princeton University Press, 1971); James W. Morley, ed., *Dilemmas of Growth in Prewar Japan* (Princeton, NJ: Princeton University Press, 1971); Bernard S. Silberman and H. D. Harootunian, eds., *Japan in Crisis: Essays on Taisho Democracy* (Princeton, NJ: Princeton University Press, 1974); and W. G. Beasley, *The Meiji Restoration* (Stanford, CA: Stanford University Press, 1971).

9. See Edwin O. Reischauer, *The Japanese* (Cambridge, MA: Belknap Press, 1977), pp. 78–87; Robert J. Smith, *Japanese Society: Tradition, Self and the Social Order* (Cambridge: Cambridge University Press, 1983), pp. 9–36.

10. Smith, *Japanese Society*, pp. 12–25.

11. Cited in Michio Nagai, "The Development of Intellectuals in the Meiji and Taisho Periods," *Journal of Social and Political Ideas in Japan*, 2 (April 1964), pp. 29–30.

12. George A. DeVos, *Socialization for Achievement* (Berkeley, CA: University of California Press, 1973), pp. 173–174.

13. David S. Landes, "Japan and Europe: Contrasts in Industrialization," in Lockwood, ed., *The State and Economic Enterprise*, pp. 100–105, 119–143. See also: on Japan, Henry Rosovsky, *Capital Formation in Japan 1868–1940* (Glencoe, IL: The Free Press, 1961); on Germany, Thorstein Veblen, *Imperial Germany and the Industrial Revolution* (New York: Viking Press, 1939). For reference to Japan, see Thorstein Veblen, *Essays in Our Changing Order* (New York: Viking Press, 1934), pp. 248–266.

14. Veblen, *Essays in Our Changing Order*, p. 251 (emphasis added).

15. As quoted in Carmi Schooler, "The Individual in Japanese History: Parallels to and Divergences from the European Experience," *Sociological Forum*, 5, no. 4 (1990), p. 569.

16. Norman Jacobs, *The Origins of Modern Capitalism in Eastern Asia* (Hong Kong: Hong Kong University Press, 1958); Schooler, "The Individual in Japanese History"; Ken'ichi Tominaga, "Max Weber on Chinese and Japanese Social Structure," in Melvin L. Kohn, ed., *Cross-National Research on Sociology* (Newbury Park, CA: Sage Publications, 1989), pp. 125–146.

17. Chalmers Johnson, *MITI and The Japanese Miracle. The Growth of Industrial Policy, 1925–1975* (Stanford, CA: Stanford University Press, 1982), especially pp. 198–304; Prestowitz, *Trading Places*, pp. 100–150.

18. Daniel I. Okimoto, *Between MITI and the Market* (Stanford, CA: Stanford University Press, 1989), pp. 11–12.

19. Louis Hartz, *The Liberal Tradition in America* (New York: Harcourt Brace, 1955).

20. Lester Thurow, *Head to Head: Coming Economic Battles Among Japan, Europe, and America* (New York: William Morrow, 1992).

21. Okimoto, *Between MITI and the Market*, pp. 11–12.

22. Quoted in Steven R. Weisman, "An American in Tokyo," *New York Times Magazine*, July 26, 1992, p. 27.

23. Douglas Moore Kenrick, *Where Communism Works: The Success of Competitive Communism in Japan* (Tokyo: Charles E. Tuttle, 1988).

24. Ibid., p. 3.

25. Chalmers Johnson, "The Japanese Economy: A Different Kind of Capitalism," in S. N. Eisenstadt and Eyal Ben-Ari, eds., *Japanese Models of Conflict Resolution* (London: Kegan Paul International, 1990), p. 44.

26. A recent survey account may be found in Bill Emmott, *Japanophobia. The Myth of the Invincible Japanese* (New York: Times Books Random House, 1993).

27. Richard Beason and David Weinstein, *Growth, Economies of Scale, and the Targeting in Japan (1955–1990)*. Discussion Paper 1644 (Cambridge, MA: Harvard Institute of Economic Research, 1993).

28. See "Picking Losers in Japan," *The Economist*, February 26, 1994, p. 69.

29. Dore, *Taking Japan Seriously*, p. 245.

30. Harumi Befu, "The Group Model of Japanese Society and an Alternative," *Rice University Studies*, 66 (Winter 1980), pp. 178–180.

31. Harumi Befu, "Four Models of Japanese Society and Their Relevance to Conflict," in Eisenstadt and Ben-Ari, eds., *Japanese Models* pp. 213–238; Robert M. Marsh and Hiroshi Manneri, *Organizational Change in Japanese Factories* (Greenwich, CN: JAI Press, 1988), pp. 8, 284–285; Woodiwiss, *Law, Labour and Society*, pp. 4–5.

32. Seymour Martin Lipset, *The First New Nation: The United States in Historical and Comparative Perspective* (New York: W. W. Norton, 1979), pp. 209–213; Lipset, *Consensus and Conflict* (New Brunswick, NJ: Transaction Books, 1985), pp. 3–5, 11–23, 33–38.

33. See pp. 35–38.

34. Charles Hampden-Turner and Alfons Trompenaars, *The Seven Cultures of Capitalism* (New York: Doubleday, 1993).

35. Johnson, "The People," p. 78. For a detailed exposition of the importance of hierarchy and seniority in Japan, see Chie Nakane, *Japanese Society* (Berkeley, CA: University of California Press, 1972).

36. Tadashi Fukutake, *The Japanese Social Structure* (Tokyo: University of Tokyo Press, 1989), pp. 44–56; Reischauer, *The Japanese*, pp. 127–137; Daniel Pipes, "Japan Invents the Future," *Society*, 2 (March–April 1992), p. 61.

37. *A Comparison of Japanese and American High School Students' Perceptions About What Their Lives Would Be Like When They Will Be Thirty Years Old* (Tokyo: Japan Youth Research Institute, 1990), p. 91.

38. *Nanakakoku Hikaku: Kokusai Leisure Chosa '89* (*International Leisure Survey '89: Comparative Survey of Seven Countries*) (Tokyo: Yoka Kaihatsu Center [Leisure Development Center], 1989), p. 47.

39. 1990 World Values Survey coordinated by Ronald Inglehart. I am deeply indebted to Professor Inglehart for access to the data.

40. Smith, *Japanese Society*, pp. 45–47.

41. Janet T. Spence, "Achievement American Style. The Rewards and Costs of Individualism," *American Psychologist*, 40 (December 1985), pp. 1287–1288. For discussions of the complexities involved in analyzing the Japanese concepts of self, see the essays in Nancy R. Rosenberger, ed., *Japanese Sense of Self* (Cambridge: Cambridge University Press, 1992). See also Ando, "Japanese View of Self," pp. 6–8.

42. William A. Caudill and Carmi Schooler, "Childrearing and Personality Formation," in Daniel I. Okimoto and Thomas P. Rohlen, eds., *Inside the Japanese System* (Stanford, CA: Stanford University Press, 1988), pp. 16–17.

43. William A. Caudill and Carmi Schooler, "Children and Their Mothers," in ibid., p. 19.

44. *Japanese Children and Their Fathers. A Comparison with the United States and West Germany* (Tokyo: Youth Affairs Administration, Management and Coordination Agency, Prime Minister's Office, 1988), p. 31.

45. Ibid.

46. Ibid., p. 33.

47. Ibid., p. 38.

48. Harry C. Triandis, "Cross-Cultural Studies of Individualism and Collectivism," in John J. Berman, ed., *Cross-Cultural Perspectives* (Lincoln, NE: University of Nebraska Press, 1990), p. 81.

49. See Takeo Doi, *The Anatomy of Dependence* (Tokyo: Kodansha International, 1973), pp. 40–44; Mitsuyuki Masatsugu, *The Modern Samurai Society* (New York: AMACOM Book Division, 1982), pp. 88–89.

50. *A Summary Report of the World Youth Survey 1989* (Tokyo: Youth Affairs Administration Management and Coordination Agency, Prime Minister's Office, 1989), p. 74. The results from the Youth Survey and some others reported here are also given in Elizabeth Hann Hastings and Philip K. Hastings, eds., *Index to International Public Opinion 1988–89* (New

York: Greenwood Press, 1990), and Sigeki Nihira and Christine Condominas, *L'Opinion Japonais: Société-Travail-Famille à travers* (Tokyo: Sudestasie, 1991).

51. *Japanese Children,* p. 38.
52. Prime Minister's Office, "International Comparisons on Youth and Family" (Tokyo: Foreign Press Center, June 1982), p. 3.
53. Dale, *The Myth of Japanese Uniqueness,* p. 44.
54. Çigdem Kagitçibas, "Family and Socialization in Cross-Cultural Perspective: A Model of Change," in Berman, ed., *Cross Cultural Perspectives,* p. 161. See C. Hayashi and T. Suzuki, "Changes in Belief Systems, Quality of Life Issues and Social Conditions in Post-War Japan," *Annals of the Institute of Statistical Mathematics,* 36 (1984), pp. 135–161.
55. G. Trommsdorf, "Some Comparative Aspects of Socialization in Japan and Germany," in I. R. Lagunes and Y. H. Poortinga, eds., *From a Different Perspective: Studies of Behavior Across Culture* (Lisse: Swets & Zeitlinger, 1985), p. 232.
56. Tatsuko Suzuki, "Ways of Life and Social Milieus in Japan and the United States: A Comparative Study," *Behaviormetrika,* 15 (1984), p. 100.
57. Veblen, *Essays in Our Changing Order,* p. 251.
58. Research Committee on the Study of the Japanese National Character, *A Study of the Japanese National Character,* Vol. 9 (Tokyo: Tokei Suri Kenkyuzyo Institute of Statistical Mathematics, 1994), pp. 523, 525, 529; Yasumasa Kuroda, et al, "The End of Westernization and the Beginning of New Modernization in Japan: Attitudinal Dynamics of the Japanese, 1953–1983," in Chikio Hayashi and Tatsuko Suzuki, eds., *Beyond Japanese Social Values: Trends and Cross-National Perspectives* (Tokyo: Institute of Statistical Mathematics, 1990), p. 253.
59. *Fortune* and Gallup Poll results from the files of the Roper Data Library, Storrs, Connecticut.
60. Scott C. Flanagan, "Value Cleavages, Contextual Influences, and the Vote," in Flanagan, et al., eds., *The Japanese Voter* (New Haven, CT: Yale University Press, 1991), pp. 84–102.
61. Ibid., p. 101.
62. Hajime Nagahama, "International Comparisons of the Public Understanding of Science and Technology Based on Opinion Surveys." Unpublished paper, National Institute of Science and Technology Policy, Science and Technology Agency, Tokyo, 1992, pp. 16–17.
63. Shin'ichi Kobayashi, *Savages in a Civilized Society: Young People's Drift Away from Science and Society* (Tokyo: National Institute of Science and Technology Policy, Science and Technology Agency, 1991), pp. 4–5.
64. Mizuno, et al., *A Study,* pp. 528, 530; Kuroda, et al., "The End of Westernization," pp. 257–259. The 1983 data on Japanese feelings of superiority are from Chikio Hayashi, "Statistical Study on Japanese National Character," *Journal of the Japanese Statistical Society,* special issue (1987), p. 77.
65. Kuroda, et al., "The End of Westernization," pp. 258–259.
66. G. J. Bamber and R. D. Lansbury, *International and Comparative Labour Relations* (London: Allen & Unwin, 1987).
67. *Japanese Working Life Profile: Labor Statistics 1993–94* (Tokyo: Japan Institute of Labour, 1992), p. 56.
68. Okimoto, *Between MITI,* pp. 121–122. See also *Labour-Management Relations in Japan 1992* (Tokyo: Japan Institute of Labour, 1992), pp. 13, 21, 27.
69. Ben-Ami Shillony, "Victors Without Vanquished: A Japanese Model of Conflict Resolution," in Eisenstadt and Ben-Ari, eds., *Japanese Models,* p. 127.
70. Hamilton and Sanders, *Everyday Justice,* p. 37.
71. Karel van Wolferen, *The Enigma of Japanese Power: People and Politics in a Stateless Nation* (New York: Alfred A. Knopf, 1989), pp. 337–339, 409–410.
72. Shillony, "Victors Without Vanquished," p. 127.
73. Walter L. Ames, *Police and Community in Japan* (Berkeley, CA: University of California Press, 1981), p. 1.

74. See U.S. Bureau of the Census, *Statistical Abstract of the United States, 1994* (Washington, D.C.: U.S. Department of Commerce, 1994), p. 198; *Asahi Shimbaum Japan Almanac 1994* (Tokyo: Asahi Shimbaum Publishing Company, 1993), pp. 224–225.

75. *Japan 1992. An International Comparison* (Tokyo: Keizei Koho Center, 1992), p. 93. For 1992 comparisons, given as bar charts, not numbers, but showing even more striking differences, see "The Secret of Japan's Safe Streets," *The Economist,* April 16, 1994, p. 39.

76. Hamilton and Sanders, *Everyday Justice,* pp. 158–159.

77. Ibid.

78. *Statistical Abstract, 1994,* pp. 407, 409; *Japan Almanac,* pp. 227–228; Nicholas D. Kristof, "Japanese Say No to Crime, Tough Methods, at a Price," *New York Times,* May 14, 1995, pp. 1, 8.

79. "The Legal Profession," *The Economist,* July 18, 1992, Survey, p. 512. See also Hamilton and Sanders, *Everyday Justice,* p. 23.

80. "The Legal Profession," p. 54.

81. Ibid., p. 513.

82. Russell Ward, *The Australian Legend* (New York: Oxford University Press, 1959), p. 27.

83. Shillony, "Victors Without Vanquished," p. 135.

84. Frank K. Upham, *Law and Social Change in Postwar Japan* (Cambridge, MA: Harvard University Press, 1987), pp. 166–227.

85. John Owen Haley, *Authority Without Power: Law and the Japanese Paradox* (New York: Oxford University Press, 1991), p. 14.

86. John Braithwaite, *Crime, Shame and Reintegration* (Cambridge: Cambridge University Press, 1989), p. 61. See also pp. 62–65.

87. George DeVos, "Dimensions of the Self in Japanese Culture," in Anthony V. Marsella, George DeVos, and Francis L. K. Hsu, eds., *Culture and Self: Asian and Western Perspectives* (New York: Tavistock Publications, 1985), pp. 145–146.

88. Kristof, "Japanese Say No," p. 8.

89. *Chugakusei no Hahaoya—Amerika no hahaoya to no hikaku* (*Mothers of Junior High School Students—A Comparison with American Mothers* (Tokyo: Somucho Seishonen Taisaku Honbu [Youth Affairs Administration Management and Coordination Agency], 1991).

90. "Japan's Missing Children," *The Economist,* November 12, 1994, p. 46; *Statistical Abstract,* p. 105.

91. William J. Goode, *World Changes in Divorce Patterns* (New Haven, CT: Yale University Press, 1993), pp. 226–228.

92. Suzuki, "Ways of Life," p. 89.

93. *Nanakakoku Hikaku,* p. 48.

94. On client relationships, see S.N. Eisenstadt and L. Roniger, *Patrons, Clients and Friends* (Cambridge: Cambridge University Press, 1984), especially pp. 145–150, 174–178.

95. Charles A. Anderson, "Corporate Directors in Japan," *Harvard Business Review,* 62 (May–June 1984), p. 30.

96. Ibid.; Prestowitz, *Trading Places,* pp. 289–317.

97. Tadao Kagano, et al., *Strategic vs. Evolutionary Management: U.S.-Japan Comparison of Strategy and Organization* (Amsterdam: North Holland Press, 1985), pp. 55–90; *Labour-Management Relations,* pp. 31–32; Masahiko Aoki, *Information, Incentives and Bargains in the Japanese Economy* (Cambridge: Cambridge University Press, 1988), pp. 61–64.

98. Hampden-Turner and Trompenaars, *The Seven Cultures,* p. 60.

99. *The World Youth Survey, 1989,* p. 60.

100. Masanori Hashimoto and John Raisian, "Employment Tenure and Earnings Profiles in Japan and the United States," *American Economic Review,* 75 (September 1985), pp. 726–727; Robert Cole, *Work, Mobility and Participation* (Berkeley, CA: University of California Press, 1979), pp. 87–90.

101. Scott A. Bass, *Productive Aging and the Role of Older People in Japan: New Approaches for the United States* (New York: Japan Society and the International Leadership Center on

Longevity and Society, 1994), pp. 22–24; Eamonn Fingleton, "Japan's Invisible Leviathan," *Foreign Affairs*, 74 (March–April 1995), p. 77.

102. Japan Institute of Labour, "Working Conditions and the Labor Market," *Japan Labor Bulletin*, March 1, 1993, p. 3.

103. Japan Institute of Labour, *Japanese Working Life Profile: Labor Statistics 1993–1994* (Tokyo: Japan Institute of Labour, 1992), p. 28.

104. Shin-chi Takazawa and Arthur M. Whitehill, *Work Ways: Japan and America* (Tokyo: Japan Institute of Labour, 1983), pp. 58–61.

105. Suzuki, "Ways of Life," pp. 88–89; Vogel, *Japan as Number One*, p. 152.

106. Takezawa and Whitehill, *Work Ways*, pp. 118–120.

107. *The World Youth Survey, 1989*, p. 62.

108. James R. Lincoln and Arne L. Kalleberg, *Culture, Control and Commitment. A Study of Work Organization and Work Attitudes in the United States and Japan* (Cambridge: Cambridge University Press, 1990), p. 88.

109. Hayashi, "Statistical Study on Japanese National Character," pp. 74–75.

110. Hampden-Turner and Trompenaars, *The Seven Cultures*, pp. 165–166.

111. See Takeshi Inagami, "The Japanese Will to Work," in Okimoto and Rohlen, eds., *Inside the Japanese System*, pp. 32–36.

112. Lincoln and Kalleberg, *Culture, Control and Commitment*, p. 56.

113. *Japan Almanac*, p. 99, and *Statistical Abstract, 1994*, p. 420.

114. *Japan Almanac*, p. 63.

115. Ibid., p. 68.

116. *The World Youth Survey, 1989*.

117. *Leisure and Recreational Activities in Japan* (Tokyo: Leisure Development Center, 1991), pp. 19–20. See also *Labour-Management Relations*, p. 38.

118. *Leisure and Recreational Activities in Japan*, pp. 20–22.

119. "The European Union," *The Economist*, October 22, 1994, Survey, p. 4.

120. Ronald Dore, *British Factory—Japanese Factory. The Origins of National Diversity in Industrial Relations* (Berkeley, CA: University of California Press, 1973), pp. 67–70. See also *Labour-Management Relations*, p. 33.

121. Kazuo Yawata, "Le recruitments et la carrière des hauts fonctionnaires japonais," *Promotions Revue de l'Association des ancients Elèves de l'Ecole Nationale d'Administration*, 113 (July–Aug., 1981), p. 5.

122. Chie Nakane, "Hierarchy in Japanese Society," in Okimoto and Rohlen, eds., *Inside the Japanese System*, pp. 10–11.

123. *The World Youth Survey, 1989*, p. 62.

124. From an analysis of the original data by the Roper Data Library.

125. Hampden-Turner and Trompenaars, *The Seven Cultures*, p. 37.

126. Elizabeth H. Hastings and Phillip K. Hastings, eds., *Index to International Public Opinion, 1980–81* (Westport, CT: Greenwood Press, 1982), pp. 606–607.

127. Ronald Dore, "Elitism and Democracy," *The Tocqueville Review*, 14(2) (1993), p. 71 (emphases in original).

128. Japan Institute of Labour, *Japanese Working Life Profile: Labor Statistics 1993–1994* (Tokyo: Japan Institute of Labour, 1992), p. 60.

129. Lincoln and Kalleberg, *Culture, Control and Commitment*, pp. 57–61.

130. Ibid., p. 61.

131. Ibid., p. 50; Dore, *British Factory—Japanese Factory*, p. 232.

132. Dore, *British Factory—Japanese Factory*, p. 218.

133. Lincoln and Kalleberg, *Culture, Control and Commitment*, p. 61; Robert E. Cole, *Japanese Blue Collar: The Changing Tradition* (Berkeley, CA: University of California Press, 1971), p. 238.

134. Ando, "Japanese View of Self," pp. 6 and 8.

135. Richard Rose, "National Pride in a Cross-National Perspective," *International Social Science Journal*, 37, no. 1 (1985), pp. 86, 93–95; Russell V. Dalton, *Citizen Politics in Western*

Democracies (Chatham, NJ: Chatham House, 1988), p. 257; "American Values," *The Economist*, September 11, 1992, p. 20.

136. Alex C. Michalos, "Optimism in Thirty Countries Over a Decade," *Social Indicators Research*, 20 (1988), pp. 178–179. The data for 1990 are from a Gallup Poll release. The poll did not ask the question from 1986 to 1989 nor from 1991 to the present.

137. The data of the 1990 World Values study show that when asked to place themselves on a 10-point scale running from "individuals have no personal effect on what happens to them" to the belief that they have a great deal of "freedom of choice and control," 77 percent of the Americans put themselves in high-control categories compared to 29 percent of the Japanese.

138. Reischauer, *The Japanese*, pp. 162–165.

139. Triandis, "Cross-Cultural Studies," p. 103.

140. William J. Goode, private communication.

141. Stephen J. Anderson, *Welfare Policy and Politics in Japan* (New York: Paragon House, 1993), p. 143.

142. *The World Youth Survey, 1989*, p. 58.

143. Hiroshi Ishida, "Educational Credentialism, Class, and the Labor Market: A Comparative Study of Social Mobility in Japan and the United States." Ph.D. Dissertation, Harvard University, Cambridge, MA, 1986), p. 176 (emphasis in original). For a discussion of the emphasis on ranking schools and universities, as well as companies, see Befu, "Four Models of Japanese Society," pp. 220–222.

144. Dore, "Elitism and Democracy," p. 70.

145. Kenrick, *Where Communism Works*, p. 152.

146. Nakane, "Hierarchy," p. 11.

147. George DeVos. "Confucian Hierarchy Versus Class Consciousness in Japan." Unpublished paper, Department of Anthropology, University of California, Berkeley, 1990.

148. Suzuki, "Ways of Life," pp. 88–89.

149. *1987 New Social Indicators* (Tokyo: Social Policy Bureau Economic Planning Agency, 1987), p. 91; *The World Youth Survey, 1989*, p. 86.

150. Mary C. Brinton, "The Social-Institutional Bases of Gender Stratification: Japan as an Illustrative Case," *American Journal of Sociology*, 94 (September 1988), p. 308; Brinton, *Women and the Economic Miracle: Gender and Work in Postwar Japan* (Berkeley, CA: University of California Press, 1993), pp. 24–70.

151. Patricia A. Roos, *Gender and Work: A Comparative Analysis of Industrial Societies* (Albany, NY: State University of New York Press, 1985), pp. 146–147.

152. Ibid., pp. 15–16, 131; Constance Sorrentino, "The Changing Family in International Perspective," *Monthly Labor Review*, 113 (March 1990), p. 53.

153. David E. Sanger, "Job-Seeking Women in Japan Finding More Discrimination," *The New York Times*, May 27, 1994, p. A9.

154. John Greenlees, "Females Say Sayonara to Job Chances," *Times Higher Education Supplement*, November 12, 1993, p. 11.

155. Robert V. Smith, "Work and Family in Contemporary Japan, Background Information" (Data distributed for a talk at the Woodrow Wilson Center for International Scholars), September 17, 1992; *Statistical Abstract, 1994*, p. 858.

156. Ibid.

157. Ibid.

158. Mary C. Brinton, "Christmas Cakes and Wedding Cakes: The Social Organization of Japanese Women's Life Course," in Takie Sugiyama Lebra, ed., *Japanese Social Organization* (Honolulu: University of Hawaii Press, 1992), p. 96.

159. Reischauer, *The Japanese*, pp. 204–212.

160. For similar findings from 1988 data, see Tatsuko Suzuki, "Cultural Link Analysis: Its Application to Social Attitudes—A Study Among Five Nations," in *Bulletin of the International Statistical Institute*, Proceedings of the 47th Session, Paris (1989), p. 368, and Brinton, *Women and the Economic Miracle*, pp. 92–93.

161. Prime Minister's Office, "International Comparison," p. 5.

162. *The World Youth Survey, 1989*, p. 86.
163. Prime Minister's Office, "International Comparison," p. 8.
164. See the Dentsu Institute's *Virginia Slims Report 1990: A Comparative Study of Opinion Polls on Women's Issues Between Japan and the United States* (Tokyo: Dentsu Institute for Human Studies, 1990).
165. *Yearbook of Labour Statistics* (Geneva: International Labor Office, 1991), pp. 108, 409, 418.
166. Cited by Greenlees, "Females Say Sayonara," p. 11.
167. *Chugakusei no Hahaoya*, pp. 1, 14–15, 34. See also Brinton, "Christmas Cakes and Wedding Cakes," p. 86.
168. Mary C. Brinton, "Gender Stratification in Contemporary Urban Japan," *American Sociological Review*, 54 (August 1989), p. 554.
169. *Japan Statistical Yearbook: 1989* (Tokyo: Statistics Bureau, Management and Coordination Agency, 1989), p. 782.
170. Brinton, "Christmas Cakes and Wedding Cakes," p. 87.
171. *The World Youth Survey, 1989*, p. 64.
172. Fumie Kumagai, "Modernization and the Family in Japan," *Journal of Family History*, 11, no. 4 (1986), pp. 371–382.
173. Glazer, "Social and Cultural Factors," p. 861.
174. Management and Coordination Agency, "The Summary of International Comparative Surveys of the Life and Opinions of the Elderly" (Tokyo: Foreign Press Center, Japan, 1986), p. 5; and *Rojin-no Seikatso to Ishiki (The Lifestyle and Attitudes of the Elderly)* (Tokyo: Somucho Chokan Kanbo Rujin Taisaku Shitsu [Elderly Affairs Administration, Management and Coordination Agency], 1991).
175. "Presentation" by Chikako Usui and "Comment" by George DeVos, in *Japanese/American National Character Conference* (Tokyo: Institute of Statistical Mathematics, and Stanford, CA: Hoover Institution, 1991), pp. 79–80. For the same data, see Management and Coordination Agency, "The Summary," p. 4; and for 1991, see *Rojin-no Seikatsu*.
176. Sorrentino, "The Changing Family," p. 52.
177. Junko Matsubara writing in *Chuo Koron*, as reported in "Japanese Society Ignores Singles' Rights," *Mainichi Daily News*, July 5, 1992, p. 2.
178. *The World Youth Survey, 1989*, p. 48.
179. Brinton, "Christmas Cakes and Wedding Cakes," p. 96.
180. Robert Bellah, *Beyond Belief: Essays on Religion in a Post-Traditional World* (New York: Harper & Row, 1970), pp. 116–118. See also Bellah, *Tokugawa Religion: The Values of Pre-Industrial Japan* (Glencoe, IL: The Free Press, 1957).
181. Masatsugu, *The Modern Samurai Society*, p. 18.
182. *The World Youth Survey, 1989*, p. 74.
83. Tatsuko Suzuki, et al., "A Study of Japanese-Americans in Honolulu, Hawaii," *Annals of the Institute of Statistical Mathematics*, Supplement 7 (1972), p. 29.
184. World Values Survey, 1990.
185. Virginia Slims–Roper Poll.
186. For evidence from the foreign traveller literature, see Lipset, *The First New Nation*, pp. 99–139.
187. Alan Wolfe, "Cultural Sources of the Reagan Revolution: The Antimodern Legacy," in B.B. Kymlicka and Jean V. Matthews, eds., *The Reagan Revolution?* (Chicago: Dorsey Press, 1988), pp. 70–71.
188. See Seymour Martin Lipset and Earl Raab, *The Politics of Unreason: Right-Wing Extremism in America, 1790–1977* (Chicago: University of Chicago Press, 1978).
189. There is much evidence of extremely high rates of ethnic and even Jewish intermarriage in America—see Seymour Martin Lipset and Earl Raab, *Jews and the New American Scene* (Cambridge: Harvard University Press, 1995), pp, 45–48, 72–73, 182–183. The best studies are Stanley Lieberson and Mary Waters, *From Many Strands: Ethnic and Racial Groups in Contemporary America* (New York: Russell Sage Foundation, 1989), pp. 162–246, and

Mary Waters, *Ethnic Options: Choosing Identities in America* (Berkeley, CA: University of California Press, 1990), pp. 102–114.

190. Suzuki, "Ways of Life," p. 100.

191. *Japan 1992*, p. 72; *Labour-Management Relations*, p. 10.

192. World Values Survey, 1990.

193. Dale, *The Myth*, pp. 105–107; Dore, *British Factory—Japanese Factory*, pp. 202–203, 219–220, 370; Michael Shalev, "Class Conflict, Corporatism and Comparison: A Japanese Enigma," in Eisenstadt and Ben-Ami, eds., *Japanese Models*, pp. 73–77; Kenrick, *Where Communism Works*, pp. 124–125.

194. Bass, *Productive Aging*, p. 16. See also Vincent A. Mahler and Claudio J. Katz, "Social Benefits in Advanced Capitalist Countries," *Comparative Politics*, 21 (October 1988), p. 40. Data taken from International Labor Office, *The Cost of Social Security. Eleventh International Inquiry, 1978–1980* (Geneva: ILO, 1985). See also Fukutake, *The Japanese*, pp. 99–201.

195. Tomoni Kodama, "Observations on the Differences and Similarities in the Japanese and U.S. Benefit Systems," *Employee Benefits Notes*, 13 (August 1992), p. 1.

196. Naoyuki Isomo, "Stimulus Size Exceeds Expectations," *The Nihon Weekly*, September 5, 1992, p. 4; T. R. Reid, "Economic Recovery Plan," *The Washington Post*, August 31, 1992, pp. A1, A13.

197. See p. 145 for wording of question.

198. T. J. Pempel and Keiichi Tsunekawa, "Corporatism Without Labor? The Japanese Anomaly," in Philippe Schmitter and Gerhard Lehmbruch, eds., *Trend Toward Corporatist Intermediation* (Beverly Hills, CA: Sage Publications, 1979), pp. 231–270; Leonard Lynn and Timothy McKeown, *Organizing Business Trade Associations in America and Japan* (Washington, D.C.: American Enterprise Institute for Public Policy Research, 1988).

199. For an analysis of these experiences, see Robert E. Cole, *Strategies for Learning Small-Group Activities in American, Japanese, and Swedish Industry* (Berkeley, CA: University of California Press, 1989).

200. Vogel, *Japan as Number One*, p. 141.

201. Quoted in Mike Millard, "After the Bashing," *The Japan Times Weekly*, July 4, 1992, p. 3.

202. James C. Abegglen and George Stalk, Jr., *Kaisha: The Japanese Corporation: The New Competitors in World Business* (New York: Basic Books, 1985), pp. 194–195.

203. Kagono, et al., *Strategic vs. Evolutionary Management*, p. 38.

204. Hampden-Turner and Trompenaars, *The Seven Cultures*, p. 32.

205. Ibid., pp. 48–49. The survey results are presented in twelve tables on pp. 26–46. The cross-national variations on well over 100 items are considerable.

206. Richard Florida and Martin Kenney, "Transplanted Organizations: The Transfer of Japanese Industrial Organization to the U.S.," *American Sociological Review*, 56 (June 1991), p. 382. See also Karen Cool and Cynthia Legnick-Hall, "Second Thoughts on the Transferability of the Japanese Management Style," *Organization Studies*, 6 (1985), pp. 1–22.

207. Florida and Kenney, "Transplanted Organizations," p. 391.

208. Fallows, "The Japanese Are Different," pp. 37–38.

209. Johnson, "The People," pp. 82–83.

210. Richard B. Freeman, ed., *Working Under Different Rules* (New York: Russell Sage Foundation, 1994), pp. 7–10.

211. Johnson, "The People," p. 82.

212. Fingleton, "Japan's Invisible Leviathan," pp. 69–85.

213. Lipset, *Continental Divide*, p. 212.

214. Paul Krugman, "The Myth of Asia's Miracle," *Foreign Affairs*, 73 (November–December 1994), p. 74.

215. "The Triumph of the West," *The Economist*, October 29, 1994, p. 74. The summarized comparative study is Arnoud De Meyer, et al., *1994 Manufacturing Futures Survey*.

216. George V. Church, "And It Hurts," *Time*, October 24, 1994, p. 51.

217. Krugman, "The Myth of Asia's Miracle," pp. 73, 74–75.

218. Jerry Jasinowski and Robert Hamrin, *Making It in America* (New York: Simon & Schuster, 1995), pp. 24–31.
219. "The Global Economy," *The Economist*, October 1, 1994, Survey, p. 38.

8. A DOUBLE-EDGED SWORD (*pp. 267–292*)

1. This chapter is elaborated from an article by Jeffrey Hayes and myself entitled "Individualism: A Double-edged Sword," in *The Responsive Community*, 4 (Winter 1993–94), pp. 69–80, and another by Seymour Martin Lipset, "American Democracy in Comparative Perspective," in Robert S. Leiken, ed., *A New Moment in the Americas* (New Brunswick, NJ: Transaction Books, 1994), pp. 1–13. I am very indebted to Hayes for agreeing to allow me to incorporate our article, as well as for his assistance on earlier drafts of a number of chapters in this book.
2. Data from "Worrying Isn't New," *The American Enterprise*, 4 (July–August 1993), p. 94.
3. See Seymour Martin Lipset and William Schneider, *The Confidence Gap: Business, Labor, and Government in the Public Mind* (Baltimore: Johns Hopkins University Press, expanded and updated ed., 1987). See also Lipset, "American Democracy in Comparative Perspective."
4. Mortimer Zuckerman, "Where Have Our Values Gone?" *U.S. News and World Report*, August 8, 1994, p. 88.
5. Robert N. Bellah, et al., *Habits of the Heart* (Berkeley, CA: University of California Press, 1985).
6. Louise I. Shelley, "American Crime: An International Anomaly?" *Comparative Social Research*, 8 (1985); V. Lee Hamilton and Joseph Sanders, *Everyday Justice: Responsibility and the Individual in Japan and the United States* (New Haven, CT: Yale University Press, 1992), p. 194. See also *Japan 1992. An International Comparison* (Tokyo: Keizei Koho Center, 1992), p. 93, and U.S. Bureau of the Census, *Statistical Abstract of the United States, 1994* (Washington, D.C.: U.S. Department of Commerce, 1994), pp. 198, 201.
7. Charles Derber, "A Nation Gone Wild," *Utne Reader* (March–April 1993), p. 69.
8. James Wilson makes this argument, although he avoids blaming individualism per se. He emphasizes an ethic of "self-expression" that he locates in America's public philosophy. See James Q. Wilson, *Thinking About Crime* (New York: Basic Books; rev. ed., 1983), pp. 234–249.
9. Robert K. Merton, *Social Theory and Social Structure* (Glencoe, IL.: The Free Press, 1957), pp. 167–169; Daniel Bell, *The End of Ideology* (Glencoe, IL.: The Free Press, 1960), pp. 116–117.
10. John Leo, "The Age of Litigation," *U.S. News and World Report*, March 30, 1992, p. 22.
11. See David Roediger, *The Wages of Whiteness: Race and the Making of the American Working Class* (New York: Verso, 1991), pp. 19–40.
12. Alan Wolfe, "Middle-Class Moralities," *Wilson Quarterly*, 17 (Summer 1993), p. 53.
13. Daniel Patrick Moynihan, "Iatrogenic Government," *The American Scholar*, 62 (Summer 1993), p. 354.
14. *Information Please Almanac and Yearbook 1994* (Boston: Houghton Mifflin, 1994), p. 466.
15. J. Hector St. John de Crèvecover, *Letters from an American Farmer* (Franklin Center, PA: Franklin Library, 1982), p. 159.
16. *Information Please Almanac*, p. 466.
17. Lloyd Johnston, "Drug use continues to climb among American teen-agers, as attitudes and beliefs about the dangers of drugs soften, U-M survey says," University of Michigan News and Information Services, December 8, 1994, p. 2, and Table I. For similar findings up to 1993 by Gallup, see "American Youth Culture: A Roper Center Review," *The Public Perspective*, 5 (January 1994), p. 23.
18. Ibid., Table I.
19. Everett C. Ladd, "The Myth of Moral Decline," *The Responsive Community*, 4 (Winter 1993–94), p. 62. Data are from Gallup Youth Surveys.
20. James Q. Wilson, *The Moral Sense* (New York: The Free Press, 1993), pp. 162–163.

21. David Popenoe, *Disturbing the Nest: Family Change and Decline in Modern Societies* (New York: Aldine de Gruyter, 1988), p. 288.

22. Ibid., p. 291.

23. "Home Alone," *The Economist*, May 15, 1993, p. 74.

24. Nancy Wood, "Unmarried . . . with Children," *MacLean's*, August 23, 1993, p. 40.

25. William J. Goode, *World Changes in Divorce Patterns* (New Haven, CT: Yale University Press, 1993), p. 82.

26. Ann Hulbert, "Home Repairs," *The New Republic*, August 16, 1993, p. 32.

27. Ibid., p. 26.

28. *Statistical Abstract, 1994*, p. 62.

29. "New Census Bureau African American Report Most Comprehensive in 20 Years," *United States Department of Commerce News* (Washington, D.C.: U.S. Department of Commerce, February 23, 1995), p. 3.

30. Christopher Jencks, "Is the American Underclass Growing?" in Christopher Jencks and Paul E. Peterson, eds., *The Urban Underclass* (Washington, D.C.: Brookings Institution, 1991) pp. 86–89. See also U.S. Bureau of the Census, *Statistical Abstract of the United States, 1944–45* (Washington, D.C.: U.S. Department of Commerce, 1945), p. 75.

31. Robert T. Michael, et al., *Sex in America. A Definitive Survey* (Boston: Little, Brown, 1994). See also Edward U. Laumann, et al., *The Social Organization of Sexuality. Sexual Practices in the United States* (Chicago: University of Chicago Press, 1994).

32. Andrew Greeley, "Marital Infidelity," *Society*, 31 (May–June 1994), p. 13, Laumann, et al., *The Social Organization*, pp. 208–216.

33. Andrew Greeley, "Review of *Sex and Morality in the United States: An Empirical Inquiry Under the Auspices of the Kinsey Institute* by Albert D. Klassen, Colin Williams, and Eugene E. Levitt and edited by Hubert J. O'Gorman (New Haven: Wesleyan University Press, 1990)," *Society*, 27 (May–June 1990), pp. 104–105. In surveying American public opinion on sex issues, William Mayer argues that since 1974, "The dominant impression is again one of stability and continuity." See William G. Mayer, *The Changing American Mind. How and Why American Public Opinion Changed Between 1960 and 1988* (Ann Arbor, MI: University of Michigan Press, 1992), pp. 36–38.

34. James H. Rutherford, *The Moral Foundations of United States Constitutional Democracy* (Pittsburgh: Dorrance Publishing, 1992), pp. 23–24.

35. In an excellent essay, Michael Walzer elaborates a complex and persuasive image of American pluralism, which is ultimately a mixed review of the societal record: "Perhaps an immigrant society has no choice; tolerance is a way of muddling through when any alternative policy would be violent and dangerous. But I would argue we have made the best of this necessity. . . ." Even though Walzer embraces America's pluralist framework, he does so reluctantly, noting that tolerance is the second best alternative. Still he recognizes the danger of the communitarian version of pluralism for American society: "communitarianism is not a plausible option; it doesn't reach to our [political and cultural] complexity." See Michael Walzer, "What Does It Mean to be an American?" *Social Research*, 57, no. 3 (Fall 1990), pp. 610–611, 613.

36. Zbigniew Rau, "Human Nature and Civil Society," *Social Philosophy and Public Policy*, 8, no. 1 (Autumn 1990), p. 178.

37. Popenoe, *Disturbing the Nest*, p. 332.

38. Alasdair MacIntyre, *After Virtue: An Essay in Moral Theory* (South Bend, IN: University of Notre Dame Press, 1981), p. 181.

39. See pp. 70–71 of this book.

40. Robert Wuthnow, *Acts of Compassion: Caring for Others and Helping Ourselves* (Princeton, NJ: Princeton University Press, 1991), p. 22 (emphasis in original). Wuthnow's data are from a national survey of 2,775 adult respondents conducted in 1988 by Gallup and reported in *Giving and Volunteering in the United States: Findings from a National Survey* (Washington, D.C.: Independent Sector, 1988), p. 37.

41. Ladd, "The Myth of Moral Decline," p. 65.

42. Peter F. Drucker, "The Age of Social Transformation," *Atlantic Monthly*, 274 (November 1994), p. 76.

43. The patterns were similar in 1981–83. See James E. Curtis, Edward G. Grabb, and Douglas E. Baer, "Voluntary Association Membership in Fifteen Countries: A Comparative Analysis," *American Sociological Review*, 57 (April 1992), pp. 143–147.

44. Mayer, *The Changing American Mind*, pp. 33, 184–185 (emphasis in original).

45. *Statistical Abstract, 1994*, p. 70.

46. Robert Putnam, "Bowling Alone: Democracy in America at the End of the Twentieth Century. Unpublished paper, Department of Government, Harvard University, Cambridge, MA, 1994; partially published as "Bowling Alone: America's Declining Social Capital," *Journal of Democracy*, 6 (January 1995) pp. 65–78.

47. Putnam, "Bowling Alone," *Journal of Democracy*, p. 69.

48. Ibid., p. 71.

49. Putnam, "Bowling Alone," unpublished version, p. 22.

50. Lipset and Schneider, *The Confidence Gap*, p. 13.

51. The (Los Angeles) *Times-Mirror* Center, *The New Political Landscape* (Washington, D.C., 1994).

52. "Measuring Crime," *The Economist*, October 15, 1994, p. 21.

53. Ibid., p. 23.

54. "The European Union," *The Economist*, October 22, 1994, Survey, p. 4.

55. Norman Ornstein, "Less Seems More: What to Do About Contemporary Political Corruption," *The Responsive Community*, 4 (Winter 1993–94), pp. 16–17.

56. The Hudson Institute, "The American Dream." Unpublished study, Indianapolis, 1994.

57. See chapter Five, pp. 65–70.

58. Richard Rose, "How Exceptional is American Government?" *Studies in Public Policy*, 150 (Glasgow: Centre for the Study of Public Policy, University of Strathclyde, 1985).

59. Tom W. Smith, "The Polls: The Welfare State in Cross-National Perspective," *Public Opinion Quarterly*, 51 (Fall 1987), p. 406.

60. "Bottom of the Heap," *The Economist*, December 11, 1993, p. 28.

61. Nathan Glazer, "Welfare and 'Welfare' in America," in Richard Rose and Rei Shiratori, eds., *The Welfare State East and West* (New York: Oxford University Press, 1986), p. 62; Harold Wilensky, *The Welfare State and Equality* (Berkeley, CA: University of California Press, 1975), pp. 28–39; Arnold Heidenheimer, et al., *Comparative Public Policy: The Politics of Social Choice in Europe and America* (New York: St. Martin's Press, 1983).

62. For a sophisticated analysis of the changes which have been attempted, and which have survived or failed, see Hugh Heclo, "The Emerging Regime," in Richard A. Harris and Sidney M. Milkis, eds., *Remaking American Politics* (Boulder, CO: Westview Press, 1989), pp. 290–320.

63. For a discussion of the complementary interrelated character of consensus and conflict in societies, see Seymour Martin Lipset, *Consensus and Conflict: Essays in Political Sociology* (New Brunswick, NJ: Transaction Books, 1985), especially pp. 1–109.

64. Samuel Huntington, *American Politics: The Promise of Disharmony* (Cambridge, MA: Belknap Press, 1981), pp. 130–131 (emphasis added), and 85–109.

65. Quoted in Sacvan Bercovitch, "The Rites of Assent: Rhetoric, Ritual, and the Ideology of American Consensus," in Sam B. Girgus, ed., *The American Self: Myth, Ideology and Popular Culture* (Albuquerque, NM: University of New Mexico Press, 1981), p. 21; see also Sacvan Bercovitch, *The American Jeremiad* (Madison, WI: University of Wisconsin Press, 1978), pp. 140–151, 176.

66. Bercovitch, "Rites of Assent," pp. 5–6 (emphasis in original).

67. Antonio Gramsci, *Selections from the Prison Notebooks* (New York: International Publishers, 1971), pp. 21–22, 272, 318.

68. Seymour Martin Lipset, "No Third Way: A Comparative Perspective on the Left," in Daniel Chirot, ed., *The Crisis of Leninism and the Decline of the Left* (Seattle: University of Washington Press, 1991), pp. 183–205.

Index

abolition, 65, 113, 176, 177, 290–91
abortion, 28, 67, 200, 204, 248
Abrams, Elliott, 195, 196
Abrams, Garry, 185
absenteeism, 233
achievement tests, 54
Acts of Compassion (Wuthnow), 277
Adams, Henry, 178
Adams, John, 13, 178
adoption, 221
affairs, extramarital, 248, 274
affirmative action, 118–31
  civil rights movement and, 120, 128, 139, 143
  as form of collectivism, 121, 128, 129
  government support for, 118–22
  liberal support for, 128–29, 131
  meritocracy vs., 121, 122, 124–25, 139, 205–6
  negative effects of, 120, 148–49
  opposition to, 117, 120–21, 124–25, 128–29, 194, 195, 204
  political impact of, 120–22, 126, 131, 139–43, 149
  poverty and, 137–38
  "problem of standards" and, 124
  public opinion on, 124–27, 139–43
  Republicans and, 120–22, 126, 131, 139, 141, 149
  women and, 121, 122, 125, 126, 127
AFL-CIO, 120, 191, 192, 194, 198
African-Americans, *see* blacks
agnostics, 152, 179
Agrarian Socialism (Lipset), 14
Alter, Robert, 186
American Association of Retired People (AARP), 281
American Association of University Professors, 178
American Civil Liberties Union (ACLU), 40
American Creed:
  blacks as exception to, 113, 115–16, 122, 143, 154
  definition of, 19, 31
  factors in, 19–28, 31
  as ideology, 18–19, 31, 83, 154, 207, 268, 291–92
  liberalism of, 31, 32, 143–44
  preferential treatment and, 127–31, 143, 149–50
  transformation of, 22, 289, 290–92
American Dilemma, An (Myrdal), 116
American Dream, 287–88
American Federation of Labor (AFL), 37, 38, 95, 97, 107, 120
American Federation of Teachers, 107
American Political Science Association, 198
American Revolution, 14, 18, 24, 31, 39, 54, 91–92, 268
American Society for the Prevention of Cruelty to Animals (A.S.P.C.A.), 158
American Sociological Association, 177
Anderson, John, 41, 86, 91, 162
Anderson, Stephen, 238
Ando, Kiyoshi, 237
Anglican Church, 19, 93
anti-communism, 65–66, 181, 190–91, 192, 194, 197, 199, 201
Anti-Defamation League, 151
Anti-Masonic Party, 249
anti-Semitism, 122, 151, 158, 159–61, 162, 163–68, 171, 172–73, 175, 205
aristocracy, 47–48, 53, 54, 62, 68, 87, 252, 268
Aronson, Bernard, 200
Articles of Confederation, 39
atheists, 179, 205
Australia, 57, 101
authority:
  opposition to, 21, 182
  respect for, 19, 24, 199, 240, 282

Baird, Zoe, 168
Baker, James A., III, 174
Banfield, Edward C., 44, 202

Baptists, 19, 64, 70
Beard, Charles, 178
Beason, Richard, 215–16
Becker, Carl, 180, 181
Befu, Harumi, 216
Bell, Daniel, 48–49, 55, 194, 196, 198, 199,
   260, 269
Bell, Linda, 60
Bellah, Robert, 50, 63, 64, 247, 250
Belmont, August, 158
Beloff, Max, 36
Bendix, Reinhard, 14
Ben Gurion, David, 167
Benjamin, Judah P., 158
Bennett, William, 195, 196
Bercovitch, Sacvan, 26, 290, 291
Berman, Paul, 204
Bernard, Jessie, 205
Bernstein, Richard, 184
Bill of Rights, 20, 21, 25, 40, 49, 116
Bismarck, Otto von, 21, 35, 84, 117
blacks, 113–50
   as Americans, 13, 113
   birth rate of, 136
   communal rights and, 121, 128, 129,
      146–47
   discrimination against, 28, 81, 113, 115–16,
      119–20, 129–30, 133, 138, 144, 175
   drug abuse by, 272
   education and, 82, 114–18, 135–36, 137
   equal opportunity for, 113–14, 130–31, 132
   as exception to American Creed, 113,
      115–16, 122, 143, 154
   fair housing laws for, 119, 121
   government assistance for, 147–48
   Jews compared with, 122, 151, 167, 175
   leadership of, 131–32
   media coverage of, 134
   in middle class, 134–35, 136
   as minority, 113, 122
   poverty of, 132–33, 134, 135, 136–37
   quotas for, 118–31, 137–38, 149, 205–6
   social progress of, 131–38
   stereotypes of, 133–34
   stratification systems and, 113–16, 151
   underclass of, 50, 113, 133–34
   work ethic and, 132, 133
   in working class, 120, 138, 139, 140, 148,
      149
boarding schools, 82, 114
Bobo, Lawrence, 146
Bok, Derek, 103
Bonaparte, Napoleon, 155
Bozell, Brent, 201
Bradley, Tom, 170
Braithwaite, John, 228

Breyer, Steven G., 168
Brinton, Mary, 241, 242
British Columbia, 105
Broder, David, 201
Brown, Henry Phelps, 93, 96–97, 102, 106
Brown v. *Board of Education,* 118
Bruce, Peter, 108
Bruckberger, R. L., 64, 67
Buchanan, James, 160
Buchanan, Patrick, 196–97
Buckley, William F., Jr., 196, 201–2
Buddhism, 226, 247
Burger, Warren, 122
Burke, Edmund, 33, 60
Burnham, James, 201
Burnham, Walter Dean, 62, 109
Bush, George, 44, 67, 121, 141, 169, 254,
   283, 284

Calvert, John, 105
Calvinism, 153, 155, 164
Cameron, Bruce, 200
Campbell, Colin, 93–94
Campbell, Kim, 99
Canada:
   authoritarianism in, 24
   Britain compared with, 33
   collectivism in, 93–94, 95, 98, 102, 146–47
   common history of, 91
   counter-revolution in, 14, 24, 91–92
   criminal justice system of, 92
   currency of, 93
   economy of, 94, 96, 98, 100
   education in, 101
   equality vs. freedom in, 101
   foreign trade of, 66
   Francophone population of, 88–89, 92,
      93–94, 96, 273
   GDP of, 55
   health care in, 99
   Jewish population of, 157, 167
   labor legislation in, 90, 102–6
   meritocracy in, 145
   prison population of, 47
   public employment in, 99
   religion in, 62, 63, 91–92, 93
   socialism in, 78, 88–108
   statism in, 19, 92–95, 97
   third parties in, 90–91
   Tory tradition in, 24, 91, 92–93, 95, 97,
      102, 108
   trade unions in, 78, 88, 89–90, 91, 95–108
   U.S. compared with, 19, 21, 24, 32–35, 78,
      88–108, 261, 291
   welfare state of, 92, 95, 99
Canadian Auto Workers, 107

Canadian Congress of Labor (CCL), 96
Canadian Jewish Congress, 157
capitalism:
  communistic, 215
  liberal, 94
  mercantile, 54, 94, 130, 211, 215
  post-, 55
  sectarianism and, 225
  socialism vs., 37–38, 88
  values of, 154
Cardoso, Fernando, 35
Carter, Jimmy, 194, 195, 197, 283, 284
Castro, Fidel, 66
Catholic Church, 19, 28, 60, 64, 65, 67, 85,
  92, 93, 157, 159–60, 165, 205
Caudill, William, 218
censorship, 49, 207–8
Champy, James, 261
Characteristics of Black Population, 137
charitable donations, 70–71, 277
Charter of Rights and Freedoms, 146–47
Chesterton, G. K., 31
children:
  black, 136–37, 273
  illegitimate, 17, 50–51, 137, 273, 274
  parents' relationship with, 218–19, 220,
    223, 240, 244, 246–47
Chile, 35
Chodorov, Frank, 201
Chomsky, Noam, 68, 207
Christian, William, 93–94
Christian Coalition, 249
church attendance, 61, 276, 279–80
Churchill, Winston, 31, 66, 251
citizenship, 154, 155
civic consciousness, 219–20
civil disobedience, 181
civil liberties, 49, 290
Civil Rights Act (1964), 120
Civil Rights Act (1991), 141
civil rights movement:
  affirmative action and, 120, 128, 139, 143
  leadership of, 131–32
  legislation for, 120, 137, 141, 170, 284
  neoconservative support for, 197
  social impact of, 116, 119, 128, 131
  student support for, 181–82
  trade unions and, 120–21
civil servants, 44, 45
Civil War, 65, 168
class consciousness, 23, 33, 38, 77, 78, 85,
  87–88, 97, 98, 108–9, 147, 251–52, 289
Clinton, Bill, 27, 67, 97, 141, 142, 168, 174,
  198, 254, 283, 284
Coalition for a Democratic Majority (CDM),
  194, 198

cocaine, 271, 272
Cohen, Steven M., 151, 169, 171, 172
Cold War, 149
Cole, Robert, 231
Cole, Stephen, 49
collectivism, communalism:
  affirmative action as form of, 121, 128, 129
  in Canada, 93–94, 95, 98, 102, 146–47
  conservative opposition to, 36, 128
  as ideology, 37, 67–68, 93
  individualism vs., 69, 102, 216–20, 275–76,
    293–96
  Japanese, 213, 216–20, 228–29, 237–38,
    240, 252–53, 256, 257
  minority rights and, 21, 121, 128, 129,
    146–47, 176
Commentary, 198, 201
Committee for Labor Law Reform, 198
Committee on Freedom of Expression, 207–8
Commons, John, 95
common schools, 54, 82, 114
Common Sense, 195
Communist International, 77, 189
communists, 31, 65–66, 77, 97, 179, 181,
  189, 190–91, 192, 194, 197, 199, 201
"communitarian" movement, 37
competition:
  collusion vs., 295
  conservative support for, 36
  education and, 53, 54, 114–15
  individualism and, 58, 102, 108, 235, 260,
    261, 267–68
  quotas and, 118–22, 130–31
  by trade unions, 107–8
Confucianism, 220, 247
Congregationalists, 91
Congress, U.S., 42, 43, 44–45, 282, 283
Congress for Cultural Freedom, 191
Congress of Industrial Organizations (CIO),
  38, 89, 95, 97, 107, 120
conscience, obedience to, 20, 65
Consensus and Conflict (Lipset), 26
conservatism:
  anti-statism of, 36, 37, 98, 289
  anti-urban sentiments of, 249
  business ideology of, 36
  collectivism opposed by, 36, 128
  comparative analysis of, 35–37
  of intellectuals, 180, 182–83
  Japanese, 250–56
  liberalism vs., 35–39, 128
  neo-, *see* neoconservatism
  progress and, 36–37
  in Republican Party, 38, 171, 183, 254
  social, 98–99, 200
  of Tories, 31, 35, 36, 37

Conservative Party, British, 153–54, 201
Conservative Party, Canadian, 92, 98–99, 105
Constitution, Canadian, 146–47
Constitution, U.S., 20, 22–23, 39, 43, 53, 86, 116, 156
Continental Divide: The Values and Institutions of the United States and Canada (Lipset), 14, 94
"Contract with America," 27–28
Cooperative Commonwealth Federation (CCF), 96
corporations:
  downsizing of, 58–60, 233, 261, 262
  Japanese, 230–38, 252–54, 257–59
  profit margins of, 257, 258, 294
  work organization of, 258–59
Coughlin, Charles, 166
Crèvecoeur, J. Hector St. John, 33–34, 271
crime:
  blacks and, 134
  control of, 49, 227, 290
  drug abuse and, 271–72
  "functional" role of, 49
  high rates of, 13, 17, 21, 26, 46–49, 267, 269–70, 285
  low rates of, 27, 46, 49, 227, 228–29
  morality and, 47, 269–70
Cruse, Harold, 122
Culley, Margo, 186–87
currency, monetary, 93
Curti, Merle, 68

Dahl, Robert, 286
Daily Forward, 163
Dale, Peter, 223
Davies, Robertson, 108
Davis, Jefferson, 158
Dawidowicz, Lucy, 163
Dearborn Independent, 165
Debs, Eugene V., 189
Declaration of Independence, 13, 14, 31, 116, 143
deficit, budget, 38, 169, 200
de Gaulle, Charles, 66
Degler, Carl, 87
Delany, Martin, 148
democracy:
  civil society in, 276–77, 280–81
  open societies and, 13, 49, 53–54, 78, 259
  stability of, 14, 17–18
  values of, 63–67, 197, 276–77
Democracy in America (Tocqueville), 17–18, 34
Democratic Party:
  affirmative action and, 120, 121, 126, 131, 139, 140, 141, 142, 149

  anti-communism in, 192
  anti-statism of, 289 ·
  black support for, 147
  electoral gains by, 101, 139–42, 147
  intellectuals as supporters of, 179, 189
  Jewish support for, 152, 169, 170, 171, 174
  liberalism of, 38, 171
  neoconservatives and, 194, 198, 199
  New Politics wing of, 192, 194
  trade union support for, 38, 97, 101
Democratic Socialists, Japanese, 254
Democratic Socialists, U.S., 89, 192
Depression, Great, *see* Great Depression
Derber, Charles, 269
DeVos, George, 228, 240
Dewey, Thomas, 180
Diggins, John, 183, 206
Dinkins, David, 170
Dionne, E. J., 197
Disraeli, Benjamin, 21, 35, 84, 117
Dissent, 193
divorce, 26, 49–50, 229, 245–46, 272–74, 289
Dole, Bob, 122
Dore, Ronald, 216, 235, 236, 239, 253
Douglas, William O., 122
Douglass, Frederick, 148, 291
Drucker, Peter, 55, 131, 277–78
drug abuse, 47, 267, 271–72
Dukakis, Michael, 169
Duke, David, 139, 140
Duke, James Buchanan, 69
Durkheim, Emile, 214–15

Economist, 59–60, 234, 261–63, 285
economy, U.S.:
  decline of, 17, 55
  equal opportunity in, 53, 72, 76, 81, 82, 92, 98, 113–15, 118–22, 130–31, 132
  foreign competition and, 58, 59–60
  government control of, 33, 37, 38, 58, 74, 76, 94–95, 97, 145–46, 215, 216, 254, 260, 290
  growth of, 17, 38, 55–60
  as market economy, 215
  as postindustrial economy, 55–57, 58
  structual variations in, 100
Edsall, Thomas, 141, 142
education:
  blacks and, 82, 114–18, 135–36, 137
  competition and, 53, 54, 114–15
  cross-national comparisons of, 21–22, 82–83, 101, 114, 117–18, 144, 213, 217, 237, 238–39, 244–45
  desegregation of, 22, 114, 118
  equal opportunity in, 21, 53–54, 82–83, 114–15, 144

higher, 26, 58, 82, 83, 114, 177, 178, 179–88
ideology and, 61, 88
Jewish involvement in, 152, 163–64, 167, 171–72
levels of, 53, 288, 289
mass, 21, 54, 59, 82, 114, 280
political correctness and, 202–8
quotas in, 123, 131, 163–64, 167
religion and, 197, 200
rote learning in, 217
social mobility and, 61, 82–83, 118
special, 145
spending on, 22, 82, 83, 117–18, 145
vocational, 82, 118
women and, 244–45
egalitarianism:
definition of, 19
economic development and, 213
equality and, 32, 235
forms of address and, 34, 53
as ideology, 19, 31, 78, 128
individualism vs., 128–29
popular support for, 14, 24, 84, 128
elderly, 200, 220, 231, 246, 254
elections:
class divisions and, 22
institutional structure of, 40–41
primary system for, 40, 43, 86
special interests and, 44–45
third parties in, 37, 41, 42, 86, 90–91, 97–98, 180, 283
two-party system in, 39, 41–42, 45, 86, 260, 282–83
voter participation in, 13, 17, 21, 26, 43–46, 85, 240, 282–83
Eliot, T. S., 178
Ellison, Ralph, 134
Emerson, Ralph Waldo, 18
employees:
blue-collar, 140, 149
dislocation of, 56–57
expectations of, 235
government, 99
Japanese, 230–38, 252–54, 257–59
loyalty of, 233, 294
white-collar, 59, 234, 288
workweek of, 60, 74, 75, 233
Encounter, 36
Engels, Friedrich, 33, 34, 54, 77, 78–81, 84
English language, 34–35, 127–28, 239
Episcopalians, 152, 169
Equal Employment Opportunity Commission, 120
equality:
egalitarianism and, 32, 235

freedom vs., 101, 145, 255–56
of groups vs. individuals, 119, 121, 143, 146–47
individualism vs., 255
meaning of, 13–14, 32, 36
natural vs. practical, 148
of opportunity vs. results, 130–31, 235, 238
equal opportunity:
economic progress and, 53, 72, 76, 81, 82, 92, 98, 113–15, 118–22, 130–31, 132
in education, 21, 53–54, 82–83, 114–15, 144
equality of results vs., 130–31, 235, 238
for immigrants, 123–24, 127
meritocracy and, 22, 25, 53, 76, 81–83, 92, 101, 114, 144–45, 195, 199, 234–35, 248, 255, 260, 289
for minorities, 21, 113–14, 123–24, 130–31, 132, 176
for women, 121, 122, 243–44
Etzioni, Amitai, 37
Europe:
Eastern, 153, 161–65, 202
economies of, 38
education in, 22, 114, 117–18, 144
postfeudal societies in, 21, 35, 79, 115, 116–17, 147, 248, 252, 288–89
religious trends in, 61–63
social evolution of, 214–15
trade unions in, 103–4
see also individual countries
European Community, 57
European Union, 22, 46, 234
exceptionalism, American:
comparative analysis of, 32–35
failure of socialism and, 77–109
historical analysis of, 23–24
Japanese uniqueness vs., 27, 28, 208, 211–63
marginalism and, 28, 176
Marxist analysis of, 33, 62, 211, 251, 291
methodology on, 23–28
negative vs. positive aspects of, 13, 26–27, 28, 267–92
organizing principles of, 13, 150, 256, 261
traditional values and, 267–68
validity of, 24, 288–92
see also American Creed
Eyerman, Ron, 187

Fallows, James, 259
families:
black, 119, 136–38, 273
crime rate and, 47
decline of, 281
independence in, 27

families: (*continued*)
    Japanese, 233, 242–43, 245–47, 260
    male-dominant, 242–43
    nuclear, 245, 260, 273–74
    single-parent, 17, 54, 136–37, 272–73, 289
    social mobility and, 81, 83
    values of, 272–74, 276
    work responsibilities vs., 233
Farber, Henry, 104, 105
Feinstein, Dianne, 139
feminism, 176, 187, 205, 207
Fifth Amendment, 120, 190
Fingleton, Eamonn, 260
Finn, Chester, 195
First Amendment, 203–4
First New Nation: The United States in
    Historical and Comparative Perspective,
    The (Lipset), 14, 34
Fish, Stanley, 203–4
Fisher, Alan, 171, 173
Flacks, Richard, 185–86, 187, 188
Flanagan, Scott, 221–22
Florida, Richard, 258
Forbath, William, 95
Ford, Henry, 165
Ford, James W., 179
"foreign traveler" literature, 17, 33–34
Foster, William Z., 179
Foucault, Michel, 184
Fox-Genovese, Elizabeth, 185
France:
    economy of, 58
    education in, 22
    Jewish population of, 155
    patriotism in, 51
    religion in, 62
    taxation in, 73
    U.S. compared with, 18
Franco, Francisco, 66, 189
Franklin, Benjamin, 60, 153
freedom, 19, 31, 101, 128, 145, 154–57, 223,
    255–56
Freeman, Richard, 60, 103
French Revolution, 17, 92, 155
Frey, William H., 135
Friedman, Milton, 36, 154, 196, 200, 202
friendship, 245, 276
Fuchs, Lawrence, 124
Fuchs, Victor, 137
Future in America, The (Wells), 33

Galbraith, John Kenneth, 85
Garfield, James, 159
Garin, Geoff, 140
Garment, Leonard, 119–20
Garment, Suzanne, 28, 177

Garrison, William Lloyd, 291
Gates, Henry Louis, Jr., 131, 132–33, 183–84,
    206
Genovese, Eugene, 204
geographic mobility, 85, 281
Germany:
    competitiveness of, 59
    economy of, 55, 57, 58
    education in, 22, 144
    Jewish population of, 160–61, 162, 165,
    166, 167
    patriotism in, 51
    productivity of, 55, 56
    religion in, 61–62
    trade unions in, 38
    U.S. compared with, 60
    welfare state in, 21, 35, 84, 117, 252
    white-collar jobs in, 59
Gershman, Carl, 195
Gilder, George, 197
Gingrich, Newt, 28, 82, 177
Ginsburg, Ruth Bader, 168
Gitlin, Todd, 204
Glazer, Nathan, 164, 194, 198, 245, 289
Glendon, Mary Ann, 23
Goldscheider, Calvin, 151, 162
Goldwater, Barry, 197
Gompers, Samuel, 37, 96
Goode, William, 50, 229
Goodman, Paul, 290
Gotlieb, Allan, 42
Gould, Stephanie, 72
government:
    affirmative action supported by, 118–22
    bureaucracy of, 58
    distrust of, 17, 27, 39, 45, 46, 68, 281–84,
    286–87
    employees of, 99
    industrial ownership by, 39
    participatory, 43–44, 289
    regulation by, 27–28, 74, 75
    separation of powers in, 39, 40, 42, 43, 44,
    46
    social programs of, 25, 37, 147–48, 196
    spending by, 38, 169, 200
    unified, 39–40
Gramsci, Antonio, 54, 61, 78, 87, 290
Grant, George, 36–37
Grant, Ulysses S., 158
Gray, John, 185, 188
Great Britain:
    civil liberties in, 49
    conscientious objection in, 65
    crime rate in, 49
    education in, 101, 144
    equal opportunity in, 83

Jewish population of, 153
parliamentary system of, 17–18
patriotism in, 51
postfeudal traditions of, 288–89
prison population of, 47
religion in, 61, 62, 65
taxation in, 73
trade unions in, 38, 103–4
U.S. compared with, 32, 33
welfare state in, 21, 35, 84, 117, 252
Great Depression, 22, 27, 37, 38, 70, 89, 95, 97, 99, 163, 166, 167, 179, 274
Greeley, Andrew, 274
Green, Martin, 69
Greenberg, Stanley, 139–40, 141
gross domestic product (GDP), 22, 55, 73, 117
gross national product (GNP), 22
Group of Seven, 55
Gulf War, 67, 284

Haley, John, 228
Hammer, Michael, 261
Hampden-Turner, Charles, 25, 217, 257–58
Hamrin, Robert, 262
Hardin, Herschel, 94
Harrington, Michael, 81, 87–88, 191, 192, 193
Hartz, Louis, 87, 108
Harwood, Richard, 134
Hashimoto, Masanori, 231
Hawkins, Augustus F., 121
Hayek, Friedrich, 36, 154, 180, 196, 200
Head Start, 119, 130, 145, 149
health care, 27, 58, 71, 75, 83, 95, 99, 253–54
Heath, Edward, 201
Hebrew Immigrant Aid Society (HIAS), 175
Helmreich, William, 173
Helms, Jesse, 139
Hess, Karl, 68
Heston, Allen, 55
Higginson, Henry Lee, 69
Higham, John, 161
Himmelfarb, Dan, 196
Himmelfarb, Gertrude, 195, 196
Himmelfarb, Milton, 169
Hispanics, 124, 127, 135, 167, 272
history:
common, 18, 31, 91, 207
consensual, 25–26
Hitler, Adolf, 67, 189
Hofstadter, Richard, 18, 26, 37, 178, 179
Holocaust, 166, 167
Hook, Sidney, 81, 87, 193
Hoover, Herbert, 38
Horowitz, Gad, 95, 96

House of Representatives, U.S., 39
housework, 242–43
Howe, Irving, 193
Hulbert, Ann, 273
Humphrey, Hubert, 120, 192, 193, 194, 195
Huntington, Samuel, 26, 54, 63–64, 290
Hussein, Saddam, 67

Image of America, The (Bruckberger), 64
immigrants:
assimilation of, 158, 165–66, 175, 249–50
equal opportunity for, 123–24, 127
Jewish, 154, 160, 162, 163
living standards of, 85
non-Protestant, 165
populism and, 154
rights of, 174
success of, 48, 135
Third World, 259
income:
discrepancies in, 72–73, 75
distribution of, 13, 26, 73, 75, 76, 84–85, 92, 145
guaranteed, 76, 145
per capita, 55
regulation of, 225–26, 234–35
individualism:
collectivism vs., 69, 102, 216–20, 275–76, 293–96
competitive, 58, 102, 108, 235, 260, 261, 267–68
culture of, 106, 114, 237–38
divorce rates and, 50
economic impact of, 74–75, 213
egalitarianism vs., 128–29
equality vs., 255
expressive, 50
as ideology, 19, 31, 96, 122, 125, 128, 143, 199, 275–76, 287
Jeffersonian, 196
legal rights and, 20–21, 139
as moral standard, 64, 267–68, 269, 275–76
possessive, 95
sectarianism and, 19–20
sexuality and, 51
social impact of, 26–27, 273, 277
statism vs., 22–23, 84
uncontrolled, 269
Industrial Revolution, 211–12
Industrial Workers of the World (IWW), 37, 95, 97, 190
infant mortality, 58, 134
inflation, 93, 97
Inglehart, Ronald, 217, 260
initiative petitions, 43–44
Innis, Harold, 93

innovation, 48, 59, 172, 213–14, 230, 258
institutions:
  corruption of, 20
  distrust of, 17, 27, 63
  religious, 63
integration, compulsory, 128–29
intellectuals, 176–208
  adversary culture of, 178
  alienation of, 28, 177–78, 188
  anti-communism of, 190–91, 192
  in anti-war movement, 177, 182, 190, 191,
    192
  as conservatives, 180, 182–83
  Jewish, 194
  as liberals, 180–81, 182, 183
  Marxism of, 184–86
  moralism of, 176–77
  political correctness and, 176, 177, 183,
    202–8
  political views of, 179–208
  radicalism of, 179–81, 182, 184, 188
  repression of, 66, 176, 180, 181, 190, 204
  socialism supported by, 177–78, 179, 180,
    181, 187–88, 189
  at universities, 177, 178, 179–88
  values of, 179–81
intolerance, 13, 113, 122, 204, 224–25
Iran-Contra Scandal, 284
Ireland, 19, 28
Israel, 154, 166, 167, 168, 174, 175, 197
Italy, 58, 159–60, 278

Jackson, Andrew, 285
Jackson, Henry, 192, 193, 194, 195, 197
Jackson, Jesse, 148
Jacobs, Norman, 215
Jaher, Frederick, 160
Jakobovits, Immanuel, 153
James, William, 178
Japan, 211–63
  agrarian society of, 211, 214, 245, 249, 260
  birth rate in, 245, 260
  civic consciousness in, 219–20
  collectivism in, 213, 216–20, 228–29,
    237–38, 240, 252–53, 256, 257
  competitiveness of, 17, 59–60, 234,
    256–63
  conflict resolution in, 225–30
  conservatism in, 250–56
  crime rate in, 27, 46, 49, 227, 228–29
  cultural biases in, 236–38
  divorce rate in, 229, 245–46
  duty and obligation in, 215, 217–20
  economy of, 17, 38, 55, 57, 58, 59–60,
    212–16, 231, 248, 251, 254, 256, 260,
    261

education in, 22, 101, 144, 213, 217, 237,
  238–39, 244–45
employment in, 59, 230–38
equality vs. freedom in, 101, 255–56
gender relations in, 241–45
GOP of, 55
health care in, 253–54
industrialization of, 211–17, 238, 245, 251,
  260
intellectuals in, 187
intolerance in, 224–25
litigiousness in, 27, 227–28, 238
marriage rate in, 241–42
modern society in, 212–17, 221–25,
  250–56
nineteenth-century barons of, 213–14
as outlier, 25, 27, 238, 263
parent-child relationships in, 218–19, 220,
  223, 240, 244, 246–47
parliamentary system of, 226, 240, 260
postfeudal traditions of, 211, 212–15, 217,
  238, 248, 252, 256, 260
postindustrial society in, 257–59, 262
prison population of, 227, 229
productivity of, 55, 56, 58
"racial purity" in, 259
religion in, 63, 213, 221, 226, 247
scientific development in, 222–23
social exchange model for, 216
socialism in, 251, 254–55
statism in, 19, 221
status-consciousness in, 213, 238–40
trade unions in, 225–26, 233, 251–52
traditional values in, 220–25, 229, 241–42,
  244, 245, 246–51, 263
uniqueness of, 27, 28, 208, 211–63
U.S. compared with, 27, 28, 38, 58, 59, 60,
  208, 211–12, 216–63
U.S. occupation of, 223, 251
volunteerism in, 27, 217, 278, 279
work ethic in, 233–37
xenophobia in, 212–13, 224–25, 259
Japanese language, 239
Jasinowski, Jerry, 262
Jefferson, Thomas, 13, 46, 93, 115–16, 150,
  155, 252, 285
Jencks, Christopher, 137, 273
Jews, 151–75
  as Americans, 13, 151, 152–54, 155,
    174–75
  assimilation of, 158, 165–66, 175
  birth rate of, 168, 175
  blacks compared with, 122, 151, 167, 175
  conservatism of, 173–74
  Conservative, 166
  discrimination against, 122, 151, 158,

159–61, 162, 163–68, 171, 172–73, 175, 205

Eastern European, 153, 161–65
education and, 152, 163–64, 167, 171–72
equal opportunity for, 123–24
forced conversion of, 159–60
German, 160–61, 162, 165
as immigrants, 154, 160, 162, 163
incomes of, 151–52, 161, 169
as intellectuals, 194
intermarriage by, 168, 175
liberalism of, 169–72, 175
in middle class, 163, 164
as neoconservatives, 194, 202
occupations of, 152, 160–61, 164
Orthodox, 162, 163, 166, 169
philanthropy of, 168–69, 170, 174
political influence of, 157–58, 162–63, 168, 169–70, 172, 174
quotas used against, 163–64, 167
Reform, 165–66
as refugees, 166, 167, 174, 175
religious freedom of, 154–57
social acceptance of, 157–60, 161
Soviet, 174
stratification systems and, 151
success of, 28, 151–54, 167, 169, 175
values of, 152–54, 164, 170–71, 172, 173, 213–14
work ethic of, 153–54, 155, 164
Jews and the New American Scene (Lipset and Raab), 14
job creation, 38, 57, 74, 75, 76, 289
job security, 101, 145
Johnson, Chalmers, 215
Johnson, Lyndon B., 66, 67, 118–19, 120, 139, 192, 285, 290
Johnson, Richard, 156
Judis, John, 107–8, 197, 201–2

Kalleberg, Arne, 233, 236
Kampelman, Max, 194, 195
Kampf, Louis, 204
Kapital, Das (Marx), 33, 80, 292
Kassalow, Everett, 103–4
kehillah, 157
Kemble, Penn, 200
Kemp, Jack, 198
Kendall, Willmore, 201
Kennan, George F., 66
Kennedy, John F., 118, 192
Kennedy, Robert F., 192
Kenney, Martin, 258
Kenrick, Douglas Moore, 215, 239
Keynesianism, 180, 254
Keyserling, Hermann, 87

King, Martin Luther, Jr., 284, 291
Kirkland, Lane, 193, 198
Kirkpatrick, Evron, 195, 196
Kirkpatrick, Jeane, 194, 195, 196, 197–98, 202
Klehr, Harvey, 80
Know-Nothing American Party, 249
Kodama, Tomoni, 253–54
Korean War, 65, 66, 191
Kosmin, Barry, 168
Kristol, Irving, 36, 194, 195–96, 197, 198, 199–200
Kristol, William, 195
Krueger, Alan, 104, 105
Krugman, Paul, 262
Kudrle, Robert T., 71
Ku Klux Klan, 165, 249

labor unions, *see* trade unions
Labour Party, British, 101, 201
Ladd, Everett Carll, 53, 64, 74, 180
LaFollette, Robert, 37, 41, 86, 91, 162
LaFollette, Suzanne, 201
laissez-faire:
    conservatism and, 36
    economic, 54, 74, 94, 96
    as ideology, 19, 31, 96, 287
    liberalism and, 153–54, 196, 202, 215, 252
    statism vs., 27, 76
Lament for a Nation (Grant), 36–37
Latin America, 35, 39
law:
    comparative analysis of, 49, 50
    due process of, 49
    obedience to, 46, 47–48, 93, 269–70, 289
    recourse to, 25, 26, 27, 40, 49, 50, 227–28, 238, 267, 270
lawyers, 25, 49, 152, 270
Lazarsfeld, Paul, 180, 181
League for Industrial Democracy (LID), 191
Left:
    conflicts in, 188–92
    New, 37, 183, 190, 191, 192, 193, 199, 204, 291
    Old, 192
    radicalism of, 179–81, 182, 184, 188
Lehning, Percy, 200
Leiken, Robert, 200
Lenin, V. I., 33, 78, 85
Leo, John, 186
Leonard, Jonathan, 137
Letters from an American Farmer (Crèvecoeur), 271
Leuba, James, 179
Levy, Uriah, 158
Liberal Democratic Party (LDP), 251, 254

liberalism:
  of American Creed, 31, 32, 143–44
  anti-statism of, 91, 95, 200, 201, 215, 252
  bourgeois, 256
  classical, 54, 91, 95, 98, 147, 200, 202,
    207, 215, 252, 253
  conservatism vs., 35–39, 128
  definition of, 35–36
  economic development and, 213
  of intellectuals, 180–81, 182, 183
  Jewish, 169–72, 175
  laissez-faire, 153–54, 196, 202, 215, 252
  mercantile, 147, 154
  neo-, 198
  neoconservatism vs., 196, 197, 200
  political impact of, 38, 171
  as possessive individualism, 95
libertarianism, 46, 89, 200
Liebman, Arthur, 162
Lincoln, Abraham, 13–14, 18, 120, 158, 285
Lincoln, James, 233, 236
litigiousness, 25, 26, 27, 40, 49, 50, 227–28,
    238, 267, 270
living standards, 38, 57–58, 76, 80, 81–82, 85,
    144, 145–46
lobbyists, 44–45
Lorwin, Val, 181
Lubell, Samuel, 97
Lutherans, 19

MacArthur, Douglas, 251
McCarthy, Eugene, 192
McCarthy, Joseph, 181, 190
McCarthyism, 66, 176, 180, 181, 190, 204
McConnell, Grant, 37
McDonald, Charles, 107
McGovern, George, 192, 194, 198
MacIntyre, Alasdair, 277
Mackenzie-Papineau Rebellion, 24
McLeod, J. T., 94
Macmillan, Harold, 24
Madison, James, 13, 155
Magnes, Judah, 157
Major, John, 153, 201
Making It in America (Jasinowski and
    Hamrin), 262
malpractice suits, 265, 238, 270
managers, business, 25, 230, 239, 257–59,
    261, 294
Marcuse, Herbert, 204
markets:
  commodities in, 211
  forces of, 130, 276
  international, 59
  share of, 257
Marmor, Theodore R., 71

marriage, 27, 50–51, 241–42
Martineau, Harriet, 34
Marx, Karl, 33, 77, 78–81, 84, 88, 215, 292
Marxism, 33, 62, 77–81, 184–86, 211, 251,
    291
Marzorati, Gerald, 186
materialism, 35, 44, 54, 77, 178, 183, 252,
    277
Matsubara, Junko, 246
Mayer, William, 279
Meany, George, 193, 194
Medoff, James, 103
Meiji restoration, 213–14, 251, 252, 254, 256
Meltz, Noah, 99–100
meritocracy:
  affirmative action vs., 121, 122, 124–25,
    139, 205–6
  equal opportunity and, 22, 25, 53, 76,
    81–83, 92, 101, 114, 144–45, 195, 199,
    234–35, 248, 255, 260, 289
Merton, Robert K., 26, 47, 115, 269
Methodists, 19, 60
metric system, 21, 93
Meyer, Frank, 201, 202
Ministry of International Trade and Industry
    (MITI), 215
Mitchell, Clarence, 121, 148
Mitchell, John, 121
Moberg, David, 106
Modern Language Association, 177, 186, 187
Molotov, V. M., 189
Mondale, Walter F., 198
morality:
  absolutism in, 63–67
  in adversarial societies, 226–27
  anti-communism and, 65–66
  conventional, 48–49
  crime and, 47, 269–70
  decline in, 17, 26–27, 28, 267–92
  foreign relations and, 20, 65–67
  human perfectibility and, 20
  individualism and, 64, 267–68, 269,
    275–76
  sectarianism and, 27
  see also values
Moral Majority, 249
Mori, Arinori, 213
Morita, Akio, 257
Mortara, Edgardo, 159–60
Mouer, Ross, 212
Moynihan, Daniel Patrick, 178, 193, 194, 196,
    198, 202, 271
Mulroney, Brian, 99
multiculturalism, 176, 183–84, 186, 206, 259
Murayama, Tomiichi, 251
Myrdal, Gunnar, 26, 116

Nader, Ralph, 194
Nakane, Chie, 234, 239
Nakazawa, Shin-ichi, 215
Napoleon Bonaparte, 155
Nasar, Sylvia, 55, 56*n*, 57
Nathan, Richard P., 135
National Academy of Sciences, 136
National Education Association, 107
National Labor Relations Board (NLRB), 108
National Review, 196, 197–98, 201–2
national service, 149
National Survey of Religious Identification, 171
National Taxpayers Union, 68–69
National Union for Social Justice, 166
Native Americans, 122
nativism, 160
Nazism, 166, 167, 171, 189
neoconservatives, 193–202
    affirmative action opposed by, 194, 195
    anti-communism of, 194, 197, 199, 201
    conservatives vs., 196–98, 200, 201–2
    Democrats and, 194, 198, 199
    emergence of, 193–98
    Jewish, 194, 202
    labeling of, 193
    liberalism vs., 196, 197, 200
    meaning of, 199–202
    Republicans and, 193–94, 195, 196, 197–200, 202
    Tories and, 200
    welfare supported by, 195, 196, 197, 199–200, 201, 202
Nettl, J. P., 40
New Deal, 27, 37–38, 95, 97, 130, 192, 193, 199, 201
New Democratic Party (NDP), 88, 89, 90, 96, 98, 99, 101, 102
New Republic, 195, 201
New York Times, 73, 228, 241
New York Times Book Review, 200
Nicaragua, 200, 284
Nisbet, Robert, 198, 202
Nixon, Richard M., 119, 120, 121, 149 194, 195–96, 198, 206
Noah, Mordecai, 158
noblesse oblige, 21, 31, 35, 68, 72, 94, 117, 252, 254
Novak, Michael, 195, 198

OECD, 73, 117, 253, 289
oil crisis (1973), 55, 59, 222
Okimoto, David, 215, 226
Ollmann, Bertell, 185
O'Neill, Thomas P. (Tip), 42
optimism, 51–52, 81, 132, 237

Organization of American Historians, 187
Ornstein, Norman, 286
Owen, Robert, 82

Page, Benjamin, 82
Palmer, John, 72
parent-teacher associations (PTA), 280
Park, Robert, 153
parliamentary system, 17–18, 42–43, 44, 45, 90–91, 226, 240, 260
particularism, 96, 102, 123, 175, 213, 217, 232–33
Parti Québécois, 88–89, 96
patriotism, 20, 51, 65, 289
Peele, Gillian, 189
pensions, 71–72, 75, 83, 230, 253
Perle, Richard, 194, 195
Perlman, Selig, 85, 95
Perot, H. Ross, 41, 86, 89, 91, 97–98, 169, 283, 287
Perry, Matthew, 259
Perutz, M. F., 186
pessimism, 267, 281–83
Peterson, Paul, 134
Phi Beta Kappa, 152
Philadelphia Plan, 120
philanthropy, 67–71, 153, 168–69, 170, 174, 277
Pierson, George, 18
Pipes, Richard, 195
Plato, 82
Podhoretz, Norman, 195, 196, 197
pogroms, 159
Poland, 19, 28
political correctness, 176, 177, 183, 202–8
Political Man: The Social Basis of Politics (Lipset), 15
politics:
    compromise in, 44–45
    free speech and, 203–4
    local, 42
    radical, 179–81, 182, 184, 188
    variables in, 39–46
Popenoe, David, 49–50, 71, 273, 276
populism:
    electoral support for, 40, 43, 45, 46
    as ideology, 19, 31
    immigration and, 154
    predominance of, 24, 40
poverty, 73–76, 119, 130, 132–38, 146, 200
pregnancies, teenage, 50–51
Presbyterians, 64
President, U.S., 39, 41, 42–43, 44, 53, 86, 90
Presthus, Robert, 92
prime ministers, 42–43
prison population, 17, 26, 46–47, 227, 229

productivity, 26, 55, 56, 57, 58–59, 79, 85, 256–57, 258, 261, 262
Progressive Conservatives, Canadian, 98–99
Progressive movement, 37, 162, 190
Progressive Party of 1924, 162
Progressive Party of 1948, 162, 190
Prohibition, 176
proletariat, 81, 88
Proposition 187, 174
Protestant Ethic and the Spirit of Capitalism, The (Weber), 60
Protestantism, 60, 63, 160, 234, 270, 279
  see also individual denominations
Protocols of the Elders of Zion, 165
Public Interest, 194, 198, 201
Puritanism, 60–61, 153, 155, 164, 238
Putnam, Robert, 280, 281

quality circles, 216, 256–67, 259
Quebec, 88–89, 92, 93–94, 96, 273
quotas, 118–31, 137–38, 149, 163–64, 167, 205–6

Raab, Earl, 14, 170, 172, 175, 249
racism, 28, 81, 113, 115–16, 119–20, 129–30, 133, 138, 144, 175
"rackets," 48, 49
Raisian, John, 231
Ranney, Austin, 44
Ransom, John Crowe, 185
Raskin, Marc, 68
Raspberry, William, 142
Rau, Zbigniew, 276
Reagan, Ronald, 36, 38, 65, 121–22, 154, 183, 187, 195–200, 202, 284
recessions, 97, 98, 132, 231, 237, 241, 254, 258, 259, 261
Reconstruction, 148
redundancy, 56–57
Reengineering Capitalism (Hammer and Champy), 261
Reform Party, Canadian, 98–99
Reich, Robert, 58
Reid, Whitelaw, 178
Reishauer, Edwin, 238, 250
religion:
  bourgeois society and, 61–62
  in Canada vs. U.S., 91–92
  churches vs. sects in, 19–20, 27, 60–67, 80, 93, 154–57, 207
  "civic," 18, 63–64
  clergy in, 19, 92, 155
  congregational, 19, 61, 157, 277
  cross-national comparisons of, 62, 63, 901–92, 93
  dogmatic, 226–27

established, 154, 155, 157
  freedom of, 154–57
  fundamentalist, 61, 160, 165, 256
  hierarchical, 61, 93, 277
  moral absolutism and, 63–67
  popular support for, 61–63, 276, 279–80, 289, 290
  in public schools, 197, 200
  state vs., 19, 62, 63, 67, 197, 200, 252
  voluntary, 19, 61, 154–55, 277
  see also individual religions
"repressive tolerance," 204
Republican Party:
  affirmative action and, 120–22, 126, 131, 139, 141, 149
  anti-statism of, 289
  conservatism in, 38, 171, 183, 254
  electoral support for, 101, 139–42
  government control opposed by, 27–28
  intellectuals as supporters of, 193–94
  Jewish support for, 162, 169, 170, 171
  neoconservatives and, 193–94, 195, 196, 197–200, 202
  origins of, 41
  WASPS in, 171, 195
Resnick, Philip, 200
retirement, 231, 254
reverse discrimination, 137, 141–42
Ribuffo, Leo, 160
Richards, I. A., 185
Richards, John, 100
Rickenbacker, Eddie, 66
Riddell, W. Craig, 100
Right, Old, 192, 196–97
Rockefeller, John D., 70
Roosevelt, Franklin D., 13, 14, 37–38, 97, 166, 189, 190, 197, 285
Roosevelt, Theodore, 37, 86, 91, 283
Ross, Aileen, 70–71, 277
Ross, E. A., 178
Russia, Czarist, 86, 159
Russian Revolution, 77
Rustin, Bayard, 193
Rutherford, James, 275

Samson, Leon, 81, 87
Samuelson, Robert, 57–58
samurai, 214, 220
savings rate, 26, 59, 235–36, 270
Schactman, Max, 191
Schaff, Philip, 54
Schattschneider, E. E., 41
Schlamm, Willi, 201
Schooler, Carmi, 215, 218
Schuman, Howard, 146
Schumpeter, Joseph, 180, 181

scientific development, 59, 222–23
Searle, John, 184–85
segregation, 115, 122–23, 128
Seligman, Joseph, 158
Senate, U.S., 39, 40
seniority, 101, 124, 234, 258
sexuality, 51, 248, 272–74, 290
Shamir, Yitzhak, 167
Shapiro, Robert, 82, 117
Shelley, Louise, 46, 47, 269
Shinto religion, 213, 226, 247
Shultz, George, 119–20, 121
Silberman, Lawrence, 120
Simms, Margaret, 137
Skerry, Peter, 127–28
slavery:
    abolition of, 65, 113, 176, 177, 290–91
    immorality of, 13, 24
    political impact of, 41, 114, 115
Smeeding, Timothy, 73–74
Smith, Adam, 215
Smith, James P., 136
Smith, Tom, 168
Snow, C. P., 180
Social Credit Party, 105, 200
Social Democratic Party, British, 201
social democrats, 22, 24, 37, 42, 78, 86,
    93–99, 108, 118, 170, 189, 192–94, 198,
    200, 201
Social Democrats USA, 192, 193, 194, 198
socialism:
    black support for, 147
    in Canada vs. U.S., 78, 88–108
    capitalism vs., 37–38, 88
    class consciousness and, 23, 77, 78, 85,
        87–88
    comparative analysis of, 78, 86–88
    contemporary sociological analysis of, 81–86
    electoral gains by, 37, 89, 97
    intellectuals as supporters of, 177–78, 179,
        180, 181, 187–88, 189
    in Japan, 251, 254–55
    market, 215
    Marxist principles of, 77–81
    modernism and, 62, 77
    party organizations for, 37, 77, 80, 85–86,
        89, 97, 181, 189, 192, 254
    paternalistic, 24, 93, 95, 154, 230, 253
    political factors and, 85–86, 192
    postfeudal societies and, 22, 109
    repression of, 86
    sectarianism vs., 79–80
    societal variables and, 84–86
    statism and, 90–96
    stratification factors and, 79, 80–81
    surrogate, 84, 87–88

trade unions and, 78, 80, 84, 85, 95–96,
    108
U.S. failure of, 14, 28, 32, 33, 37–39, 76,
    77–109
worker support for, 22, 33, 78, 80, 84,
    85–86, 95–96, 108
Socialist International, 89
Socialist Party, Japanese, 254
Socialist Party, U.S., 37, 80, 89, 97, 181, 189,
    192
Socialist Workers Party, 190
social mobility, 14, 26, 53, 61, 81–82, 83, 84,
    149, 168
Social Mobility in Industrial Society (Lipset
    and Bendix), 14
society:
    adversarial, 25–26, 178, 199, 216, 225–27,
        276, 290–91, 296
    agrarian, 62, 211, 214, 245, 249, 260, 288
    bourgeois, 32, 54, 61–62, 147, 211, 225,
        238, 256, 291
    civil, 276–81
    communal, *see* collectivism, communalism
    heterogeneous, 54
    modern, 62, 77, 79, 84, 212–17, 221–25,
        248–56
    new, 79, 84
    open, 13, 49, 53–54, 78, 259
    paternalistic, 24, 93
    pluralistic, 176, 183–84, 186, 206, 259,
        275–76
    postfeudal, 21, 22, 35, 79, 109, 115,
        116–17, 147, 211, 212–15, 217, 238,
        248, 252, 256, 260, 288–89
    postindustrial, 257–59, 262
    stratification of, 79, 80–81
sociology, 178, 181, 187
Sombart, Werner, 33, 78, 84
Soviet Union, 174, 185, 189–91, 202
Spanish-American War, 65, 178
speech, freedom of, 203–8
Spence, Janet, 218
Staats, Elmer, 120
Stalin, Joseph, 66
Stalinism, 189
Stanford, Leland, 178
Stanton, Elizabeth Cady, 291
"State as a Conceptual Variable, The" (Nettl),
    40
statism:
    conservative opposition to, 36, 37, 98, 289
    cross-national comparisons of, 19, 92–95,
        97
    individualism vs., 22–23, 84
    institutional structures and, 40–41
    in Japan, 19, 221

statism: (*continued*)
  laissez-faire vs., 27, 76
  liberal opposition to, 91, 95, 200, 201, 215, 252
  socialism and, 90–96
  Tory support for, 87, 91, 93–94, 97, 102, 153–54, 200, 253
Statistical Abstract of the United States (1994), 58
Steele, Shelby, 148–49
Strauss, Leo, 39
Students for a Democratic Society (SDS), 185, 191
success:
  conditions for, 28, 151–54, 167, 169, 175, 287
  ends vs. means in, 47, 230
  as goal, 47–48, 135
Summers, Robert, 55
Sunday Mails Law, 156
Supreme Court, U.S., 39, 118
Suzuki, Tatsuko, 220–21, 250–51
Swartz, Donald, 107
Sweden, 62, 73, 118
Switzerland, 40, 45

Taft, Robert, 197
Talmud, 153
Tax, Sol, 65
taxation, 26, 38, 68–69, 72, 73, 169, 227–28, 253
television, 219, 281, 285–87
Thatcher, Margaret, 153–54, 200, 201, 292
"There's No Such Thing as Free Speech and It's a Good Thing Too" (Fish), 203–4
Thielens, Wagner, Jr., 180, 181
Thomas, Norman, 189
Thomas, W. I., 78, 178
Tiryakian, Edward, 155
Title VII, 137
Tocqueville, Alexis de, 13, 17–18, 34, 60–61, 62, 77, 80, 81, 154, 228, 270, 276, 277, 280
Tocqueville and Beaumont in America (Pierson), 18
Tokugawa Shogunate, 212
Tominaga, Ken'ichi, 215
Tories:
  in Canada, 24, 91, 92–93, 95, 97, 102, 108
  conservatism of, 31, 35, 36, 37
  elitism of, 95, 235, 252
  neoconservatives and, 200
  paternalistic socialism supported by, 24, 93, 95, 154, 230, 253
  political party of, 42

  statism of, 87, 91, 93–94, 97, 102, 153–54, 200, 253
  U.S. failure of, 32
  values of, 31–32
  welfare supported by, 20, 153
tort, 26, 49, 50, 227–28
Trades and Labour Congress (TLC), 96
trade unions:
  business opposition to, 103
  in Canada vs. U.S., 78, 88, 89–90, 91, 95–108
  civil rights movement and, 120–21
  class consciousness and, 97, 98, 108–9, 251–52, 289
  collective bargaining by, 102, 103–4, 225–26
  competition by, 107–8
  decline of, 33, 89–90, 98
  density of, 89, 90, 96–108
  "Europeanization" of, 38
  for government employees, 99
  growth of, 22, 38, 89–90
  in Japan, 225–26, 233, 251–52
  leadership of, 107–8
  legislation for, 90, 102–6
  membership of, 103, 104, 107–8, 289–90
  non-member support for, 104–5, 106, 191, 192
  organizing by, 90, 102–5, 107–8
  political influence of, 38, 97, 100–102
  socialism and, 78, 80, 84, 85, 95–96, 108
  strikes by, 107, 225, 233
  for teachers, 107
Trompenaars, Alfons, 25, 217, 257–58
Trotsky, Leon, 33
Trotskyism, 188–89, 190, 191, 192, 195
Trow, Martin, 53
Troy, Leo, 99
Truman, Harry S., 180, 190, 192, 197
tzedekah, 170

"un-American" beliefs, 207, 291
Underhill, Frank, 24
unemployment, 38, 56–57, 145–46, 231
unemployment benefits, 83
unemployment insurance, 71–72, 94
Unitarians, 152, 177
United Auto Workers (UAW), 107
United Church of Canada, 93
United States:
  as adversarial society, 25–26, 178, 199, 216, 225–27, 276, 290–91, 296
  as Anglophonic society, 34–35, 127–28
  as bourgeois society, 32, 54, 147, 211, 225, 238, 256, 291
  colonial period of, 18

decentralization in, 18
economy of, *see* economy, U.S.
exceptionalism of, *see* exceptionalism, American
feudal structures lacked by, 19, 54, 79, 87, 109, 211
foreign perspectives on, 17–18, 33–34
foreign policy of, 20, 43, 65–67
industrialization of, 28, 55, 60, 260
as "melting pot," 249–50
as new society, 79, 84
as open society, 13, 49, 53–54, 78, 259
as outlier, 13, 18, 25, 26, 27, 73, 234, 263
revolutionary basis of, 14, 18, 24, 31, 39, 54, 91–92, 268
trade deficit of, 59
wealth of, 26, 33, 47, 53, 69–70, 84, 88
universalism, 115, 154, 172, 175, 228, 249
utopianism, 63, 66, 84, 177

values:
  attitudes vs., 24–25, 101, 102, 221, 236, 250–51
  bourgeois, 32, 54, 61–62, 147, 211, 225, 238, 256, 291
  capitalistic, 154
  change in, 267–68, 271
  consensus vs., 290–91, 296
  democratic, 63–67, 197, 276–77
  family, 272–74, 276
  individual rights and, 116
  of intellectuals, 179–81
  Judaic, 152–54, 164, 170–71, 172, 173, 213–14
  secular, 63
  social, 47, 54–55, 87
  Tory, 31–32
  traditional, 220–25, 229, 241–42, 244, 245, 246–51, 263, 267–68
Van Buren, Martin, 156
Veblen, Thornstein, 172, 180, 181, 214, 221
Vernoff, Edward, 185
Vietnam War, 65, 66, 177, 182, 190, 191, 192, 286
Visser, Jelle, 100, 106
volunteerism, 27, 28, 61, 67–68, 71, 217, 268, 276–81
voter participation, 13, 17, 21, 26, 43–46, 85, 240, 282–83
voter registration, 45–46
voting rights, 85–86, 205
Vulnerable, The (Gould and Palmer), 72

wages, 25, 57, 74, 75, 80
Wald, Kenneth, 62
Wallace, George, 41, 86, 91

Wallace, Henry, 190
war:
  opposition to, 20, 65, 66, 176, 177, 182, 190, 191, 192
  support for, 14, 20, 65
  unconditional surrender in, 65, 66, 67
  veterans of, 123
Washington, George, 13, 53, 115–16, 155
Washington, Harold, 170
Washington Post, 134
Watergate scandal, 27
Watson, Tom, 165
Wattenberg, Ben, 195
Weber, Max, 23–24, 34, 54, 61, 77, 153, 211, 250, 277
Weiler, Paul, 99, 104
Weinstein, David, 215–16
Welch, Finis R., 136
welfare:
  in Canada, 92, 95, 99
  entitlements of, 22–23
  as institution, 71–75, 84
  neoconservative support for, 195, 196, 197, 199–200, 201, 202
  reduction of, 38, 98
  revenues for, 83, 92
  Tory support for, 20, 153
  viability of, 24, 26, 27, 33, 68, 92, 117, 169, 170
Wells, H. G., 31–32, 33, 35, 87
Wesley, John, 60
Where Communism Works (Kenrick), 215
Whigs, 24, 41, 46, 91, 108
Why Is There No Socialism in the United States? (Sombart), 33
"Why We Are Not Republicans" (Kirkpatrick), 195
Wiener, Jonathan, 187
"wilding," 269
Wilhelm II, Kaiser of Germany, 251
Wilson, Clyde, 197
Wilson, Edmund, 185
Wilson, James Q., 44, 272
Wilson, Pete, 139
Wilson, William Julius, 134, 137, 149
Wilson, Woodrow, 197
Wolfe, Alan, 248, 270
Wolff, Edward N., 55, 56*n*, 73
women:
  affirmative action and, 121, 122, 125, 126, 127
  black, 136–37, 138
  discrimination against, 205, 246
  education and, 244–45
  equal opportunity for, 121, 122, 243–44
  gender as viewed by, 221, 244

women: (*continued*)
  Japanese, 241–45
  quotas for, 205, 206
  working, 57, 205, 241, 242–44, 281
Woodward, C. Vann, 208
work ethic, 54, 60, 81–82, 87, 132, 133,
    153–54, 155, 164, 233–37, 287, 295
working class:
  blacks vs. whites in, 120, 138, 139, 140,
    148, 149
  class consciousness of, 33, 98, 108–9, 147,
    252
  living standards of, 79, 80, 81–82, 84, 118
  see also trade unions
Workingmen's Party, 78, 82, 114

World Economic Forum, 59, 262
World War I, 65, 178, 190
World War II, 20, 65, 123, 189–90, 191
Wuthnow, Robert, 277

Yale University, 177
Yankelovich, Daniel, 282
Yarborough, Ralph, 121
Yiddish, 153, 162
Yoshio, Sugimito, 212
Young, John, 117
Yulee, David, 158

Zionism, 162, 163, 167
Zuckerman, Alan, 151, 162